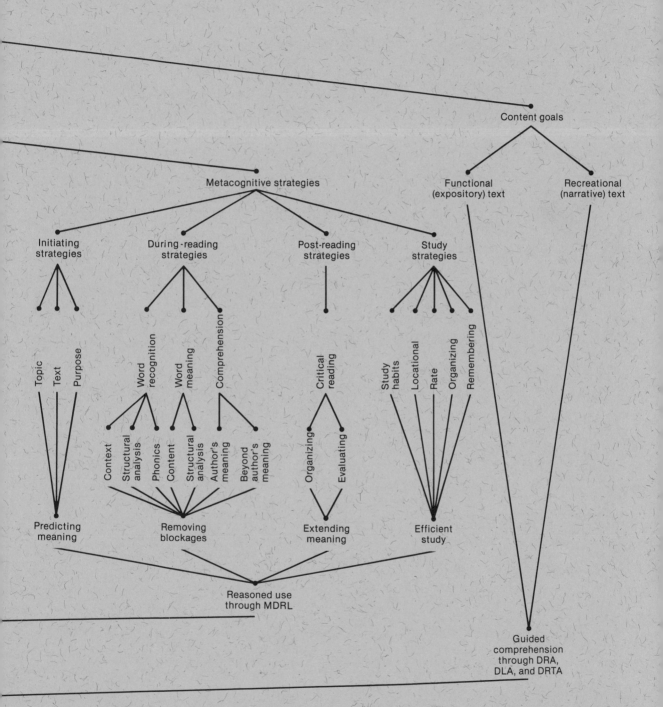

IMPROVING CLASSROOM READING INSTRUCTION

A Decision-Making Approach

IMPROVING CLASSROOM READING INSTRUCTION

A Decision-Making Approach
THIRD EDITION

Gerald G. Duffy
Whitworth College

Laura R. Roehler
Michigan State University

McGRAW-HILL, INC.
New York St. Louis San Francisco Auckland Bogotá Caracas
Lisbon London Madrid Mexico Milan Montreal New Delhi
Paris San Juan Singapore Sydney Tokyo Toronto

This book was developed by Lane Akers, Inc.

IMPROVING CLASSROOM READING INSTRUCTION
A Decision-Making Approach

1 2 3 4 5 6 7 8 9 0 DOC DOC 9 0 9 8 7 6 5 4 3 2

ISBN 0-07-018034-2

This book was set in Caledonia by Publication Services.
The editor was Lane Akers;
the production supervisor was Leroy A. Young.
The cover was designed by Karen K. Quigley.
The photo editor was Inge King.
Project supervision was done by Publication Services.
R. R. Donnelley & Sons Company was printer and binder.

Cover photo by Richard Hutchings/Info Edit.

Library of Congress Catalogin-in-Publication Data

Duffy, Gerald G.
    Improving classroom reading instruction: a decision-making
approach / Gerald G. Duffy, Laura R. Roehler—3rd ed.
        p.   cm.
    Includes bibliographical references and index.
    ISBN 0-07-018034-2
    1. Reading.   I. Roehler, Laura R., (date).   II. Title.
LB1050.D755   1993
372.41—dc20   92-26490

Photo Credits
2: Susan Lapides/Design Conceptions 7: Courtesy of Michigan State University 9: Robert Bawden 19: Susan Lapides/Design Conceptions 28: McGraw-Hill photo by Peter Vadnai 31: Elizabeth Crews 45: Susan Lapides/Design Conceptions 56: Elizabeth Crews 63: Elizabeth Crews 74: David Strickler/Monkmeyer Press 82: Sybil Shelton/Peter Arnold 88: Susan Lapides/Design Conceptions 102: Rick Friedman/The Picture Cube 106: McGraw-Hill photo by Peter Vadnai 117: Peter Menzel/Stock, Boston 133: Robert Bawden 162: Elizabeth Crews 165: Robert Bawden 182: Robert Bawden 188: McGraw-Hill photo by Peter Vadnai 196: Robert Bawden 201: Robert Bawden 204: Robert Bawden 212: Robert Bawden 220: Elizabeth Crews 222: McGraw-Hill photo by Peter Vadnai 224: Susan Lapides/Design Conceptions 231: Elizabeth Crews 246: Elizabeth Crews 253: McGraw-Hill photo by Peter Vadnai 265: Will McIntyre/Photo Researchers 269: Burt Glinn/Magnum Photos 280: Robert Bawden 283: Frank Siteman 306: Susan Lapides/Design Conceptions 315: McGraw-Hill photo by Peter Vadnai 326: George Bellerose/Stock, Boston 329: John R. Maher/EKM Nepenthe 348: Elizabeth Crews 365: Courtesy of Michigan State University 391: Susan Lapides/Design Conceptions 409: Burt Glinn/Magnum Photos 426: Elizabeth Crews 446: Susan Lapides/Design Conceptions 455: Robert Bawden 472: Alan Carey/The Image Works 476: Elizabeth Crews 481: Robert Bawden 482: Robert Bawden

To

Danise, Bob, and Jack
Michael
Susinn, Xavier, and Matthew
Christopher and Anna
Kathy, George, and Max
Anne
Byrch and Yvonne

Contents

Part 3 Getting Organized for Instruction   197

Preface for Students

This book is written to help you become a professional teacher of reading. Professional teachers are in control of classroom instruction; they make the decisions. Control comes from knowledge and from a willingness to use knowledge. This book provides the knowledge and sets the expectation that you will use this knowledge to make instructional decisions.

Because the information load is heavy, the book has been carefully organized to assist your learning. Part 1 provides basic information about reading and explains what it's like to be a teacher. Part 2 describes how to teach reading to achieve various goals. Part 3 tells how to get organized for instruction; Part 4 provides specifics for teaching reading at various grade levels; and Part 5 provides the basis for future professional growth.

The chapters are not separate and isolated. In a cumulative manner, each succeeding chapter uses information from previous chapters as a starting point. Similarly, concepts are continually developed throughout the book. For instance, *instruction* is discussed in virtually every chapter; as the book progresses, the meaning of the term becomes more and more refined as it is used in a variety of contexts and with a variety of examples.

To help you comprehend the content of the book, the following learning aids have been included:

1. *Advance organizers* Each of the 20 chapters begins with an overview, or Getting Ready, section. These overviews are followed by Focus Questions that direct you to specific information to be learned. Together these sections will help you activate the appropriate background experience needed to understand the chapter content.

2. *Chapter headings and subheadings* Headings and subheadings have been designed to guide your reading. They not only signal where important points are discussed, but, wherever possible, they are cued to the focus questions at the beginning of each chapter.

3. *Figures, tables, and examples* Numerous summarizing figures, tables, and examples have been provided to aid you in acquiring and reviewing key material. In addition, chapter photographs help you construct mental pictures of classroom reading instruction.

4. *Vocabulary aids* All professional terms are printed in boldface in the text and are also defined in the glossary.

5. *Chapter summaries*   The essential chapter content is summarized at the end of every chapter to help you review major points and answer the Focus Questions.

6. *Activities for reflecting, observing and teaching*   Each chapter ends with activities designed to help you use the concepts developed in the chapter.

One additional aid could not be built into the book. This is the opportunity for you to use what you learn with real students in real classrooms. Perhaps a supervised field practicum is part of your course work. If it is, use that situation as an opportunity to test and to apply what you learn in this book. If no such practicum is available, try to arrange classroom visits on your own so you can observe the teaching of reading and can try out the content of this book. The more you use the content, the better you will understand it.

You are embarking on a difficult task. Although teaching reading is complex, the rewards are satisfying and fulfilling. We hope this book—together with your real-world experience with students—will help you become a professional decision maker who reaps the rewards of being a classroom teacher of reading and literacy.

Gerald G. Duffy

Laura R. Roehler

Acknowledgments

As a third edition, this book has changed partly because of the comments of various reviewers of earlier editions, all of whom were noted in the acknowledgments section of those earlier books. In addition, this book has continued to evolve because of the intellectual stimulation we have received from our colleagues at Michigan State University and at the National Reading Conference. Finally, this edition of the book has profited from the comments of our graduate and undergraduate students who have provided us with helpful critiques in the past. We gratefully acknowledge the contributions of all. But we are particularly grateful to Lane Akers, whose patience during difficult times was the difference between getting this edition done and not getting it done.

In addition to our students, who have been a constant source of ideas and encouragement, we would like to thank the following users of the previous edition. Their generous feedback has helped shape the changes that, hopefully, make this the most practical and useful edition yet.

Robin Erwin Jr., Niagara University

Cullita Grindstaff, Morehead State University

Beth Ann Hermann, University of South Carolina

Tim Miller, Morehead State University

Betty Newman, Athens State College

Jerry Niles, V.P.I.

Dixie Peterson, Wichita State University

Christine Swager, University of South Carolina

Gail Tompkins, California State University, Fresno

Gerald G. Duffy
Laura R. Roehler

IMPROVING CLASSROOM READING INSTRUCTION

A Decision-Making Approach

Part 1

Perspectives on Reading Instruction

This section introduces you to the themes and terminology of reading instruction. Chapter 1 identifies the major theme—that we need a new kind of literacy and a new kind of teacher. With this as a base, Chapters 2, 3, and 4 develop fundamental concepts of students' learning, reading curricula, and instruction. The themes and terms introduced here will be returned to again and again as the specifics of classroom reading instruction are developed in subsequent sections of the book.

1 Breaking with Tradition in Reading Instruction

GETTING READY

Teachers make a difference. This is not a wishful statement or hopeful rhetoric; it is a fact established by more than 20 years of painstaking research, which shows that when teachers do certain things they produce higher achievement, and when they do not do these things, they produce less achievement. Being an instructionally effective teacher, however, is not easy. Teaching is extremely demanding, and the constraints and realities of classroom life often cause teachers to favor mechanical instruction, which, although less effective in producing reading achievement, is easier and makes classroom life more manageable.

To help you get ready for real classroom teaching of reading, we start this book by discussing these realities, describing current instructional practices in reading, and explaining how classroom life encourages these practices. We then describe characteristics that you need to acquire to overcome the constraints of classroom life and to become a professional decision maker who is in control of your own instruction.

FOCUS QUESTIONS

- What is the challenge for teachers of reading in the years to come?

- How is reading currently taught in today's schools?

- Why is it taught this way?

- What do teachers need to do to avoid teaching like technicians?

- What are the characteristics associated with teacher decision making in reading?

4

One of the most alarming results of recent educational research is the finding that most preservice teachers believe that they already know how to teach before their teacher education ever begins! What these prospective teachers mean is that, when they themselves were elementary and high school students, they accumulated hours and hours of experience watching teachers teach. They remember what their favorite teachers did, and they plan to do likewise.

Unfortunately, this practice perpetuates the status quo. The children of new generations are educated in the same manner as the children of past generations. In a rapidly changing world that will change even more rapidly in the decades to come, perpetuating the educational status quo is woefully inadequate.

Consequently, this book challenges you to break the cycle. It challenges you to prepare students for a new world by teaching a new literacy in new ways. It challenges you to temporarily put aside the ways you were taught when you were in school until you can combine that old knowledge with new knowledge; it challenges you to prepare yourself to become a new kind of teacher—an independent decision maker who teaches reading in ways that prepare students for a new age.

The New Literacy

Literacy changes as the world changes. Not too long ago, you were considered literate if you could read and write your name. More recently, the term "functional literacy" has been used; it refers to the reading level needed to function in society at any particular time. Functional literacy in 1950 was a fourth grade reading level; ten years or so later, it was a seventh grade reading level.

But those definitions of literacy were formulated in a different age. We were still basically an industrial society, and education was geared to serve the huge middle class of Caucasians that comprised the major part of our society. The major job of schools in those days was to produce citizens who could function as workers in an industrialized society and become productive members of the middle class.

However, as we approach the year 2000, the world is different. We are no longer an industrial society. We have moved into the Information Age, where knowledge proliferates at a previously unimaginable rate, where service-related jobs are the major source of employment, and where people will need to be able to restructure their job tasks every few years in order to keep pace with technological advances. Additionally, our population has moved gradually from a society dominated by the middle class to one in which the lower economic class is growing ever larger and in which cultural and racial diversity will soon be the norm.

Under these circumstances, the old literacy will no longer do. Being able to read and write is no longer sufficient. Nor is it sufficient to measure our success by how well we do with middle class Caucasian children.

What we need is a new literacy—a literacy in which children not only read and write but are in control of their language and enthusiastic about its use; in which they do not passively receive and send messages but *use* reading and writing to control their destinies; in which they not only comprehend and compose but also interpret, adapt, analyze, frame and solve problems, and persuade using higher forms of thinking.

And, because of the changing demographics of our society, it is not enough to develop this new literacy with only the advantaged segments of society. We must also learn to be successful in educating the economically deprived, culturally diverse, and disadvantaged students who have traditionally fallen through the cracks in our schools and who are now rapidly becoming the dominant social class in our society. Unless we succeed in helping this segment of our citizenry develop the new literacy, society as we know it is likely to collapse, because we will not have enough citizens who can do the interpretive, adaptive, analytical problem framing and solving required of workers in the coming technological age, and we will not have enough people working to generate the taxes needed to support existing social institutions.

The New Teacher

The new literacy cannot be developed by old-style teaching. The dominant instructional practices that you probably experienced when you were learning to read and write in the elementary school are not particularly effective in producing interpretive, adaptive, analytical problem solvers, especially among economically deprived, culturally diverse, disadvantaged students.

The instruction you probably experienced as an elementary school student is often called a "recitation" mode of teaching. Students are asked to do tasks and then to recite what they learned. In reading, for instance, the dominant instructional practices have required students to read stories, often in an oral turn-taking format known as "round robin reading," to answer comprehension questions, and to follow directions for completing a workbook page or worksheet. The task is to provide answers the teacher wants to hear. Students' mastery of the answers is periodically evaluated with a test. Students do very little interpretation, adaptation, analysis, or problem framing or solving. Instead, what students learn is memory, recall of facts and compliance with standard ways of doing things.

Typically, this kind of teaching is based in a commercial reading program sold complete with a set of prescriptions contained in a teacher's guide that, often, is not a guide at all but is, rather, a script to be followed. Hence, the teacher follows someone else's directions when teaching students to read a story, to answer comprehension questions, and to do workbook pages or worksheets. The teacher corrects students' papers by referring to what the teacher's guide

Students learn what teachers emphasize.

says the correct answer is. Teachers using these materials behave like technicians, following directions laid out by others.

Although a teacher's guide may give lip service to higher-order thinking and other elements of the new literacy, higher forms of literacy actually receive less attention than memory and recall because higher-order thinking is difficult to prescribe when you do not know the students and is virtually impossible to test with traditional paper-and-pencil tests. Consequently, commercial reading programs continue to emphasize memory tasks and recall associated with the old literacy because it is easier to put into a teacher's guide.

To develop the new literacy, a different kind of teaching is needed. Instead of moving to the next reading selection simply because it is the next one in the book, teaching must revolve around the framing and solving of real problems such as those solved by literate people in the real world; instead of focusing on getting answers from the text, teaching must focus on how the reader can adapt text information to the problem being solved; instead of answering prepared problems unrelated to students' concerns, teaching must revolve around analyzing real problems and determining what the problems are; instead of measuring teaching by testing to see whether students get correct answers, teaching must measure the quality of students' interpretation and application of the messages embedded in text.

This kind of teaching requires a new kind of teacher—a teacher who does not depend on the prescriptions of a commercially prepared teacher's guide.

These new teachers are themselves interpretive, adaptive, analytical problem framers and solvers. They interpret the instructional situation, they adapt instruction, they are analytical about how students are responding to instruction, and they frame and solve problems concerning how to adapt instruction to ensure that all students become interpretive, analytical problem solvers.

It is this kind of teacher that this book is designed to develop. We focus on decision making because teachers developing a new literacy cannot afford to be technicians, passively following directions prescribed in advance. Instead, teachers must make decisions—decisions about what to teach various students at various times in order to promote a new literacy, decisions about how to embed instruction in real-life problems, decisions about how to help students learn what they need to know, and decisions about how to determine whether instruction has been successful or whether alternative instruction must be provided.

THE GOALS OF THIS BOOK

Given the above, our goals in writing this book are clear. We want you to develop

- An understanding that *literacy* is the proactive, enthusiastic use of language and higher-order thinking in the service of controlling and enriching one's destiny

- A commitment to educating the culturally different, economically deprived, disadvantaged students who will soon represent a majority of our population

- A faith in your ability to develop your own literacy instruction on the basis of students' needs and your professional knowledge rather than depending on teachers' guides to give you directions to follow

The book is organized to achieve these goals. The following chapters in Part 1 provide you with information you can use to construct fundamental conceptions about language, students, curriculum, and instruction. Part 2 expands on these fundamentals, providing specifics about *what* to teach. Part 3 further elaborates on the fundamental conceptions by detailing *how* to teach. Part 4 is a supplement, with each chapter providing elaborations and a storehouse of instructional activities for early reading, primary grades, middle grades, and upper grades, respectively. Part 5, consisting of a single chapter, describes how you can ensure that you continue growing professionally.

WHAT MAKES DECISION MAKING DIFFICULT?

If it were easy to be an instructional decision maker when teaching reading, there would be little need for this book. However, it is not easy; it is extremely difficult because of the constraints under which teachers work. Two of the main categories of constraints are the complexity of the classroom and the dominant use of the basal reading textbook.

The Complexity of Classroom Life

One of the unfortunate myths of our culture is that "anybody can be a teacher." The truth is that being a teacher is very difficult, especially if by "teacher" we mean a person who develops understandings and positive attitudes about reading. A major difficulty is the complexity of effectively managing daily classroom life. The energy expended on classroom management too often leaves little energy for the kind of instructional decision making advocated in this book.

What is so difficult about managing classroom life? First, teachers must organize and smoothly manage the activities of 25 or 30 youngsters for five or six hours every day. It is difficult enough to keep one seven-year-old child occupied for five or six hours; it is incredibly more difficult to deal with 25 or 30 because of the social interactions that occur. Consequently, one of the first jobs a teacher

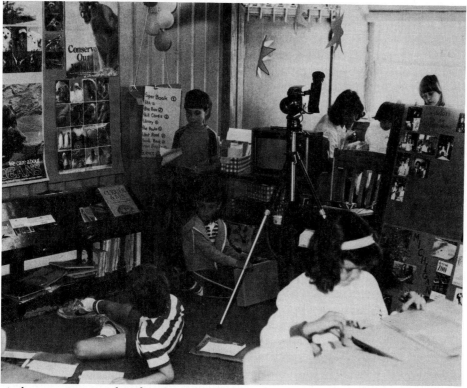

A classroom is a complex place.

faces is to create a socially acceptable environment where 25 or 30 distinct and captive personalities can exist in close proximity to each other for extended periods of time.

The problem is further compounded by the fact that in our society going to school is a serious business in which schools and teachers are held accountable for student achievement. To ensure this achievement, state and local boards of education require various kinds of achievement tests, and if the test scores are low the teacher is held accountable by parents and school officials. This **accountability** for good achievement test scores can be handicapping to teachers because achievement growth is affected by many factors outside the teacher's control, and because what is measured by tests often differs from what teachers know to be important.

Accountability pressures on students also add to the complexity of classrooms. For instance, students exchange performance in classrooms for grades, a fact that influences their classroom behavior. Students often avoid responding in class so they will not expose themselves to errors, and they negotiate for easier tasks to get better grades. This makes the teacher's job that much more difficult.

Classroom life is further complicated by the fact that teachers must constantly deal with dilemmas as well as with problems. Although problems can be resolved by rational problem solving, dilemmas have no "right" answers and create an ongoing climate of uncertainty. For instance, if you are teaching a reading group of ten students and you notice that two are whispering together while you are explaining something to another, you are faced with a dilemma. If you turn your attention to the two whispering students, the one you are interacting with suffers; if you ignore the whispering and attend to the student you are instructing, the whispering tends to spread.

Similarly, if you are teaching the same group of ten students and it becomes clear that five of them understand the task and five do not, you are faced with a dilemma. If you hold all ten until they have all learned satisfactorily, the five who can already do the task correctly will lose interest; if you dismiss them, you may embarrass the five remaining students because of their inability to perform as well. Such dilemmas are endless in the daily life of teachers and dealing with them makes teaching complex.

The problem of dilemma management is further complicated by the fact that teachers are often led to expect simple answers, as, for example, when they are required to use certain instructional materials or certain procedures. These directives imply that problems of teaching can be solved if you use the right set of materials or procedures. Nothing could be further from the truth. Teaching is simply too complex; no one set of procedures or materials can possibly anticipate all the situations you will confront.

Classroom teaching is also difficult because of the constant need to adjust and adapt to changes. For instance, as our world changes we find that we are faced with more language and learning problems than ever before, and that there are more and more innovations to which teachers must adapt. To cope with such continuous change, teachers need to be flexible and adaptable.

Of all the difficulties of classroom life, perhaps none is harder to deal with than the isolation of teaching. The classroom is a crowded social environment, but it is an environment of children; as a classroom teacher, you are virtually isolated from other adults during the hours you are teaching. Consequently, you endure a professional loneliness as you try to cope with the dilemmas and difficulties of classroom life.

These are not the only difficulties classroom teachers face; they merely illustrate the complexity of the job. Contrary to public opinion, not everybody can be a teacher. Not everybody can deal with the complexities of classroom life and have the energy left to be effective decision makers when providing reading instruction.

The Basal Reading Textbook

The normal constraints of classroom life are more than enough for some teachers. After wrestling with them, they have little energy left to organize an instructional program in reading, so they look for something that will organize it for them. For 85 to 95 percent of American elementary school teachers, the answer lies with the basal reading textbook.

Whether or not you have recently been in elementary schools, you are probably familiar with **basal reading textbooks,** those carefully structured reading books that virtually every American identifies as the focus of reading instruction. These texts normally contain a series of fiction, nonfiction, and poetry reading selections, with fiction given the most emphasis. Each child in a reading group has the same book; children in different reading groups usually have different levels in the same series of books. During reading group time, students read the selections in the basal (either orally or silently), discuss the stories with the teacher, and complete the skill exercises in the workbook that accompanies the basal text. Most teacher questioning during elementary reading instruction focuses on what happens in the basal text selection being read, and most teacher monitoring focuses on the work sheets provided in the accompanying workbook.

Basal textbooks become a constraint because of the way so many teachers use them. The complexities of classroom life often cause teachers to feel overloaded—there just seems to be too much to attend to and do. When this happens, many teachers turn to the basal textbook as a way to simplify their lives. They say, in effect, "I'll deal with all this complexity by simply following the 'expert' directions provided for me in this textbook." In saying this, they relinquish control of instruction, abdicating instructional decision making to the authors of the basal textbook. They stop thinking about their instruction and making their own decisions and start following: The teachers' guide becomes their leader. Merely having students "cover" the material—that is, correctly answer the questions in the basal textbook—becomes their goal.

The basal text thrives for two reasons. First, for teachers who have difficulty dealing with the complexity of classrooms and who consequently have little energy left to plan their own instruction, the basal text provides an organizational structure. It tells them what to do and say, puts materials in students' hands to keep them busy, and provides tests to determine whether progress is being made. In the fast-paced environment of classroom life, it seems to be a lifesaver because, by providing routines, procedures, and activities, it structures the program and promotes the smooth flow of classroom life.

Second, the basal text provides what appears to be a systematic and coordinated reading sequence from kindergarten to eighth grade. With its progression of levels, its skills sequence, and its massive assistance to teachers, it seems to be tailor-made for conducting instruction. In fact, the basal text is so ingrained in our educational system that even good teachers begin to doubt themselves if they are not religiously following the basal "system." For instance, despite tangible evidence that her students are not only in control of the reading process but are excited about it, the teacher in the following example feels guilty because she is not faithfully and mindlessly following the dictates of the basal system. Such is the pervasiveness of the basal text's influence!

> I sometimes feel I am struggling against odds to give my kids a worthwhile reading program. I have tried a different approach this year by balancing basal skills with children's literature. We read anything from Arnold Lobel and Shel Silverstein to Beverly Cleary and Judy Blume. Although I'm aware there is more to reading than the recreational end, I feel a small miracle has taken place with my kids. They sit on the edge of their seats, they laugh out loud, they hold their breath, they get angry but they can't wait to get to the next page! It never happened that way with the basal stories. Yet, I go through doubtful periods as I leaf through basal manuals wondering what horrible gaps I may be creating in these children's reading development.

Despite its systematic characteristics and its apparent usefulness in making classroom life more manageable, the basal text is not a panacea. There are problems associated with its use. As previously mentioned, too many hard-pressed teachers are willing to transfer responsibility for instruction from themselves to the basal. They expect the basal to provide the instruction, and if students do not learn, it is the basal's fault, not the teacher's. In other words, they operate on the principle that the basal program makes the difference, not that the teacher makes the difference.

Also, when teachers assign instructional responsibility to a basal text program, they stop teaching for understanding. They cover basal material mechanically, doing what the teachers' edition says to do and making sure that students "complete" the material. They focus on whether students get the right answer, assuming correct responses mean students are learning what the basal says they are supposed to learn. Such teachers seldom try to think of alternative strategies or activities because all the prescriptions are presumably in the teachers' edition. Hence, these teachers become technicians who follow someone else's plans rather than professionals who make their own instructional decisions.

The faith teachers place in basals is unwarranted. Recent studies indicate that basal materials often present information in confusing ways, that they emphasize practice and assessment exercises associated with answer-oriented instruction, and that the accompanying workbook exercises are often misleading or inaccurate.

It is unlikely that the content of basal texts will change dramatically in the near future. The reason is simple: They sell the way they are. Because teachers feel they need help in ordering classroom life, they favor basals; because publishers are in business to sell books, they include the routinized, answer-oriented materials some teachers favor. In short, since basals are going to be around for awhile, you must learn to teach reading effectively while using them.

The constraints of classroom life that drive teachers in the direction of basal text programs are summarized in Figure 1.1.

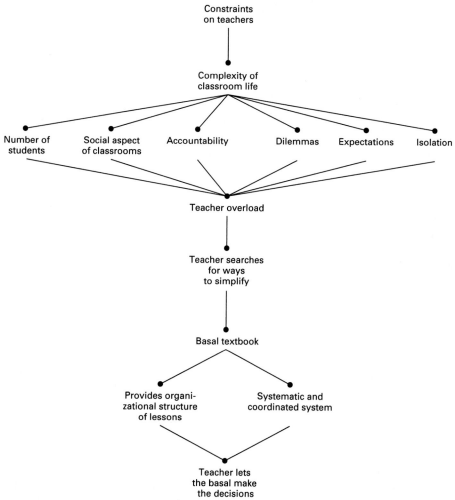

FIGURE 1.1 Why Teachers Teach Like Technicians.

CURRENT INSTRUCTIONAL PRACTICE IN READING

When teachers are controlled by constraints, they fill instructional time with activities that merely keep students busy. Positive attitudes, understanding, and conscious awareness of how to comprehend text receive relatively little emphasis.

This phenomenon appears to be prevalent at all grade levels. For instance, primary grade teachers spend much of their time monitoring students through workbook pages and work sheets without providing information about how to do a task or why it is being pursued. The work sheet directions to students in the following example are typical. Not only is there an absence of assistance to students, but the teacher defines the task as one of accurate answer getting. There is little concern about why the work sheet should be completed or how it contributes to the students' understanding of reading:

T: Okay. In the little paragraph that begins there, I would like to have you read the first one to yourselves and put a line under every word you can see that has the word *play* in it. Even if it has an *s* added to it. We're looking for the word *play*. Okay. Mary?

S: Look.

T: Okay. There's the word *look*, looked. But we're looking for *play*. John?

S: Playing.

T: Yes, *Playing* has *play* in it. How about the next one? Sue?

To illustrate an alternative, the teacher could have initiated the lesson by providing substantive information about what is to be learned, when it will be used, and how to do it:

T: Okay, today we are going to read a story that has lots of hard words in it. These words are alike because they end with either *s*, *ed*, or *ing*. I'm going to show you a strategy for figuring out these words. Where are we going to use this strategy, John?

S: In the story we read today?

T: Yes. Words like these will be in the story we read today. Now, let me show you a strategy for figuring out these words. Let's say we come to this word. [Writes *plays* on the board.] Okay, what I do is look at the word to see if it has one of my endings on it. Does it, Sarah?

S: Yes. It ends in *s*.

T: Okay. So then I cover the *s* and see if I know the root word. Do you know this word, Sam?

S: Play.

T: Yes. The root word is *play*. Now I uncover the *s*, say *play* and add the *s*. Plays. Does that word make sense in the sentence?

S: Yes.

T: Okay, then it is probably the right word. Now let's say we are reading along and we run into this word. [Writes *looked* on the board.] Can you use my strategy to figure out that word, Mary?

A similar pattern is seen in the other elementary grades. In these classrooms, there is heavy emphasis on asking questions to assess whether students understand what the selection is about. The following excerpt from a third grade classroom is an example of how teachers "interrogate" during reading without providing instruction in how to answer the questions. This emphasis on time-filling activities such as oral reading followed by a period of questioning or monitoring students through work sheets is reflected in virtually all studies of classroom instructional practice.

S   [reading orally]: It was morning. The sun was in the—

T: You can stop there. It was a good morning for doing something. What is it a good morning to do?

S: Jump.

T: Ed, will you read for me?

S: Hop, hop, hop—

T: He is going to talk to a rabbit, isn't he? Is it a small rabbit?

S: No, kind of big. Kind of big and kind of small.

T: It's Bill's turn to read.

S: The rabbit did not look happy. The rabbit had lost two little rabbits on the hill.

T: Why is the rabbit unhappy, Bill?

S   [long pause]: I don't know.

T: Let's see if someone else knows.

S: I don't know.

T: Because he lost his two rabbits. You have to pay better attention.

Despite the fact that such tasks probably cause students to conclude that reading is answering questions rather than knowing how to answer questions, teachers persist in asking questions without telling students how to answer the questions. The driving force seems to be not what students will conclude about reading but, rather, occupying students' time. However, the teacher in the previous example could have inserted explanations that would have provided the information the students needed to answer the question about why the rabbit was unhappy:

T: Why is the rabbit unhappy, Bill?

S [long pause]: I don't know.

T: Let me show you a strategy you can use to figure out the answer to questions like that. First, go back and look at what the text says. For instance, it says, "The rabbit did not look happy. The rabbit had lost two little rabbits on the hill." When the question is asked, you have to ask yourself, What do I know about things like that? What if I were the rabbit and I had lost two little rabbits, how would I feel?

S: You'd probably feel sad.

T: Yes. Now what would have made me sad? It was the fact that I lost the two little rabbits. Right? And that's why the rabbit was unhappy. You can figure out the answer to these kinds of questions by putting yourself into the story and thinking about how you would feel if you were in his place.

Our task in this book is to put you in control of your reading instruction. The goal is for you to make your own decisions about your reading instruction despite the constraints and complexities that make teaching difficult.

BECOMING AN INSTRUCTIONAL DECISION MAKER

The point here is not that teachers lack dedication and diligence. On the contrary, nearly all the teachers we encounter want to help students, want to be better teachers, and want to improve. Neither do we believe that teachers are unable to become professional decision makers who are in cognitive control of their instruction; we believe that teachers can and should.

This textbook emphasizes two important functions of being a decision maker when teaching reading. It puts a premium on (1) helping you become a good organizer and manager of reading curricula and instruction so you can reduce the complexities of classroom life and (2) teaching you how to make your own decisions about reading instruction even though you may be using basal textbooks. In the process, we hope you will develop the following eight characteristics emphasized in this book because they are associated with instructional decision makers.

First, teachers who are instructional decision makers view reading broadly. They see it not as a skill or series of skills, nor as an isolated subject, but as part of a literacy system whose purpose is communication and comprehension for genuine purposes. Therefore, their reading instruction emphasizes language and the communication function of language in pursuit of authentic goals.

Second, these teachers think in terms of what students should learn, not in terms of assignments for students to complete. In reading, the ultimate goal is for students to be in control of "real" reading as pursued by literate people. Therefore, instruction focuses on real reading, not on skill exercises. Similarly, instruction is not effective when practice sheets are answered accurately; it is effective when students use reading to attain authentic goals.

Third, these teachers understand that positive attitudes are as crucial as skills in learning to read. Teachers do many important things, but teaching children to like to read is especially important.

Fourth, teachers who are decision makers understand that comprehension is the result of cognition, awareness, and strategic thinking, not memory, rote, and accuracy. Therefore, a central question to students is not "Are you correct?" but rather "How do you know you are correct?"

Fifth, these teachers understand that basal textbooks cannot dominate reading instruction. They use them as tools, not as infallible guides; they do not organize their reading program around an assigned basal but modify, adjust, and innovate according to chosen goals and the needs of their students.

Sixth, these teachers know that teachers' guides mainly provide tasks, activities, and directions. If students are to understand *how* to do tasks successfully, teachers must explain them and work hard to analyze them, using these analyses to create explicit "how-to" explanations.

Seventh, these teachers are not looking for "the" answer to reading instruction. They know that reading instruction is complex, classrooms are complex, and students and teachers are complex. There can be no panacea when so many complexities interact.

Eighth, these teachers know they must be life-long students of reading instruction. They will become more proficient from year to year, but they will never do things exactly the same. They are constantly thinking, changing, modifying, innovating, and looking for ways to improve instruction. The following list summarizes the ways in which decision makers think about reading instruction.

1. They think of reading in terms of its uses in the real world, not as a narrow skill.

2. They think in terms of what students learn, not activities they complete.

3. They think that learning to like reading is as important as knowing how to read.

4. They think about the reasoning process involved in comprehending, not just getting the answer.

5. They think that their job is to modify basal materials, not to follow them blindly.

6.   They think that teachers should explain, not just assign tasks.

7.   They think that there are many ways to teach reading, not just one way.

8.   They think they should change and grow each year, not do the same thing from one year to the next.

Teachers who are decision makers are in control of their own instruction. One way to dramatize the difference between teachers who are in control from those who are not is to note how each one reacts to the same instructional task. In each of the following two examples, the teacher has presented a lesson and students' answers indicate a lack of understanding. The difference in what the two teachers do illustrates the difference between technicians and professional decision makers. The first teacher is a technician. She follows the teachers' guide and its prescriptions. When the need to explain arises, she does not know what to do, so she continues asking for the correct answer.

T: When you add an apostrophe *s* to boy, it shows that the boy has something. Can you make up a sentence for kitten? Something belongs to the kitten.

S: There's a basket full of kittens.

T: You added just an *s*. That's more than one kitten. This time make it ownership. Something belongs to this right here. Troy?

S: The kitten always owns the basket.

T: All right, but can you change your sentence around? You're saying the kitten owns the basket. Let's use kitten and basket.

S: Kitten basket.

T: But with the apostrophe *s*.

S: The kitten's basket.

T: The kitten's, that's the kitten's basket. All right. What belongs to the kitten? Troy?

S: The basket.

In contrast, the second teacher is not under the control of the basal. She possesses professional knowledge about reading and about how to instruct, and she uses this knowledge to generate a spontaneous explanation. As a result, the students' misconceptions are corrected, they become aware of how to do the task, and they achieve.

T: Connector words are what, David?

S: Two words put together.

T: What are connector words, Josh?

s: Two words hooked together.

t: They are not two words. Maybe I explained that incorrectly. A connector word is a word that connects one or more ideas. Okay, in this sentence, "They always walk to school together and they always walk home together," there are two ideas. They always walk to school and they always come home. Of the two connector words I put on the board [*and, but*], which word is connecting the two ideas, David?

s: And.

t: And. Do you see that? And. I have it underlined here. See how it is connecting the ideas of walking to school together and coming home together? It is sort of like a bridge that connects these two. Bridges connect different places, words connect ideas. Connector words connect ideas.

Reading instruction requires more than drilling children, asking them for right answers, and demanding that directions be followed accurately. Sense making must be emphasized. Students must understand what reading is, what they are trying to do when they read, how to get right answers, how reading works, and how to be in conscious control of their own cognitive processing as they

Sense making is promoted when the teacher asks students questions about the meaning of their reading.

on reading in the real world, not reading for school assignments only. What this requires is a teacher who adapts instructional materials by making appropriate decisions—a teacher who is in control of instruction and can modify it in ways that put students in control of their reading.

SUMMARY

Reading instruction in elementary schools ought to be characterized by sense making, awareness, positive attitudes, and using reading for authentic purposes. Unfortunately, many teachers emphasize fragmented, meaningless, and mechanical elements of reading. This kind of reading instruction often occurs because of the constrained conditions of teaching, some of which are associated with the pervasiveness of basal textbooks and school policies about how these materials are to be used. In turn, these constraints cause teachers to follow the material technically rather than to make decisions about how to adapt it. To avoid teaching like a technician, you must assume regulatory control of your instruction by making your own decisions; doing so is the essence of being a professional.

SUGGESTED ADDITIONAL READING

BOWMAN, B. (1989). Educating language-minority children: Challenges and opportunities. *Phi Delta Kappan, 71*(2), 118–120.

DREHER, M., & SINGER, H. (1989). The teacher's role in students' success. *Reading Teacher, 42*(8), 612–617.

DURKIN D. (1984). Is there a match between what elementary teachers do and what basal reader manuals recommend? *Reading Teacher, 37*(8), 734–744.

HARRIS, L., & LALIK, R. (1987). Teachers' use of Informal Reading Inventories: An example of school constraints. *Reading Teacher, 40*, 624–631.

KIRST, M. (1991). View on America 2000: New American Schools Component of President Bush's Education Strategy. *Educational Researcher, 20*(7), 27–29.

LEHR, F. (1982). Teacher effectiveness research and reading instruction. *Language Arts, 59*(8), 883–887.

MIKULECKY, L. (1990). National adult literacy and life long learning goals. *Phi Delta Kappan, 72*(4), 304–309.

SHANKER, A. (1990). The end of the traditional model of schooling—And a proposal for using incentives to restructure our schools. *Phi Delta Kappan, 71*(5), 344–357.

SHANNON, P. (1982). A retrospective look at teacher's reliance on commercial reading materials. *Language Arts, 59*(8), 844–853.

SHANNON, P. (1982). Some subjective reasons for teachers' reliance on commercial reading materials. *Reading Teacher, 35*(8), 884–889.

SHROUFE, G. (1991). New American Schools Development Corporation: Open for business. *Educational Researcher, 20*(7), 26–27.

STERN, P., & SHAVELSON, R. J.   (1983). Reading teachers' judgments, plans, and decision making. *Reading Teacher, 37*(3), 280–286.

VENEZKY, R., WAGNER, D., & CILIBERT, B.   (Eds.) (1987). *Towards defining literacy.* Newark, DE: International Reading Association.

THE RESEARCH BASE

ANDERSON, L., BRUBAKER, N., ALLEMAN-BROOKS, J., & DUFFY, G.   (1984). *Making seatwork work* (Research Series No. 142). East Lansing: Michigan State University, Institute for Research on Teaching.

BAILEY, T.   (1991). Jobs of the future and the education they will require: Evidence from occupational forecasts. *Educational Researcher, 20*(2), 11–20.

BRICE-HEATH, S.   (1991). The sense of being literate. In R. Barr, M. Kamil, P. Mosenthal, & P. D. Pearson (Eds.), *Handbook of reading research, volume II* (pp. 3–25). New York: Longman.

DUFFY, G.   (1983). From turn-taking to sense-making: Toward a broader definition of teacher effectiveness. *Journal of Educational Research, 76*(3), 134–139.

DUFFY, G. G., & ROEHLER, L. R.   (1982). The illusion of instruction. *Reading Research Quarterly, 17,* 438–445.

DURKIN, D.   (1978–1979). What classroom observation reveals about reading comprehension instruction. *Reading Research Quarterly, 14,* 481–533.

DURKIN, D.   (1981). Reading comprehension instruction in five basal reader series. *Reading Research Quarterly, 16*(4), 515–544.

MIKULECKY, L.   (1982). Job literacy: The relationship between school preparation and work place actuality. *Reading Research Quarterly, 17*(3), 400–419.

MIKULECKY, L., & DREW, R.   (1991). Basic literacy skills in the workplace. In R. Barr, M. Kamil, P. Mosenthal, & P. D. Pearson (Eds.), *Handbook of reading research, volume II* (pp. 669–689). New York: Longman.

PALLAS, A., NATRIELLO, G., & MCDILL, E.   (1989). The changing nature of the disadvantaged population: Current dimension and future trends. *Educational Researcher, 18*(5), 16–22.

RESNICK, D., & RESNICK, L.   (1985). Standards, curriculum and performance: A historical and comparative perspective. *Educational Researcher, 14*(4), 5–21.

ACTIVITIES FOR REFLECTING, OBSERVING, AND TEACHING

Reflecting On When I Learned How To Read

Purpose: One of the major influences on how you teach reading is your experience as a student. If your teaching is going to be a break with tradition, you must analyze how you were taught to read and decide how you are going to teach differently.

Describe what you remember about being taught to read in the elementary school.

_____

_____

_____

Think of one of your elementary school teachers whom you remember particularly well. Rate him or her on the eight characteristics emphasized in this book.

1. Thought of reading as something to use, not as a narrow skill

       No   Yes

2. Thought in terms of what you learned, not in terms of the assignments you completed

       No   Yes

3. Emphasized liking to read

       No   Yes

4. Emphasized reasoning rather than getting the right answer

       No   Yes

5. Modified the prescribed materials to fit the situation

       No   Yes

6. Explained rather than just assigning

       No   Yes

7.   Used many techniques to teach reading, not just one

        No   Yes
        ⌐_____⌐

8.   Probably changed how reading was taught the next year rather than doing the same thing over again

        No   Yes
        ⌐_____⌐

What will you do the same as that teacher did? What will you try to change?
_____

_____

_____

Interviewing a Teacher

Purpose: Being a good teacher means knowing both what instruction ought to be and the realities under which teachers work. Interviewing a teacher will help you bring these two things together.

Directions: Ask the teacher to rate herself or himself on the eight characteristics emphasized in this book. After she or he rates each characteristic, ask the teacher to elaborate on why she or he rated it that way, probing particularly to find out how the complexities of classroom life and the basal textbook influenced the rating.

1.   Do you teach reading as something to be used as opposed to a skill?

        Never   Sometimes   Always
        ⌐_____⌐_____⌐

Notes on teacher's elaborations:

2.   Do you count students' successful completion of assignments as the major indicator of success in learning to read?

        Never   Sometimes   Always
        ⌐_____⌐_____⌐

Notes on teacher's elaborations:

3.   Do you emphasize liking to read?

Never   Sometimes   Always

Notes on teacher's elaborations:

4.   Do you want students to give you the right answer to comprehension questions?

Never   Sometimes   Always

Notes on teacher's elaborations:

5.   Do you modify the basal text materials?

Never   Sometimes   Always

Notes on teacher's elaborations:

6.   Do you explain the thinking needed to do a reading skill or strategy?

Never   Sometimes   Always

Notes on teacher's elaborations:

7.   Do you stick primarily to a single technique when teaching reading?

Never   Sometimes   Always

Notes on teacher's elaborations:

8.   Is your reading instruction next year going to be basically the same as it was this year?

               No   Maybe   Yes

Notes on teacher's elaborations:

Summarize below what you learned from the interview about how the eight characteristics are influenced by the realities of classroom life.

_____

_____

_____

What will you do the same way this teacher does? What will you do differently?

_____

_____

_____

2 The Reading and Writing Curricula

GETTING READY

To be in control of reading instruction, you must know what to teach and why you are teaching it. This chapter describes the overall goal of reading instruction and how this goal must be the dominant theme in the curriculum. It then defines reading, describes the reading curriculum and its relationship to writing, and provides a rationale for the reading curricular goals. At the end of this chapter, you should have a global picture of the reading and writing curricula.

FOCUS QUESTIONS

- What is the overall goal of reading instruction?

- How does this goal relate to the reading curriculum?

- How can whole language be a guide to curriculum building?

- What is reading?

- How does it work?

- What is the role of concepts? prior knowledge? text? inferencing? strategies? context?

- How are reading and writing related?

- Given the nature of reading, what are the goals of reading instruction?

- How is the reading curriculum organized?

- How are the reading curriculum and the writing curriculum related?

- What do you teach when you teach reading?

- Why do you teach what you teach in reading?

We define literacy as "the proactive, enthusiastic use of language and higher-order thinking in the service of controlling and enriching one's destiny." Consequently, the goal of reading and writing instruction is the development of students who proactively and enthusiastically use language and higher-order thinking to control and enrich their lives.

If reading instruction in our schools is successful, this kind of literacy should be evident in our communities. In fact, the best way to measure the success of a school literacy program is to look in the community for evidence of a literate citizenry. What kind of evidence might you find if the school literacy program developed "proactive, enthusiastic users of language and higher-order thinking to control and enrich one's destiny"? Certainly, circulation of books in the local library would increase, more people would subscribe to the local newspaper, and bookstores would thrive. You would see more letters to the editor published in the local newspaper, the community's political figures would receive more written commentary from their constituencies, and written correspondence of all kinds would be evident. But most of all, you would see citizens using reading and writing to adapt to their world. As job demands changed, people would use reading and writing to keep current and to make the changes necessary to fit into new positions; as the increased complexity of our society threatened the quality of one or another aspect of our lives, community members would read, write, and discuss as a means for becoming informed about the issues and for taking appropriate action; as opportunities for travel or recreation present themselves, people would read and write to inform themselves and to ensure that they get the most out of an experience; and as individuals encountered difficulties in life, reading and writing would be a major resource for deciding how to frame and resolve the difficulties.

If this is what we mean by "a literate citizenry," then we must develop this kind of literacy in school. That is, the school should be a place where students engage in "proactive, enthusiastic use of language and higher-order thinking in the service of controlling and enriching one's destiny."

As noted in Chapter 1, however, this is not easy to do. Schools are artificial institutions in which students are artificially grouped together in order to meet society's mandate that they become educated. This artificiality often causes the daily instructional activities to be artificial. That is, reading and writing activity in school seldom engages students in proactive, enthusiastic use of language and higher-order thinking in the service of controlling and enriching their lives. More typically, school reading and writing activity involves the reading of teacher-selected passages and drill and practice on language components, both done without regard for whether those activities serve to help students control or enrich their current lives. As a result, students seldom have experience with genuine literacy in school. And with no experience in being literate, students are unable to be literate when they get out of school.

A **curriculum** is a description of what to teach. In this case, we are concerned about what to teach to develop genuine literacy. The temptation is often to begin immediately looking for the bits and pieces of skills and strategies associated with reading and writing because that is what we remember learning in school. But a curriculum cannot be just the bits and pieces of what to teach. A curriculum must, instead, be dominated by the goal. In this case, the goal is to develop literate people. This means that the school must be a place where, first and foremost, students experience what it is to be literate. Therefore, the reading and writing curriculum must, first and foremost, provide experiences in proactively and enthusiastically using language and higher-order thinking in the service of controlling and enriching their lives. All the bits and pieces that are also taught as part of the curriculum must be dominated by that overall goal.

WHOLE LANGUAGE AS A GUIDE TO CURRICULUM BUILDING

This book uses the philosophy of **whole language** as a guide in thinking about the reading and writing curriculum. This philosophy focuses on the wholeness of the reading and writing curriculum—that it should not be broken into isolated bits and pieces. This wholeness takes three forms.

Wholistic reading encounters emphasize listening, speaking, reading, and writing.

First, the curriculum should be whole in the sense that what is taught is always taught within the context of the pursuit of meaningful activity—that is, what is taught is always taught as part of an authentic activity in which students are controlling or enriching their lives. By always teaching reading and writing in this context, we are assured that students experience being literate.

Second, the curriculum should be whole in the sense that language is message-sending—the function is communication. For communication to occur, there must be someone to send a message and someone to receive it. If a message is not worth sending or is of little interest to the receiver, there is little communication. Hence, instruction is whole in that it involves all the **language arts**—reading, listening, speaking, and writing.

Third, the curriculum should be whole in the sense that the bits and pieces that are the component parts of language—that is, the skills and strategies—remain subordinate to the function of language as message-sending and -receiving in the pursuit of one's life. Consequently, individual language components must never obscure the whole—the use of language to achieve authentic goals.

Comprehension is the goal of all communication. In the **expressive language modes** of speaking and writing, comprehension means understanding the message well enough to compose it clearly. In the **receptive language modes** of listening and reading, comprehension means interpreting the message accurately enough to understand its meaning. Consequently, reading instruction focuses on getting meaning from text; writing instruction focuses on creating meaning in text. Because the various language modes are so inextricably bound up with one another, it is almost impossible to teach one in isolation from the others. Comprehension must be whole.

Comprehension makes the world of literacy available. When creative writers compose messages that cause us to see the world differently, as with good literature, literacy is a recreational (and often aesthetic) experience. When writers share functional knowledge, as with written directions or textbooks, literacy is a practical experience. Therefore, the main purpose of reading instruction is to teach students to eagerly engage in literate activities using both **recreational text** and **functional text**. Again, it must be whole. It will be if your reading instruction reflects the following:

- Reading instruction should be integrated in natural ways with the other language arts of listening, speaking, and writing.

- Students' reading and writing should always involve messages that are sent and received in pursuit of controlling or enriching their lives.

- Reading instruction should develop students who eagerly read all kinds of written text.

Figure 2.1 summarizes the relationships among the major language concepts that are central to a **whole language approach** to reading.

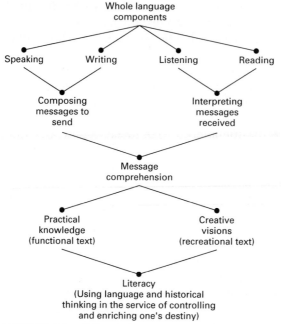

FIGURE 2.1   Relationships among Major Language Concepts.

DESCRIBING READING

Traditionally, reading was described as a series of competencies or skills to be mastered. These competencies were identified by breaking the reading act into its component parts. It was logically assumed that the smallest unit in reading was the alphabet letter and its associated sound, and descriptions of reading often began with letters and letter sounds, then progressed to syllables, then to words, then to phrases, then to sentences, and so on. The idea was that the best way to understand reading was to isolate its individual aspects. Reading instruction consisted of teaching each of these separate parts, and students were considered good readers if they mastered each one. It was assumed that reading would result when all the separate parts had been learned. Given this point of view, it is understandable why many teachers emphasize isolated skill instruction during reading.

However, reading is not performing a series of independent skills, but rather is the simultaneous interaction of various kinds of information in the pursuit of authentic purposes. Neither does reading begin with the alphabet and proceed in an orderly progression to meaning; it starts by seeking meaning, and it uses a variety of sources, including the letters of the alphabet, to create meaning. Additionally, reading is not a matter of determining a single correct meaning in text; it is a matter of interpreting the text based on what the reader already knows.

Humans organize what they know about a topic (from **direct** or **vicarious experiences**) into categories or mental structures called **schemata**. Whenever you begin talking or writing about a particular topic, you compose your message by drawing on the information you have in that schema. Whenever you read or listen to someone else talk about a topic, you interpret the message in terms of what you already know about the topic. The amount of information you have organized into a given schema depends on your experience with or prior knowledge about that topic. The more you know about a topic, the richer your schema is and the better you will understand messages about that topic; the less you know, the more barren your schema is and the less you will understand about that topic. For instance, the authors of this book have spent years studying effective reading instruction and, consequently, have a richer schema for reading instruction than you do. Hence, when we read a text on reading instruction, we comprehend more and detect more fine-grained levels of meaning than you do.

Concepts about Reading

Supporting any understanding of reading are your concepts about its essential functions. For instance, you conceptualize reading as a message-sending, message-receiving activity. You know that at one end is a person (an author)

Teachers want students to understand what reading can do for them.

who has a message to send, and at the other end is another person (a reader) who wants to understand the message. You want your students to demonstrate a similar understanding of this author-reader relationship. If they do not—if, for instance, they think reading is saying each word on a page correctly or that it is sounding out words—then they will have difficulty becoming truly literate.

Similarly, you want your students to articulate that reading is communication and that writing and reading are related. You want to know that they understand what reading can do for them and how important it is. And you want them to conceptualize reading as something that is controllable: to know that reading ability is not a matter of being smarter than someone else but of knowing how the comprehension system works and that they can use this knowledge to get meaning from text.

These concepts are essential because they provide motivation for learning to read. If students develop the understanding that reading is something done only in school and that it is an arbitrary and mysterious process over which they have little control, they probably will not want to learn to read and will not read outside school. On the other hand, if you ensure that your students receive messages they really want to understand and that they feel empowered to make sense of these messages, they will develop accurate concepts for reading, will want to learn to read and will read outside school. These early concepts about reading form the basis of students' attitudes and responses toward it.

Making Sense Out of Reading

Language is the communication and clarification of thought from one person to another. In the case of this book, we (the authors) want to communicate to you (the reader) our thoughts about reading instruction so your schema will be richer. We want you to understand reading instruction as we do. Your ability to comprehend our text depends upon a variety of factors, which we will now examine.

The Role of Prior Knowledge

Various kinds of **prior knowledge** influence readers' ability to comprehend what they read about a topic. For instance, you have much prior knowledge about the topic of reading instruction simply by virtue of having gone to school. However, your prior knowledge about reading instruction differs somewhat from that of your classmates who went to different schools. When the information each of you gets from this book interacts with your prior knowledge about reading instruction, each of you actively interprets what you read in terms of what you have previously learned. Consequently, you and your friends construct slightly different meanings from this text.

In addition to prior knowledge about a topic, readers also use prior knowledge about language and how it works. For instance, you know from experience that certain language conventions are followed when you read (starting at the left side of the page and moving right); that certain combinations of letters (c-o-m-b) represent specific words; that certain words (because, next) signal particular relationships (cause-effect, sequence); that certain kinds of text (newspaper articles) are structured differently from other kinds of text (sonnets); that the meaning in one sentence can often provide clues to specific word meanings in another sentence; and that common meanings can by synthesized across large segments of text.

Some of this prior knowledge about language is automatic. That is, because some aspects of language are stable and are used in the same form all the time, you memorize them. Examples include left-to-right directionality across the page, letter sounds, and instant recognition of common words. Other aspects of prior knowledge about language are strategic. That is, because comprehension of text demands flexibility, you must reason, must be aware metacognitively of how to figure out what makes the most sense. Good examples include predicting what is to come, using context clues to establish the meaning of an unknown word, inferencing, and synthesizing.

Readers also use their prior knowledge about the social situation within which comprehension takes place. For instance, when prior knowledge of a certain school situation tells you that the purpose of a reading assignment is to pass a factual test, you read differently than if the purpose is to solve a problem important to you.

Similarly, prior experience with an author, such as Ernest Hemingway, or with a particular type of text, such as directions for completing tax returns, will influence how readers comprehend. Because of prior knowledge about Hemingway and tax forms, you use different comprehension strategies for each.

In a sense, even readers' prior feelings influence comprehension. If your previous experiences with reading have been generally positive, you tend to have a better attitude toward reading, are more motivated about it, and expect it to be a good experience. If, on the other hand, your previous experiences with reading have been negative, you either try to avoid it altogether or to develop strategies that allow you to minimize the amount you do.

The Role of Text   Readers make sense out of text. The **text** is the printed matter an author creates to convey his or her ideas. The meaning is the author's, and the text carries that meaning. In composing text, authors use conventions of the language system to signal meaning to the reader. You use your understanding of those conventions as well as prior knowledge about the topic, purpose, and reading to reconstruct the author's message. Because your background knowledge is different from the writer's, you always construct a slightly different message than the author intended. Again, the meaning is not in the printed text; it is constructed by each reader, who uses prior knowledge about the topic, purpose, and language conventions to interpret the author's message.

The Role of Inferencing   Because comprehension depends on interpreting new knowledge in terms of what readers already know about a topic, virtually all comprehension is inferential. Whenever you receive a spoken or written message, you make **inferences** or predictions about the intended meaning—that is, you infer or predict what the author is trying to communicate to you. These inferences are based on prior knowledge about language, the topic, the purposes for reading the text, and the strategic reasoning required to comprehend language.

It works like this, First, you look at the print (letters and words) for cues about the topic. You establish what the topic is and then use what you already know about that topic (your schema for that topic) to infer what the author intends to convey. You make inferences based on what you know about the author's purpose in writing the selection and your own purpose for reading it. Finally, you strategically adjust meaning as you are reading on the basis of your understanding of language. For instance, knowing that the text you will read is a political speech and knowing that the meaning of political speeches is different from that of a comedian's monologue, you expect a certain type of meaning from the text.

The Role of Metacognitive Strategies   Rather than constructing meaning randomly, readers use metacognitive strategies to reason about the author's meaning. **Metacognitive strategies,** in contrast to routine skills, require awareness, conscious thought, and reasoning. When *beginning to read*, you use initiating strategies to **activate background knowledge** and make initial predictions. When something does not make sense *while reading*, you stop, analyze the situation in terms of what is known about the reading system, and try to repair the blockage by using fix-it strategies. *After reading*, you use post-reading strategies to determine larger meanings. For instance, a reader who has a strong background in unions will initially predict that a passage titled "The Strike" is going to be about unions and will activate that schema and make appropriate predictions. However, when the first line of text starts out, "When Anne rolled her last ball and got her twelfth strike in a row...," the reader will stop, confirm that the message is about a game instead of a union, and "fix" the situation by substituting a "bowling" schema for the "union" schema. After finishing the passage, the reader will reflect on it, perhaps drawing conclusions about the concentration demanded to roll 12 strikes in a row.

The Role of Situation   Inferencing and **strategic behavior** result from interactions between reader and text; the situation or context in which reading occurs is also important. If the situation is a casual look at a magazine while waiting to be picked up by a friend, the meaning you get will be different from reading the directions for your tax forms. Similarly, the school context influences meaning. For example, the meaning you get from reading a social studies text for a multiple choice test will be different from reading done to solve a genuine, real-world problem. Hence, the context of the reading situation plays an important part in comprehension.

See Example 2.1 for an illustration of text comprehension.

EXAMPLE   2.1   Comprehending Text

The Rotation

The rotation in a Piper Cherokee occurs at 60 miles an hour. When achieving that IAS, apply back pressure on the yoke and step on the right rudder. Soon you will achieve your best angle of climb.

When reading this text you use prior knowledge from a variety of sources simultaneously. You use what you know about print to identify the words "the rotation" in the title and probably predict a meaning associated in some way with turn taking or revolving. However, by the time you read the first line, you encounter other words, such as "Piper Cherokee" and "60 miles an hour," which cause you to revise that prediction. If you have enough prior knowledge about airplanes to include Piper Cherokee in your airplane schema, you probably predict an airplane topic at this point, although unless you have a very rich airplane schema you may not yet be able to construct a meaning for *rotation.* However, if you knew that this passage appeared in a chapter entitled "How to Take Off and Land a Small Plane," your choice of predictions for rotation narrows to airplanes landing and taking off. On the other hand, if this passage appeared in a book on Favorite After Dinner Jokes of Famous Toastmasters, you would start forming hypotheses about where the punch line is in relation to the word *rotation*—you abandon the schema "how to fly an airplane" and get your mind in gear for a joke. You use all these various knowledge sources almost simultaneously, monitoring your sense making as you proceed and being strategic about building meaning. Every time you encounter unknown terminol-

ogy, such as "IAS," or identify a word having a meaning you associate with a totally different topic, such as "yoke," you generate new hypotheses.

By testing hypotheses that are triggered by combinations of your knowledge of language and the topic, you gradually build a meaning for "The Rotation." You probably construct a message about the steps involved in getting a small airplane to take off. Depending on the richness of your small plane schema, you may correctly infer that rotation is that point when the plane first leaves the ground, or you may remain unclear about the precise meaning of rotation while still comprehending the essential message about taking off.

Differences in schemata are crucial. For instance, those who build a meaning for "The Rotation" based on a sparse schema for airplanes may get the essential sense of what is happening but will not have a clear understanding of where the yoke is, what a rudder looks like, what the best angle of climb is, and so on. Most licensed pilots, however, will not only construct those additional meanings but will be critical of the use of the term "best angle of climb" because they will feel it is not precise enough to describe that situation. In short, they go beyond the text passage and make a judgment.

Defining Reading

The focus of reading is meaning getting, or comprehending the content of a text for practical or aesthetic purposes. Meaning results from the simultaneous interaction of a variety of information that is available from the reader, from the text, and from the situation that directs the reading act. When reading is initiated, these knowledge sources interact simultaneously. The reader predicts the meaning of the text, revises predictions on the basis of additional knowledge, and gradually constructs an interpretation of the message, employing **fix-it strategies** when the sense breaks down and reflective strategies following the completion of reading. We define reading as *purposeful reconstruction of an author's printed message for recreational, aesthetic, or functional purposes.*

RELATING READING AND WRITING

Because reading is part of a whole language process, it should be taught in close association with oral language (listening and speaking) and writing. The relationship between reading and writing is particularly important because both are based on print; consequently, reading instruction should be closely tied to writing instruction.

Writing is important to reading growth for three reasons. First, readers and writers use the same set of written language signals. Writers must understand and manipulate these signals when composing a message that readers can reconstruct by interpreting the same signals. Thus, students' understanding of the system of language signals is enhanced when they use them in writing as well as in reading.

Second, there is a close relationship between what readers do and think as they reconstruct meaning from text and what writers do and think as they compose text. For instance, both good readers and good writers understand that the purpose of written language is to communicate a message to someone who is not physically present to receive it. Consequently, both the act of composing and the act of comprehending require an empathy for the person at the other end of the communication channel, a monitoring of the sense-making process as it proceeds, and the use of strategies to clarify (in the case of writing) and to reconstruct (in the case of reading) meaning.

Third, writing is important to the development of reading because a good writing program increases the amount of time spent on text. No matter how much time is spent in the reading program, student learning is enhanced if additional time is devoted to composing text, a task that requires much the same kind of thinking. Consequently, good reading teachers work hard to integrate writing instruction into their reading programs.

BUILDING A READING CURRICULUM

As noted earlier in this chapter, the dominant force in building a reading curriculum should be the overall goal—what you want the student to become ultimately. In this case, we want the students to become literate—to proactively and enthusiastically use language and higher-order thinking in the service of controlling and enriching their destinies. However, although the overall goal must dominate, building a curriculum is aided by thinking in terms of subgoals.

SUBGOALS OF WHOLISTIC READING INSTRUCTION

There are three major subgoals for reading instruction. Because the function of language is to communicate, the first subgoal is to have students comprehend what they read. They should understand the **content** of the selections they read. The second subgoal is students with positive **attitudes** about reading: They should be enthusiastically involved in literacy events, they should love to read, and they should understand what reading can do for them. Finally, because the best learners are in conscious control of their reading, the third subgoal is to produce students who comprehend and are also aware of *how* they comprehend. They should be metacognitive about the **process** of reading. When students are consciously aware of how reading works, they are able to figure out the meaning of difficult text when no teacher is available to guide them.

All three subgoals involve both cognition and metacognition. **Cognition** refers to the various mental processes you go through to comprehend the meaning of a text. **Metacognition**, as noted, is awareness of the mental processing you go through. Therefore, when you read a text, you are metacognitive if you not only comprehend the meaning but are aware of the mental processes that produced comprehension and use this awareness to regulate your comprehension.

To summarize, the three subgoals of reading instruction have two dimensions: the cognitive acts associated with reading and being metacognitive about these acts. Acquiring an awareness of these two dimensions puts students in conscious control of the process of constructing meaning from text, which is a key to being enthusiastic readers. Enabling students to develop such control is what reading instruction is all about. Figure 2.2 summarizes the goals of reading instruction.

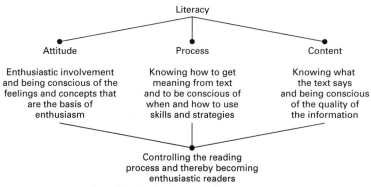

FIGURE 2.2   Subgoals of Wholistic Reading Instruction

Although these three subgoals are separated for instructional purposes (both in this book and when planning reading instruction), they are not separated in reality. On the contrary, they are interactive—that is, each of the three subgoals influences and is influenced by each of the others. During classroom instruction, you will seldom focus on one subgoal to the total exclusion of the others. A particular lesson may have a process goal as a primary focus (the observable layer of the lesson) and still develop attitude and content goals (the hidden layers of the lesson). This is particularly true when instruction is examined in units or clusters of related lessons.

Figure 2.3 illustrates the nonlinear, interactive nature of reading. Note that the figure begins with attitude goals. This is not because attitude goals are necessarily taught first, but because students' attitudes about reading interact in a fundamental way with all the other goals. The process goals are listed next, not because they necessarily precede the reading of real text, but to illustrate the means-ends relationship that exists between process and content goals. Process goals have value only when they are applied to the content of real text. Finally, content goals are connected to attitude goals in order to illustrate that what students learn about comprehending text influences their understanding of reading and their attitudes toward it. The arrows are double-headed to emphasize the interrelationships among these outcomes.

We teach reading to develop the attitude, process, and content subgoals that together help students achieve the ultimate goal of being literate. These subgoals are imbedded in the reading **curriculum**—the planned learning experiences you design to produce motivated, independent readers.

Decisions about the reading curriculum, about what to teach in reading, are determined by the subgoals of reading instruction. Because students need to understand and enjoy reading, part of your curriculum focuses on building accurate concepts and positive responses to reading (attitude goals). Because students need to be conscious of how they get meaning from text, part of your curriculum focuses on how reading works (process goals). Because students need to understand the messages in texts, part of your curriculum focuses on helping them get content from text (content goals). Figure 2.4, an elaboration of Figure 2.3, shows how the three subgoals interact and contribute to the development of reading. A more extended discussion of the three subgoals follows.

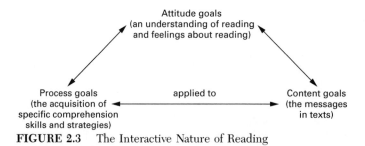

FIGURE 2.3   The Interactive Nature of Reading

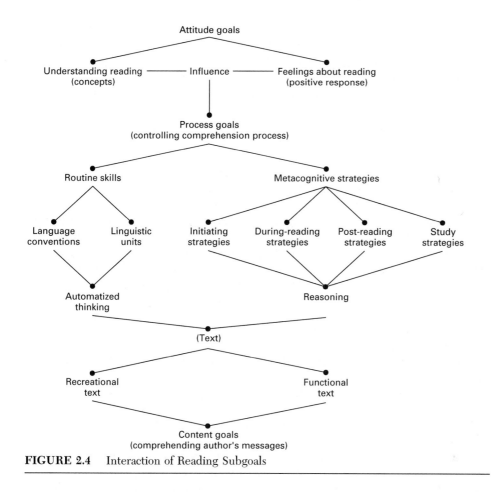

FIGURE 2.4 Interaction of Reading Subgoals

Attitude Goals

Students must have a positive attitude about reading. That is, they cannot have incomplete or erroneous concepts about reading or perceive reading negatively. You will need to help them develop their concepts of reading and to instill positive responses.

Concepts A **concept** is the combination of all the characteristics you associate with something. Every concept has an identifying word or label. For example, a familiar word like *dog* probably brings to mind many characteristics. For the word *platypus*, however, you may generate only a few characteristics and, as a result, your concept of platypus is not as rich as your concept of dog. Because everyone has had different experiences, everyone generates slightly different characteristics for identical concepts. Even a common word like *dog* results in slightly different mental images because of different background experiences.

Similarly, different students have different concepts of reading. For instance, if school reading experiences primarily emphasize work sheets, drill, and correct answers, students will think reading is work sheets, drill, and correct answers. If, in contrast, school reading experiences emphasize meeting needs and solving problems, students will think reading is meaning getting, sense making, and problem solving.

One of the fundamental goals in reading instruction is to help students understand that reading is a meaning-getting activity. Such a concept of reading contributes to a positive attitude about reading by setting for students accurate expectations about what real readers actually do. To build this concept, teachers provide positive experiences with reading that highlight the fact that text is produced by a writer who has a message to convey and that all reading involves interpreting the writer's message. Students' encounters with reading should emphasize the relationship among all four language modes: listening, speaking, reading, and writing. They will then learn that both speaking and writing involve a message sender who composes a message; that listening and reading involve a message receiver who interprets the message; and that reading and writing are not different subjects but opposite ends of the communication process.

Positive Responses   Positive responses are closely tied to a conceptual understanding of reading, because it is difficult for people to feel good about something when they have misconceptions about it. The chances of creating positive attitudes become better when students' reading experiences deal with messages of interest to them and are easy enough to be performed successfully. Hence, to create positive responses to reading you should provide reading experiences that have interesting content and that can be completed successfully. When these conditions are present, your students will develop positive responses to reading. Details for teaching attitude goals are provided in Chapter 5, and suggestions for developing attitudes at various grade levels are provided in Chapters 16 through 19.

Process Goals

The second subgoal of reading instruction focuses on how reading works—that is, on the development of routine skills and metacognitive strategies.

Routine Skills   Good readers do some things automatically and they think carefully (or reason) about other things. Those things done automatically are **routine skills** and include both language conventions and various linguistic units.

Language conventions are arbitrary rules that govern text. In English, examples include reading from the front of a book to the back, from the top of a page to the bottom, from the left side of the page to the right, and from the left side of a word to the right. Expert readers take such conventions for granted, but beginning readers who have no previous experience with English text may start reading at the back of a book, at the bottom of a page, or at the right-hand side of a page or word. Indeed, text in languages other than English may begin not at the front but at the back of the book, not at the top but at the bottom of the page, and not at the left but at the right sides of the page and word. To be in control of the reading process, students need to automatically apply these conventions when reading.

Linguistic units are letter combinations that students should learn to recognize without conscious effort, such as sight words, letter-name and letter-sound associations, and the meanings of common prefixes and suffixes. **Sight words** appear so frequently in English text that students should identify them instantly. It would be inefficient to expect readers to figure out common words such as "have" or "the" every time they encounter them. Instead, reading is more fluent when readers recognize most of these words at sight. That is, they memorize them through frequent use. Similarly, students should not have to consciously figure out the sound associated with every alphabet letter or letter-sound combination (such as *tr* or *th*). That would also be inefficient, if not impossible. Consequently, you should teach letter sounds as routine skills to be memorized so they can be recalled automatically when needed. The same is true of common prefixes and suffixes, as well as other linguistic units.

Metacognitive Strategies   Although routine skills are important, an even more important part of reading involves metacognitive strategies. Four kinds of metacognitive strategies are particularly important.

Initiating strategies are used as you begin to read; they involve activating background knowledge about the topic, the type of text, and purpose in reading it and making appropriate predictions.

During-reading strategies are used while comprehending and consist of two substrategies. The first is **monitoring,** in which you check the accuracy of your predictions and prepare to stop and generate new predictions if the text cues do not conform to your expectations. Monitoring refers to the constant test readers apply to what they read: "Is this the meaning I expected and does it make sense in terms of what I know about the world?" This strategy is the heart of comprehension; readers who do not monitor their meaning getting are not aware when their reading fails to make sense. Once monitoring reveals a problem with getting the meaning, readers must use **fix-it strategies** to generate new predictions or to remove the blockage to meaning. Ideally students would always be able to construct accurate meaning using initiating strategies. Such is not always the case, however. Frequently students will encounter words they cannot identify in print, will be unable to interpret the relationships being communicated by the author, will lose track of the gist of the message, or will be unable to make the inferences or draw the conclusions essential to the author's message. In such cases they need strategies they can apply to fix their comprehension—to remove the blockage, restore the meaning, and allow for the continuation of fluent reading.

Post-reading strategies are used after reading to organize, restructure, and make judgments about the author's message.

These three metacognitive strategies interact: a reader makes initial predictions about meaning, uses during-reading strategies to monitor meaning getting to confirm or reject these predictions and to fix or construct new interpretations whenever needed, and uses post-reading strategies to reflect on the author's message. This interactive process happens almost instantaneously. Following is an illustration of how these three metacognitive strategies might work in comprehending a book about the rules of baseball.

On the basis of previous experience with the topic (the rules of baseball), the kind of text it is (an information book on "How to Play the Game of Baseball"), and the purpose (to convey the basic procedures in playing the game), the reader initiates meaning getting by activating appropriate schemata and making predictions regarding what will be learned about baseball. In a sense, it is a getting-ready step in which the reader activates appropriate background knowledge to prepare for making sense out of an author's message. Second, while reading, the reader monitors meaning getting. As each word or group of words on the page is identified, the reader attaches meaning based on his or her schemata for that topic, type of text, and purpose. The reader then confirms or rejects these predicted meanings by testing them against the **syntactic** or **semantic** cues imbedded in the text. If the prediction is confirmed, the reader goes on; if it is rejected in view of subsequent syntactic and semantic cues, the reader uses fix-it strategies to repair the blockage so that meaning getting can continue. Finally, after completing the reading, the information about baseball is organized and evaluated, particularly in view of the reader's purpose.

Study strategies, a fourth set of metacognitive strategies, are specialized strategies readers use to locate, organize, and remember text information, particularly the information found in textbooks, encyclopedias, and other functional text. For instance, expert readers locate information by using tables of contents, indexes, and card catalogs; they organize information by taking notes and outlining; and they remember information by using systematic study techniques. Because study strategies are usually used in association with content areas such as social studies and science, they are usually taught at the upper elementary grades.

Some people think of all the metacognitive strategies as "skills." However, skills are procedures to be memorized in isolation, and as a result, students use them automatically rather than thoughtfully and strategically. Although skills are useful and important for language conventions and linguistic units, comprehension of text requires flexible and adaptive reasoning—as opposed to routine and unvarying procedures—to reconstruct an author's meaning. So metacognitive strategies are not skills; rather, they are flexible and adaptable plans to be learned consciously. Once learned, the strategies may be applied automatically in highly familiar text situations that are easy for the reader to comprehend, but they will become conscious again when the reader encounters difficult text.

Details for teaching process goals associated with words are provided in Chapter 7, and Chapter 8 describes how to teach process goals associated with the strategies for comprehension. Suggestions for developing process goals at various grade levels are provided in Chapters 16 through 19.

Content Goals

The ultimate goal of reading is to interpret the author's message; therefore, readers have achieved the content subgoal when they can state what the author's message is. Process and content goals represent a means-ends relationship: Getting meaning from content is the end, and understanding how reading works is a means to that end.

Functional texts are those texts in which the content is utilitarian information. Normally, they are written as **expository text.** Textbooks are a good example; others are newspapers, catalogs, recipes, application forms, encyclopedias, various kinds of written directions, and so on.

When presenting such functional texts to your students, you should orient them to specific terminology or unknown words being employed, help them activate the appropriate **topic** schemata, provide information about the author's purpose in writing the text and the students' **purpose** in reading it, and help them anticipate and interpret the **text structure.**

Recreational texts are those texts in which the content is entertaining or enriching. Normally, recreational writing takes the form of **narrative texts.** These include nearly all forms of fiction, such as short stories, novels, and fictionalized biographies; other forms include fables, mythology, fairy tales, other folk literature, and poetry.

A major strategy used to involve students in recreational text is **uninterrupted sustained silent reading** (USSR) in which students and teachers quietly read books of their choice. Many teachers also plan daily sessions in which they orally read good literature to students, and teachers frequently have students share their favorite recreational reading with each other. The basal reading textbook typically contains numerous selections of recreational reading, many of which are excerpts from excellent examples of children's literature. When presenting such text to your students, you should provide guidance similar to that noted for functional text: Prepare students for the selection by helping them activate relevant background knowledge. In addition, you should often use recreational reading activities to teach such literary devices as metaphors, symbolism, and others.

It is important to note that the instructional focus of content goals is not so students can identify particular examples of text as "functional" or "recreational," but so they can get meaning from both kinds of text. Getting meaning in recreational text, which is primarily narrative, is a different task from getting meaning from functional text, which is primarily expository. Details for teaching content goals appear in Chapter 6. Suggestions for developing content goals at various grade levels are provided in Chapters 16 through 19.

Summary of Reading Curriculum Subgoals

A good reader is one who chooses to read independently, possesses the routine skills and metacognitive strategies to control the process of getting meaning, and applies what is known about how reading works to get the messages in functional and recreational text. No one of these three subgoals is more important than another, nor do you teach one as a prerequisite to another. Rather, all three are developed together and interact in support and encouraging reading growth.

The reading curriculum, then, is a direct reflection of the three subgoals that contribute to the goal of literacy. To build attitude goals, you create instructional encounters designed to build desired concepts and positive responses to reading; to develop process goals, you directly teach the routine skills and metacognitive strategies your students need to fluently generate predictions about the author's meaning and to restore meaning when the predictions are rejected; and to develop content goals, you guide your students' attempts to get the messages in functional and recreational text.

INTEGRATING THE WRITING CURRICULUM

Although this is a book about reading instruction, the close relationship between reading and writing means that reading teachers often integrate writing instruction with reading instruction. To help you accomplish such integration, we provide a brief description of the writing curriculum here and mention writing in subsequent chapters where appropriate.

There are many similarities between the reading and writing curricula. Just as the ultimate outcome of reading instruction is using text to control and enrich one's life, the ultimate outcome of writing instruction is creating text to control and enrich one's life. Your students should know how to compose the functional and recreational messages they wish to write. To accomplish this, you must help students develop positive attitudes toward writing, knowledge of the content to be communicated, and an understanding of how the writing process works.

Attitude Goals

Like reading, writing growth depends upon good attitudes about writing. These attitudes are based in students' concepts about writing, which grow from their encounters with writing.

These concepts are virtually the same as those in reading. Students should understand the reader-writer relationship. That is, they should understand that writers are the first to read their own composed text; writing is message sending and always involves an audience; the audience can be oneself as well as others; writing is similar to speaking except that the audience is not physically present; and writing fulfills both functional and recreational needs.

When students enjoy reading their own writing, the experience will be positive.

Similarly, you should make sure students have positive encounters with writing. They should associate writing with enjoyment, fulfillment, and meaningful activity rather than with fear, work, and defeat. To develop accurate concepts and positive experiences you must provide students with writing experiences that are useful, pleasant, satisfying, and reasonably natural. If this does not happen—if their writing encounters are useless, unpleasant, and contrived—students will develop inaccurate concepts and negative feelings about writing.

Content Goals

The content of writing is whatever message the writer wants to send. For instance, students should be able to compose such functional messages as business letters, friendly letters, simple expository text, reports, newspaper articles, and formal term papers. For recreation messages students should be able to compose diaries, journals, stories, poems, riddles, and jingles, among others. Before composing various kinds of text, however, they must decide upon the purpose and content of the message. When students have clear and meaningful reasons for writing, they seldom have difficulty knowing what to say.

You should also help students distinguish between writing for oneself and writing for others. The content of personal writing (diaries, journals, reflections, recipes) is different from the content of writing produced for an outside audience. Text written for personal use is not so concerned with clarity or adherence to the mechanics of language, because there is little chance that writers will fail to understand their own messages to themselves, even when inaccuracies are present. When writing for others, however, both clarity and language mechanics must be emphasized to assist readers in reconstructing the message. In short, the content goals in a writing curriculum should help students identify the message they want to send, distinguish between writing for oneself and writing for others, and distinguish the text structures associated with various kinds of functional and recreational text.

Process Goals

Process goals in writing are divided into two categories: knowledge of the stages in the composing process and strategies for implementing each stage.

Knowledge of the Stages of Writing To be in control of the writing process, students must first know what stages writers go through in composing text. All writers must plan, draft, and edit.

The **planning stage** emphasizes reflection. A writer decides upon the purpose of a message, the central meaning to be conveyed, and the supportive information to be included. An important part of the planning stage is to think about who will read the message and how to adapt it to that audience. For instance, when writing about a complex topic for a knowledgeable audience, elaborate background information is not needed. On the other hand, when the intended audience is relatively unsophisticated about the topic, it is necessary to build a background before launching into the central message. Consequently, the planning stage must take into account the intended reader's values and schemata.

The planning stage also includes organizing the message into an appropriate text structure. For instance, in composing a story, the text structure usually follows a progression from the setting to the main character, to the character's problem, to a series of events that occur, to a resolution of the problem. In contrast, in composing a news article, the usual text structure is to have all the relevant information in the first paragraph and to assign the details to subsequent paragraphs. Planning is especially crucial when the audience is someone other than oneself, since the text structure helps the reader reconstruct the message.

In the **drafting stage** the writer composes a message in rough form, concentrating on producing a coherent and cohesive text. Coherence (the ideas fit together) and cohesiveness (the central message is maintained throughout the text) are important whether the writer is producing functional or recreational text.

In the **editing stage** the writer critically reads his or her text, trying to anticipate where readers might have difficulty. All stages of the composing process are important, but editing is particularly important because it is here that the message is honed and polished to ensure that the reader makes an interpretation close to what the writer intends. Editing encompasses all aspects of the writing process: The writer edits in terms of the planning stage (content and audience), the drafting stage (text structure, coherence, and cohesiveness), and the finer points of the editing stage (word and phrase choice, punctuation, grammatical accuracy, and spelling).

These stages are not necessarily linear. Writers often move from planning to drafting and back again before all the planning is complete. Similarly, editing often occurs before the drafting stage is complete. This is particularly true when writing for an audience other than oneself. Nevertheless, the typical progression is as follows: A writer plans for the content, the audience, and the basic text structure; this plan is then used to produce a coherent and cohesive first draft; the draft is then edited for content, clarity, and the mechanics of written language, a process which often proceeds through several additional drafts.

Strategies to Be Used at Each Stage   The strategies used in writing are similar to those in reading. Whereas readers consciously monitor their understanding of an author's message and stop when there is a blockage and activate a fix-it strategy, writers consciously monitor what they are composing for potential blockages to readers' comprehension. When a potential blockage is detected, the writer calls on a planning, drafting, or editing strategy to remove it.

Three strategies are helpful at the planning stage. The first planning strategy involves getting the necessary information, either by brainstorming, reading, interviewing, or observing. An important distinction must be made here: When students complain that they do not know what to write about, it is often because the writing task is not meaningful to them—it is busy work. The problem is not a lack of information but a meaningless assignment; the solution, then, is to give students a good reason for writing rather than strategies for getting more information. If students do lack information about a real message that will be sent to someone, then ways to gather information must be taught. The second planning strategy involves focusing on what is to be said, which often involves clarifying the purpose of the writing. Students can accomplish this by grouping or categorizing gathered information. The third planning strategy focuses on organizing: It calls for procedures such as outlining, in which related concepts are grouped together in a chosen text structure.

Drafting-stage strategies focus on creating coherence and cohesion in the message. To ensure coherence, the age-old method of adding introductory and summary statements and wrapping them around the central message is a reliable remedy. This solution can be adapted to both functional and recreational writing. It is most often associated with expository text, in which it is used to provide coherence to paragraphs, sections, and entire texts. Another way to make expository text coherent is to carefully use headings and subheadings to guide the reader. For narrative text students can follow a story map, which sequences the events. To ensure cohesion students may insert transition statements between paragraphs and sections and insert signal words that key one section of text to another. Particularly useful is the strategy of including periodic summaries. In functional text summaries remind readers of key points, concepts, or the main idea; in recreational text summaries can remind readers of the problem, the sequence of events relating to the problem, or the theme.

Editing-stage strategies focus on helping the reader reconstruct the intended meaning. Editing requires the writer to play two roles simultaneously: During this process the writer is also a reader. Although multiparagraph organizational characteristics are sometimes modified at the editing stage, most editing focuses on the sentence and word levels. For instance, writers use synonyms and a thesaurus to make more precise word choices, syntactic changes to improve meaning through word order, punctuation to help the reader understand what the author intended, and spelling to help the reader identify the words. These strategies are often referred to as the mechanics of writing and are sometimes incorrectly taught as skills to be memorized through synonym and antonym drills, sentence diagramming, punctuation drills, and weekly spelling tests. When students are taught writing mechanics in this way, they seldom apply them to the actual task of composing. When taught as strategies to be used when editing a real message, however, mechanics become more meaningful and useful.

Summarizing, the writing curriculum involves giving students information about how the writing process works, just as the reading curriculum involves giving information about how the reading process works. In both cases the intent is to have students who are in cognitive control of the communication process and who can apply appropriate strategies to repair actual or potential blockages to meaning getting. Suggestions for integrating writing into various reading goals are provided in Chapters 5 through 9, and suggestions for using writing when teaching various grade levels are provided in Chapters 16 through 19.

THE IMPORTANCE OF WHY

Professional teachers understand why they teach what they teach. Technicians who have no such rationale blindly follow directions contained in teachers' manuals and workbook pages. They do not know why they are doing what they do, so they have no basis for making their own decisions. Knowing why things are done in a certain way provides the cohesiveness that glues the instructional reading program together. The technician's emphasis on isolated tasks, mechanics, and surface answers, in contrast, tends to create a disjointed and mechanical instructional program.

Knowing why you are doing things is the first step in becoming a professional decision maker. You must know why reading and writing are related and why particular content, attitude, and process goals contribute to literacy.

This book emphasizes justifying instructional decisions by referring to the desired literacy goal. Although many classroom constraints limit what teachers can do and the materials they can use, professionals rise above these constraints. They shape instructional encounters to create genuine occasions for literacy. Thus, professional teachers are in cognitive control and are prepared for continuous modification, refinement, and improvement of instruction.

SUMMARY

Writers purposefully construct text so their messages will be read and readers purposefully reconstruct text to receive messages. To get messages from text, readers simultaneously combine cues the author embeds in the text and cues from their own prior knowledge about the topic and about reading itself, strategically inferring the meaning the author intended. Consequently, the reader must have a positive attitude based on a conceptual understanding of reading and its function; an understanding of the mental processing good readers engage in to construct meaning; and ultimately an understanding of the content of the message. These three components—positive attitudes about reading, awareness of the processes involved, and understanding the content of text—are the subgoals of reading instruction: When you teach a reading curriculum, you teach attitudes about reading, mental processes employed by good readers, and comprehension of text content. Because reading and writing are so closely related, analogous attitude, process, and content goals are developed during writing instruction. Both reading and writing curricular subgoals are embedded in experiences with genuine literacy.

SUGGESTED ADDITIONAL READING

ARTLEY, A. S. (1980). Reading: Skills or competencies? *Language Arts, 57*(5), 546–549.

AUTEN, A. (1985). Focus on thinking instruction. *Reading Teacher, 38*(4), 454–456.

BABBS, P. J., & MOE, A. J. (1983). Metacognition: A key for independent learning from text. *Reading Teacher, 36*(4), 422–426.

BERGERON, B. (1990). What does the term whole language mean? Constructing a definition from the literature. *Journal of Reading Behavior, 22*(4), 301–329.

CANADY, R. J. (1980). Psycholinguistics in a real-life classroom. *Reading Teacher, 34*(2), 156–159.

CHOMSKY, C. (1971). Write now, read later. *Childhood Education, 47*, 296–299.

CHOMSKY, C. (1976). After decoding, what? *Language Arts, 53*, 288–296.

DIONISIO, M. (1983). Write? Isn't this reading class? *Reading Teacher, 36*(8), 746–750.

DOWNING, J. (1982). Reading—skill or skills? *Reading Teacher, 35*(5), 534–537.

FITZGERALD, J. (1983). Helping readers gain self-control over reading comprehension. *Reading Teacher, 37*(3), 249–253.

FITZGERALD, J. (1989). Enhancing two related thought processes: Revision in writing and critical reading. *Reading Teacher, 43*(1), 42–48.

GAMBRELL, L. B. (1985). Dialogue journals: Reading-writing interaction. *Reading Teacher, 38*(6), 512–515.

GARNER, W. I. (1984). Reading is a problem-solving process. *Reading Teacher,* 38(1), 36–47.

GEMAKE, J. (1984). Interactive reading: How to make children active readers. *Reading Teacher,* 37(6), 462–466.

GOLDEN, J. M. (1984). Children's concept of story in reading and writing. *Reading Teacher,* 37(7), 578–584.

GOODMAN, Y. (1989). Roots of the whole language movement. *Elementary School Journal,* 90(2), 113–127.

GUTHRIE, J. T. (1984). Comprehension instruction. *Reading Teacher,* 38(2), 236–238.

GUTHRIE, J. T. (1984). Writing connections. *Reading Teacher,* 37(6), 540–542.

HELLER, M. (1991). *Reading-writing connections: From theory to practice.* New York: Longman.

JONES, L. L. (1982). An interactive view of reading: Implications for the classroom. *Reading Teacher,* 35(7), 772–777.

LAMME, L. (1989). Authorship: A key facet of whole language. *Reading Teacher,* 42(9), 704–710.

MOORE, S., & MOORE, D. (1990). Reading through writing through reading through writing . . . *Reading Teacher,* 44(2), 158–159.

PEARSON, P. D. (1989). Reading the whole language movement. *Elementary School Journal,* 90(20), 232–241.

RAND, M. K. (1984). Story schema: Theory, research and practice. *Reading Teacher,* 37(4), 377–383.

RONEY, R. C. (1984). Background experience is the foundation of success in learning to read. *Reading Teacher,* 38(2), 196–199.

SHANAHAN, T. (1990). *Reading and writing together.* Norwood, MA: Christopher-Gordon.

SHANKLIN, N., & RHODES, L. (1989). Comprehension instruction as sharing and extending. *Reading Teacher,* 42(7), 496–500.

SMITH, C. (1989). Emergent literacy: An environmental concept. *Reading Teacher,* 42(7), 528.

SPODEK, B. (1988). Conceptualizing today's kindergarten curriculum. *Elementary School Journal,* 89(2), 204–211.

STRICKLAND, D., & MORROW, L. (1989). Creating curriculum: An emergent literacy perspective. *Reading Teacher,* 42(9), 722–723.

TIERNEY, R. (1990, March). Redefining reading comprehension. *Educational Leadership,* 37–42.

TIERNEY, R., & PEARSON, P. D. (1983). Toward a composing model of reading. *Reading Teacher,* 37, 568–580.

WALMSLEY, S., & WALP, T. (1990). Integrating literature and composing into the language arts curriculum: Philosophy and practice. *Elementary School Journal,* 90(3), 252–274.

WATSON, D. (1989). Defining and describing whole language. *Elementary School Journal,* 90(2), 129–141.

WILSON, C. R. (1983). Teaching reading comprehension by connecting the known to the new. *Reading Teacher,* 36(4), 382–390.

WINN, D. (1988). Develop listening skills as part of the curriculum. *Reading Teacher,* 42(2), 144–146.

WITTROCK, M. C. (1991). Generative teaching of comprehension. *Elementary School Journal,* 92(2), 169–184.

THE RESEARCH BASE

ALEXANDER, P., & JUDY, J. (1988). The interaction of domain-specific and strategic knowledge in academic performance. *Review of Educational Research, 58*(4), 375–404.

ALEXANDER, P., SCHALLERT, D., & HARE, V. (1991). Coming to terms: How researchers in learning and literacy talk about knowledge. *Review of Educational Research, 61*(3), 315–343.

ANDERSON, R. C., & PEARSON, P. D. (1984). A schema-theoretic view of basic processes in reading comprehension. In P. D. Pearson (Ed.), *Handbook of reading research.* New York: Longman.

DOLE, J., DUFFY, G., ROEHLER, L., & PEARSON, P. D. (1991). Moving from the old to the new: Research on reading comprehension instruction. *Review of Educational Research, 61*(2), 239–264.

GOODMAN, K. (1991). Whole language research: Foundations and development. In J. Samuels & A. Farstrup (Eds.), *What research has to say about reading instruction,* 2nd edition (pp. 46–69). Newark, DE: International Reading Association.

HALLER, E., CHILD, D., & WALBERG, H. (1988). Can comprehension be taught? *Educational Researcher, 17*(9), 5–8.

KING, M., & REUTEL, V. (1981). *How children learn to write: A longitudinal study.* Final report. Columbus, OH: Ohio State University.

PARIS, S., OKA, E., & DEBRITTO, A. (1983). Beyond decoding: Synthesis of research on reading comprehension. *Educational Leadership, 41,* 78–83.

PEARSON, P. D. (1984). Twenty years of research in reading comprehension. In T. Raphael (Ed.), *Contexts of school-based literacy* (pp. 43–62). New York: Random House.

PEARSON, P. D., & TIERNEY, R. (1984). On becoming a thoughtful reader: Learning to read like a writer. In A. Purves & O. Niles (Eds.), *Becoming readers in a complex society.* Eighty-third Yearbook of the National Society for the Study of Education. Chicago: University of Chicago Press.

TAYLOR, B. (1992). Text structure, comprehension and recall. In J. Samuels & A. Farstrup (Eds.), *What research has to say about reading instruction,* 2nd edition (pp. 220–235). Newark, DE: International Reading Association.

TIERNEY, R., & SHANAHAN, T. (1991). Research in the reading-writing relationship: Interactions, transactions and outcomes. In R. Barr, M. Kamil, P. Mosenthal, & P. D. Pearson (Eds.), *Handbook of reading research, volume II* (pp. 246–280). New York: Longman.

TIERNEY, R., SOTER, A., O'FLAHAVAN, J., & MCGINLEY, W. (1989). The effects of reading and writing upon thinking critically. *Reading Research Quarterly, 24*(2), 134–173.

ACTIVITIES FOR REFLECTING, OBSERVING, AND TEACHING

Reflecting on What It Means To Be Literate

PURPOSE: Whether or not your reading instruction produces literate students depends on what you think it means to be literate. This activity is designed to help you clarify your meaning of literacy.

Describe things you have done recently that are examples of literate behavior. Do NOT include school or university tasks.

_____

_____

_____

Think back to your childhood. What out-of-school activities did you pursue that demanded literacy?

_____

_____

_____

Think ahead in time. Consider the increasing complexity of society and the rapidity of change. What on-the-job literacy will be required of the students you teach as they enter the work force?

_____

_____

_____

Think about your classroom and the students you teach. What activities can they pursue in school that will provide them with the experience of being literate?

_____

Observing In A Classroom

PURPOSE: This chapter emphasized what to teach—what activities and experiences to provide to students for them to become literate. One of the first steps in being able to work with a reading curriculum is the ability to recognize various goals and subgoals when you see them. This observation is designed to help you accomplish this.

DIRECTIONS: While watching the teacher teach reading, describe in the space provided below an example of each curriculum goal and subgoal.

Overall Literacy Goal   Describe activities or instruction designed to provide students with experiences with being literate.

Subgoal of Attitude   Describe activities or instruction designed to develop in students a positive response to reading.

Describe activities or instruction designed to develop in students conceptual understandings about the nature and function of reading.

Subgoal of Process   Describe activities or instruction designed to develop in students routine skills.

Describe activities or instruction designed to develop in students metacognitive strategies.

Subgoal of Content   Describe activities or instruction designed to develop students' abilities in getting meaning from recreational text.

Describe activities or instruction designed to develop students' abilities in getting meaning from expository text.

3 Learning and Student Diversity

GETTING READY

While it is important to understand the curriculum of reading and writing in order to control your instruction, the most important single ingredient in the teaching-learning process is the student. Consequently, this chapter is devoted to students and learning. Specifically, this chapter focuses on student diversity because our survival as a society may well depend on our ability to develop literacy among all students; on our ability to develop cognitive, emotional, and social aspects of learning (which apply to the learning of all students); and on our understanding of stages of developmental reading growth (as a means for thinking about students and how they learn to read). The basic message of the chapter is that teachers must set high expectations for all students regardless of their culture, their economic status, or their academic standing.

FOCUS QUESTIONS

- Why is it important to learn to teach students by using their unique diversities?

- What kinds of diversity can we expect as we work with students?

- How can giving students "voice" help diversity concerns?

- How does conceptually meaningful learning occur?

- What is the role of the social situation in learning?

- How do stages of developmental reading growth help us think about problems of reading instruction?

- What is the role of expectations in teaching reading?

A basic fact of life in American education is that the current minority will soon be the the majority. The number of cultural, economic, physical, mental, and emotional differences in our classrooms are growing larger and larger as our society itself becomes more pluralistic. Where students with minority backgrounds used to represent about one-third of the enrollment in a typical elementary classroom, half the students in many of our current classrooms are representative of what used to be thought of as minorities.

It is a sad fact of life that, in the past, students with minority backgrounds have all too frequently ended up in the low reading groups. That is, teachers have thought that, because these students were different from the majority, they would not learn to read well. Given that expectation, teachers effectively "picked winners and losers." That is, by associating student cultural differences with low academic achievement and by placing culturally different students in low reading groups and students of the majority in high reading groups, teachers increased the chances that students who were different would be the losers and that students of the majority would be the winners.

Such practices were never just. In this day and age, however, we need to teach all students to be literate. Teachers need to use the diversities of students to improve instruction. Student differences are assets and should be viewed as ways to strengthen teaching and learning. Failure to teach certain students because of their diversity means that literacy in our society will never reach its potential. If our society is not literate, a majority of the people will be unable to perform useful work. As work in our society becomes increasingly complex, it becomes more difficult for people to contribute intellectually, emotionally, socially, or financially. The result will be a fatal weakness of our economy and, ultimately, our society.

The stakes are high. We must build on diversities. We must teach *all* students to be literate. That means that we must learn to teach all students by using their diversities.

KINDS OF DIVERSITY

There is no limit to the ways in which children can be different. However, when we talk about the diversities of students, we are usually referring to differences associated with cultural, economic, language, and physical-mental-emotional differences.

Cultural Diversity

Cultural diversity is one of the most visible kinds of differences in our society. Because America is an immigrant country, schools have been dealing with cultural differences and ethnicity for a long time. However, there is a serious question as to whether schools have ever done well in providing education for students whose racial and ethnic backgrounds are different. Contrary to popular belief, for instance, the waves of Irish, Italian, and German immigrants who migrated to America during the nineteenth century did not have much more success in school than do today's culturally different children. However, today's problem is much more visible, since it is evident to one extent or another in virtually every school district in the country, rather than confined to a few cities along the eastern seaboard.

The two most evident cultural groups in today's schools are the Afro-Americans and the Hispanics. In recent years, large numbers of Asians have also immigrated to America and comprise a large part of the school population in some parts of the country. In most cases, cultural diversity is most prevalent in urban schools.

Children who are culturally different can learn to read just as well as any other child. However, such children may have initial difficulty learning to read if a language other than English is spoken in the home, or if home life promotes values and beliefs which are perceived to be in conflict with the undergirding principles of instruction provided in the school. However, these difficulties can be overcome. Culturally different children are capable of learning what is needed for the 21st century. In fact, their diversities can enrich and strengthen instructional situations.

Diversity Enhances Classroom Life.

Economic Diversity

Economic diversity is not confined to urban centers. While many of the culturally different people of our country who live in urban centers may also experience economic deprivation, rural America also has many people living in poverty.

Awareness of economic diversity is important because economically-deprived people tend to provide sparse home literacy experiences. School is generally not high on the priority list. Problems such as hunger or lack of sleep often accompany poverty, making it more difficult for these children to learn to read. Again, the problem is not an innate lack of capacity to learn to read. Rather, the problem is associated with the difference between the realities of the home and the values of the school, and the way teachers use those differences. Children from economically-deprived backgrounds can learn how to read. However, teachers must take into account the fact that economic deprivation also often means hunger, other physical deprivations, and different literacy backgrounds. Steps must be taken so that the school can work collaboratively with families and communities to use these differences productively and build ways to have home and school environments become more compatible.

Language Diversity

In one way or another, both cultural diversity and economic diversity end up also being related to language. Culturally different people, for instance, often speak a language other than English in the home, which means that the children come to school with difficulties with the language of the school. Some cultures use an English dialect. For instance, Afro-Americans often speak a form of Black English and Creoles often use their own dialect, as do some native Hawaiians. Similarly, children of economically-deprived families often come to school speaking a dialect of English that is not generally used in the school.

There was a time when language differences such as these were considered to be a liability. The idea was to eradicate the different language as soon as possible. Recently, however, educators have come to understand that different languages and different language forms are strengths rather than weaknesses. That is, when a child has a firm grasp on one language or language form, it is easier to learn another language or language form. Consequently, the emphasis recently is often on using the language of the home as a foundation for building a language of the school. The expectation is that both languages will be equally valued, but one will be more appropriate in one setting and the other more appropriate in another setting.

Again, language differences do not mean that a child cannot learn how to read English. On the contrary, the fact that a child has already learned one language suggests that he or she will certainly be able to learn a second language. However, teachers must be alert for cultural conflicts when working with language-different children. For instance, the Mexican-American culture sanctions cooperation, and Mexican-American children are likely to seek help from friends while in the classroom. However, if the teacher's cultural tradition is that such help in school is cheating, there is now the potential for a cultural conflict. For instruction to be effective, teachers must be sensitive to such cultural differences and accommodate them.

Physical, Mental, and Emotional Diversity

In 1977, Public Law 94-142 took effect. Called the Education for All Handicapped Children Act, it specified that all children in the United States were entitled to appropriate public education. The immediate effect of this law was to increase the diversity of the classroom, because students with physical, mental, and/or emotional impairments who were formerly taught in special classrooms were now expected to be **mainstreamed** into regular classrooms.

Not all physically, mentally, and emotionally impaired students were mainstreamed. The key term in the law was "least restrictive environment," which meant that students had to be provided an environment which involved them as much as possible in the regular routines of daily life. In schools, this meant that those physically, mentally, and emotionally impaired students who can learn in regular classrooms must be taught in those classrooms rather than being segregated and ostracized.

The idea of mainstreaming is certainly a humane one. Forcing physically-mentally-emotionally different students to live and learn in an isolated ghetto of their own has little to commend it. And there is no pedagogical reason for segregating those students while their physical, mental, or emotional impairment is such that they can operate in a regular classroom. These children, like the others discussed above, can learn how to read. What is required from teachers is sensitivity to children's handicaps and willingness to be accommodating.

Summary

Diversity is a fact of life in American schools today. To teach, one must be prepared to handle diversity. To teach reading specifically, one must be prepared to develop true literacy in all students—that is, all students, with their diversities, are entitled to become "proactive and enthusiastic users of language and higher-order thinking in the pursuit of being responsible for and enriching their destinies." The fact is that all students with their cultural, economic, language, and physical or mental and emotional differences can be literate. In fact, it is essential that these students become literate.

"VOICE" AS A KEY TO DIVERSITY

As was noted in Chapter Two, comprehension does not mean that there is meaning in the text and that students must get that precise meaning. Rather, the reader's experiences are themselves one of the sources of text meaning, because the reader interprets text meaning in light of personal background experience. This personal aspect of reading comprehension is sometimes referred to as **voice.** That is, reading instruction should provide an environment in which students' voices, as well as authors' voices, may be heard.

The concept of student "voice" is relevant to all aspects of reading instruction. The more students are involved in interpreting meaning of text, the more they themselves are transformed by text. That is, they are more likely to be able to "control and enrich their destinies."

But, while voice is important for all students, it is particularly important when considering the diversity issue. Students *are* different. As such, they often feel that they are on the outside looking in. The teacher is responsible for creating ways to help students who feel like outsiders become insiders. Not being part of the learning community in the classroom is a serious inhibitor to learning.

This condition can be countered by working to give all students "voice," and by working particularly hard to ensure that the voices of all students, especially those with widely different characteristics, are valued and heard. In doing so, students with diverse experiences, cultures, beliefs, and morals can become exciting sources of information as students search for meaning in texts. Consequently, by ensuring that the voices of all students are heard, diversity becomes a strength.

NATURE OF MEANINGFUL LEARNING

Traditionally, learning was thought to be synonymous with simple remembering, and memorization skills were highly valued. For instance, do you remember the Friday spelling tests you took in elementary school? If you are like many people, you probably studied very hard on Thursday night, memorized all the target words, kept reciting them to yourself on the way to school on Friday, spelled them correctly on the test, and then promptly forgot how they were spelled because you did not use them. Psychologists call that kind of learning "short-term" memory. That is, you memorize something, and for a short time, you "know" it. However, most memorized information is forgotten because it is isolated from other actively used information and is relatively meaningless. Once forgotten, it is of no further use.

Cognitive Aspects of Learning

To be remembered in future situations, most learning must be conceptually meaningful—that is, you must understand individual concepts and the relationships among them. The human mind expedites meaningful learning by organizing experiences (such as experiences with restaurants) into networks of interlocking and related concepts called **schemata.** For example, your experiences with restaurants provide you with a restaurant **schema** that includes all your "restaurant" experiences, ranging from how the drive-through window at McDonald's works to the role of the maitre d' in a four-star restaurant. All that restaurant knowledge is effortlessly remembered because it is meaningfully organized in your long-term memory. What students learn during reading instruction also should be meaningfully organized so that it too can be easily retrieved. In this sense, learning is cognitive.

Meaningful learning occurs when you create a new schema or modify an old one. For the learning to be meaningful, the concepts stored in the schema must be linked together in sensible ways, as they are in the figures in this chapter, for instance. To illustrate, if someone encounters a Japanese restaurant for the first time, that person will integrate procedures such as sitting on tatami mats instead of at a table into his or her existing restaurant schema, probably under a category "Oriental restaurants, Japanese." Long-term learning occurs when this new knowledge about restaurants is integrated meaningfully into a person's existing restaurant schema; that is, when it is linked in sensible ways with prior restaurant knowledge so that it can be remembered and used when needed. What students learn about reading in school should be integrated in similar ways into their prior schemata for reading.

Unfamiliarity with a Japanese restaurant's way of doing things may at first result in disorientation and frustration. If the disorientation and frustration are great enough, the person's motivation to eat there may disappear, and he or she may leave. In such a case, the restaurant schema remains unmodified, and no learning occurs. On the other hand, if the person stays and looks for analogous relationships from existing restaurant and Oriental culture schema or receives instruction from someone—a waiter, for example—the existing restaurant schema is successfully modified. Similarly, during reading instruction, students learn things on any given day that are modifications of the reading schemata they all brought to class. Effective instruction either corrects a previously held misconception about reading or embellishes an existing reading schema by adding new concepts.

Motivation, or the enthusiasm and perseverance a learner brings to a task, is obviously important in learning. We all want our students to be motivated. Motivation occurs if two factors are present—if there is a reasonable chance of success and if the end result is valued. In the case of the Japanese restaurant, the newcomer will enthusiastically persist in learning the etiquette of Japanese restaurants as long as it does not become too difficult to learn and as long as he or she continues to want to eat there. The same thing happens during reading instruction. Students are motivated if the work is not too hard and if the goal of being a reader is genuinely useful.

Learning depends on more than motivation, however. The way a learner **mediates,** or thinks about, an experience is also important. For instance, one customer new to Japanese restaurants may think about the experience as a matter of making a few perfunctory adjustments, whereas another may think about the experience as the beginning of new cultural understandings and appreciations that go well beyond simple restaurant behavior. Because each person's schema for a particular topic is unique, each person uniquely mediates experiences and **restructures** them to create unique understandings. That is why no two people possess precisely the same conceptual understanding about any given topic. In the classroom, individual students mediate the reading instruction provided and restructure the understandings so they are unique to each of them. Consequently, every student comes up with slightly different understandings from identical learning experiences.

Learners mediate experiences better when they have been provided with information that helps them understand how to think about these experiences. For instance, the learner who has been taught how to apply existing schemata to new experiences is more likely to create broader cultural understanding from the Japanese restaurant experience, whereas the learner who has not been taught how to activate existing schemata will probably be satisfied with "getting by" behavior. This awareness of how one thinks is called **metacognition.** Reading instruction focuses on providing students with information about how they think as they read. The result is readers who are metacognitive about how they read—who are aware of how to think when making sense out of text so they can control the comprehension process.

Social Aspects of Learning

However, information is not provided in a vacuum. It is always provided in the context of a social situation. The nature of the social situation determines to a large degree how students restructure learning experiences. That is, when students are restructuring experiences, they are constructing their own meaning for experiences which, in their perception, fit the social situation they are in. In that sense, learning is always **socially constructed.**

Consequently, teachers must always be aware of the effect the social situation is having on learning, knowing that students are constructing their understandings partly in response to the social situation they find themselves in. To return to the Japanese restaurant example, students will construct one set of meanings if they are simply learning about Japanese restaurants as an academic exercise and will construct a dramatically different set of meanings if they are really going to go to a Japanese restaurant and have dinner. In the former situation, for instance, students might simply memorize some facts in a short-term learning mode because the social situation calls for them to merely spit back those facts on a test, whereas in the latter situation students might develop long-term understandings because the social situation calls for them to actually use what they learn while dining in a Japanese restaurant. In Chapter Four, we will talk about the importance of teachers "situating" learning for students so that the social situation encourages students to construct the desired understandings and not some other understandings.

Learning Summarized

To summarize, learning can be short-term or long-term. Short-term learning is a relatively meaningless process of remembering isolated bits of information for short periods of time. Long-term learning is the active combining of new and old knowledge in meaningful ways so that a modified understanding results. Long-term learning is what teachers strive for, because students can recall and use it when needed. It is influenced by (1) metacognition, or how conscious the learner is in making linkages in the mind; (2) motivation, or how much or how little frustration and value is attached to the task; (3) the information teachers provide to help the learner know how to mediate experiences in intended ways; and (4) the social situation in which the learning is embedded.

You will help students become enthusiastic readers if your reading instruction reflects the following characteristics of learning:

- Because learning occurs gradually, understanding about reading develops over time, not in a single lesson or a single experience.

- Because learning is an active process, students must be active participants, not passive recipients of knowledge.

- Because learning occurs by integrating old and new knowledge, students must have opportunities to integrate new content with existing schemata and thereby generate restructured understanding.

- Because metacognitive awareness of how one learns influences learning, students should be taught to be aware of how they read so they can control their own comprehension.

- Because humans are motivated when they are successful and when they value a task, reading instruction should emphasize activities that are low in frustration and high in value.

- Because humans construct meaning to fit the social situation in which they find themselves, reading instruction should be situated in tasks which call for students to engage in authentic literacy.

STAGES OF DEVELOPMENTAL READING GROWTH

Learning progresses developmentally. Learning to read, for instance, progresses gradually from **emergent literacy** in the preschool and kindergarten years when children first encounter written language to adulthood when people continue to "use language and higher-order thinking to control and enrich their lives." In this sense, we are always in the process of becoming more literate, and learning to read is a process that never ends. We can always learn more about how to be better readers and writers.

In a general sense, the developmental progression from emergent literacy to adult literacy can be predicted. Common sense dictates, for instance, that preschool students will be learning different aspects of becoming literate than will normally progressing eighth graders. Because this is so, the reading and writing curriculum is usually presented as a developmental continuum. This continuum is often referred to as **stages of developmental reading growth** and is often reflected in school curriculum guides and in the scope and sequence charts of basal textbooks.

It is helpful to think of learning as progressing developmentally and to organize curriculum in terms of developmental stages. Doing so brings some order and sequence to a process that would otherwise be extremely complex and difficult to think about. Consequently, we refer in this book to five stages of developmental reading growth.

However, before describing those stages, we must identify three potential dangers of developmental stages. The first danger relates back to diversity. Because students of diversity are, in fact, different, they do not always learn to read in exactly the progression described in a particular development sequence. Consequently, development stages cannot be used as absolute standards for progress, with students who do not match those standards being branded failures.

Second, developmental stages cannot be mixed up with grade levels. This is so for two reasons. First, the fact that a child is in kindergarten does not necessarily mean that the child is at a particular developmental stage. For instance, some kindergartners come to school reading very well. Consequently, they are at a stage of developmental reading growth which is higher than that of typi-

Cognitive Development May Be Well Ahead of Reading Levels for Many Minority Students Not Familiar with English.

cal kindergartners. Similarly, the fact that a child is in the eighth grade does not necessarily mean that the child will be at a particular stage. For instance, if the child is a 14-year old newly arrived from Vietnam, he may be placed in the eighth grade, but because he speaks no English, his developmental stage of reading growth will probably be closer to that of a typical kindergartner than to that of a typical eighth grader. Another reason why developmental stages cannot be mixed up with grade levels is that from kindergarten to eighth grade there are nine grade levels, but only five developmental stages.

A third danger of developmental stages occurs when teachers expect the boundaries from one stage to another to be clear-cut. In fact, however, stages of developmental reading growth often overlap. A child may simultaneously be near the end of one developmental stage while learning certain things normally associated with the next developmental stage. This is perfectly natural. Consequently, teachers need to avoid thinking of developmental stages as rigid demarcations from one point to another.

In sum, developmental stages are useful as guides in thinking about how students progress in learning to become literate. They are not useful, however, if they are used rigidly.

Given that, this book refers to five stages of developmental reading growth as a way of thinking about what might be a logical learning sequence, and as a means for assessing what students have already learned and what they have yet to learn. However, the labels we provide are ours; they are arbitrary and not universally used. Consequently, while the stages themselves are accurate representations of the progression in learning to read, the labels are used to communicate among ourselves and may or may not communicate with persons who have not read this book.

The first level, the **emergent literacy stage,** includes preschool, kindergarten, and first-grade students. At this level, most students are not actually reading, but are preparing to do so. Oral language activities are generally used to help them learn the attitude, process, and content goals needed to begin actual reading. In writing, there is an emphasis on **preliterate writing** in which students begin to use their individual, nonstandard language systems to create and share written messages.

The second level, the **initial mastery stage,** ordinarily begins in first grade and continues into second grade. At this stage, most students actually begin to read and write print. During the initial mastery stage, students learn to read preprimers, primers, and other materials associated with beginning reading. Attitude, process, and content goals are taught with a particular emphasis on word identification.

The third stage, the **expanded fundamentals stage,** ordinarily begins in second grade and continues into fourth grade. At this stage students' reading levels expand into second, third, and fourth grade materials due to increased mastery of the fundamentals of reading. The curriculum continues to include attitude, process, and content outcomes, but the emphasis on word identification diminishes and emphasis on comprehension increases.

The fourth stage, the **application stage,** ordinarily begins at about fourth grade and continues into eighth grade. Along with basal reading textbooks, students increasingly use textbooks for other curricular areas such as social studies, science, and mathematics. They apply what they have learned about reading to these other content areas. At this stage, emphasis is on attitude, process, and content goals that support such application.

The fifth stage, the **power stage,** typically begins in eighth grade and can continue long after formal schooling ends. Readers at this level can handle almost any kind of reading. Because it typically occurs at the post-elementary school level, the power stage is not emphasized in this book.

As Table 3.1 illustrates, the relative emphasis given the three curricular goals varies according to the stages of developmental growth even though all three goals are taught at every developmental stage. For instance, a kindergarten teacher expects to emphasize attitudes almost 50 percent of the time

TABLE 3.1   Relative Curricular Emphasis across Developmental Stages*

	READINESS	INITIAL MASTERY	EXPANDED FUNDAMENTALS	APPLICATION
Attitude goals				
Concepts and positive responses	Stressed in listening comprehension	Stressed	Continued development	Maintained
Process goals				
Routine skills	Stressed in print awareness			
• vocabulary		Stressed	Maintained	Maintained
• word recognition		Stressed	Continued development	Maintained
Metacognitive strategies	Stressed in listening comprehension			
• initiating strategies		Stressed	Continued development	Continued development
• during-reading strategies		Stressed	Continued development	Continued development
• post-reading strategies		Introduced	Introduced	Continued development
• study strategies	Not dealt with	Introduced	Introduced	Stressed
Content goals				
Recreational text	Stressed	Stressed	Continued development	Continued development
Functional text	Introduced	Introduced	Stressed	Stressed

*The power stage is not discussed in this book.

and content less than 25 percent of the time, whereas a twelfth-grade teacher reverses this emphasis. Similarly, the emphasis within any particular goal varies from one developmental level to another. Content goals heavily emphasize recreational reading at the readiness and initial mastery levels where narrative text is frequently used, and heavily emphasize functional reading at the application and power levels where expository text is frequently used. Process goals are heavily emphasized at the initial-mastery and the expanded-fundamentals levels, where many fix-it strategies are taught, and are emphasized less at higher levels.

EXPECTANCIES AND STUDENT DIVERSITY

There is no question that learning to become literate is a complex process. Teaching others to become literate is even more complicated when our students have diverse characteristics. It would certainly be a lot easier to teach reading if all our students were alike.

However, all our students are not alike. To the contrary, they differ in many ways. And we have learned from past experience that segregating students into groups of like ability only tends to widen the gap between those who are literate and those who are not.

When all students are taught together, however, students with diverse characteristics do better. This is so because grouping students together changes the **expectations** for students with diverse characteristics.

This concept of expectations is one of the strongest influences on learning. Simply stated, this concept refers to the tendency of humans to perform at an expected level. If someone expects much of you, you tend to rise to that level; if someone does not expect much of you, you tend to do less well.

Expectations are particularly powerful in school. By grouping students regardless of diverse characteristics, all students rise to expected levels; by grouping them according to similarities, they tend to do less well. In other words, when students are grouped with others like themselves, their teachers tend to have lower expectations for them and they cannot learn from their classmates who have different backgrounds; when students with diverse characteristics are grouped with all other students, however, their teachers tend to expect them to perform like anyone else and the students with diverse characteristics are able to collaborate with and learn from other students.

Consequently, the basic message of this chapter is that students with diverse characteristics and backgrounds can strengthen the learning of all students—*if* the expectation is set that they will learn. That expectation includes giving all students their voice—promoting opportunities for them to use their diverse experiences, beliefs, and characteristics in the on-going activities of the classroom—and making clear that learning for understanding and long-term memory is not something reserved for a select few. All students can learn.

SUGGESTED ADDITIONAL READING

AUTEN, A. (1983). The ultimate connection: Reading, listening, writing, speaking-thinking. *Reading Teacher, 36*(6), 584–587.

BOYLE, O., & PEREGOY (1990). Literacy scaffolds: Strategies for first- and second-language readers and writers. *Reading Teacher, 44*(3), 194–200.

CLAY, M. (1986). Constructive processes: Talking, reading, writing, art and craft. *Reading Teacher,* 764–770.

D'ALESSANDRO, M. (1990). Accommodating emotionally handicapped children through a literature-based reading program. *Reading Teacher, 44*(4), 288–293.

GUTHRIE, J. T. (1983). Students' perceptions of teaching. *Reading Teacher, 37*(1), 94–95.

KOPFSTEIN, R. M. (1978). Fluent reading, language, and the reading teacher. *Reading Teacher, 32*(2), 195–197.

LAMINACK, L. (1990). "Possibilities, Daddy, I think it says possibilities": A father's journal of the emergence of literacy. *Reading Teacher, 43*(8), 536–540.

LIPSON, M. Y. (1984). Some unexpected issues in prior knowledge and comprehension. *Reading Teacher, 37*(8), 760–764.

MOORE, S., & MOORE, D. (1991). Linguistic diversity and reading. *Reading Teacher, 45*(4), 326–327.

OTTO, J. (1982). The new debate in reading. *Reading Teacher, 36*(1), 14–18.

PEARSON, P. D. (1976). A psycholinguistic model of reading. *Language Arts, 53*(3), 309–314.

PURCELL-GATES, V. (1989). What oral/written language differences tell us about beginning instruction. *Reading Teacher, 42*(4), 290–293.

QUINTERO, E., & HUERTA-MACIAS, A. (1990). All in the family: Bilingualism and bi-literacy. *Reading Teacher, 44*(4), 306–312.

ROSER, N., HOFFMAN, J., & FAREST, C. (1990). Language, literature, and at-risk children. *Reading Teacher, 43*(3), 554–559.

SANACORE, J. (1984). Metacognition and the improvement of reading: Some important links. *Journal of Reading, 27*(8), 706–712.

STRANGE, M. (1980). Instructional implications of a conceptual theory of reading comprehension. *Reading Teacher 33*(4), 391–397.

STRICKLAND, D., & MORROW, L. (1988). New perspectives on young children learning to read and write. *Reading Teacher, 42*(1), 70–71.

STRICKLAND, D., & MORROW, L. (1989). Young children's early writing development. *Reading Teacher, 42*(6), 426–427.

STRICKLAND, D., MORROW, L., EDWARDS, P., BEASLEY, K., & THOMPSON, J. (1991). Teachers in transition: Accommodating reading curriculum to cultural diversity. *Reading Teacher, 44*(6), 436–437.

SUTTON, C. (1989). Helping the non-native English speaker with reading. *Reading Teacher, 42*(9), 684–688.

WALKER-DALHENSE, D. (1992). Using African-American literature to increase ethnic understanding. *Reading Teacher, 45*(6), 416–423.

WEISS, M. J. (1986). Writers and readers: The literary connection. *Reading Teacher, 39,* 758–763.

WILDE, S.J. (1979). The experience and consequences of literacy: A case study. *Lanuage Arts, 56*(2). 141–145.

THE RESEARCH BASE

COMMINS, N., & MIRAMONTES, O.   (1989). Perceived and actual linguistic competence: A descriptive study of four low-achieving Hispanic bilingual students. *American Educational Research Journal, 26*(4), 443–472.

DUFFY, G. G., ROEHLER, L. R., & MASON, J.   (Eds.) (1984). *Comprehension instruction: Perspectives and suggestions.* New York: Longman.

HOFFMAN, J. V.   (Ed.) (1986). *Effective teaching of reading: Research and practice.* Newark, DE: International Reading Association.

LANGER, J., BARTHOLOME, L., VASQUEZ, O., & LUCAS, T.   (1990). Meaning construction in school literacy tasks: A study of bilingual students. *American Educational Research Journal, 27*(3), 427–471.

NURSS, J., & HOUGH, R.   (1992). Reading and the ESL Student. In J. Samuels & A. Farstrup (Eds.) *What research has to say about reading instruction,* 2nd edition. (pp. 277–313). Newark, DE: International Reading Association.

OLSEN, M.   (1992). Ethnic identity development and literacy education. *Reading Psychology, 13*(1), 91–98.

PEARSON, P. D.   (Ed.) (1984). *The handbook of reading research.* New York: Longman.

ROEHLER, L.   (1991, December). *Increasing learning for understanding for elementary at-risk ESL students.* Paper presented at the National Reading Conference, Palm Springs, CA.

ROEHLER, L. R., & DUFFY, G. G.   (1991). Teachers' instructional actions. In R. Barr, M. L. Kamil, P. Mosenthal, & P. D. Pearson (Eds.), *Handbook of reading research, volume II.* New York: Longman.

WEBER, R.   (1991). Linguistic diversity and reading in American society. In R. Barr, M. L. Kamil, P. Mosenthal & P. D. Pearson (Eds.) *Handbook of reading research, volume II,* (pp. 97–119). New York: Longman.

WITTROCK, M.   (Ed.) (1986). *Handbook of research on teaching.* New York: Macmillan.

ACTIVITIES FOR REFLECTING, OBSERVING, AND TEACHING

Reflecting on Diversity

PURPOSE: Things that are different are often frightening for humans. We like to think of ourselves as "normal" and of anything different as "abnormal." However, teachers must be accepting of many kinds of differences. This activity gives you an opportunity to think about yourself and your beliefs in light of the reality that, as a teacher of reading, you must be able to use diverse characteristics and backgrounds as you develop literacy among all students.

Think about your experiences with people who are different from you. How much experience have you had with people who are different from yourself?

People who are culturally different?

People who are economically different?

People who are language different?

People who are physically or mentally or emotionally different?

Assess your ability to work with students who have diverse characteristics and backgrounds. What do you consider to be your strengths in this regard? Your weaknesses? How can you use their diversities productively?

Reflecting on How You Learn

PURPOSE: One cannot teach well if one does not understand how learning occurs. This activity provides you with an opportunity to examine your own learning and to think about your learning in light of the principles developed in this chapter as a means for developing a better understanding of learning how it works.

Think about your own learning in elementary or high school. List some things that were examples of short-term memory learning.

List some things that were examples of long-term memory learning.

Describe one school learning experience in which you think you created a new schema or modified an old one.

Describe a school experience in which you think the teacher intended the learning to be conceptually meaningful, and describe why it was successful or failed to achieve the intended results.

Describe a situation in which the social situation you were in caused you to restructure a school learning experience in a way that probably was inconsistent with the teacher's intention.

Describe a situation in which you were motivated to learn and what it is that you think caused you to be motivated.

Did your motivation change depending on your social situation?

Observing Children Learn to Read and Write

PURPOSE: Since the learner is the most important participant in the teaching-learning enterprise, it is important that you are familiar with students at various stages of development and the way they are learning. This observation activity is designed to help you develop a better understanding of students.

DIRECTIONS: Arrange to observe in a kindergarten, a second grade, a fourth grade, a sixth grade, and an eighth grade. In the kindergarten, identify a child who you think is at the emergent literacy stage, in the second grade identify a child who you think is at the initial mastery stage, in the fourth grade identify a child who you think is at the expanded fundamentals stage, in the sixth grade identify a child who you think is at the application stage, and in the eighth grade identify a child who you think is at the power stage. For each student, describe (1) the student's observed reading and writing activity which is typical of that developmental stage and (2) the kind of learning in which the student is engaged.

Student from the emergent literacy stage—

Student from the initial mastery stage—

Student from the expanded fundamentals stage—

Student from the application stage—

Student from the power stage—

Motivation and Instruction: What Philosophy, Approach, or Method Should Be Used?

4

GETTING READY

Some students learn to read with a minimum of assistance; others need extensive help. Generally speaking, students from emotionally stable, economically advantaged homes learn to read with relatively little difficulty; culturally different, economically deprived, and emotionally and/or mentally handicapped students often have relatively more difficulty learning to read. The more difficulty a child has learning to read, the more the teacher must strategically orchestrate instruction. This chapter introduces you to the instructional components the teacher must orchestrate if *all* students are to achieve literacy. Five major topics are discussed: the nature of direct and indirect instruction, motivating, approaches to organizing reading instruction, whole language, and instructional decision-making which leads to assuming strategic control of your instruction.

FOCUS QUESTIONS

- What is the distinction between teaching and instruction?

- What are the five main properties of instruction?

- How does the way instruction is situated influence what students learn?

- What is the distinction between direct instruction and indirect instruction?

- How can you motivate students?

- How does organizing lessons into units enhance motivation?

- What is the distinction between the whole language approach, the basal textbook approach, the language experience approach, the literature-based approach, and a combined approach?

Teachers expedite the learning of students. That is, teachers instruct. According to Lee Shulman:

> A teacher is someone who knows something not understood by others, presumably his students. He is capable of transforming his own comprehension of the subject matter, his own skills of performance or desired attitude values, into pedagogical representations and actions. There are ways of talking, showing, enacting or otherwise representing the ideas so that the unknowing can come to know, those without understanding can comprehend and discern, the unskilled can become adept.[1]

The Distinction between Teaching and Instruction

The first step in understanding instruction is to distinguish it from other elements of teaching. Although learning, teaching, and instruction tend to occur together, they are not synonymous. Learning can occur without teachers or any formal instruction. **Teaching** encompasses all that you do in the course of the school day, including instruction. What you do to keep your class moving smoothly, to keep up morale, and to make children feel good about themselves are not instructional activities. They are part of the important general activities associated with teaching school but are not specifically tied to intentional efforts to develop specific curricular outcomes. This does not mean that these more general classroom activities are unimportant. Collecting milk money, taking lunch count, supervising recess, consoling an injured child, and countless other activities that make up the daily classroom routine are essential for effective operation of a classroom. However, they are noninstructional because they do not involve intentionally using professional knowledge to achieve curricular goals.

Instruction is intentional and goal directed. As a teacher, you plan an encounter between your student's schema and a specified experience with the intention that your student will modify that schema. **Instruction,** therefore, is a conscious attempt to modify another's understanding (or schema) in a specified way, with the intention of producing specific curricular outcomes. It may or may not cause your students to modify their schemata, which is to say it may or may not result in learning.

PROPERTIES OF INSTRUCTION

Instruction is characterized by five properties: expectations, caring, situating, informing, and mediating student construction of meaning.

Expectations have already been discussed in Chapter Three. As noted there, humans tend to meet the expectations set for them. Consequently, a crucial property of instruction is the setting of high expectations.

[1]Shulman, L. (1986). *Knowledge and teaching. Foundations of the new reform.* Unpublished paper, Stanford University.

Second, teachers must genuinely care about their students. They must do more than simply tell students what they need to know or give them an activity to do, because students are not passive participants in learning. They have feelings, and they already possess conceptions (and, sometimes, misconceptions) about what is being taught. While you certainly need to provide students with knowledge, you must also account for students' feelings as human beings and for their active role in redefining, on the basis of their conceptions and misconceptions, what it is that you are teaching them. The second property of instruction is sensitivity to learners' thoughts and feelings in accomplishing the desired goal.

By **situating** instruction, we are referring to the social situation a student is in when learning to do something. All too often, students are put in a situation where they are learning something for no reason other than the fact that the teacher tells them to learn it. Alternatively, however, they can be put in a social situation where they are learning something because they are going to use it immediately to pursue a genuinely literate activity. The situation is usually determined by the student's **academic task**—that is, the work teachers give students to do and what is really important about that work. By looking at a student's work, you can tell how it is situated. For instance, when a student's task is to complete a ditto sheet on letter sounds simply because the teacher is the boss in that social situation and says it is important to learn letter sounds, it is artificially situated—what counts is getting the task done to the teacher's satisfaction. In contrast, when a student's task is to complete a ditto sheet on letter sounds because the class is writing a letter to the President as part of a "Save the Whales" campaign and needs to know certain sounds to spell the words in the letter, it is situated in genuinely literate activity—what counts is the class's success in writing a convincing letter to the President. Because our primary curricular goal is to develop literate students, a third crucial property of instruction is situating learning in genuinely literate activity.

A fourth property of instruction is information giving. Learning occurs when students modify an existing schema or create a new schema from information they receive. Students can receive information directly, as when you **model,** that is, show them exactly how to do a task; or less directly from the classroom environment as they participate in activities intended to encourage them to infer the information. In either case students must receive information in order to build schemata about curricular goals.

The fifth property of instruction is mediation of student restructuring of the information provided. Students mediate what happens during instruction. That is, they filter information through their minds and, in the process, restructure the message so that it fits their respective schemata.

This is not the way instruction has always been viewed. People used to think of instruction as a single cycle in which the teacher "poured" information into students' minds. Research has shown, however, that students are not passive recipients of instructional information, but active mediators of experiences that they encounter. They pass instructional information through their existing schemata and, in the process, negotiate a meaning consistent with those

Teachers must allow students time to express their understanding of instruction.

schemata. This modern view of learning and instruction requires teachers to do more than care and more than simply "pour in" information. They must also allow time for students to express their restructured understandings and then decide what instructional elaborations, if any, to provide to help students reach the intended curricular goal.

How students mediate instruction is determined by how instruction is socially situated because they interpret or reconstruct the lesson in light of the situation. For instance, when the academic task is to complete a ditto sheet on letter sounds because the teacher says to do so, students may think of this task as a social situation that calls for finishing quickly. Acting upon this interpretation of the situation, they will learn how to get the ditto done quickly (but perhaps will not learn letter sounds). The teacher's intention was for students to use letter sounds when reading and writing, but because instruction is situated in social activity which does not call for using letter sounds in reading and writing, students will interpret that what really counts is getting done. In contrast, if the task is situated in genuine activity (such as writing a letter to the President as noted above), students are more likely to mediate instruction in the way intended by the teacher—that is, they are more likely to learn to use letter sounds in reading and writing because they have been placed in a social situation where they will use them in actually writing a real letter in an attempt to achieve a real goal. In short, they are learning letter sounds in situations where they are being genuinely literate, so they come to understand what it means to be literate and how letter sounds contribute to that end.

Good instruction, then, can be summed up with the following four points:

1. Instruction is the intentional provision of academic tasks designed to help students modify their schemata in ways specified in the curriculum.

2. Academic tasks must be embedded in (or situated in) authentic literacy experiences and activity.

3. Instruction involves an interaction between information provided either directly or indirectly by the teacher, and student mediation or interpretation of that information.

4. All instructional interactions must be conducted within an aura of care and concern for the well-being of the individual student.

DISTINCTION BETWEEN DIRECT AND INDIRECT INSTRUCTION

Instruction can be direct, indirect, or a combination of both. **Direct instruction** occurs when teachers present an academic task to students. For example, a mother teaching a baby to say the new word *Daddy* and a teacher teaching a student to read the printed word *Daddy* are examples of direct instruction. **Indirect instruction** occurs when academic tasks are embedded in activities in the classroom environment to lead students to some desired goal. Leaving computer catalogs in the classroom so students will examine them and, hopefully, understand that reading includes catalogs as well as the more traditional books typically found in school is an example of indirect instruction. Most instruction contains elements of both direct and indirect instruction. The following discussion gives details on using these types of instruction.

Direct Instruction

Teachers who instruct directly play a structured and active role. They rely on what they say to ensure that students interpret academic tasks in the intended way. That is, they provide information to students directly and expect students to respond. Each response provides an opportunity for students to express their understanding of the information the teacher provides, and each of these expressions offers the teacher a window into students' minds. By looking through this window you then interpret to see how students have restructured the task; you use what you learn through each interaction as a basis for providing elaboration. Consequently, successful direct instruction depends as much on your spontaneous elaborations as on your initial presentation of information. Hence, direct instruction is an ongoing process of reciprocal mediation. Caring teachers plan encounters to provide students with information about the curricular goal that is mediated and restructured by students, fed back to the teacher, and, when necessary, followed by elaborated information keyed to this feedback. This interactive cycle continues until students reach the desired goal, whether during a single lesson or, in the case of more complex understandings, after a series of lessons. (See Figure 4.1.) Four characteristics are associated with direct instruction: assessment, explanation, practice, and application.

Assessment involves collection of the data used to make decisions. It is crucial to all instruction, especially direct instruction because teachers cannot make good decisions unless they assess student performance.

Data can be collected either formally (using standardized tests) or informally (using teacher-made measures). Clinicians and reading specialists make much use of **formal tests,** but most classroom teachers rely on **informal tests.** That is, they observe their students, question and talk with them, examine their written work, and make instructional decisions from these data. One example of informal assessment is the teacher's observation of students' restructuring in the

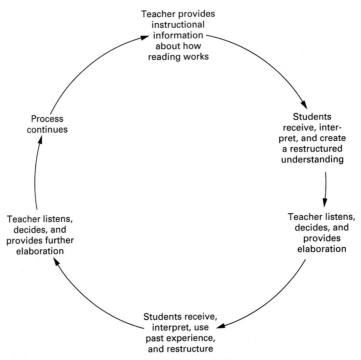

FIGURE 4.1   Instructional Interaction in Direct Instruction

description of instructional mediation. Chapter 11 provides details about how to assess.

Explanation is verbal assistance. It is extremely important in direct instruction because it is during explanation that teachers initially provide the information students need to construct an understanding of what is being taught. Explanation provides the "how-to" bridge between not knowing and knowing. It plays a major role in determining how students will interpret a task, because they tend to think about tasks in the ways teachers talk about them. In short, students learn what teachers emphasize.

Explanation consists of two parts. First is the initial instructional presentation—a series of brief teacher statements about what is to be learned, why it is to be learned, and how to do it. This information giving usually includes explicit teacher modeling of how to do a task and, as such, relies greatly on teacher talk. Second is the interaction between teacher and students as students restructure the teacher's presentation. This is where teachers gradually shift the responsibility for doing and understanding a task to their students by providing a series of opportunities for students to express their understanding. Students complete succeeding items in the series of opportunities with less and less assistance from the teacher (with less and less teacher talk and more and more student talk). The goal is for students to comprehend without teacher assistance. This interactive part of instruction calls for much flexibility from teachers, since students constantly restructure explanations in terms of their prior knowledge. Chapter 13 provides details about how to explain.

Practice is repetition, and its function is to make habitual, or solidify, initial understanding developed during explanation. For instance, explanation helps students understand how to figure out the theme of a story, but practice makes the strategy a habit. Practice is generally characterized by repetition and drill, whereas explanation is characterized by information giving and sense making.

Practice usually consists of activities rather than teacher talk. To give students practice, teachers involve them in activities with either controlled or natural text. **Controlled text** is intentionally structured to include many repetitions of whatever knowledge or strategy is being taught; **natural text** is an unaltered example of text, such as a library book, that includes sufficient examples of what is to be practiced. In most reading classrooms, practice activities employ controlled text such as workbook pages or ditto sheets in which students respond several times to a similar kind of task because it is efficient and easy to use. However, controlled-text practice activities do not encourage application of the learning to natural text. Since the ultimate goal is "real" reading, natural text is often a more useful practice, despite the relative scarceness of examples.

Whereas explanations must be teacher led, practice can be either teacher guided or independent. Practice is guided when teachers directly supervise it: for instance, monitoring each student's response to practice items or listening to each student read aloud during the reading group. Practice is unguided when teachers have students work independently: for instance, giving students unsupervised seatwork or assigning practice sheets for homework.

Along with assessment and explanation, practice is part of the bridge teachers provide during direct instruction to help students achieve the desired goal. It is intentional (you decide what the practice is to be) and **strategic** (you design the practice to solidify a specific curricular goal). However, practice is distinct from explanation. Explanation comes first, and then practice solidifies what has been explained and understood. Because it would be foolish to practice something one does not understand, explanation is a prerequisite to practice. More information on practice is provided in Chapter 13, and examples of practice appropriate for various goals are provided in the chapters devoted to specific grade levels (Chapters 15 through 18).

Application is designed to help students **transfer** what has been learned from an instructional setting to a real world setting. Whereas teachers' explanations develop students' understanding of a goal and practice provides repetition in using that understanding in a somewhat artificial situation (the text is controlled rather than natural), application helps students apply to natural settings what was understood and practiced. For instance, explanation helps students understand how to figure out the meaning of an unknown word from context, and practice helps them use what has been learned when reading self-selected material. When students use what they learn when reading a newspaper or reading a library book, they are applying what they learned. To accomplish this, teachers must provide opportunities for such application.

Assessment, explanation, practice, and application in direct instruction are distinguished from each other by their functions. If you intend to develop initial understanding, explanation is needed; if you intend to solidify understanding, practice is needed; if you intend to test understanding, assessment is needed; and if you intend to help students transfer understanding to real reading, application is needed.

Example 4.1 is an illustration of a typical direct instruction lesson, including examples of assessment, explanation, practice, and application. Detailed directions for planning and teaching direct instruction lessons are provided in Chapter 13.

Indirect Instruction

In contrast to direct instruction, indirect instruction depends more on classroom activities than on teacher talk. That is, the activities themselves provide the information, shaping students' interpretations of the task and leading them to discover the intended instructional goal. Since the activities in the environment contain information that is self-evident, teachers assume a relatively covert role. A strength of this approach is that student interest and motivation increase with independent (or semi-independent) pursuit of activities. A weakness is that because students are not working as closely with teachers there are fewer teacher-student interactions and, as a result, fewer opportunities to monitor and respond to students' restructuring.

EXAMPLE 4.1 Direct Instruction

This example of direct instruction is designed to develop students' understanding about how to make predictions while reading. The instruction is based on the teacher's assessment that the students do not actively predict what meanings will come next.

The teacher's instructional plan calls for a task that requires predicting and a two-part explanation. First, the teacher presents initial information by explicitly stating what is to be learned (how to make predictions), why it is important (because good readers think along with the author), and when it will be used (in a story to be read that day, which the teacher shows to the students). Then the teacher models what good readers think about as they make predictions while reading. In the second part of the explanation the teacher listens to students' interpretations of how to make predictions, decides if additional elaboration is needed to guide students to the desired goal, and provides such elaboration as needed.

The teacher then provides practice in making predictions, using excerpts from real text, which have been put together on a single practice sheet. The teacher has the students complete the practice under guidance and provides corrective feedback as appropriate.

Once the students understand how to make predictions, the teacher introduces them to the targeted text and cites the importance of applying what has been learned when reading that text. Students are then directed to read the text and to make predictions as they read. The subsequent discussion focuses not only on what the selection was about but also on the students' application of their newly acquired prediction strategy.

When using indirect instruction, teachers build a **literate environment** that features activities—academic tasks—that contain information students can use to build schemata about instructional goals. For instance, teachers might encourage students to send handwritten notes to each other at any time during the school day. This is an academic task. The task has embedded in it the information that writing and reading are message-sending, message-getting activities. By engaging students in the task of passing notes, the teacher hopes that students will infer the information about these characteristics of language and will use it to revise their schemata for reading and writing.

Teachers orchestrate activities in three aspects of the environment: the physical, the social-emotional, and the intellectual.

The **physical environment** refers to what is seen in the classroom. It includes such things as seating arrangements, types of furniture, decorations on the wall, work that is displayed, and bulletin boards. Teachers can structure a physical environment to highlight certain activities that stimulate specific reading goals. For instance, a positive response to reading could be developed by including in the physical environment lots of attractive books and inviting places to read them, such as bean bag chairs; this physical environment invites the activity of pausing and relaxing with books. Because such an arrangement is intended to stimulate activities that contain self-evident information about appreciation of reading as a recreational activity, it is a form of indirect instruction.

The **social-emotional environment** refers to activities that involve social interactions among classroom participants. For instance, teachers may wish to develop the concept that reading is a form of communication between reader and writer similar to the speaker-listener relationship. Although the teacher does not directly explain it, the social activity of pairing students to exchange first oral and then written messages demonstrates that all language is a process of sending and receiving messages. Such teacher orchestration of a classroom's social-emotional activities is an example of indirect instruction.

The **intellectual environment** refers to activities in which teachers model, set expectations, challenge, and stimulate interests. For instance, to develop the concept that reading is an enjoyable leisure-time pursuit, teachers may provide pleasure-reading activities and personally model their own enjoyment of reading, or they may read a story to their students. The instruction is not overt; there is little or no direct teacher talk about how to enjoy books. Instead, these teachers arrange for activities to carry the message that reading is an enjoyable leisure-time activity. This is indirect instruction.

Instruction is indirect when you intentionally orchestrate classroom activities to lead students to specific goals. It may not appear that you are providing information students can use to build schemata about reading when you are sitting and reading a library book or quietly observing students interacting in pairs, but you are. It is, therefore, an example of indirect instruction, because you assume a relatively passive and covert role and permit the activities to do the instructing. Example 4.2 provides an example of indirect instruction. Detailed suggestions for building a literate environment in your classroom are provided in Chapter 10, and suggestions for planning and teaching lessons that are indirect are provided in Chapter 13.

Summary of Direct and Indirect Instruction

Both direct and indirect instruction are intentional efforts by teachers to achieve specified curricular goals; both employ academic tasks, presentations, and interactions with students, and both are teacher led. The difference is one of degree. In direct instruction a teacher presents the academic task in a more direct and straightforward manner (usually through teacher talk) to achieve desired goals; in indirect instruction a teacher's intervention is through involving students in activities. Good teachers use both direct and indirect instruction.

The decision to employ direct or indirect instruction depends on two things. The first is the desired curricular goal. If you want to develop a conceptual understanding about reading or good feelings about reading (that is, attitude goals), indirect instruction is usually best. If you want to develop knowledge about how reading works or the ability to get meaning from a text (that is, process and content goals), direct instruction usually works best. The second condition is the aptitude of the student. If a student learns to read easily, indirect instruction

EXAMPLE 4.2 Indirect Instruction

This example of indirect instruction is designed to develop students' appreciation for how books can produce a sense of wonder.

The teacher first engages the students in a task of book sharing. Children's books that typically stimulate a sense of wonder are collected — examples include McCloskey's *Time of Wonder,* Sperry's *Call It Courage,* L'Engle's *Wrinkle in Time,* and Lewis's *Moment of Wonder.* The teacher displays these books prominently in the classroom as part of the physical environment, reads certain excerpts aloud, and features the theme of wonder on a bulletin board.

Then the teacher discusses the books with the students. This activity combines the intellectual and social-emotional environments. To an observer, the academic task looks casual, informal, and unplanned. In reality, however, the teacher has deliberately selected the books, carefully selected which segments to read, and planned what to say to students to draw unusual experiences described in the books to their attention.

Then the teacher involves the students in choosing and reading books, guiding them as they talk about passages that stimulate interest and reinforcing them as they respond positively to the chosen passages. This task again reflects both the intellectual and social-emotional environment.

is often effective; if a student has difficulty learning to read, better results are usually obtained with direct instruction.

Whether instruction is direct or indirect, however, it always reflects your intention and involves information-giving through an academic task. In direct instruction, you take more responsibility for providing information about what is to be learned; in indirect instruction, the information is implicit in the activity students engage in.

Combining Direct and Indirect Instruction

Direct and indirect instruction are not mutually exclusive. Rather, instruction is a continuum, ranging from extreme examples of direct instruction in which teacher talk is dominant, through gradually diminishing amounts of teacher intervention, to a point where student involvement in activities is dominant. Hence, you may choose to teach in more or less direct or indirect ways depending on what the curricular goal is and on how difficult you expect it to be for a particular group of students.

Because effective teachers combine direct and indirect instruction, the classroom reflects both a literate environment and direct teacher guidance. The literate environment emphasizes activities that literate people pursue, rather than the typical classroom "work." For instance, the physical environment includes many reading and writing opportunities, and students use them for genuine communication: students read books of their choice, write real messages to

Instruction can be direct, indirect, or a combination of both.

real people, and use reading and writing to achieve both aesthetic and pragmatic goals. In short, classroom activities indirectly instruct students in both the joys and practicalities of literacy. The teacher actively guides students' evolving understanding about how reading works. While exhibiting humaneness and sensitivity in responding to students, the teacher provides explicit information students can use to construct accurate concepts about reading and teaches them how to gain metacognitive control of meaning getting. Figure 4.2 summarizes the important components of instruction.

MOTIVATING

One of the major instructional concerns of teachers is motivation, and a frequently asked question is, "How do you get kids to *want* to learn to read?" There are two keys to motivation. The first is success. As human beings, we all enjoy doing things successfully, and we all dislike doing things we cannot do well. To motivate students you must make sure their encounters with reading

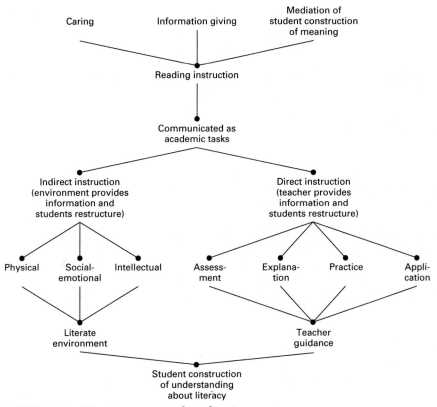

FIGURE 4.2   Key Components of Reading Instruction

are reasonably successful ones by assigning tasks at which students can succeed. Chapter 11 discusses this in detail.

The second key to motivation is whether the instructional situation emphasizes the usefulness of reading. Human beings all enjoy learning things they can use in some important way, and they dislike doing things that seem to be busy work. You must make sure your students' encounters with reading lead to some useful end as opposed to isolated tasks with little perceived value. Creating useful reading tasks means you must **integrate** or combine reading with something else your students value. The two following examples of integration are illustrative.

Integration within a Single Lesson

The simplest way to illustrate the usefulness of reading is to integrate within a single lesson. When you present a skill or strategy in isolation from real reading, students are not able to understand why it is useful and, consequently, are not motivated to learn it. For instance, a lesson about prefixes that is limited to finding and circling prefixes in lists of words has little perceived usefulness. Students conclude that the task is busy work, and they are not motivated by it. However, if you situate the prefix task in the reading of an interesting story containing unknown prefixed words, your students will conclude that the task is worthwhile, and they will be inclined to learn the prefixes. By situating the skill or strategy in real reading, you create usefulness and resulting motivation.

Integration across Lessons

Another more elaborate kind of usefulness involves integrating tasks across lessons. Teachers often teach several related aspects of reading and writing in a series of connected lessons that are planned as cohesive and wholistic units of instruction. For instance, if your students participate in a series of lessons about how to read directions in order to build and fly kites and they are interested in flying kites, the task of learning to follow directions possesses usefulness. It helps them build kites so they conclude that the series of lessons are useful, and they are motivated. By situating the series of lessons in a project the students value, you show them the usefulness of the lessons, and motivation results.

Examples of integration are virtually endless. You can integrate reading with writing, listening, speaking, previously learned reading content, or a variety of different subject areas. In all cases, your intent is to hook reading content to another activity where it will be immediately used. This is a much more powerful motivator than telling students that what they learn in reading will help them at some vague time and place in the distant future.

APPROACHES TO ORGANIZING READING INSTRUCTION

Instruction, whether it is direct or indirect, has to be organized. Teachers call their year-long series of organized reading activities the **reading program.** Every classroom has such a program; that is, every teacher organizes the teaching of reading into a set of year-long activities. The different ways to organize programs are usually discussed in terms of approaches to the teaching of reading. Although there are many such approaches, the three major ones are: the basal text approach, the language experience approach, and the personalized reading approach. In practice, the basal text approach is used by most classroom teachers.

Basal Text Approach

As noted in Chapter 1, basal reading textbooks are used in the **basal text approach** in almost all elementary classrooms in the United States. For many teachers a basal textbook *is* the reading program, and their year-long set of activities comes primarily from the teacher's guide that accompanies the text.

Publishers invest millions of dollars in developing, packaging, and marketing these instructional materials. Despite publisher competition, however, the differences among the major basal reading programs are marginal. All follow essentially the same format including a multilevel series of 15 to 20 books beginning with **readiness** books for kindergartners and proceeding through **preprimers** and **primers** to texts designed for use in the eighth grade. Usually a publisher provides two separate books, one slightly more difficult than the other, for use at each grade level. In actuality, however, several levels may be in use in any given classroom at any time because of the wide differences in students' reading abilities. This explains why U.S. schoolchildren identify each other's relative reading status by asking the question, "What book are you in?"

Each level of a basal reading series includes a student text containing the selections to be read, a workbook with exercises to be completed, and a teachers' edition with extensive teaching suggestions and directions. The teachers' edition for any given level is a massive book that contains:

1. Copies of both the selections and the workbook pages that appear in the student's edition.

2. Extensive descriptive material regarding the philosophy of the basal program.

3. Organizational procedures teachers should follow in implementing the program.

4. Specific directions to follow in presenting prescribed skills.

5. Suggested questions to ask when discussing selections with students.

6. Enrichment activities for use as follow-up or culminating activities.

7. End-of-unit tests that can be used to evaluate student achievement.

In addition, most basal reading series provide supplementary charts, work sheets, games, and other instructional devices useful to a teacher, as well as an elaborate **scope-and-sequence chart,** which details the development of every skill and strategy across all levels of the program. Example 4.3 outlines the procedure of a typical lesson using the basal text approach.

There are advantages to the basal text system. From the teachers' standpoint, a basal simplifies the complexity of teaching reading. All the techniques, activities, and materials are provided and have been organized into manageable three- to four-day units. Consequently, the demands on teachers are lessened. When one considers the complexity of the classroom, as noted in Chapter 1, this advantage is compelling.

However, the basal also has disadvantages. First, because the basal is organized into a set of routine activities, teachers tend to conduct instruction in a technical manner; they assign the instructional responsibility to the basal and

EXAMPLE 4.3 Basal Text Lesson

Typically, teachers use basal texts in the following way. They call the reading groups together often referring to the group by the title of the basal text being used (e.g., "Would the Windchimes come to the reading table now?"). The lesson typically begins with the teacher introducing the reading selection using the suggestions provided in the teachers' edition. The teacher then introduces and teaches the vocabulary words, gives students a purpose for reading the selection, and has them read the story (often orally in the very early grades and silently once students are in second grade or beyond).

After the selection has been read, the teacher discusses the content with students by asking questions suggested in the teachers' edition and often has students do oral or silent rereading of certain parts to elaborate on some point. Then the teacher refers to the teachers' edition for suggestions regarding what skills to teach, uses these in introducing the skills, and assigns students to the associated workbook pages to give them practice in the skill. Finally, the teacher closes the lesson using one or more of the teachers' edition suggestions for enrichment activities and pupil evaluation. Ordinarily, this series of activities requires three or four days for each selection. Once the cycle is completed with one selection, it is repeated with the next. In this way each basal reading textbook is completed, and reading instruction gets accomplished.

become technicians who follow directions rather than professionals who maintain control of their own instruction. Second, because of the emphasis placed on the stories in the basal, teachers tend to believe that all children learn how to read simply by reading. While high-aptitude students sometimes learn to read by reading, low-aptitude students seldom do. Third, despite the emphasis on stories, basal programs provide little opportunity for sustained reading of text. Instead, reading is often disrupted by the need to respond to teacher questions or by requests to read orally in turn. Finally, basals emphasize isolated workbook-type activities more than real comprehension outcomes and, as a result, tend to convey the impression that reading is a mechanical process of getting answers rather than a cognitive process of making sense out of an author's message.

Language Experience Approach

The **language experience approach** (LEA) is organized around personal experiences that students translate into written text and then read. Consequently, what students read describes personal experiences using familiar words. Students are in control of comprehension because the words, prior knowledge, author purpose, and text structure are all familiar.

The language experience approach is most frequently associated with beginning reading. However, because of the dominance of the basal text approach, it is seldom used exclusively.

More than any other approach, the language experience approach emphasizes the interrelationships among the language modes. It starts with an experience (such as a field trip), continues with oral language (students talk about the field trip and listen to others express their thoughts), results in a written product (the talk about the field trip is written down), and culminates in students reading what they have written (their own stories). Students learn the role of reading within the overall language system: that thoughts can be communicated in spoken messages, that what can be spoken can be written down, and that what is written can be read.

In the early grades the language experience approach usually involves taking dictation from children, since young students cannot yet write. However, young students can write their own stories using **invented spelling** to make up for what they have not yet formally learned about spelling. In later grades, students do their own writing. Language experience stories for primary grades are frequently composed in the following sequence.

1. Start with an experience—a holiday, the weather, a story they read, or any other common experience.

2. Discuss the experience with students.

3. Suggest that the students' ideas be written by the teacher on a large piece of chart paper displayed at the front of the room.

4. Direct students to suggest a title and a first line, and write these on the chart paper.

5. Solicit subsequent contributions from others in the group and write these on the chart paper.

6. When complete, read the product orally to the group.

7. Direct students to read the story or parts of the story on the chart to you.

8. Have students copy the story for themselves and illustrate it.

9. Make the resulting book part of the growing library of material students can read.

Language experience stories for upper-elementary grades are somewhat different in that students can write and do not need to copy a group story. The pattern for upper grades usually follows the following sequence.

1. Discuss an experience with students—a field trip, a sporting activity, a visitor to the classroom, an adventure they have had.

2. Brainstorm with students about ideas regarding the topic—sequences of action, descriptive words, conclusions.

The language experience approach emphasizes the interrelationships among speaking, writing, and reading.

3.   Write ideas so they can be seen visually, such as on a chalkboard.

4.   Guide students in developing an opening and possible plots or sequence of events.

5.   Have students complete their own stories.

6.   Edit completed stories—editors can be students or teachers.

7.   Prepare final copies as books for the room or school library, or for home.

The language experience approach has many advantages. It emphasizes the language concepts that undergird reading (the relationship between reading and writing, for instance). It also puts students in control of the reading process (they know the words because they were used in the oral discussion, they have prior knowledge because the text is based on a shared experience, and they understand both the author's purpose and the text structure, because it was self-written). In addition, it is always fresh and motivating, since the experiences that are the basis for the stories are real, not contrived. As such, it is probably the best single approach to early reading instruction.

However, there are disadvantages to language experience. The most serious one is that it does not have the built-in organization of materials and activities found in the basal text. Instead, teachers and children generate all the reading materials, and teachers are totally responsible for creating both the curricular structure and the necessary materials. A teacher's organizational task is therefore very difficult and the energy demands on teachers are high.

Another disadvantage of the language experience approach is its heavy reliance on indirect instruction. Although effective for developing positive attitudes and an understanding of language, it is less effective in developing an understanding of specific skills and strategies, especially for low-aptitude students. Instruction that is more direct is most effective in developing these outcomes, and there is little emphasis on direct instruction in the language experience approach.

A final disadvantage of the language experience approach is that very few schools allow teachers the latitude to use it as the primary means for organizing the reading program. Instead, they either mandate a specific basal text or provide several different basals, thereby setting the expectation that a reading program should be organized around basal materials and activities.

Literature-based Approach

The **literature-based approach,** sometimes called the **personalized reading approach** or **individualized reading,** is based on self-selection in which children choose the library books they wish to read and the words they wish to learn. Students read these selections independently, and the teacher instructs each student through individual conferences. During these conferences the teacher discusses the book currently being read by the student, assesses the student's needs and achievements, and provides individual instruction. Because students must be independent readers to employ this approach, it tends to be associated with the middle and upper grades but is seldom used exclusively. The following list shows the key points involved in organizing a literature-based program.

1. Start collecting a variety of books. For the average classroom, try to collect 100 books, or at least three different books per pupil. If there are not enough available in your school, borrow, trade, and ask for donations.

2. Set up an interesting library area with a rug, pillows, and some furniture. Try to arrange the books with the covers facing the students.

3. Teach your students the "rule of thumb." If they are primary age, tell them to select a page in the middle of the book and begin reading it silently. Each time they miss a word, they should put up a finger. If all their fingers are up before the page is finished, the book is too hard. Older students can just count up to five words missed.

4. Teach them to get books quietly.

5. Teach them how to get help with a word. They could go to the dictionary, an aide, experience charts, other books that they know, a friend, or the teacher, or they could try to figure it out for themselves.

6. Teach them to prepare for a conference with the teacher by:
   a. Selecting a book.
   b. Reading silently to themselves or reading aloud to a friend.
   c. Signing up for the conference.

7. During the conference, which should last five to ten minutes, discuss with the student interesting information, the author's purpose, and how the story can be applied to other situations. Finally, to check performance, have the student read a portion of the story aloud.

8. Meanwhile, the rest of the class are reading their books or doing an original activity to follow up something they have read. Examples of creative activities are writing for a class newspaper, keeping track of books, choral reading, dramatization, writing letters, and creative writing.

9. Occasionally you may form temporary groups to work on a particular reading goal.

The literature-based approach has many advantages. It is highly motivating, since the students are personally involved in selecting their reading materials. Vocabulary control is not imposed by an outside source; instead, students expand their vocabulary as they read a variety of books. This approach, through the use of teacher-student conferences, promotes personal interaction between students and teacher. Most important, however, a literature-based approach encourages the reading habit, promoting reading as reading and not as some boring school task that has no relation to the real world.

Literature-based reading also has disadvantages, however. There is a lack of emphasis on systematic instruction. Strategies, for instance, are not taught systematically, but are taught as they happen to appear in self-selected materials. It takes a highly skilled teacher to determine needs as quickly and as accurately as demanded by this approach, and it takes a highly organized teacher to find the time to conduct conferences and also to teach the strategies once the need is recognized. Most teachers feel they cannot do this adequately because other demands of the classroom are just too great.

While a literature-based approach is seldom used as the only reading program in a classroom, elements of it are often incorporated into existing programs. For example, many classrooms have regular free reading periods in which students select what they read and occasionally have conferences with the teacher about them.

Basing Instruction in Whole Language

As you can see from the above, each of the three major approaches to reading instruction has advantages and disadvantages. None is totally satisfactory in itself. Consequently, many teachers use a **combined approach** for organizing their reading programs. Typically, because use of a basal textbook is mandated (either explicitly or implicitly) and because most teachers appreciate the organizational comfort of basals, teachers may base their instruction on a basal text. Then they integrate elements of language experience and literature-based programs into the basal program. For instance, a portion of each school day may be used for free reading of self-selected books or for having individual students or groups of students create and read text based on real experience.

However, we recommend that you use **whole language** as the basis for your reading and writing instruction. Whole language is not an approach—it is a philosophy. Consequently, whole language is not a set of procedures for how to teach reading as much as it is a set of beliefs about the "whole-ness" of literacy. Chief among these beliefs are: (1) the child should be a user of language; (2) language should be used to achieve authentic goals; and (3) language should not be isolated from genuine use. We recommend that you use a whole language philosophy because implementation of the above three beliefs will ensure that students' experiences with literacy reflect what literacy really is, not an artificial, school version of literacy.

What we learn—and what we think is most important about what we learn—reflects our experiences. Our schema for reading, for instance, reflects our experiences with reading. Consequently, getting students to build accurate schema for reading requires that they have experiences with reading which, because they are "whole," are accurate reflections of what reading really is and what it is used for in real life.

Consequently, the first task in creating effective reading instruction is to provide students with "whole" reading experiences which will cause them to build accurate conceptions (or schema) for what reading is in the real world. The best way to accomplish this is to think in terms of situating instruction in meaningful social situations—that is, providing reading instruction within the framework of the pursuit of authentic goals.

For instance:

- Kindergartners may want to write a letter to grandparents to tell them what they want for their birthday—within this authentic goal, they could learn to "read" newspaper advertisements, and mail-order catalogs and to write letters;

- First graders may want to have a bake sale to raise money to buy library books for their classroom—within this authentic goal, they could read and write about various kinds of cookies and cookie recipes;

- Second graders may want to do something with the bare spot outside their classroom window—within this authentic goal, they could read and write about various kinds of plants which could be grown there;

- Third graders may want to get a certain piece of playground equipment added to the schoolyard—within this authentic goal, they could read and write about how to accomplish this goal;

- Fourth graders may be concerned about a student injured in a bicycle accident and want to prevent additional accidents—within this authentic goal, they could read and write about bicycle safety and how to communicate safety tips to others;

- Fifth graders may be interested in world peace and the efforts of the United Nations to achieve this goal in the Near East—within this authentic goal, they could read and write about the United Nations' efforts to ensure peace in the Near East;

- Sixth graders may be concerned about environmental abuse and the dangers to health in their community—within this authentic goal, they could read and write about environmental efforts and what they could do to help in their community.

Pursuit of authentic goals such as these ensure that students' experiences with literacy will be life-like. That is, when they learn skills and strategies, it will be because they are going to use them to accomplish an important goal, not because the teacher says to do it or because it is the next activity in the workbook. Consequently, chances are increased that they will build accurate concepts about the nature and purpose of reading—that is, they are more likely to learn that being literate means "proactive and enthusiastic use of language in the pursuit of controlling and enriching one's own destiny."

In sum, we recommend that you think about your reading instruction in terms of the philosophy of whole language—in which the child's pursuit of authentic goals using language is the primary focus and in which nitty-gritty skills and strategies associated with reading are embedded (or situated) in authentic literate activity. In the process of pursuing authentic goals, you may wish to use basal textbooks, language experience activities, or literature. However, your instructional decisions are not determined by the material you use. Instead, your instructional decisions are determined by whether students are engaged in authentic activity and are, therefore, likely to develop accurate conceptions of literacy.

INSTRUCTIONAL DECISION MAKING

To help your students achieve literacy, you must be able to make your own decisions about instruction as you teach. As we mentioned in Chapter 1, this is not easy. You must possess professional knowledge about language, learning, and instruction. This book starts you on the road to obtaining that knowledge. For this knowledge to be stored in your long-term memory, however, you must build a meaningful schema for "teaching reading" in which many concepts are linked together into a meaningful whole. This means creating an integrated mental structure for teaching reading in which you link, in sensible ways, the content from one chapter of this book with the content from other chapters.

You must be in metacognitive control of your knowledge so you can control your instruction just as you want your students to be metacognitive of how reading works so they can control the reading process. You must be conscious of how you organize your knowledge about the teaching of reading, and you must reflect on how the different categories of knowledge in your knowledge structure relate to one another.

You must also be flexible. Teaching reading is a highly complex endeavor; there are no pat answers. What works in one situation with one group of students may not work in another situation with another group of students. Therefore, change is a constant. The knowledge structure you create today will be adjusted or embellished tomorrow, not only while you are learning how to teach but throughout your entire career.

Decision making demands constant assessment. You must assess the students you are teaching, the situation you are in, and yourself. Assessment provides the basis for the decisions you make. Without assessment data, you cannot know whether things are going well or poorly or whether any decisions need to be made.

Finally, decision making requires hard work and courage. It is easy to follow the directions someone else provides, and it is easy to justify doing so if you assume that the people who wrote the teachers' guide know more about teaching than you do. It is much harder to acknowledge that, in the reality of the classroom, you are in a far better position to judge how well students understand instructional content than the author of the teachers' guide. And it takes courage to steadfastly refuse to abdicate your responsibility for instructional decisions even when you make mistakes, as we all do.

Despite the difficulties, however, being a decision maker is worth the effort. The payoff comes in two ways. First, you will be more effective. You will help more students achieve literacy. Second, and equally as important, you will not "burn out" as a teacher. Instead, you will discover the joy and pride of creative work, of rarely doing anything the same way twice, and of striving to improve. Figure 4.3 summarizes the main points about decision making.

SUMMARY

Teaching is used in this book to encompass all the classroom roles and responsibilities a teacher assumes in the normal course of a day; *instruction,* in contrast, refers to those roles and responsibilities specifically associated with developing curricular goals. There are five main properties of instruction: setting high expectations; a humane caring about children and their well-being; situating learning

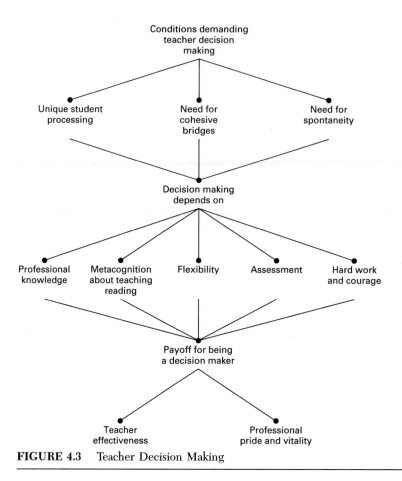

FIGURE 4.3   Teacher Decision Making

in authentic activity; a provision of information that students can use to build a schema for a curricular goal; and mediation of students' restructuring as they build understanding about a curricular goal. These characteristics can be developed directly by having a teacher provide information for student use in creating schemata or less directly by including activities in the classroom environment that contain implicit information students can use to build curricular schemata. In any case, students must be motivated and instruction must be organized. Teachers motivate by giving students tasks they can succeed at and by integrating what is to be learned with activities that are meaningful. Teachers organize reading instruction by employing a basal text approach, a language experience approach, a personalized reading approach, or a combination of these. In this book, however, we recommend basing instruction in whole language—a philosophy which puts priority on students using language in the pursuit of authentic tasks.

SUGGESTED ADDITIONAL READING

ALLEN, E. G., & LAMINACK, L. L. (1982). Language experience reading—It's a natural! *Reading Teacher, 35*(6), 708–714.

ALLEN, R. V. (1968). How a language experience program works. In E. C. Vilscek (Ed.). *A decade of innovations: Approaches to beginning reading.* Newark: International Reading Association.

ASHTON-WARNER, S. (1963). *Teacher.* New York: Bantam Books.

BARR, R. (1991). Toward a balanced perspective in beginning reading. *Educational Researcher, 20*(4), 30–82.

BLAIR, T. R. (1984). Teacher effectiveness: The know-how to improve student learning. *Reading Teacher, 38*(2), 138–142.

CRISCUOLO, N. P. (1979). Effective approaches for motivating children to read. *Reading Teacher, 32*(5), 543–546.

DUFFY, G., & ROEHLER, L. (1982). The illusion of instruction. *Reading Research Quarterly, 17*(3), 543–546.

DURKIN D. (1990). Delores Durkin speaks on instruction. *Reading Teacher, 43*(7), 472–476.

FARRAR, M. T. (1984). Asking better questions. *Reading Teacher, 38*(1), 10–20.

FUHLER, C. (1990). Let's move toward literature-based reading instruction. *Reading Teacher, 43*(4), 312–318.

HALL, M. (1979). Language-centered reading: Premises and recommendations. *Language Arts, 56*(6), 664–670.

HELLER, M. (1988). Comprehending and composing through language experience. *Reading Teacher, 42*(2), 130–135.

HERRMANN, B. (1988). Two approaches for helping poor readers become more strategic. *Reading Teacher, 42*(1), 24–28.

HIEBERT, E., & COLT, J. (1989). Patterns of literature-based reading instruction. *Reading Teacher, 43*(1), 14–20.

HILL, S. E. (1985). Children's individual responses and literature conferences in the elementary school. *Reading Teacher, 38*(4), 382–386.

HUNT, L. C. (1971). Six steps to the individualized reading program (IRP). *Elementary English, 48*(1), 27–32.

KARNOWSKI, L. (1989). Using LEA with process writing. *Reading Teacher, 42*(7), 462–465.

LAMBIE, R. A., & BRITTAIN, M. M. (1983). Adaptive reading instruction: A three-pronged approach. *Reading Journal, 37*(3), 243–248.

MALLON, B., & BERGLUND, R. (1984). The language experience approach to reading: Recurring questions and their answers. *Reading Teacher, 37*(9), 867–871.

MCKENNA, M., ROBINSON, R., & MILLER, J. (1990). Whole language: A research agenda for the nineties. *Educational Researcher, 19*(8), 3–6.

MOSS, J. (1984). *Focus units in literature: The handbook for elementary school teachers.* Urbana, IL: National Council of Teachers of English.

MOSS, J. (1990). *Focus on literature.* Katonah, NY: Richard C. Owen.

NEWMAN, J., & CHURCH, S. (1990). Myths of whole language. *Reading Teacher, 44*(1), 20–26.

NORTON, D. (1990). Teaching multicultural literature in the reading curriculum. *Reading Teacher, 44*(1), 28–40.

PAPPAS, C., KIEFER, B., & LEVSTIK, L.   (1990). *Integrated language perspective in the elementary school: Theory into action.* New York: Longman.

PEARSON, P. D., & DOLE, J.   (1987). Explicit comprehension instruction: A review of research and a new conceptualization of instruction. *Elementary School Journal, 88,* 151–166.

ROEHLER, L., & DUFFY, G.   (1981). Classroom teaching is more than an opportunity to learn. *Journal of Teacher Education, 32*(6), 7–13.

ROEHLER, L., & DUFFY, G.   (1982). Matching direct instruction to reading outcomes. *Language Arts, 59*(5), 476–481.

ROSENSHINE, B.   (1983). Teaching functions in instructional programs. *Elementary School Journal, 83,* 335–352.

SLAUGHTER, H.   (1988). Indirect and direct teaching in a whole language program. *Reading Teacher, 42*(1), 30–34.

TUNNELL, M., & JACOBS, J.   (1989). Using "real" books: Research findings on literature based reading instruction. *Reading Teacher, 42*(7), 470–477.

YOPP, R., & YOPP, H.   (1992). *Literature-based reading activity.* Boston: Allyn & Bacon.

ZARILLO, J.   (1989). Teachers' interpretations of literature-based reading. *Reading Teacher, 43*(1), 22–28.

THE RESEARCH BASE

BARR, R.   (1984). Beginning reading instruction: From debate to reformation. In P. D. Pearson (Ed.), *Handbook of reading research.* New York: Longman.

BROPHY, J. E., & GOOD, T. L.   (1986). Teacher behavior and student achievement. In M. Wittrock (Ed.), *Handbook of research on teaching.* New York: Macmillan.

BROWN, J., COLLINS, A., & DUGUID, P.   (1989). Situated cognition and the culture of learning. *Educational Researcher, 18*(1), 32–42.

DOLE, J., DUFFY, G., ROEHLER, L., & PEARSON, P. D.   (1991). Moving from the old to the new: Research or reading comprehension instruction. *Review of Educational Research, 61*(2), 239–264.

DUFFY, G. G., ROEHLER, L. R., MELOTH, M. S., & VAVRUS, L.G.   (1986). Conceptualizing instructional explanation. *Teaching and Teacher Education, 2,* 197–214.

HOFFMAN, J.   (1991). Teacher and school effects in learning to read. In R. Barr, M. L. Kamil, P. Mosenthal, & P. D. Pearson (Eds.) *Handbook of reading research, volume II.* (pp. 911–950). New York: Longman.

PEARSON, P. D., ROEHLER, L., DOLE, J., & DUFFY, G.   (1992). Developing expertise in reading comprehension. In J. Samuels & A. Farstrup (Eds.) *What research has to say about reading instruction,* 2nd edition (pp. 145–199). Newark, DE: International Reading Association.

PRAWAT, R.   (1989). Promoting access to knowledge, strategy and disposition of students: A research synthesis. *Review of Educational Research, 59*(1), 1–42.

PRAWAT, R.   (1991). The value of ideas: The immersion approach to the development of thinking. *Educational Researcher, 20*(2), 3–10.

ROEHLER, L. R., & DUFFY, G. G.   (1990). Teachers' instructional actions. In R. Barr, M. L. Kamil, P. Mosenthal, & P. D. Pearson (Eds.), *Handbook of reading research, volume II.* New York: Longman.

SCHICKEDANZ, J. (1990). The jury is still out on the effects of whole language and language experience approaches for beginning reading: A critique of Stahl and Miller's Study. *Review of Educational Research, 60*(1), 127–131.

STAHL, S., & MILLER, P. (1989). Whole language and language experience approaches for beginning reading. A quantitative research synthesis. *Review of Educational Research, 59*(1), 87–116.

ACTIVITIES FOR REFLECTING, OBSERVING, AND TEACHING

Reflecting on the Nature of Instruction

PURPOSE: A primary characteristic about instruction is that it is intentional. That is, specific curricular outcomes are intentionally sought; in the pursuit of these outcomes, the teacher intentionally orchestrates various conditions. To be a teacher who is in control of your reading instruction, you must be metacognitive about these various conditions. This activity is designed to help you achieve that goal.

Think about the distinction between "teaching" and "instruction" developed in this chapter. As a teacher, what activities might you engage in that are part of the general act of "teaching" but which would not be examples of "instruction?"

Think back on the teachers you had in school. Were there some who engaged in teaching without providing any instruction? If so, explain why their actions as teachers fail to qualify as instruction.

Think back on your favorite teacher when you were in school. Rate this teacher on each of the five properties of instruction:

1. Expectancies

    Excellent   Poor
    └──────────────────────────────────┘

2. Caring

    Excellent   Poor
    └──────────────────────────────────┘

3. Situating

    Excellent   Poor
    └──────────────────────────────────┘

4. Informing

    Excellent   Poor
    └──────────────────────────────────┘

5. Mediating

    Excellent   Poor
    └──────────────────────────────────┘

Using your ratings above as a basis, what do you think was the most important reason why this person was your favorite teacher?

Continuing to think about your favorite teacher, did this person rely most on direct instruction or indirect instruction? Illustrate by giving examples of what this teacher did.

How did your favorite teacher motivate?

In teaching reading, did this person use:

A basal textbook?

Language experience?

A literature-based approach?

A whole-language philosophy?

Still thinking back on your favorite teacher, what will you try to emulate? What will you try not to emulate?

A major concern in providing whole-language instruction is the ability to situate students' learning in authentic social activity—activity which calls for students to be literate (i.e., to proactively and enthusiastically use language and higher-order thinking in the pursuit of controlling and enriching one's destiny). What can elementary students do in school to "control and enrich their destiny?" List below projects you might have your students pursue which would require them to use language and higher-order thinking in controlling and enriching their lives.

Watching the Instruction of Other Teachers

PURPOSE: One of the most effective ways to understand instruction is to observe and analyze the instruction of other teachers. This activity is designed to help you do this.

DIRECTIONS: Select a teacher for observation and watch him or her teach reading for several days. Analyze the teacher's instruction in terms of the following content of Chapter 4.

The Five Properties of Instruction   What did you observe about the teacher's use of the five properties of instruction?

Expectancies—

Caring—

Situating—

Informing—

Mediating—

Direct and Indirect Instruction

Describe the teacher's use of direct instruction.

Describe the teacher's use of indirect instruction.

Did you observe instances when the teacher was using both direct and indirect instruction? If so, describe these.

Whole Language   Judging by what you observed, to what degree does the teacher you visited reflect the philosophy of whole language?

Provide below specific examples of the teacher's instruction which reflects (or does not reflect) the philosophy of whole language.

Use of Approaches and/or Materials

Did this teacher use:

a basal textbook?

language produced by students?

literature books?

other approaches and/or materials?

What drove the teacher's instruction? Were decisions based primarily on the approach or materials being used? Or on the teacher's philosophy?

Part 2

Structuring and Teaching the Reading Curriculum

A teacher must possess a vast amount of professional knowledge. Of fundamental importance is knowledge about what to teach and how to teach it. The chapters in this section will help you build this understanding. The chapters are organized around the major subgoals of reading: Chapter 5 develops attitude goals, Chapter 6 develops content goals, and Chapters 7, 8, and 9 develop various kinds of process goals.

5 Helping Students Feel Good about Reading: Attitude Goals

GETTING READY

This chapter describes in greater detail the attitude goals for each stage of developmental reading growth in elementary school. Both what attitude goals to teach and how to develop them are discussed. More detailed suggestions for developing positive attitudes are described in the appropriate chapters in Part 4.

In this chapter you will meet four teachers who will illustrate how attitude goals can be developed at various grade levels. Ms. Chang is a kindergarten teacher, Ms. Walters teaches first grade, Mr. Gutierrez teaches third grade, and Ms. O'Malley teaches fifth grade. These teachers will help illustrate points in Chapters 6 through 9 also.

FOCUS QUESTIONS

- What are the components of attitude?

- Why are attitude goals important?

- Why should students be metacognitively aware of their concepts and feelings about reading?

- What role does the literate environment play in developing attitude goals?

- What role does direct teacher guidance play in developing attitude goals?

- What are the major attitude goals developed at the emergent literacy stage? at the initial mastery stage? at the expanded fundamentals stage? at the application stage?

WHAT ARE ATTITUDES AND WHY ARE THEY IMPORTANT?

"Attitude" is a frequently misunderstood word in education. Often, it is used to describe unmotivated students, as in "Sam has a poor attitude." In this book, however, attitude refers to students' conceptual understandings and feelings about reading; the goals are accurate concepts and positive feelings. A "bad attitude" can be changed by determining whether the difficulty lies with misconceptions about reading or bad feelings about it, or both, and then developing the needed concepts or positive feelings.

Students' attitudes often determine whether they develop reading ability, for misconceptions and negative feelings about reading rarely lead to reading competence. Consequently, attitude goals are the curricular foundation to a good elementary school reading program.

At the emergent literacy and initial mastery stages, the foundation for reading should be that reading is a joyful and useful activity. For this reason, preschool, kindergarten, and first and second grade teachers spend much of their instructional time and effort developing attitude goals. Although this emphasis lessens in later years, it nevertheless remains a permanent part of the elementary reading curriculum. Kindergarten teachers may spend as much as 50 percent of their instructional time developing attitude goals, whereas seventh and eighth grade teachers may spend only 20 percent.

DEVELOPING METACOGNITIVE CONTROL

To reach attitude goals, you want students to become metacognitive about what reading is and about the value of reading. Such metacognitive awareness is often revealed in student interviews. For instance, when asked what reading is, students who answer, "Reading is getting an author's message" possess a more accurate concept of reading than those who say, "Reading is sounding out words." Similarly, when asked what reading is used for, students who answer, "It's used for sending messages" possess a more accurate concept than students who say, "It's used in school." Interview responses also reveal students' metacognitive awareness of their own feelings about reading. We know that when students are aware of what reading is and of their own positive feelings toward reading, they understand why they are learning to read. This provides a motivational basis for learning.

Metacognitive awareness is an intermittent rather than a permanent state of mind, of course. For instance, students with positive attitudes may routinely enjoy reading without being consciously aware of it; when questioned about their concepts and feelings, however, they should be able to access and articulate them. This ability to be metacognitive results only if early instructional experiences develop awareness.

INSTRUCTIONAL EMPHASIS IN ATTITUDE GOALS

Attitudes are sometimes discussed as if they are inherent in students and beyond the teacher's control, but this is not the case. Poor student attitudes in reading are usually tied to misconceptions and negative feelings about it. If you can change these, your students' attitudes about reading will change.

It is crucial that you be as systematic and as dedicated to developing attitude goals as you are to teaching other aspects of reading. At any stage of developmental reading growth, you must include attitude development as an integral part of your reading curriculum.

Instruction in attitude goals, like all reading instruction, involves two kinds of academic tasks. One centers around the literate environment (or indirect instruction), and the other around teacher-directed activities (or direct instruction).

The Literate Environment

The literate environment plays a major role in developing attitude goals by emphasizing activities that provide natural opportunities for students to communicate personally meaningful messages. In this way students come to view reading and writing as useful, not artificial. For instance, classrooms with a

When students communicate personally meaningful messages, they learn that reading and writing are satisfying activities.

literate environment typically display different kinds of reading materials and include opportunities for students to use them to solve real problems. Similarly, opportunities for composing, sending, and receiving meaningful written messages are provided.

The intention is that the activities of the classroom itself, by virtue of emphasizing literate encounters, will cause students to conclude that reading and writing are valued pursuits that fulfill genuine functions. Even though this is an indirect form of instruction, it is nevertheless a powerful way to help students develop their reading schemata.

Direct Teacher Guidance

Direct instruction plays a relatively minor role in developing attitude goals, basically because actions speak louder than words where attitudes are concerned. Direct teacher guidance does play a role in developing attitude goals, however, since students are influenced by what teachers say. It is crucial that teachers look for every opportunity to make statements that reflect accurate concepts of reading and provide tangible evidence of their own enthusiasm for literate activities. In doing so, teachers help students construct accurate understandings and enthusiastic responses to reading.

TEACHING ATTITUDE GOALS AT VARIOUS DEVELOPMENTAL LEVELS

The following sections provide initial suggestions for teaching attitude goals. More specific suggestions for teaching attitude goals are provided in Chapter 16 for preschool and kindergarten, in Chapter 17 for primary grades, in Chapter 18 for middle grades, and in Chapter 19 for upper grades.

Emergent Literacy Stage

At the preschool and kindergarten levels, teachers want students to develop fundamental conceptual understandings, such as that reading is talk written down by someone and that it communicates entertaining and useful messages. It is also crucial that students begin to associate reading with good feelings. Consequently, teachers of young children plan and conduct a variety of activities designed to cause students to conclude that reading can be a satisfying, exciting, and useful activity.

Because students at the emergent literacy stage are not yet reading print independently, attitude goals are primarily developed through oral language activities. Teachers read stories to students, have them listen to recordings of stories, create stories with them on the basis of shared experiences (language experience activities), or help them tell stories they have composed using their own preliterate form of writing. Just because students are not yet reading independently does not mean they cannot engage in communication using written language. Moreover, because of the close relationship between reading and writing, teachers develop children's positive attitudes about writing as they develop attitudes about reading. Example 5.1 illustrates how to develop positive reading and writing attitude goals at the emergent literacy stage.

Initial Mastery Stage

As students begin to read print in first and second grade, teachers continue to devote about half their time to developing conceptual understandings and positive feelings about reading. The major difference between teaching attitude goals at the initial mastery stage and teaching them at the emergent literacy stage is that students can now read simple text. Even though stories, as opposed to functional text, are widely used at the initial mastery stage, teachers can begin developing the concept that reading is also used to satisfy curiosity and provide information. They continue simultaneous development of positive attitudes about writing by having students act out the role of author as well as reader.

EXAMPLE 5.1 Developing Attitude Goals at the Emergent Literacy Stage

I. Attitude goals
  A. *Concepts—reading is*
    1. Talk written down
    2. Someone saying something
    3. For enjoyment

  B. *Positive responses—readers feel*
    1. Excitement
    2. Satisfaction

Linda Chang began the afternoon session of her kindergarten class with a lesson using Leo Leonni's *Swimmy.* This delightful story describes the adventures of a little black fish who thwarts the eating habits of bigger fish by arranging little red fish in the shape of one big fish with Swimmy becoming the eye.

Ms. Chang used the oral reading of Leonni's *Swimmy* to develop the attitude goal that reading is someone saying something. To stress that books are written by someone who wants to send a message to others, Ms. Chang described Leo Leonni as a real person who liked friends and wanted to tell others about his feelings. Therefore, he took his message and put it into a book to be shared with them.

The following afternoon, Ms. Chang illustrated to her students that they, too, could share a message with others. After recalling how Leo Leonni had shared with them his message about liking friends, the children decided they wanted to share similar messages, and Ms. Chang recorded it. Afterward, Ms. Chang read their messages about liking friends to them and gave each student a copy to take home for the parents to read aloud. In this way, Ms. Chang developed attitude goals about what reading is, especially the close relationship between reading and writing.

Language experience activities continue to play a major role in building the reading-writing connection. Students and teachers spend much time talking about shared experiences, writing down these experiences, and reading what they have written down. These language experience activities help develop accurate concepts about what reading and writing are all about and demonstrate that communication through written language can be useful and fun. Example 5.2 illustrates how to develop positive attitude goals at the initial mastery stage.

Expanded Fundamentals Stage

At the expanded fundamentals stage, third and fourth grade students begin developing the flexibility and independence associated with expert reading. Although attitude goals no longer dominate instruction, they continue to be important despite three noticeable changes.

The first change involves the time devoted to attitudinal instruction. Teachers in these grades devote about a third of their energies and resources to these goals, rather than the earlier 50 percent. This does not mean that attitudes di-

---

EXAMPLE 5.2   Developing Attitude Goals at the Initial Mastery Stage

I. Attitude goals

   A. Concepts—reading is
1. A message written by an author for a reader
2. For enjoyment
3. For information

   B. Positive responses—readers feel
1. Excitement
2. Satisfaction
3. Knowledgeable
4. Their curiosity satisfied

In Kelly Walters' first grade room, the morning reading period began with the sharing of Judith Viorst's *Alexander and the Terrible, Horrible, No Good, Very Bad Day.* Alexander had a day where everything went wrong. He counted wrong, lost his best friend, and the dentist discovered he had a cavity. Ms. Walters chose this book to develop the attitude goal that reading brings satisfaction. Ms. Walters read the book to the class, and they discussed their own horrible days and how reading about Alexander's horrible day made them feel that they were not the only ones who have bad days.

Ms. Walters used a follow-up activity to help her students realize the connection between reading and writing as well as the satisfaction and pleasure that comes with sending a written message. When she told them that their principal, Mr. Jennings, had had a day like Alexander, the students decided to send him a letter about their horrible days to help make him feel better. After dictating a letter that Ms. Walters printed on the board, the children copied the sentences and added at least one more of their own. Then all the letters were sent to Mr. Jennings. After reading his letters, Mr. Jennings strengthened the students' understanding and positive responses by coming to the classroom and telling them how much better he felt because of their letters.

EXAMPLE 5.3   Developing Attitude Goals at the Expanded Fundamentals Stage

I. Attitude goals

A. *Concepts—reading is*
1. Communication between a writer and a reader
2. For enjoyment
3. Predicting meaning
4. Making sense
5. A tool for gathering information

B. *Positive responses—readers feel*
1. Excitement and joy
2. Satisfaction in solving problems
3. Knowledgeable
4. Curious
5. A sense of power

John Gutierrez's third graders were busily preparing for a visit from an opthamologist. Before the visit, they read Ellen Raskin's *Spectacles,* a story about Iris, who sees strange things because she is nearsighted. However, visits to the opthamologist and the optician enable Iris to see like everyone else.

As his attitude goal, Mr. Gutierrez wanted to teach the concept that reading is a tool for gathering information. In addition, he chose to illustrate the connections between oral language and written language by having each student write a question and send it to the opthamologist prior to her talk. As the opthamologist presented her information, the students listened for the answers to their questions and, if the answers were not provided, asked them in person. After the opthamologist's talk, the students wrote informational booklets about a first visit to the optometrist. These books were then read to students in another third grade classroom.

---

minish in importance once students begin reading at the third and fourth grade levels. But because solid attitudinal foundations have already been developed at the emergent literacy and initial mastery stages, teachers at the expanded fundamentals stage can maintain that foundation while devoting proportionately more time and energy to their instructional goals.

The second difference focuses on how reading works. At this stage, conceptual understandings are expanded to include the concepts that reading is part of a language system, the system is based on making sense of written messages by making predictions based on prior knowledge of both topic and language, and reading can be controlled by using the language system strategically. This conceptual awareness, and its related feelings of self-control, is the heart of developing metacognitive readers.

The third difference involves the transition from narrative to functional text. Whereas students' initial understanding of reading is based primarily on stories, there is a movement at the expanded fundamentals stage to develop the concept that reading provides information and know-how. That is, the concept about reading being a message-sending and message-getting activity is expanded from narrative story telling to include a variety of expository text forms, such as textbooks, newspapers, and printed directions. While this conceptual understanding is being built, the teacher simultaneously attempts to develop positive feelings about reading as a functional tool. Example 5.3 illustrates how to develop positive attitude goals at the expanded fundamentals stage.

EXAMPLE 5.4   Developing Attitude Goals at the Application Stage

I. Attitude goals

A. Concepts—reading is
1. Authors have purposes for writing text; readers have purposes for reading text
2. Reading can clarify knowledge, feelings, and attitudes
3. Reading can expand knowledge, feelings, and attitudes
4. Reading is a valuable tool that meets needs

B. Positive response—readers feel
1. Excitement
2. Satisfaction
3. Knowledgeable
4. Curious
5. A sense of power

As part of a fifth grade unit on animal behavior, Donna O'Malley had a small group of students read Jean George's *Julie of the Wolves.* Julie survived alone in an area of the Arctic Circle known as the Northern Slope because she developed an understanding of wolves' social behavior and, as a result, was allowed by the wolves to share their food and become a member of the wolf pack.

After a lengthy discussion of the wolves' social behavior as it affected Julie, the group prepared a written report for the entire class to read and use. For her attitude goal, Ms. O'Malley developed the concept that reading is a tool for information gathering that enables one to become knowledgeable from reading. In discussions with the group, she illustrated how they had used reading to gather information about wolves' social behavior. In addition, the students saw the natural relationship between reading and writing.

Application Stage

If attitude goals have been properly developed at earlier stages, attitude development at the application stage is often a matter of maintenance. That is, teachers of students reading at the fifth through eighth grade levels ensure that the accurate concepts and positive feelings developed at earlier levels are reinforced and strengthened. Within that general framework, however, there is a transition from reading stories to reading informational material such as that found in social studies and science. Example 5.4 illustrates how to develop positive attitude goals at the application stage.

SUMMARY

Students are not likely to develop control of their reading if they feel negative about it. Positive attitudes for reading depend on students being metacognitively aware of concepts about what reading is and about their feelings for participating in reading activities. The major instructional technique for developing attitude goals is the literate environment, in which students develop accurate concepts and good feelings by engaging in meaningful reading and writing activities. While you may occasionally develop attitude goals through direct teacher guidance, this form of instruction generally plays a relatively minor role. As students move through the grades, instructional emphasis on attitudes moves gradually from simple concepts of reading and enjoyment of stories to more complex concepts about the function of reading and the variety of responses one can have to reading.

SUGGESTED ADDITIONAL READING

CLAY, M. (1989). Concepts about print in English and other languages. *Reading Teacher, 42*(4), 268–275.

FREDERICKS, A. D. (1982). Developing positive reading attitudes. *Reading Teacher, 36*(1), 38–40.

GENTILE, L. M., & HOOT, J. L. (1983). Kindergarten play: The foundation of reading. *Reading Teacher, 36*(4), 436–439.

HEATHINGTON, B. S., & ALEXANDER, J. E. (1984). Do classroom teachers emphasize attitudes toward reading? *Reading Teacher, 37*(6), 484–488.

MADDEN, L. (1989). Improve reading attitudes of poor readers through cooperative reading teams. *Reading Teacher, 43*(3), 194–199.

MAGER, R. (1960). *Developing attitudes toward learning.* Palo Alto, CA: Fearon.

MASS, L. N. (1982). Developing concepts of literacy in young children. *Reading Teacher, 35*(6), 670–675.

ROETTGER, D. (1980). Elementary students' attitudes toward reading. *Reading Teacher, 33*(4) 451–453.

TEMPLETON, S. (1980). Young children invent words: Developing concepts of "wordness." *Reading Teacher, 33*(4), 454–459.

TRELEASE, J. (1989). Jim Trelease speaks on reading aloud to children. *Reading Teacher, 43*(3), 200–206.

THE RESEARCH BASE

BEACH, R. & HYNDS, S. (1991). Research in response to literature. In R. Barr, M. Kamil, P. Mosenthal, & P. D. Pearson (Eds.) *Handbook of reading research, volume II* (pp. 453–489). New York: Longman.

BROPHY, J. E. (1983). Research on the self-fulfilling prophecy and teacher expectations. *Journal of Educational Psychology, 75,* 631–661.

BROPHY, J. E. (1986). *Socializing student motivation to learn* (Research Series No. 169). East Lansing: Michigan State University, Institute for Research on Teaching.

FREPPON, P. (1991). Children's concepts of the nature and purpose of reading in different instructional settings. *Journal of Reading Behavior, 23*(2), 139–163.

WEINSTEIN, R. (1983). Student perceptions of schooling. *Elementary School Journal, 83,* 287–312.

WIGFIELD, A., & ASHER, S. (1984). Social motivational influences on reading. In P. D. Pearson (Ed.), *Handbook of reading research* (pp. 423–452). New York: Longman.

ACTIVITIES FOR REFLECTING, OBSERVING, AND TEACHING

Reflecting on How to Help Students Feel Good About Reading

PURPOSE: The hardest thing about developing students' attitudes about reading is thinking analytically about the relationship between *liking* reading and *understanding what reading is*. You can be a better teacher and do a better job of developing students' attitudes if you think carefully about what attitudes are. This activity is designed to help you do this.

DIRECTIONS: Develop an interview you can administer to school children to determine their attitudes about reading. Divide it into two sections. The first section should try to determine how students *feel* about reading. For instance, you might ask questions such as: What is your favorite free-time activity? How do you feel about reading a book on a rainy Saturday morning? What is your favorite book? What is your favorite part of the book you are reading now?

The second section should try to determine students' *conceptions* about reading. For instance, you might ask questions such as: What *is* reading? Why is it important for people to learn to read? How does the print on a page get there? Why are books written?

Administer this interview to an elementary school student. Examine the responses. Is there any relationship between the answers to one section and the answers to the other? Is there any evidence that bad feelings about reading are associated with misconceptions about reading and that students who like reading also have accurate concepts about what reading is and what it is for?

Watching Others Teach Attitudes

PURPOSE: You can learn a lot about how to develop students' attitudes about reading by watching teachers teach reading and interviewing them afterwards about what they were doing. This activity is designed to help you do that.

DIRECTIONS: Arrange to watch a teacher teach reading to an elementary school class. Before observing, review the examples provided in this chapter regarding the teaching of attitude goals at various stages. During the observation, note whether there is any relationship between the kind of activity suggested in the appropriate example in the chapter and what you saw the teacher doing. If not, when you talk to the teacher following the lesson, describe the example and ask the teacher to explain the difference between what you saw and what is described in this chapter. In discussing your observation with the teacher, try to determine whether the teacher was consciously trying to develop good feelings about reading and/or accurate conceptions of what reading is.

Trying It Yourself: Teaching Attitude Goals

PURPOSE: Learning how to develop attitudes is difficult to do if you never have an opportunity to try it yourself. Arrange an opportunity to do a brief activity with a group of elementary-age students. Even something as simple as reading them a story will suffice.

DIRECTIONS: In planning the activity, think about how you can develop the students' attitudes about reading. That is, think about what you could do during the activity to help students feel good about reading and what you could do to develop specific concepts about reading. List the feelings and concepts you hope to develop. Then, after the activity is over, ask the students what they learned.

Helping Students Comprehend Text: Content Goals

6

GETTING READY

This chapter describes the content goals that are taught at each stage of developmental reading growth in elementary school. Again, both what content goals to teach and how to teach them are discussed. More detailed suggestions for teaching content goals are described in the appropriate chapters in Part 4. Ms. Chang, Ms. Walters, Mr. Gutierrez, and Ms. O'Malley again provide illustrations for various grade levels.

FOCUS QUESTIONS

- What should students be able to do as a result of being taught content goals?

- What three factors influence student comprehension of text content?

- What should students be metacognitive about when pursuing content goals?

- How does a literate environment contribute to the development of content goals?

- What direct teacher actions contribute to the development of content goals?

THE COMPONENTS OF CONTENT GOALS

Understanding the content of written messages depends on three components: prior knowledge of topic, text structure, and purpose. How these components influence understanding of content is the focus of this chapter.

Role of Prior Knowledge of Topic

Students' ability to comprehend the content of written messages depends heavily on how much they already know about the topic. If students know a lot about the topic, they also know the meaning of most words associated with that topic and will therefore understand the content of the message; if students have limited experience with the topic, they will not know many words, and chances are good that they will not understand the content.

When teaching to develop content goals, you should try to make sure students know the meaning of all the words used and, if some words are not known, provide them with experiences designed to develop those word meanings.

Role of Text Structure

The print that contains a written message is called the text and takes various forms. Narrative text (referred to as recreational text in this book) entertains and includes stories, plays, and poems. Expository text (referred to as functional text in this book) informs or persuades and includes textbooks, newspapers, encyclopedias, recipes, etc.

Text is a major concern when you teach content goals because each kind places different demands on the reader. One of the demands relates to text structure, that is, to the overall pattern followed when writing a particular kind of text. For instance, when writing stories, writers use narrative structures such as the following.

1. Establish the setting.

2. Introduce the main character.

3. Describe the problem or conflict.

4. Describe the events related to resolution of the problem.

5. Resolve the problem.

When writing textbooks, they use expository structures such as the following.

1. Introduction (tell them what you're going to tell them)

2. Body (tell them)

3. Conclusion (tell them what you told them)

Similarly, when writing Haiku poetry, writers follow a structure in which five syllables appear in the first line, seven syllables in the second line, and five syllables in the third line; when writing a business letter, managers use a business letter structure; and when writing a news story, reporters state the main points about what, who, where, when, and why in the first paragraph, with subsequent paragraphs offering supporting facts in descending order of importance.

To help students comprehend various kinds of text, you should provide opportunities for them to read them and then guide their reading by informing them about the text structure employed.

Role of Purpose

A newspaper account of a baseball game can be read to find out who won, or how the teams ranked as a result of the game, or what the hero of the game said in the post-game interview, or all of these things. What students actually understand depends largely on their purposes for reading. When teaching, you should help students understand the content of the text by providing them with purposes or by helping them select their own purposes.

Textbook and recreational reading place different demands on a reader.

WHO IS IN METACOGNITIVE CONTROL?

When developing content goals, your role is to organize students' encounters with text to focus on understanding the content, not on improving their strategies for understanding. Therefore, you should have students focus on the author's message and on being aware of whether their purposes for reading are being met. When planning instruction to meet content goals, the teacher examines the text, decides what type of text it is and what words are unknown (and, sometimes, what the purpose for reading should be), and then presents the lesson in ways that emphasize understanding the content. As a result, students are focused on the content, and they learn the content, which was your intention.

INSTRUCTIONAL EMPHASIS IN CONTENT GOALS

Content-oriented instruction centers around both indirect instruction, which employs the literate environment, and direct instruction, in which the teacher actively guides.

The Literate Environment

To develop content goals, a literate environment physically demonstrates to students the role played by reading and various kinds of recreational and functional text. The classroom and the library include many examples of recreational and functional text appropriate for the grade level being taught, and teachers encourage students to use these texts both for pleasurable reading and for solving problems.

In a literate environment, the importance and function of various kinds of text become self-evident. Because students are surrounded by a variety of functional and recreational text matched to their reading levels, interests, and assignments, they are encouraged to pursue independent reading. This kind of indirect instruction is crucial to developing content goals.

Direct Teacher Guidance

In content-oriented reading, teachers guide students' understanding of text. This means they assume metacognitive control of the task, figuring out ahead of time the word meanings to be developed, the structure of the material to be read, and (sometimes) the purposes for reading the text. Then they decide what assistance students will need to understand the content of the selection.

This assistance is usually provided in three phases: things to do before, during, and after the reading assignment. Before the reading, teachers help students activate prior knowledge about the topic, develop necessary word meanings, and establish purposes for reading that particular text. During the reading, they help students monitor their meaning getting, especially in terms of established purposes. After the reading, they help students demonstrate their understanding by summarizing and clarifying the message. The most common tool for conducting this kind of instruction is the **directed reading lesson** (DRL), which is summarized as follows.

1. *Introduce the selection to be read:* Activate students' background knowledge about the topic, direct student attention to necessary words, and establish appropriate purposes.

2. *Have students read the selection:* Ask questions to monitor students' meaning getting.

3. *Discuss the selection:* Ask clarifying and summarizing questions, check to see that the purposes of the reading have been met, and extend students' understanding of the meaning of the text.

There are several variations on the directed reading lesson, all of which begin with teachers analyzing the demands of the text and then providing their students with guidance to help them focus on the text's content.

Role of Teacher Questioning

The questions teachers ask play a crucial role in developing students' understanding of text content. It is often the teacher's questions that get students to focus on a particular meaning.

You can ask *literal questions* when you want students to comprehend an author's explicit meaning. You can ask *inferential questions* when you want students to understand implied meanings found between the lines of a text and to construct meanings the author only hints at. You can ask *critical questions* when you want students to understand meanings that go beyond what the author said—such as to analyze the author's message critically or to pass judgment on the validity of what the author was saying. In the Aesop fable "The Tortoise and the Hare," a literal question would ask who the participants in the race were; an inferential question would ask why we expect the hare to win the race; and a critical question would ask whether such a race is likely to occur in reality. These three types of teacher questions are crucial to content goals since they focus students' attention on the kind of meaning you want them to get from the text.

However, while teacher questioning helps students focus on the level of meaning, questions do not necessarily result in student metacognitive control of comprehension. In a directed reading lesson *you* are in metacognitive control, deciding what prior knowledge needs to be activated and then asking questions designed to access it. Likewise, during the reading it is *you* who decides what meaning must be monitored and asks questions that focus students on that meaning. Finally, it is *you* who decides what meaning needs to be clarified and summarized after the reading. In all three instances, students merely follow your lead. You are in metacognitive control of comprehension, not they. In short, the reasoning involved in knowing what prior knowledge to activate as reading begins, what inferences to make during reading, and what critical judgments to make following reading is directed by you, not your students. Questioning is a crucial teacher action to focus students' attention on particular levels of text meaning. But such questions will not help students learn how to do the reasoning associated with answering the questions. Chapters 7 and 8 provide details on using questions to teach the reasoning associated with process goals.

CONTENT GOALS AND WRITING

Although writers are concerned with composing rather than interpreting the content of a message, the components remain the same. Just as background experience, text structure, and purpose are the keys to interpreting a message, so they are the keys to composing a message. Writers must match the words they use with their audience, must arrange those words into familiar patterns or structures, and must maintain a consistent focus or purpose for their message. Since much of a written message's content is determined at the planning stage, content goals in writing are developed mainly during the planning of the written text.

Integrating content goals into writing helps students understand the reciprocal author-reader relationship while also reinforcing the roles of prior knowledge of topic, text structure, and purpose in written literacy.

TEACHING CONTENT GOALS AT VARIOUS DEVELOPMENTAL LEVELS

Emergent Literacy Stage

Even though most preschool and kindergarten children cannot read yet, they can understand the meaning of text read to them. Content goals in preschool and kindergarten focus on helping students get meaning from the simple narratives they listen to.

The major instructional tool at this stage is the directed listening activity (DLA). Basically the **directed listening activity** is the same as the directed reading lesson except that students listen while the text is read to them. Before listening, the teacher activates appropriate background experience, develops word meanings, and sets the purpose. During the lesson, the teacher asks questions to help students monitor their meaning getting. After the lesson, the teacher helps students answer questions related to the purposes for the reading. The goal, of course, is student understanding of the content of the text that was read to them. Example 6.1 illustrates how to develop content goals at the emergent literacy stage.

EXAMPLE 6.1   Developing Content Goals at the Emergent Literacy Stage Using a DLA

I. Introduce the selection
   A. *Activate background knowledge*
   B. *Direct attention to necessary words*
   C. *Establish purpose*
II. Read the selection
   A. *Ask questions to check comprehension*

III. Discuss the selection
   A. *Ask clarifying and summarizing questions*
   B. *Check that purposes for listening have been met*
   C. *Expand on students' understanding of text*

Linda Chang had prereading, during-reading, and after-reading purposes when she read *Swimmy* to her kindergarten children. She first activated her students' background knowledge about oceans or large bodies of water by conducting a short discussion on fish and where they live, the different sizes of fish, and what it feels like to be small and alone. Then Ms. Chang developed an understanding of new words (such as *mussel, shell, marvel,* and *school of fish*) by talking about what they are and what they are for and by providing some examples and nonexamples of each. Finally Ms. Chang directed students' attention to the purpose for listening to the book by alerting them to any information that would help them understand what Swimmy did when he found himself alone with big fish around him.

During the reading, Ms. Chang stopped at several places to help students monitor their own meaning getting. She asked literal questions about what was happening and inferential questions about how Swimmy was feeling.

After the story was read, Ms. Chang asked questions to clarify and summarize the story. She wanted to be certain students understood why Swimmy arranged the little fish in the shape of a big fish and why he acted like the big fish's eye. Activities were complete when the students answered critical questions about how working together can help get a task done and how belonging to a group can help combat the fears associated with being alone and small.

The following day, Ms. Chang used *Swimmy* as the basis for creating a class-written story entitled "When I Feel Alone and Small." She helped students during prewriting activities by reminding them of what Swimmy did when he felt alone and small, and by emphasizing words that the children contributed as description words. Ms. Chang helped the children create their story by providing a text structure as follows: "When I feel alone and small, I _____. Then I feel _____." After the story was written, Ms. Chang read the story to the children, asking them to listen carefully to see if it made sense and if it told how they feel and what they did when they were feeling alone and small.

Initial Mastery Stage

It is at the initial mastery stage, usually during the first grade, that most students first learn to read independently. This transition from emergent literacy to initial mastery is a gradual one in which the focus shifts from understanding content of text read orally to understanding content of text students read themselves. Of course, first and second graders often have many listening activities as they begin to read simple books on their own. Although teachers continue to emphasize recreational text (especially narrative text) at the initial mastery stage, students also read simple expository text and other forms of functional text.

Teachers of first and second grade rely heavily on two techniques for guiding student comprehension of the texts they read. The first technique is the directed reading lesson. Example 6.2 illustrates how to use DRL to guide student understanding of content at the initial mastery stage.

The second technique is the language experience approach, in which students and teacher collaboratively write a story based on a common experience. Because the story involves a shared experience (and thus shared word meanings) and because all the students shared in constructing the text, understanding the content is virtually assured. Example 6.3 illustrates how to use the language experience approach to teach content goals.

EXAMPLE 6.2   Developing Content Goals at the Initial Mastery Stage Using a DRL

I. Introduce the selection
  A. *Activate background knowledge*
  B. *Direct attention to necessary words*
  C. *Establish purpose*
II. Have students read the selection
  A. *Ask questions to check comprehension*

III. Discuss the selection
  A. *Ask clarifying and summarizing questions*
  B. *Check that purposes for reading have been met*
  C. *Expand on students' understanding of text*

The first graders in Kelly Walters' room were settling down for a reading lesson using Judith Viorst's *Alexander and the Terrible, Horrible, No Good, Very Bad Day.* During the prereading activities to activate their background knowledge, Ms. Walters led her students through a discussion of bad days in which everything seems to go wrong. Students quickly contributed to the discussion so Ms. Walters began introducing words with which she felt they would have difficulty. Finally, the purposes were set when Ms. Walters asked her students to answer literal and inferential questions about how Alexander helped himself feel better when it seemed like everything was going wrong. As the group read the book aloud together, Ms. Walters periodically asked questions to see if students understood the story. After the story ended, she asked students other questions—such as, "What do you think this story is about?"—to see if students understood how Alexander made himself feel better about his bad day.

On the next day, the students decided to help Mr. Jennings feel better about his bad day by sending him letters (see Example 5.2). The students began their prewriting activities by remembering Alexander's horrible day, and then they generated a list of the horrible things that had happened to Mr. Jennings. Then they created their letters. Using the text structure of a friendly letter, each student wrote about at least two bad incidents. For the post-writing activities, the students edited each other's letters for content and mechanics.

EXAMPLE 6.3   Developing Content Goals at the Initial Mastery Stage Using the LEA

I. Introduce common experience — initiate a direct experience
 A. *Field trip*
 B. *Classroom visitor*
 C. *Vicarious experience, such as a story*

II. Discuss the experience
 A. *Solicit student ideas about topic*
 B. *Write down key ideas and words*

III. Help students write a story
 A. *Help students devise title and opening*
 B. *Solicit more ideas*

IV. Read the story with students and help them produce copies to take home.

The first graders eagerly gathered around Ms. Walters to hear Judith Viorst's story of *Alexander and the Terrible, Horrible, No Good, Very Bad Day*. After quickly introducing the book and its characters, Ms. Walters read the story using an opaque projector so the children could join in during the repetition parts. Afterward the children discussed the story with Ms. Walters, highlighting visually and auditorily the repetitive pattern found in the story. The discussion then moved into bad days experienced by the students. Incidents were recorded on the board and words that described the incident were added. Ms. Walters then had the students select certain incidents and the class created their own story, *Ms. Walters' Class and Their Terrible, Horrible, No Good, Very Bad Day*. Ms. Walters typed the story and made each student a copy. Students illustrated their own books, and then took the books home to read to their families, showing and explaining their illustrations.

Expanded Fundamentals Stage

At the expanded fundamentals stage, which usually occurs in third and fourth grade, students significantly expand the kinds of text they read. The earlier focus on narrative stories broadens to include various literary genres. Students now encounter text structures associated with poetry, with various kinds of folk tales, and with simple drama, as well as traditional narrative stories. Similarly, functional reading expands beyond the simplest form of expository text to include textbooks, newspapers, magazines, and other common forms of informational text. Consequently, content goals at the expanded fundamentals stage focus on helping students understand the content of various types of text.

Teachers at the expanded fundamentals stage continue to rely heavily on the directed reading lesson to develop understanding of content, often with modifications. One example is the **directed reading-thinking activity** (DRTA), which actively involves students in setting purposes by having them predict what the content of the text will be. Example 6.4 illustrates how to use a DRTA to teach content goals at the expanded fundamentals stage.

EXAMPLE 6.4 Developing Content Goals at the Expanded Fundamentals Stage Using a DRTA

I. Introduce the selection
  A. *Activate background knowledge about topic, purpose, and type of text*
  B. *Teach new vocabulary words*
II. Make predictions
  A. *Have students survey the selection's illustrations, headings, and other clues*
  B. *List their predictions on the board*

III. Have students read the selection and check their predictions
IV. Discuss the selection
  A. *Have students discuss the accuracy of their predictions*
  B. *Provide follow-up activity that involves story content or predicting skills*

The All Stars reading group joined Mr. Gutierrez at the third grade reading circle. He handed every student a copy of Ellen Raskin's *Spectacles* and asked them to examine the front of the book only. He activated background knowledge by a discussion of eyeglasses—who wears them, what they are for, what types there are, and so on. He then carefully related the unknown word spectacles to eyeglasses. On the basis of their discussion, Mr. Gutierrez asked every student to make a prediction about the content of the book. [This book is particularly good for making predictions because the strange creatures that Iris thinks she sees are exposed on the following pages when an adult corrects her.] After the predictions were recorded, Mr. Gutierrez established the purpose of the lesson by telling students they were going to see if their predictions about the the story were accurate. After the first two pages were

read, he had each student note the accuracy of their prediction, and, if necessary, make a new prediction. As the story was read students predicted, verified, and made new predictions. When the story was finished, the students discussed how Iris' nearsightedness created problems, and they all checked to see how accurate they had become in making predictions.

Because an ophthalmologist was coming to provide information on eye examinations, all students in the group used their predicting ability while reading informational books about opthamology. The students took notes on what they read and contributed their notes to the group. From the notes, the group created an outline for a book on eye examinations, and each student wrote a section. The group compiled their book, edited it, and shared it with the rest of the class in preparation for the ophthalmologist's visit.

Application Stage

Content goals are particularly important at the application stage (grades 5 through 8) because it is here that the instructional emphasis shifts from learning how to read to using reading as a tool to get meaning from a variety of text. Now, students learn about various forms and genres of literature and begin in-depth study of content areas such as social studies and science. Not only are students expected to understand various story, poetry, and drama forms, but also they are expected to understand expository text containing heavy conceptual loads (such as encyclopedia articles, information books, specialized directions, and technically oriented texts). Figure 6.1 illustrates the progression of content goals from the readiness to the application stages.

FIGURE 6.1   Content Goals across Developmental Stages

Emergent literacy
Recreational text
    Getting meaning from narrative text read to students
Functional text
    Getting meaning from simple expository text read to students

Initial mastery stage
Recreational text
    Getting meaning from narrative text
Functional text
    Getting meaning from simple expository text

Expanded fundamentals stage
Recreational text
    Getting meaning from various forms of narrative text
    Getting meaning from various genre of literature
Functional text
    Getting meaning from expository text (e.g., textbooks)
    Using question-answer relationships to get meaning from content

Application stage
Recreational text
    Getting meaning from various forms of narrative text
    Getting meaning from various genre of literature
Functional text
    Getting meaning from expository and content-area text
    Using question-answer relationships to get meaning from content
    Getting meaning from text with heavy conceptual content

Because of the increased conceptual load and the variety of texts encountered at the application stage, teachers work hard at providing guidance in these texts. The DRL and DRTA continue to be used heavily. In addition, other specialized techniques are used, some of which focus on word meanings (such as **structured overviews** and **semantic maps**), some on how to locate answers to the questions posed (such as **question-answer relationships**, or *QARs*)[1], and some on the structure of the text itself (**story maps**). Example 6.5 illustrates how to use a QAR, which is a variation of the DRL, to help students understand a reading selection at the application stage.

SUMMARY

Content goals focus on helping students understand the message in written texts. Understanding the content of written text depends on the reader's background

---

[1]Raphael, T. Question-answering strategies for children. *Reading Teacher, 36*(2), 186–191.

EXAMPLE 6.5   Developing Content Goals at the Application Stage Using QAR

I. **Introduce the lesson**
   A. *Activate background knowledge*
   B. *Direct attention to necessary words*
   C. *Discuss how to use QARs to find answers to questions*

II. **Demonstrate (model) how you identify what type of question is used**
   A. *Right there—answer is found on page*
   B. *Think and search—answer requires information from more than one sentence or paragraph*
   C. *On my own—answer is not in the selection but is found in the reader's own knowledge*

   D. *Explain how you thought about the question, the information in the text, and where to find the answer*

III. **Interaction with students**
   A. *Give students samples of text and related questions*
   B. *Have students explain how they looked through the text information to decide how to answer the question*
   C. *Gradually increase text complexity as students become more proficient at answering questions*

IV. **Closure—have student apply their understanding of QARs to another assignment**

The Max Headroom reading group in Ms. O'Malley's fifth grade class was preparing to read Jean George's *Julie of the Wolves*, a story of how an Eskimo girl survives in the wilderness with the help of a wolf pack. Because Ms. O'Malley wanted her students to gain information from the text about the social behavior of wolves, she developed lessons using question-answer relationships (QARs). The lesson began as Ms. O'Malley led the students through the lesson introduction where motivation, background, purpose, directions, and word meanings were developed. Motivation was high because the task focused on wolf behaviors that were like human behaviors, so the students knew the story would be helpful in developing their reports on animal social behavior.

With the background in place, Ms. O'Malley directed students to questions about how human parents feed their young, how they reprimand others for inappropriate behavior, how they show affection, and so on. The students examined questions and predicted whether they would find the answer explicitly stated in the text ("right there"), whether the answer would be implied by the author ("think and search"), or whether the answer required them to make an independent judgment ("on-your-own"). Then students read the selection and answered the questions. When the students were ready to write their reports on the social behavior of animals, they were able to refer to their questions and answers about wolves. Ms. O'Malley's strategy succeeded in teaching both reading and writing content goals.

experience for the topic, the type of text, and the purpose for reading the selection. When teaching content goals, you want students to be conscious of the content of the text, and you are less concerned about whether your students understand the process by which they came to understand the text. Consequently, you develop content goals by establishing a literate environment, which calls for the reading of meaningful text, and asking students questions and employing directed reading techniques that make you responsible for the comprehension process while freeing your students to focus on content. The curricular emphasis on content goals gradually increases from one grade level to the next as students encounter more and more difficult types of text.

SUGGESTED ADDITIONAL READING

BLANTON, W., WOOD, K. & MOORMAN, G. (1990). The role of purpose in reading instruction. *Reading Teacher, 43*(7), 486–493.

CHOATE, J., & RAKES, T. (1987). The structured listening activity: A model for improving listening comprehension. *Reading Teacher, 40,* 194–200.

NESSEL, D. (1987). The new face of comprehension instruction: A closer look at questions. *Reading Teacher, 40,* 604–607.

OGLE, D. (1986). K-W-L: A teaching technique that develops active reading of expository text. *Reading Teacher 39,* 564–571.

PALINSCAR, A. M. (1986). Interactive teaching to promote independent learning from text. *Reading Teacher, 39,* 771–777.

POOSTAY, E. J. (1984). Show me your underlines: A strategy to teach comprehension. *Reading Teacher, 37*(9), 828–830.

RAPHAEL, T. E. (1984). Teaching learners about sources of information for answering comprehension questions. *Journal of Reading, 27*(4), 303–311.

RICHGELS, D. J., & HANSEN, R. (1984). Gloss: Helping students apply both skills and strategies in reading content texts. *Journal of Reading, 27*(4), 312–317.

ROEHLER, L., DUFFY, G., & MELOTH, M. (1986). What to be direct about in direct instruction in reading; Content-only versus process-into-content. In T. Raphael (Ed.), *Contexts of school-based literacy.* New York: Random House.

SMITH, M., & BEAN, T. W. (1983). Four strategies that develop children's story comprehension and writing. *Reading Teacher, 37*(3), 295–301.

STAUFFER, R. G., & HARREL, M. M. (1975). Individualized reading-thinking activities. *Reading Teacher, 28*(8), 765–769.

WIXSON, K. K. (1983). Questions about a text: What you ask about is what children learn. *Reading Teacher, 37*(3), 287–294.

WONG, J. A., & HU-PEI AU, K. (1985). The concept-text application approach: Helping elementary students comprehend expository text. *Reading Teacher, 38*(7), 612–618.

WOOD, K. D., & ROBINSON, N. (1983). Vocabulary, language and prediction: A prereading strategy. *Reading Teacher, 36*(4), 392–395.

THE RESEARCH BASE

AU, K. H. (1979). Using the experience-text-relationship method with minority children. *Reading Teacher, 32,* 677–679.

BECK, I., & MCKEOWN, M. (1981). Developing questions that promote comprehension: The story map. *Language Arts, 58,* 913–918.

BECK, I. L., OMANSON, R. C., & MCKEOWN, M. G. (1982). An instructional redesign of reading lessons: Effects on comprehension. *Reading Research Quarterly, 17*(4), 462–481.

BLOOM, B. (1956). *Taxonomy of educational objectives: Cognitive domain*. New York: McKay.

CARLSEN, W. (1991). Questioning in classrooms: Associolinguistic perspective. *Review of Educational Research, 61*(2), 157–178.

DOLE, J., VALENCIA, S., GREER, E., & WARDROP, J. (1991). Effects of two types of prereading instruction on the comprehension of narrative and expository text. *Reading Research Quarterly, 26*(2), 142–159.

GUZAK, F. J. (1967). Teacher questioning and reading. *Reading Teacher, 21*, 227–234.

PEARSON, P. D. (1981). *Asking questions about stories*. Occasional Paper Series. Lexington, MA: Ginn.

RAPHAEL, T. (1987). Research on reading: But what can I teach on Monday? In V. Koehler (Ed.), *Educator's handbook: A research perspective* (pp. 26–49). New York: Longman.

ACTIVITIES FOR REFLECTING, OBSERVING, AND TEACHING

Reflecting on Helping Students Comprehend Text

PURPOSE: A crucial distinction in this chapter is the difference between getting students to understand the content of written messages (this chapter) and helping them become aware of the process they use to independently determine the content of written messages (Chapter 8). This activity is designed to help you make this distinction.

DIRECTIONS: Locate a student and arrange to have half an hour with him or her. Give the student a passage to read. After the student is finished, ask questions to determine whether the student got the message (this would be a good opportunity to practice asking literal, inferential, and critical questions). If the student seems to understand the written message, ask questions to determine whether he or she understands the process used to figure out the message, such as "How did you figure that out?'" and "How did you know the answer to my question?" Then reflect on the difference. As a teacher, what would you do to help the student comprehend the content better? If the student had difficulty understanding the process used to figure out the content of the message, use that to get ready to learn the content of Chapter 8 of this book.

Watching Others Teach Content Goals

PURPOSE: You can learn a lot about how to help students learn to comprehend the content of printed messages by watching experienced teachers. Regarding the content of this chapter, you want to watch teachers as they give guidance to students' attempts to read and understand text.

DIRECTIONS: Arrange to watch a teacher teach a lesson in which students read a textbook selection in order to learn the content of the lesson. Note what the teacher does to help the students comprehend that textbook selection. What guidance does the teacher provide? Compare the activities of the teacher with the sample activity at the appropriate stage as provided in this chapter. Given the content of this chapter, note what guidance you would provide that you did not see the teacher do. Then interview the teacher following the lesson. Ask questions about the teacher's intentions in conducting the lesson and what strategies were used to help students comprehend the content of the text.

Trying It Yourself: Teaching Content Goals

PURPOSE: It is one thing to watch someone else try to get students to comprehend text; it is another to do it well yourself. The purpose of this activity is to give you an opportunity to try out the ideas in this chapter yourself.

DIRECTIONS: After watching a teacher teach a lesson in which the goal is to get students to understand the content of the text, try to arrange an opportunity where you can do a similar lesson. Using this chapter as a guide, decide how you would structure the lesson to ensure that students will understand the content of the text they are to read. What would you do to guide the students' comprehension of the text? You should definitely try to employ some variation of a directed reading-lesson format. After the lesson, ask students questions or otherwise check to determine the extent to which they understood the content of the selection. Then examine the content of this chapter to determine how you might do things differently next time to ensure that students comprehend even better.

Helping Students Use Words: Process Goals

7

GETTING READY

A major part of reading involves words—decoding what they say and attaching meaning to them. These are process goals and are commonly labeled word recognition and vocabulary. This chapter describes the process goals for teaching word recognition and vocabulary at each stage of developmental reading growth in elementary school. Related writing goals are also described. Again, both what word recognition and vocabulary goals to teach and how to teach them are discussed. More detailed suggestions for teaching are described in the appropriate chapters in Part 4. Ms. Chang, Ms. Walters, Mr. Gutierrez, and Ms. O'Malley again provide illustrations for various grade levels.

FOCUS QUESTIONS

- What is the difference between word recognition and vocabulary?

- What are some examples of routine word recognition skills and metacognitive strategies for word recognition?

- What is an example of a routine vocabulary skill and a metacognitive strategy for vocabulary?

- What is fluency?

- In word recognition and vocabulary, when should students be in metacognitive control and when should these functions be automatic?

- How do instructional actions differ in teaching routine skills and metacognitive strategies for word recognition? in teaching routine skills and metacognitive strategies for vocabulary?

- What role does teacher questioning play in developing word recognition and vocabulary goals?

- What word recognition and vocabulary goals are emphasized at the emergent literacy stage? at the initial mastery stage? at the expanded fundamentals stage? at the application stage?

THE WRITTEN CODE

One way to describe reading is to say that it is "talk written down." Writing down talk creates the need for written symbols and a system of conventions to ensure that the symbols are employed in uniform ways. The symbols and the governing conventions are like a code. A message is encoded in print and the resulting text is sent to the reader in various forms (letters, newspapers, books, etc.). Both the writer and the reader must be in agreement about the code, or the messages cannot be communicated.

Understanding the written code is an important part of the reading curriculum. If your students are unfamiliar with the written symbols (letters and words), and with the conventions governing their use (how to examine the letters, how letters form words, what sounds go with what letters, how words are separated in print, and so on), they cannot reconstruct messages authors embed in text.

This chapter focuses on what parts of the code to teach at various grade levels. Because the smallest meaningful product of the code is a word, word recognition and word meaning (vocabulary) are the focus.

DISTINGUISHING BETWEEN WORD RECOGNITION AND VOCABULARY

Readers can have two different kinds of problems with words. First, they may encounter a word they have never seen in print before and are thus unable to identify, even though they may know what it means when someone says it to them. This is a **word recognition** problem. A good example is the word *know*. A reader who understands this word in conversation may not recognize it in print because it sounds like it should be spelled *no*. This is a word recognition problem—the word is not recognized in print.

Readers can also encounter words for which they have no meaning. This is a **vocabulary** problem. For instance, you can pronounce the word *aglet*, but you probably do not know the meaning of the word. This is a vocabulary problem— you do not know the meaning for a word.

In order to focus instruction, it is important to know whether you want students to recognize words unknown in print but known in oral language or whether you are trying to teach them the meaning of words.

COMPONENTS OF WORD RECOGNITION

The ability to recognize words in print consists of both routine skills and metacognitive strategies. Routine skills are associated with recognizing words instantly; metacognitive strategies are associated with figuring out unknown words.

Routine Skills

Routine skills are those skills that expert readers perform automatically with little thought or reasoning. In word recognition, they consist of both language conventions and linguistic units that contribute to recognizing words instantly.

Language Conventions   Language conventions associated with word recognition govern how printed language works. For instance, to recognize words instantly, readers must know how to examine print—that is, to start at the top left-hand side of the page and move across the lines in a left-to-right direction from the top of the page to the bottom. Further, readers must know that the beginning and end of words are marked by a space on either side of the word and that words start at the left and go to the right. These conventions are part of the written language code, and readers must use them routinely in order to recognize many words instantly.

Linguistic Units   Linguistic units associated with word recognition consist of both words and letters. To read text easily, the reader must instantly recognize most of the words on the page. Such instantly recognized words are called **sight**

Integrating word recognition and vocabulary ensures that students will be able to both pronounce and understand unfamiliar words.

words. Teaching readers to recognize words at sight—or instantly—is an important part of word recognition. A list of 325 basic sight words, organized into four lists starting with the easiest and moving to the hardest, is provided in Figure 7.1.

Letters are also important linguistic units. For instance, to figure out unknown words young readers can sound out each letter or letter combination in turn and then blend the sounds together. In order to use such a strategy, how-

---

FIGURE 7.1   325 Basic Sight Words

List 1: Easiest

I	green	mother	on	but	what
and	blue	girl	some	an	all
the	yellow	look	you	be	been
a	one	on	jump	they	her
to	two	after	little	for	much
was	three	get	then	were	them
in	four	is	we	out	about
it	five	not	did	him	too
of	six	she	father	us	baby
my	seven	who	make	or	
he	eight	boy	cat	have	
white	nine	go	get	new	
black	ten	good	sit	sad	
red	saw	like	hot	this	

List 2: More difficult

something	other	old	day	when	full
from	laugh	there	our	talk	horse
house	ball	again	with	today	orange
want	some	his	bigger	as	keep
went	pretty	chair	do	off	table
where	surprise	push	know	child	which
door	water	any	put	take	guess
dog	woman	by	will	tell	give
shall	word	how	are	children	right
pull	write	song	busy	walk	find
if	before	very	just	wash	would
long	please	am	apple	first	

List 3: Still more difficult

draw	does	ready	build	miss	ear
feet	family	store	break	nice	lion
many	funny	end	drink	air	point

---

ever, they must first recognize, without conscious effort, the individual letters and their associated sounds. This associating of letter and sound is commonly called **phonics**. (See pp. 112–114 for a list of phonic elements.)

Metacognitive Strategies

Metacognitive word recognition strategies are used to figure out what a word says while in the midst of reading a text.

FIGURE 7.1   325 Basic Sight Words   *(continued)*

their	bread	brother	slow	because	together
your	milk	ask	near	careful	wild
over	more	quiet	match	done	tried
well	away	read	mice	felt	post
sure	doll	school	ride	heavy	voice
into	good-bye	own	should	love	war
may	could	car	listen	poor	warm
upon	morning	only	money	also	wonder
color	friend	once	most	believe	breakfast
street	hurry	shoe	next	catch	

List 4: Most difficult

feather	fire	floor	heard	through	minute
else	hello	clothes	learn	thought	monkey
umbrella	hair	paw	carry	tomorrow	people
nothing	honey	quite	sign	brought	log
field	piece	animal	splash	enough	build
held	roll	every	spring	head	soft
already	turtle	turn	station	lie	beautiful
quick	more	kept	turkey	answer	care
always	both	large	soup	balloon	year
roar	bowl	noise	squirrel	watch	vegetable
arrow	uncle	wolf	wear	cross	great
bump	egg	world	cover	engine	picture
country	hurt	worm	across	front	
elephant	climb	cried	buttom	bear	
board	end	pennies	automobile	calf	
caught	circus	cabbage	buy	eye	
early	kind	cage	dear	left	

Source: These sight words are taken from Duffy, G., & Sherman, G. *Systematic reading instruction*, Harper & Row, 1971.

If you are using a particular basal reader program, you can develop a similar sight word list for your program by taking the new words introduced at each level (usually found at the back of the teachers' edition) and listing them in order of appearance in the basal series.

Monitoring　　Monitoring is the key to word recognition strategy use. That is, the reader is always alert for situations in the text that do not make sense and is always ready to say something like, "Oh, oh, something's wrong here." In the case of word recognition, the problem is an unrecognized word. In monitoring for unrecognized words, readers consciously acknowledge that they do not recognize a word and pause momentarily to decide what to do about it. This is a conscious reasoning process and is therefore a metacognitive strategy.

Fix-It Strategies　　Once they are conscious of an unrecognized word, readers must **decode,** or figure out, the word. Decoding is also sometimes called **word analysis** or **word attack.** To decode, readers apply fix-it strategies, of which there are three.

The first way of decoding is using **context clues:** That is, the reader quickly uses the words around the unknown word to figure out its meaning. Context is usually the most efficient method to decode unrecognized words because it is usually the fastest. Examples of the most common context clues are provided in Figure 7.2.

FIGURE 7.2　Types of Context Clues

Each of the following explanations describes how the unknown word in a sentence is defined or identified.

Direct definition clue: Directly defined in the passage.

Ex: The first goal of a serious photographer is a perfect *exposure*, or the amount of light actually hitting the film.

Experience clue: Using one's own experience to make a prediction (or inference).

Ex: The perfect exposure will show the most *intricate* detail in the picture, down to the thread used to sew on a button.

Synonym clue: Reference to a synonym in the text.

Ex: Maria is a *fortunate* person. I wish I could be as lucky.

Sentence structure clue: Reference to its function in the sentence (as a noun, a verb, an adjective, and adverb, and so forth).

Ex: Our baseball game was canceled because of *inclement* weather.

Summary clue: Reference to the gist of the text.

Ex: Jenny has had several unhappy things happen to her lately. But she has a *resilient* nature. After a week she seemed to be her old self again, sunny and cheerful.

Mood clue: Reference to the mood of the passage.

Ex: I stood in the hateful slime of the Great Swamp. Before this, I had always felt that there was something beautiful about every place on earth. Now I knew there wasn't. Its *malevolence* seeped around me like a deadly fog. I felt that its stench of evil and decay brought me a message of ill will.

If using the context clues does not work (and if the unrecognized word contains an **affix**), the expert reader will often try structural analysis since it is the next fastest means of decoding. **Structural analysis** is the breaking apart of an unrecognized word by its structural units (prefixes, suffixes, inflectional endings, and root words) and then identifying the word by pronouncing each

---

FIGURE 7.3   Some Common Structural Units

Some common prefixes

Prefix	Meaning
dis-	not; the opposite of
in-, im-, il-, ir-	not
pre-	before
re-	again, back
un-	not; the opposite of
anti-	against; opposed to; stopping
inter-	together; between
under-	below; beneath

Other prefixes

mal-	pro-
mid-	super-
mis-	

Some common suffixes

Suffix	Meaning
-age	act or result of; cost of
-dom	position or rank of being; condition of being
-hood	state or condition of being
-ist	person who does or makes or works

Other suffixes

-able	-ful
-an; -ian	-ic
-ant	-ly
-em	-meter

Some Latin roots

Root	Meaning	Example
cred	believe	credence, credo, incredible
cur	run, flow	current, curriculum
fac, fec	do, make	factory, defect
gen	kind, type	generation, generic
mit, miss	send	admit, dismiss, transmission
scrib, script	write	describe, inscribe, prescription
stat	stand, put in place	stature, station
struc	build, prepare	construction, instruct
voc	call	vocal, vocation
volv	roll, turn	evolve, revolve

separate structural unit in turn. For instance, if *unhappy* is an unrecognized word, it could be pronounced un-happy. A list of common structural units and their meanings is provided in Figure 7.3.

Finally, the reader might use **phonics,** which is the blending together of individual letter sounds as a means of figuring out an unrecognized word. That is, the individual letter sounds learned routinely (see Figure 7.4) are consciously combined and blended. Phonics is the slowest of the three decoding methods because it requires that each separate letter-sound unit be retrieved from memory and then blended together. *Unhappy,* for instance, would be pronounced u-n-h-a-p-p-y. Further, phonics is not always reliable because letter sounds are not always consistent and predictable.

FIGURE 7.4   Common Phonic Elements in English

Consonants: *b, c, d, f, g, h, j, k, l, m, n, p, q, r, s, t, v, w, x, y, z.* The letters *b, d, f, h, j, k, l, m, n, p, r, s, t, v, w, y,* and *z* have corresponding sounds that are quite consistent in English. The letters *c* and *g* have two associated sounds. One is referred to as hard and the other as soft:

Hard *c* cane, cat, cow	Soft *c* cent, certain, city
Hard *g* go, good, gone	Soft *g* gene, gent, gem

Consonant blends: A consonant blend or cluster is a combination of two or three consecutive consonants in one syllable. When the blend is pronounced, each letter in the blend has its own distinct sound. The following blends occur frequently in English:

bl	*cr*	*fl*	*gr*	*sc*	*sn*	*str*	*tw*
br	*dr*	*fr*	*pl*	*sk*	*sp*	*sw*	
cl	*dw*	*gl*	*pr*	*sm*	*st*	*tr*	

Consonant digraphs: Two consecutive consonants that represent only one sound are called consonant digraphs. The following are examples of consonant digraphs:

ch	*sh*	*wh*	*gh*
ph	*th*	*ck*	*ng*

The *th* may occur voiced or voiceless (if your vocal cords vibrate, it is voiced; if they do not, it is voiceless):

voiced *th*   there, *this*
voiceless *th*   *thin, thing*

Silent consonants: Certain consonants sometimes have no sound value in spoken English.

gh	*ghost*	*kh*	*khaki*	*pn*	*pneumonia*	*rh*	*rhubarb*
gn	*gnat*	*kn*	*knot*	*ps*	*psalm*	*wr*	*wrong*
h	*honor*						

Vowels: There are two categories of vowel sounds that most frequently occur in English:

Long vowels		Short vowels	
ate	*rode*	*am*	*odd*
eel	*use*	*end*	*us*
ice		*ill*	

Expert readers seldom use just one decoding strategy at a time but combine them, simultaneously using surrounding meanings (context clues), initial letter sounds (phonics), and inflectional endings (structural analysis) to figure out an unknown word. For instance, if *umbrella* is an unknown word in the sentence "I put up my umbrella when it rains," a good reader would use both the context (what do you "put up" when it rains?) and phonics (what are the initial sounds in the word?) to figure out the word.

To summarize, teachers teach metacognitive word-recognition strategies to help students develop a reasoning response to unrecognized words encountered in print. This reasoning response puts the reader in the position of being a problem solver. When reading, you want readers (1) to monitor what they read in order to identify problems (in this case, unrecognizable words), (2) to have access to an appropriate strategy to solve the problem (for unrecognized words, the

---

FIGURE 7.4   continued

Vowel digraphs: Two consecutive vowels that represent only one sound are called vowel digraphs. The following are examples of the most common vowel digraphs:

ai	rain	*ee*	meet	*au*	August	*oa*	boat
ay	play	*ei*	ceiling	*aw*	awful	*oe*	toe
ea	easy	*ie*	pie	*ow*	grow	*ue*	true

Diphthongs: Two consecutive vowels with one sound but in which the tongue starts in one position and moves rapidly to another are called diphthongs. The following are examples of diphthongs:

oil   *boy*   *owl*   *out*

Schwa: The *schwa* sound an best the described as an unstressed short *u* sound and is symbolized phonetically by / ə /. The *schwa* sound is the most frequently occurring vowel sound in the English language and occurs with all vowels. The vowels in the following *unstressed* syllables stand for the *schwa* sound:

a	e	i	o	u
com*a*	beat*e*n	im*i*tate	butt*o*n	col*u*mn
bedl*a*m	tak*e*n	nostr*i*l	summ*o*n	

Syllable: A syllable is the smallest pronounceable unit of a word. In defining a syllable, direct the emphasis at the idea of vowel sounds. Children will be able to recognize that *all* of the following words have only one syllable because there is only one vowel sound:

so   *two*   *seed*   *charge*   *stretch*   *straight*

All of the following words have two syllables because they have two distinct vowel sounds:

hotel   *picnic*   *country*   *preacher*

Phonetic and syllabic generalizations: Syllabication rules and phonetic generalizations have been the subject of some controversy at various times throughout the course of educational history. Whereas many of the rules or generalizations are quite useful, the utility of others is open to question. What is of utmost importance is that a teacher of reading be familiar with the commonly taught generalizations and realize the limitations that the various rules have.

strategies would be context clues, structural analysis, phonics, or a combination of these), (3) to implement the strategy, and (4) to check to see if the problem is removed (for unrecognized words, to see if implementing the strategy results in a word that makes sense in the sentence).

FIGURE 7.4   continued

Phonetic generalizations for vowels
1.   When a syllable has one vowel and that vowel is not in final position, the vowel *generally* sounds short (unglided):

cat, cut, cot, in-dex

2.   When a syllable has one vowel and that vowel is in final position, the vowel *generally* sounds long (glided):

me, my, hel-lo

3.   When a syllable has two digraph vowels, the long sound of the first is generally pronounced:

meat, plain

4.   The vowel digraph *oo* stands for both a long and a short sound.

room, wood

Syllabication generalizations
1.   Most affixes and inflections are syllables:

un-like, tell-ing

2.   When two consonants in a root are preceded and followed by vowels a syllabic division *generally* occurs between them:

bul-let, af-ter

Certain basic reading series have adjusted this rule to state that the syllable division occurs *after* the *second* consonant:

happ-en.

3.   When vowels precede and follow a single consonant, a syllabic division *usually* occurs between the preceding vowel and the consonant:

ho-tel, po-lice.

4.   When a root ends in a consonant followed by *le*, the consonant plus *le generally* make up its final syllable:

tum-*ble*.

5.   For purposes of syllabication, consonant digraphs *generally* function as if they were one consonant:

o-*ther*

6.   For purposes of syllabication, vowel digraphs *generally* function as if they were one vowel:

de-*tail*, aw-ful

COMPONENTS OF VOCABULARY

As discussed in Chapter 6, knowing the topic and thus the meaning of words is crucial to understanding the content of written messages. The more word meanings a reader knows, the better comprehension will be. Some word meanings are known instantly through routine development of vocabulary; others must be figured out through the use of metacognitive strategies.

Routine Vocabulary Skills

Many new word meanings are learned routinely when new experiences are encountered. For instance, when teaching content goals (see Chapter 6) such as a unit on community helpers, a first grade teacher includes direct and vicarious experiences to help students routinely build concepts for key words such as *community, mayor,* and *utilities.* Similarly, a sixth grade social studies teacher who wants students to read and understand a textbook chapter on ancient Egypt helps students routinely build concepts for key words such as *pharaoh, pyramid,* and *sphinx.* The goal in such cases is for students to know instantly the meaning of necessary words. They may not be conscious of how they know the meanings, but they do know them.

Metacognitive Vocabulary Strategies

Knowing a word meaning from experience with a topic such as ancient Egypt is one thing; figuring out word meanings on your own is another. Consequently, teachers help students develop metacognitive strategies that can be applied to figure out word meaning. For instance, they teach students to monitor in order to spot words for which they have no meaning. And once such unknown words have been spotted, students can begin thinking of ways to figure them out. Just as in decoding, the two most commonly used strategies are context clues and structural analysis. Just as context clues can be used to decode a word's pronunciation, they also can be used to figure out a word's meaning (refer to Figure 7.2). And as students can use root words, prefixes, suffixes, and inflectional endings to identify a printed word, they can use these same structural elements to figure out what an unknown word means. For instance, *un-*happy, is *not* happy.

As with word recognition strategies, you teach metacognitive vocabulary strategies to help students reason about words that are unknown in meaning. Again, it is a problem-solving situation in which readers monitor to locate unknown words, choose an appropriate strategy (context, structural analysis, or a combination of these) to solve the problem, implement the strategy, and then check to see if the problem (the unknown word meaning) has been solved.

Developing Student Metacognitive Control

Metacognitive control is a primary emphasis in word recognition and vocabulary. However, its role varies. It is of central concern when teaching metacognitive strategies, but it has little to do with teaching routine skills. In word recognition, for instance, students need not be metacognitive (i.e., conscious) of their use of linguistic units and language conventions. They should be automatic about such things as reading pages from left to right and also in their recognition of letter names and sight words. However, students should be metacognitive about monitoring and decoding unknown words. Consequently, instruction in monitoring and fix-it strategies emphasize conscious reasoning.

Similarly, in vocabulary instruction there are some things that receive a metacognitive emphasis and some things that do not. The routine development of new vocabulary when reading for content goals, for instance, is not done with a metacognitive emphasis. Students develop new word meanings as they engage in such reading, but they are not particularly conscious of how they are learning these words. In contrast, strategies for how to figure out unknown word meanings found in print *are* taught with a heavy metacognitive emphasis. Students should be consciously aware of what they do when they encounter an unknown word so that, in future situations, they will be able to think through the problem themselves and resolve it independently.

Teaching with a metacognitive emphasis requires that you recast as reasoning processes those skills that are traditionally taught as memorized routines. In word recognition, for instance, context clues, structural analysis, and phonics are commonly presented to students as skills—that is, as certain rules to memorize and follow exactly the same way each time. Unfortunately, this does not work very well because readers must construct meaning flexibly. To teach context clues, structured analysis, and phonics as metacognitive word recognition strategies, you must present them as something other than routine and fixed rules. Specifically, you must present them as reasoning processes that are modified and adapted to fit a problem to be solved. Structural analysis, for instance, is not presented as a routine matter of dividing root words from prefixes and suffixes, but rather as an adaptive process of consciously thinking about how the meaning of a prefix and suffix are combined with a root word meaning and about the reasoning that must be done to arrive at the new meaning.

It is important to understand that expert readers are not forever metacognitive when faced with word recognition and vocabulary problems. In fact, as students become more and more expert, there is less need for conscious word recognition and vocabulary strategies because experience with reading makes virtually all situations routine. However, metacognitive control is essential at the earlier stages of reading when problems are encountered frequently. At the later developmental stages when faced with occasional unrecognized or unknown words, if your students' original instruction emphasized conscious awareness they will be able to access the knowledge and assume control over the situation. However, in order for this to happen, word recognition and vocabulary must be initially taught as metacognitive strategies, not as routine skills.

INSTRUCTIONAL EMPHASIS IN WORD RECOGNITION AND VOCABULARY

As with other goals, instruction for word recognition and vocabulary instruction is discussed in terms of (1) the indirect instruction associated with a literate environment and (2) the direct instruction associated with the teacher's role as a mediator.

The Literate Environment

The major function of the literate environment is to promote conceptual understanding of reading and positive feelings about literacy. Because word recognition and vocabulary focus on words (sometimes in isolation), it is particularly crucial that a literate environment be much in evidence to counter indications that reading is just a matter of knowing words. In the absence of a literate environment, your students are likely to develop the misconception that the most important thing about reading is knowing isolated words. Consequently, your classroom should provide tangible evidence that word recognition and vocabulary are used as part of the message-sending, message-getting function of reading.

To enhance word recognition and vocabulary, the literate environment should provide a word-rich environment. Written words, and messages composed of written words, should be much in evidence, whether through labeling various objects in the room, bulletin boards with written messages, a classroom postal system in which the teacher and students exchange written messages, or other ways. Similarly, oral vocabulary games and the sharing of special words, funny words, strange words, and so forth can help students develop positive attitudes about words generally and about word recognition and vocabulary in particular.

Direct Teacher Guidance

There are two kinds of direct instruction in word recognition and vocabulary, depending on whether the goal is to develop routine skills or metacognitive strategies. Because routine skills should be automatic, there is a **drill and practice model,** which emphasizes repetition to teach these skills. However, the repetition is sandwiched between other crucial elements. First, provide an explanation in which you activate students' background knowledge, make explicit statements about what is to be learned and when it will be used, and model what is to be learned so students have a tangible example to follow. Second, provide an opportunity for students to practice under your guidance. Finally, provide an opportunity for students to apply the routine skills. To illustrate, consider instruction in a routine skill such as learning the sight word *the*. You would drill and practice as follows. To provide an explanation, make sure students' background knowledge of the word *the* is activated—they recognize it when it is spoken; then tell them that they are going to learn to recognize the printed version of the word so they can say it instantly when they encounter it in the story you

---

FIGURE 7.5   Drill and Practice Model

Step 1   Explanation
          Teacher activates students' background knowledge, specifies what is to be
          learned and when it will be used in the immediate future.

          Model-repetition cycle
          Teacher demonstrates what is to be learned, and students repeat demonstration.

Step 2   Guided practice cycle
          Student practices under teacher's guidance.
          Student has repeated opportunities to do the task.
          Teacher provides corrective feedback and re-models as needed.

Step 3   Application
          The learning is immediately applied to a real reading situation.

---

are going to read together. To model, show students the word in context (such
as in the sentence,"*The* doll is mine"), say the sentence, point to *the* and say it.
Then have your students do the same. Practice the procedure repeatedly with
other sentences until students display accuracy in recognizing the target word.
Finally present the story to be read and direct your students to use their newly
acquired sight word knowledge of *the* when they encounter it in the story. You
employ a similar procedure when teaching other linguistic units and language
conventions. A three-step drill and practice lesson model is shown in Figure 7.5.

A modification of this three-step lesson can be adapted to the direct teaching of vocabulary (see Figure 7.6). To illustrate this procedure, consider a situation in which you want to teach the meaning of *platypus* to fifth graders. First,
give students experiences with a platypus, perhaps by showing them a picture
of one, and use the experience (the picture, in this case) to identify characteristics of a platypus. It is often helpful to organize these characteristics according
to the class it belongs to, its identifying properties, some examples of it, and
some nonexamples of it (a duck, for instance, which shares some properties of a
platypus, but it is not a platypus). As you do so, say the word to associate it with
the experience. You might say, "This is called a platypus. An animal with these
webbed feet and a broad bill is called a platypus." Finally, have your students
use the new word in oral or written expression.

FIGURE 7.6   Teaching Vocabulary Using a Modified Drill and Practice Lesson

---

Step 1   Provide an experience.

Step 2   Identify the properties or characteristics associated with the concept.

Step 3   Say the name of the concept.

Step 4   Give students opportunities to express themselves using the new word.

The routine drill and practice model is not appropriate for metacognitive strategies. Instead, you should use a **modified directed reading lesson** (MDRL) (see Figure 7.7). You will remember from Chapter 6 that the directed reading lesson (DRL) is used for developing content goals, and is structured to get students thinking about the content of the text. In contrast, when developing metacognitive strategies, students should think not so much about the content, but instead about the reasoning they do in order to understand the content. Consequently, you modify the DRL so that your students will think about *how* they get meaning rather than the meaning itself.

For instance, when teaching context clues, you would introduce a selection to be read, state (or show) that it will contain unknown words, and set as a main purpose of the lesson learning how to figure out those words when they are encountered in the selection. Next, you would model the reasoning expert readers employ when using context clues to figure out unrecognized words and would provide opportunities for your students to practice that reasoning. Then you would introduce the selection to be read, set the dual goals of understanding the selection's content and using context to figure out any unrecognized words, have your students read the selection, and then discuss both the content of the selection and how context was used to figure out the unrecognized words. Hence, the DRL with its emphasis on understanding the content of a selection is modified to focus mainly on the process used to overcome problems related to understanding that content.

Direct instruction in word recognition and vocabulary, then, depends on whether the goal to be developed is an automatic, memorized response (a routine skill) or conscious reasoning to solve a problem of getting meaning (a metacognitive strategy). When the goal is routine skill, a drill and practice model is used; when the goal is strategic reasoning, a modified directed reading lesson is used.

FIGURE 7.7   Teaching a Process Goal Using MDRL

Step 1	Introduce the selection to be read (activate prior knowledge about topic) and introduce the reading problem to be encountered.
Step 2	Model the use of the strategy to be used, guide students' practice solving similar problems, and set the purpose that the strategy will be used for in the selection to be read.
Step 3	Reintroduce the selection to be read, set the dual goals of understanding the content (content goal) and applying the newly learned strategy (process goal), and have students read the selection.
Step 4	Discuss the selection in terms of the content and application of the strategy to solve the problem.
Step 5	Close the lesson by summarizing both the content of the selection and the strategy used to solve the problem.

Integration of Word Recognition and Vocabulary

There is obviously some overlap between word recognition and vocabulary. Both focus on words, both demand monitoring, both make use of context clues and structural analysis as strategies, and neither is "reading" in the true sense of constructing meaning from text because the focus is individual words, not connected text. Both, therefore, are prerequisites to the process of creating meaning.

Because word recognition and vocabulary focus on different functions (what the printed form of a word says and what it means), we present each separately here. However, because they are so closely associated, when we present them to children it is best to teach them together. Integrating word recognition and vocabulary is not only efficient in terms of time, but also helps ensure that students will not become **word callers** who pronounce words they read but do not understand what they mean.

Role of Fluency

A term frequently associated with word recognition and vocabulary is **fluency,** which usually refers to how smoothly and expressively a student orally reads a text. If students can read text with no hesitations or mistakes and can use intonation patterns consistent with the text's meaning, they are said to be fluent readers. If, on the other hand, they read in a slow, choppy manner characterized by many errors and poor intonation patterns, they are not fluent. The typical instructional activity associated with fluency is **oral round robin reading,** in which each student in the reading group takes a turn reading orally.

Fluency is an important but complex goal of reading instruction. It involves much more than oral round robin reading. In fact, oral round robin reading is probably a destructive instructional activity since it often causes students to conclude that the goal is for them never to hesitate, and to know every word instantly. In actuality, you want your students to conclude that reading involves thoughtful reconstruction of meaning from text.

A student's poor fluency may be rooted in routine skills (not knowing enough words and word meanings) or in metacognitive strategies (not knowing how to figure them out). The skill most commonly associated with poor fluency is sight word recognition, because when students instantly recognize all the words in a selection, they tend to read smoothly. Similarly, prior knowledge of topic affects fluency since students with rich conceptual networks about a topic know more word meanings and are better able to create meaning fluently. Finally, students' ability to apply metacognitive strategies to text blockages also affects fluency because the better they are with strategies, the faster and smoother they are in removing blockages to meaning.

Fluency, then, results when students possess both routine skills and metacognitive strategies associated with all aspects of reading, not just word recognition and vocabulary, and it really means smoothness of meaning getting, not smoothness of oral reading. Consequently, fluency is better defined as smoothness in constructing meaning from text using all aspects of the reading process, not just those relating to words.

Role of the Dictionary

Dictionary usage is frequently associated with word recognition and vocabulary instruction. This is because students are often told to look up unknown words in the dictionary. However, dictionaries are virtually useless for figuring out unrecognized words until the application stage (which usually occurs in grades 5 through 8). Using a dictionary for word recognition purposes requires so many skills (use of alphabetizing, guide words, entry words, pronunciation keys, and so forth) that it is virtually impossible to teach its use for pronunciation purposes before the fifth grade. By this time relatively few words need to be decoded because so many are known as sight words.

Dictionaries are more easily used to determine word meanings. However, even when used for this purpose, the disruption they produce poses a serious disadvantage. When a reader stops reading to look up the meaning of a word in a dictionary, so much time is consumed that the train of thought is interrupted, and sometimes the reader loses the text's message.

Dictionaries are most useful in study strategies, particularly at the application and power stages of developmental reading growth. Consequently, dictionary usage is emphasized in Chapter 9.

Role of Teacher Questioning

As noted in Chapter 6, teacher questions serve to focus students' attention on particular aspects of an instructional task. For content goals, your questions focus students on the desired level of meaning (literal, inferential, or critical). For word recognition and vocabulary goals, your questions focus students on the specific goal. Your questions help students determine, for example, whether the lesson is on how to say a word (word recognition) or on what a word means (vocabulary). Similarly, your questions help focus a lesson on automatized responses (as with routine skills) or on reasoning (as with metacognitive strategies).

However, these kinds of questions do not cause students to develop the desired reasoning associated with metacognitive control of word recognition and vocabulary. For instance, asking your students the meaning of an unknown word will not develop their reasoning associated with how to use context to figure it out. Even asking what metacognitive strategy was used to figure out a word meaning will not by itself cause your students to develop the desired reasoning. For reasoning to develop, two conditions must be present. First, you must ask questions about the reasoning students used, not about the word's meaning. Therefore, the relevant question to ask is not, "What does the word mean?" but, rather, "How did you figure out what the word meant?" Second, your question about the reasoning must follow an explanation and demonstration of how to figure out word meanings. It is assumed that your students do not have adequate schemata for figuring out word meanings, so you must explain and demonstrate the metacognitive strategy before asking questions about it.

Integration with Writing

Word recognition and vocabulary are equally important in writing, but the perspective shifts from interpreting to composing text. The more vocabulary words a writer knows, the more clearly the message can be composed, just as the more vocabulary words a reader knows, the more clearly the message can be interpreted.

Similarly, metacognitive strategies can be used when composing text. For instance, context strategies, usually associated with reader comprehension, can be inserted by the writer into written messages as clues designed to help the reader construct the writer's intended meaning.

Word recognition skills and strategies such as sight words and phonics also have analogous uses in writing. In spelling, for instance, it is important to be able to remember visually (at sight) some words that do not use phonetic principles (such as *come* and *pneumonia*) while also using phonetic and structural analysis principles strategically when spelling words that do conform to these principles (*rabbit* and *hat*).

TEACHING WORD RECOGNITION AND VOCABULARY AT VARIOUS DEVELOPMENTAL LEVELS

Emergent Literacy Stage

In preschool and kindergarten, both vocabulary and word recognition are developed through listening and language experience stories, since few students at this stage can read text independently. Many of the skills and strategies taught at this level get students ready to read independently.

The preschool and kindergarten emphasis on vocabulary development is twofold. First, teachers provide students with direct and vicarious experiences that both broaden their backgrounds and, in the process, increase their meaning vocabulary. Preschool and kindergarten teachers often take their students on field trips or engage in other activities to bring students into contact with new experiences; as a follow-up, they then use these activities to create language experience stories using newly acquired vocabulary. Simultaneously, and often as part of the same language experience activity, teachers show students how context can be used to predict meaning. For instance, a teacher might show students how to predict the next word in a sentence.

Word recognition instruction at the emergent literacy level emphasizes routine skills. Students are taught about the basic conventions of language such as left-to-right movement, linguistic units such as letters and letter sounds, and general **print awareness**. Emphasis is placed on visually distinguishing between letters (called **visual discrimination**) and auditorily distinguishing between letter sounds (called **auditory discrimination**). In addition, students at this stage learn high utility sight words, such as their own name. Example 7.1 illustrates how to teach vocabulary and word recognition at the emergent literacy stage.

Initial Mastery Stage

Word recognition and vocabulary are heavily emphasized at the initial mastery stage. This is the time when most students independently read text for the first time, and, consequently, knowing words is a major concern. In vocabulary development, there continues to be a heavy emphasis on providing both vicarious and direct experiences that result in development of new vocabulary. Additionally, however, there is an increase in the emphasis on fix-it strategies, such as context clues and structural analysis, to figure out the meaning of unknown words. The goal is to increase the number of word meanings the students know.

In word recognition, the emphasis shifts from emergent literacy skills associated with visually discriminating print conventions and auditorily discriminating letter sounds to increasing the number of words the student can recognize in print. This is done in three ways. First, a heavy emphasis is placed on sight word recognition, in which more and more of the high-utility words in English are instantly recognized. As part of this effort, students are taught to discriminate visually among easily confused words such as *was-saw, them-then,* and *there-where.* Second, students are taught during-reading strategies, specifically to monitor their reading so that they are conscious of encountering unrecognized words and, if they become aware of a word they do not recognize, to stop and apply an appropriate fix-it strategy to identify the word. At the initial mastery stage, there is a heavy emphasis on all three decoding strategies for word recognition: context clues, structural analysis, and phonics.

Fluency of word recognition receives some emphasis at the initial mastery stage. However, the focus is less on fluency in saying every word accurately than on effective monitoring and the efficient application of fix-it strategies when unrecognized words are encountered. In short, stopping to fix blockages is encouraged. It is during these pauses in reading that the student accesses the repertoire of available strategies and selects an appropriate one for application in the particular situation. Example 7.2 illustrates how to teach vocabulary and word recognition at the initial mastery stage.

Expanded Fundamentals Stage

Word recognition and vocabulary instruction continue at the expanded fundamentals stage (grades 3 and 4), but the emphasis shifts from the most basic skills and strategies to more sophisticated ones.

Vocabulary development shifts from learning new word meanings through direct experiences to learning new word meanings from more formal word-study

EXAMPLE   7.1   Developing Word Recognition and Vocabulary at the Emergent Literacy Stage

I. Word recognition
  A. Routine skills
    1. Print awareness regarding conventions of letter and word usage
    2. Visually discriminate among letters and words
    3. Auditorily discriminate among letter sounds
    4. Associate letters and sounds
    5. Identify the highest utility words at sight
  B. Metacognitive strategies
    1. Monitor language experience text for words that are recognized and unrecognized
    2. Access fix-it strategies for unknown words
      a. Using context to identify words in a language experience activity
      b. Blend sounds together in combination with context to identify simple words

II. Vocabulary
  A. Routine skills
    1. Build vocabulary by discussing experiences that employ new words
    2. Build meaning of concrete words
  B. Metacognitive strategies
    1. Monitor oral language and language experience stories for words that are unknown in meaning
    2. Access fix-it strategies for meaning getting
      a. Use context in oral language to predict unknown word meanings
      b. Use context in language experience stories to predict unknown word meanings

Linda Chang, who planned to read *Swimmy* to her kindergarten class, decided to introduce the vocabulary associated with oceans before reading the story to them. As she introduced concrete words such as *jelly fish, seaweeds, sea anemones, school of fish,* and *eel,* she used illustrations in *Swimmy* to help explain what each word meant: "Seaweeds are plants that grow in the ocean." Next, she introduced some of the identifying characteristics of these new concepts: "Seaweeds are like the weeds around us except they grow under the water, are soft, and float in water." Next, she showed how seaweeds are different from the local weeds: "Local weeds have hard stems, have firm leaves, and stand upright by themselves, whereas seaweed stems are not hard, the leaves are not firm, and the plants can't stand by themselves; they float in the water." Finally, Ms. Chang showed how all the new words were connected to living things found in the ocean.

As Ms. Chang began the story about Swimmy, she told the children that books are read from left to right, and as the story progressed, she periodically showed them how she was doing this. Then she questioned them about left-to-right progression, and finally she supported their responses when they showed her where to start and which way to go. As she read the story, Ms. Chang also showed the children pictures to illustrate new vocabulary words.

In subsequent days, after the children had created their language experience story about feelings of friendship (described in Chapter 5), Ms. Chang read their story back to them, deliberately leaving out words that could be predicted from context. Following a short lesson on predicting, the children predicted words that would fit in the empty spots in their story. All the children then took their story home to read to their families. Ms. Chang had achieved the word recognition and vocabulary objectives of developing language conventions (left to right), building vocabulary through discussions of vicarious experiences found in *Swimmy,* and developing an understanding about the role of prediction in reading.

EXAMPLE 7.2   Developing Word Recognition and Vocabulary at the Initial Mastery Stage

I. Word recognition
  A. Routine skills
    1. Identify words at sight
    2. Recognize easily confused words
    3. Fluently recognize sight words in connected text
  B. Metacognitive strategies
    1. Monitor for unrecognized words and fluently access appropriate fix-it strategies
    2. Access fix-it strategies for unknown words
      a. Identify words by using the context of a sentence
      b. Identify words by using common structural units such as compound words, contractions, prefixes, and suffixes
      c. Identify words by using initial and final consonant sounds and common phonogram units

      d. Use context clues, structural analysis, and phonics in combination
II. Vocabulary
  A. Routine skills
    1. Build vocabulary through discussion of vicarious and direct experiences
    2. Continue emphasis on concrete words
  B. Metacognitive strategies
    1. Monitor for words unknown in meaning and fluently access appropriate fix-it strategies
    2. Access fix-it strategies for meaning getting
      a. Using context to predict the meaning of unknown words in print
      b. Using structural analysis to predict the meaning of unknown words in print

Kelly Walters decided to teach her first grade students how to use phonics as a decoding strategy to identify unknown printed words. She also decided to build their vocabularies by discussing both vicarious and direct experiences. *Alexander and the Terrible, Horrible, No Good, Very Bad Day* had many examples of closed, short vowel words (*bad, get,* etc.) and multiple opportunities to build vocabulary.

While reviewing the book, Ms. Walters picked out words that fit a simple phonic pattern (*gum, get, bed, bad, box, kit, let, got,* etc.). She grouped the words (*bed* and *bad, got* and *get, kit* and *sit,* etc.), and taught a phonics lesson of letter substitution in closed, short-vowel words. She taught students that you can pronounce an unknown word by recognizing the pattern it belongs to, substitute a new letter in it, and say it. Immediately after

the phonics lesson, the students, each with their own paperback version of Viorst's book, went through the story looking for words that fit. When a word was found, they pronounced it, and then discussed the part of the story in which the word was used. As they discussed the parts of the story, each event was listed. Using all the events listed, they brainstormed descriptive words that fit each event. For instance, for the event where one student was blamed for getting the library books out of order when she was only trying to help a friend who didn't know how to check a book out of the library, the students developed the descriptive words of *quiet, orderly,* and *librarian.* These events and descriptor words were then used when the entire class wrote their letter to the principal about their bad days (as described in Chapter 5).

I. Word recognition
  A. Routine skills
    1. Recognize a wide variety of words instantly
    2. Fluently recognize sight words in connected text
  B. Metacognitive strategies
    1. Monitor for unrecognized words and fluently access appropriate fix-it strategies
    2. Access fix-it strategies for unknown words
      a. Identify words by using the context of surrounding sentences and paragraphs
      b. Identify words by using less common prefixes and suffixes
      c. Identify words by using vowel generalizations and common syllabication principles
      d. Use context clues, structural analysis, and phonics in combination

II. Vocabulary
  A. Routine skills
    1. Build vocabulary through direct study of words associated with content being studied
    2. Shift emphasis from concrete words to multiple meaning words, homonyms, synonyms, antonyms, and other special categories of words
  B. Metacognitive strategies
    1. Monitor for words unknown in meaning and fluently accessing appropriate fix-it strategies
    2. Access fix-it strategies for meaning getting
      a. Use large chunks of context around the unknown word to figure out meaning
      b. Use less common prefixes and suffixes to figure out meaning
      c. Introduce the dictionary for determining word meaning

John Gutierrez's third grade students were completing lessons that helped to develop understanding about vocabulary and word recognition skills. For the word recognition parts of his lessons, he decided to teach students how to recognize unknown words that had the relatively uncommon suffix of *-er* since the book *Spectacles* had many examples of such words. After presenting information about *-er* words, modeling how to say unknown words that end in *-er,* and helping students learn to use the *-er* endings with unknown words on their own, he had them read *Spectacles* for content goals as well as to note *-er* words. Since some of the students included words like *Chester* and *mother,* Mr. Gutierrez took that opportunity to clarify that all *-er* words do not fit the pattern and broadened their understanding of the uses of both phonics and structural analysis.

Because an ophthalmologist was coming to visit the classroom, Mr. Gutierrez taught a vocabulary lesson with words taken from the story that were directly associated with eye examinations. Using the words *prescribed, contact lens, glasses, frames,* and *spectacles,* he took the students through a four-step lesson. First, Mr. Gutierrez provided experiences with these words by bringing in some contact lenses for the students to examine. Second, he used the experiences to generate characteristics associated with the words: For contact lens they generated words like *small, not flat, clear,* and *bendable sometimes.* These characteristics fit into four categories: They decided contact lenses were a way to see, they were small, they were not flat, and they were clear. They also decided that some contact lenses were rigid while others were flexible or soft. Third, the students visually connected the printed words *contact lens* with its characteristics, and finally they discussed possible questions they might ask the ophthalmologist about contact lenses. After meanings for all the words were developed, the students generated and wrote questions to ask the ophthalmologist about eye examinations.

efforts. That is, as students begin to encounter difficult terminology associated with content areas such as social studies and science, the teacher directly teaches the meanings of these words (refer to Figure 7.6). Simultaneously, efforts to teach monitoring and fix-it strategies for figuring out unknown word meanings continues.

In word recognition, the emphasis shifts from basic to more sophisticated metacognitive strategies. Consequently, teachers of students reading at third and fourth grade levels continue to teach word recognition, but the more difficult elements are emphasized.

Example 7.3 illustrates how to teach word recognition and vocabulary at the expanded fundamentals stage.

EXAMPLE 7.4   Developing Word Recognition and Vocabulary at the Application Stage

I. Word recognition
 A. *Routine skills*
  1. Not emphasized
 B. *Metacognitive strategies*
  1. Maintain monitoring for unrecognized words and fluent accessing of appropriate fix-it strategies
  2. Maintain fix-it strategies for recognizing words unknown in print

II. Vocabulary
 A. *Routine skills*
  1. Build vocabulary through direct study of words encountered in content area subjects
  2. Emphasize abstract words
 B. *Metacognitive Strategies*
  1. Maintain monitoring for words unknown in meaning and fluently accessing appropriate fix-it strategies
  2. Maintain fix-it strategies for figuring out the meaning of unknown words

Donna O'Malley's fifth grade students in the Max Headroom reading group were completing lessons that combined understandings about vocabulary and word recognition with the attitude and content goals. Ms. O'Malley decided to teach her students how to identify unknown words using a variety of fix-it strategies, since the book *Julie of the Wolves* has several unknown words, such as *predicament, kayak, Nunivak, gussaks, ilaya,* and *ulo.* After a brief discussion that activated the students' knowledge about phonics, structural analysis, and context clues, Ms. O'Malley taught them to use a combination of all three strategies when encountering unknown words. She presented information to the students, modeled how to use a combination of the strategies, and provided opportunities for student practice. Students were asked to jot down any words they figured out using their new skill as they continued to read *Julie of the Wolves.*

For the vocabulary portion of the lesson, Ms. O'Malley taught them how to use context clues to figure out the meaning of an unknown word. *Julie of the Wolves* contains many passages where context can be used to figure out unknown words, such as *warily, quickened,* and *vaulted.* After the lesson, the students applied the strategy as they read *Julie of the Wolves,* and finally they used their new vocabulary as they wrote reports on the social behavior of animals.

Application Stage

By the time students move into the application stage (fifth through eighth grade), they should have most of the skills and strategies associated with word recognition and vocabulary. Word recognition and vocabulary tasks at this level are primarily a matter of maintaining and extending the skills and strategies developed earlier.

In vocabulary, the emphasis is on learning specialized vocabulary associated with content-area subjects such as social studies, science, and literature. In word recognition, the emphasis is on maintaining students' fluency in reading, monitoring, and applying fix-it strategies. Example 7.4 illustrates how to teach word recognition and vocabulary at the application stage.

SUMMARY

Readers need to decode and understand the meaning of words in order to read. Word recognition focuses on decoding; vocabulary focuses on word meaning. Some of what students must learn consists of routine skills. For instance, students must routinely and automatically know letter sounds to decode and must routinely and automatically know the meaning of words associated with their background experience. Similarly, some of what students must learn about words consists of metacognitive strategies. For instance, students must be conscious of how they use context to decode a word unknown in print, and they must be conscious of how they use prefixes to determine the meaning of unknown prefixed words. Your instructional role differs depending on whether you are teaching routine skills, in which case you will use a drill and practice model, or metacognitive strategies, in which case you will use a modified directed reading lesson. In any case, instruction on words requires that you do more than simply develop fluency in reading orally or ask students questions about content. Instead, you must teach the routine skills and metacognitive strategies, question students about how they used those skills and strategies, and check to see that students are applying them when reading. While word recognition and vocabulary are most heavily emphasized in the early developmental stages, words continue to receive some emphasis even at the application stage.

SUGGESTED ADDITIONAL READING

BECK, I. L., & MCKEOWN, M. G. (1983). Learning words well—A program to enhance vocabulary and comprehension. *Reading Teacher, 36*(7), 622–625.

BLACHOWICZ, C. L. (1978). Metalinguistic awareness and the beginning reader. *Reading Teacher, 31*(8), 875–882.

BLACHOWICZ, C. (1987). Vocabulary instruction: What goes on in the classroom? *Reading Teacher, 41*, 132–137.

BLACHOWICZ, C. (1985). Vocabulary development and reading: From research to instruction. *Reading Teacher, 39*, 876–881.

BURKE, E. M. (1978). Using trade books to intrigue children with words. *Reading Teacher, 32*(2), 144–148.

CLYMER, T. (1963). The utility of phonics generalization in the primary grades. *Reading Teacher, 41,* 252–258.

CULYER, III, R. C. (1979). Guidelines for skill development: Word attack. *Reading Teacher, 32*(4), 425–433.

CUNNINGHAM, J. W. (1979). An automatic pilot for decoding. *Reading Teacher, 32*(4), 420–424.

CUNNINGHAM, P. M. (1980). Teaching were, with, what, and other "four-letter" words. *Reading Teacher, 34*(2), 160–163.

DICKERSON, D. P. (1982). A study for use of games to reinforce sight vocabulary. *Reading Teacher, 26*(1), 46–49.

GROFF, P. (1986). The maturing of phonics instruction. *Reading Teacher, 39,* 919–923.

GROFF, P. J. (1984). Resolving the letter name controversy. *Reading Teacher, 37*(4), 384–388.

JIGANTI, M., & TINDALL, M. (1986). An interactive approach to teaching vocabulary. *Reading Teacher, 39,* 444–451.

MARZANO, R. J. (1984). A cluster approach to vocabulary instruction: A new direction from the research literature. *The Reading Teacher, 38*(2), 168–173.

MEMORY, D. (1990). Teaching technical vocabulary: Before, during, or after the reading assignment? *Journal of Reading Behavior, 22*(1), 39–53.

MORRIS, D. (1982). "Word sort": A categorization strategy for improving word recognition ability. *Reading Psychology, 3*(3), 247–259.

OLSON, M. (1990). Phonemic awareness and reading achievement. *Reading Psychology, 11*(4), 347–353.

RASINSKI, T. (1989). Fluency for everyone: Incorporating fluency instruction into the classroom. *Reading Teacher, 42*(9), 690–693.

RIBOVICH, J. K. (1979). A methodology for teaching concepts. *Reading Teacher, 33*(3), 285–289.

SCHWARTZ, R., & RAPHAEL T. (1985). Concept of definition: A key to improving students' vocabulary. *Reading Teacher, 39,* 198–205.

TAYLOR, B. M., & NOSBUSH, L. (1983). Oral reading for meaning: A technique for improving word-identification skills. *Reading Teacher, 37*(3), 234–237.

WHITE, T., SOWELL, J., & YANAGIHARA, A. (1989). Teaching elementary students to use word-part clues. *Reading Teacher, 42*(4), 302–307.

THE RESEARCH BASE

ANDERSON, R. & NAGY, W. (1991). Word meanings. In R. Barr, M. Kamil, P. Mosenthal, & P. D. Pearson (Eds.) *Handbook of reading research, volume II* (pp. 690–724). New York: Longman.

BECK, I., & JUEL, C. (1992). The role of decoding in learning to read. In J. Samuels & A. Farstrup (Eds.) *What research has to say about reading instruction,* 2nd edition (pp. 101–123). Newark, DE: International Reading Association.

BECK, I., MCKEOWN, M., & MCCASLIN, E. (1983). Vocabulary development: All contexts are not created equal. *Elementary School Journal, 83,* 177–181.

EHRI, L. (1991). Development of the ability to read words. In R. Barr, M. Kamil, P. Mosenthal, & P. D. Pearson (Eds.) *Handbook of reading research, volume II* (pp. 383–417). New York: Longman.

GOODMAN, K.   (1972). Reading: The key is in the children's language. *Reading Teacher, 25* (7), 505–508.

GRIFFITH, P.   (1991). Phonemic awareness helps first graders invent spellings and third graders remember correct spellings. *Journal of Reading Behavior, 23*(2), 215–233.

JOHNSON, D., & PEARSON, P. D.   (1984). *Teaching reading vocabulary* (2nd edition). New York: Holt, Rinehart & Winston.

KLESIUS, J., & SEARLS, E.   (1991). Vocabulary instruction. *Reading Psychology, 12*(2), 165–171.

LABERGE, D., & SAMUELS, J.   (1974). Toward a theory of automatic information processing in reading. *Cognitive Psychology, 6*, 293–323.

LIE, A.   (1991). Effects of a training program for stimulating skills in word analysis in first grade children. *Reading Research Quarterly, 26*(3), 234–250.

PARIS, S., LIPSON, M., & WIXSON, K.   (1983). Becoming a strategic reader. *Contemporary Educational Psychology, 8*, 293–316.

ACTIVITIES FOR REFLECTING, OBSERVING, AND TEACHING

Reflecting on Helping Students Use Words

PURPOSE: There are two crucial distinctions in this chapter. The first relates to the distinction between word recognition and vocabulary; the second relates to the distinction between skills and strategies. This activity is designed to focus your attention on these distinctions.

DIRECTIONS: In the space provided below, answer the questions posed.

1. Give an example of when a child would be said to have a "word recognition" problem.

2. Give an example of when a child would be said to have a "vocabulary" problem.

3. In your own words, what is the crucial distinction between word recognition and vocabulary?

4. Give an example of a lesson in which the major focus is the teaching of a skill.

5. Give an example of a lesson in which the major focus is the teaching of a strategy.

6. In your own words, what is the crucial distinction between a skill and a strategy?

Watching Others Teach Process Goals

PURPOSE: We all remember from our own childhoods the task of learning words in school. However, helping students use words is much more complicated than our memories might suggest. This activity is designed to help you become conscious of what teachers do to teach process goals regarding words.

DIRECTIONS: Arrange to watch a teacher teaching a reading lesson. Answer the following questions as you watch:

1. Is the teacher helping students use words?

2. Is the focus on word recognition? vocabulary? both? How do you know?

3. Is the emphasis on routine skills? strategies? both? How do you know?

Following the lesson, interview the teacher about the teacher's intentions and instructional strategies. Compare what the teacher did with the appropriate grade-level examples provided in this chapter.

After talking to the teacher, reflect on what you might have done differently. Use the content of this chapter to assist you.

Trying It Yourself: Teaching Students To Use Words

PURPOSE: To become confident of your own teaching ability, it is important that you get a chance to try out what you are learning. This activity is designed to give you an opportunity to try teaching yourself the process goals associated with words.

DIRECTIONS: Arrange to be able to teach a small group of students at a developmental stage you are interested in. Teach two lessons: the first should try to develop a routine skill; the second should try to develop a metacognitive strategy. In teaching the skill, use the drill and practice model; in teaching the strategy, use a modified directed-reading lesson.

Helping Students Use Comprehension Strategies: Process Goals

8

GETTING READY

Comprehension is what reading is all about. Consequently, comprehension is the most important process goal. This chapter describes the process goals for comprehension taught at each stage of developmental reading growth in elementary school. Related writing goals are also described. Again, both what comprehension goals to teach and how to teach them are discussed. More detailed suggestions for teaching are described in the appropriate chapters in Part 4. Our sample teachers again provide illustrations for various levels.

FOCUS QUESTIONS

- How are comprehension processes distinguished from what was learned in earlier chapters about attitude, content, and word recognition and vocabulary goals?

- What strategies help students become self-regulated comprehenders?

- What comprehension strategies are used as one begins to read? during reading? after reading?

- What can teachers do to develop student understanding of comprehension processes?

- How are reading comprehension processes related to writing?

- What are the curricular emphases when teaching comprehension processes at various levels of developmental reading growth?

IMPORTANT DISTINCTIONS ABOUT COMPREHENSION

Comprehension is the essence of reading. The writer creates a text to communicate a message; the reader's task is to comprehend that message. To teach comprehension effectively, however, you must make three important distinctions.

Distinguishing Comprehension from Word Recognition and Vocabulary

Word recognition and vocabulary (see Chapter 7) usually receive heavy instructional attention in the beginning stages of reading acquisition. This is because both recognizing and knowing the meanings of words are basic to comprehension. Because students must recognize and attach meaning to individual words when reconstructing printed messages, word recognition and vocabulary are actually part of the comprehension process.

Understanding this subtle interrelationship is important when teaching reading because it is the key to achieving balance between word knowledge and comprehension instruction. Although word recognition is a prerequisite to comprehension, it is only a small part of the overall process. Being able to pronounce the word *halberd*, for instance, does not necessarily mean that you comprehend its meaning.

Distinguishing Comprehension from Remembering

Some teachers equate comprehension and **remembering,** particularly remembering factual information. These teachers require students to answer questions about information contained in the reading selection, with recall being the primary focus.

However, comprehension and remembering are not synonymous. Comprehension is reconstruction of an author's message. As detailed in Chapter 2, it involves combining new information from text with old information from prior experiences and actively building new understandings. While recall of what was read is important, it is distinct from reconstructing a message. When you recall, you do not construct; you memorize. Good readers use comprehension processes to reconstruct an author's message. They then employ memory strategies to remember that message for a test or other purpose. Remembering strategies are separate from comprehension strategies and are taught as study strategies (see Chapter 9).

Distinguishing Comprehension Processes and Content Goals

Distinguishing between process and content is crucial in comprehension instruction. To comprehend the content of a text, the author's message (see Chapter 6), you must engage in mental processes, or reasoning. Although the two goals are interrelated, they are distinct, and you must always remember that knowing the content, repeating it on a test for instance, does not always mean students understand the process of reasoning. This book emphasizes throughout that you want your students to learn how they process rather than simply recall facts.

There is a means-ends relationship between process and content. Although the end product of comprehension is understanding specific content, the means to that understanding is the reasoning used to reconstruct text. If you limit comprehension instruction to the content of the immediate text, then your students receive no explicit information about *how* to comprehend. Consequently, you will be unable to gradually shift control of the comprehension process to students.

Although teacher-posed comprehension questions are useful in guiding students to important content, they do relatively little to focus students on comprehension reasoning. To ensure that your students learn how expert readers comprehend, you must explicitly teach both the reasoning employed by experts when making sense of text and how to apply these mental processes while reading. Some students, particularly those with rich language backgrounds, incidentally discover these mental processes while reading. Other students, however, find it is too confusing to answer questions about a selection's content while simultaneously figuring out for themselves how comprehension works. They need explicit demonstrations of how good readers comprehend, and they need practice in using these reasoning processes.

This chapter focuses on the mental processes involved in comprehension. While these processes are discussed separately from content here, they are not taught in isolation from content. As you explain comprehension processes to your students, you should immediately help them apply these processes to the context of texts they are reading.

TYPES OF COMPREHENSION STRATEGIES

In contrast to word recognition and vocabulary, comprehension has no routine skills that, once mastered, are forever automatic. Instead, all **comprehension strategies** are metacognitive. That is, you teach your students to be conscious of when and how to use them so they can access them when reading text on their own.

This does not mean that comprehension strategies never become automatic. On the contrary, through repeated use, comprehension reasoning becomes increasingly automatic, especially when reading easy or familiar text. This is another form of fluency (see Chapter 7) in which students smoothly construct meaning from text without hesitations, false starts, and errors. This fluency develops after your students have had extensive experience in consciously adapting strategies to a variety of text situations. However, even the best readers occasionally encounter a difficult text and, consequently, must be able to consciously access these strategies.

Like all metacognitive activity in reading, comprehension strategies are based in monitoring. That is, readers expect the message in the text to make sense, and as they read, they listen to see if it does.

Word recognition receives much attention in the beginning stages of reading instruction.

Within the framework of monitoring, comprehension strategies can be described in terms of strategies readers employ as they begin to read (initiating strategies), as they are in the midst of reading (during-reading strategies), and when reflecting on meaning after reading (post-reading strategies).

Initiating Strategies

When initially encountering text, readers immediately become strategic. They examine the text (and the situation in which the text is to be read) for clues about its meaning, and they predict what the content will be about. These are called initiating strategies.

There are three sources of clues for making predictions about the selection. One is topic clues, which are often found in a selection's title, in its pictures, or in the first or second paragraph. Using a story about rainfall, for instance, you could model by saying, "I see that the title is about rainfall, and the pictures all show people standing around looking sad in the rain, so I think the topic must be something about rain and how it affects people." Also teach students to recall what they already know about those clues—what their background experience tells them. You could model by saying, "I know from my own experience that too much rain can make things messy and even cause floods, which hurt people." Then teach students to use topic clues and prior experiences to make predictions about what the author's message will be. You could model by saying, "I think this story is about the bad things that can happen to you when you get too much rain."

A second source of clues for making predictions about a selection is text clues. A selection on rain will stir different expectations if it is found in a collection of humorous tales, a geography book, or a poetry book. You could model by saying, "This story about rain is in a section of our textbook that has the theme 'courage,' so I think this story, like the others in this section of the book, must be about courage." Then show your students how to predict on the basis of that information, saying, "Because the topic is rain and appears in a section of the book about courage, maybe this selection is going to be about the ways people are courageous when there is lots of rain." Another kind of text clue is the internal text structure. Teach your students to identify whether a selection to be read is a story, an expository article, a poem, or some other kind of text. Then, teach them to use what they know about each type of text structure to predict what will happen in the selection. You could model by saying, "Since this is a story, and stories usually start by describing the main character and the problem, I think the next page or so should tell me who the main character is and what problem the main character is going to have with the rain."

A third source of clues for making initial predictions is the purpose for reading the text. Your students may be reading a text for enjoyment, for a homework assignment, to solve a particular problem, or for other reasons. Purpose shapes perceptions, whether one is looking for a particular person in a crowd or looking for meaning in a text. For instance, when you read a newspaper article, you predict different meanings depending on what you are looking for. You could model how readers use purpose to make predictions about meaning by saying, "Because we are reading the stories in this section of our book to learn about different kinds of courage, I think I'm going to find that this is a story about a different type of courage."

To summarize, initiating strategies focus on what readers think about to make predictions as they begin to read. You should provide your students with explicit information about how to generate predictions using topic, text, and purpose clues. These are the first steps in reconstructing the author's message.

During-Reading Strategies

No matter how strategic a reader is when initiating reading, some predictions may prove to be inaccurate. During-reading strategies are used to check and, if necessary, to modify initial predictions when something unexpected is encountered. The essence of being metacognitive is the reader's regulation of these unexpected blockages to meaning. The reader stops and says, "Oh, oh, something's wrong here. This doesn't seem right in light of what I expected," and then consciously activates a fix-it strategy to correct the situation. This regulation of meaning getting is repeated frequently when reading a difficult selection.

During-reading strategies for comprehension are used to resolve two kinds of problems. The first focuses on the author's message—what the author wants readers to understand. This can include information the author explicitly states in the text or implies. In either case, the focus of the problem is on what the author intended. The second focuses on meaning that goes beyond the author's message. What meaning does the reader construct beyond that intended by the author?

Continuing the illustration from the preceding section on initiating strategies, assume that your students made initial predictions that the story was going to be about one boy's courage in the face of floods caused by excessive rainfall. However, while reading the opening paragraphs of the story, cooperative rather than individual action is favored. Readers must use strategies for determining the author's message to identify this subtle change. For instance they may use strategies they have been taught for making inferences to identify the author's implication that cooperative rather than individual effort is to be the focus. Similarly, when reading this passage readers can use what they have been taught about how to construct meaning beyond what the author intended. They might draw conclusions about whether cooperative effort would be more or less efficient than individual effort, regardless of whether the author intended that they create this meaning or not.

As was noted in Chapter 7 regarding word recognition and vocabulary, many traditional reading comprehension skills typically learned in isolation can be recast as during-reading strategies. For instance, skills such as noting details; determining pronoun referents, main idea, and author purpose; classifying; recognizing relationships (e.g., causal, sequencing, compare-contrast); identifying character traits; and constructing inferences based on author cues can be taught as strategies for determining an author's message. And constructing inferences based on reader background knowledge, drawing conclusions, and making critical judgments can be recast as strategies for going beyond the author's meaning.

To accomplish such recasting, you present what is to be learned not as a rule-driven procedure to be routinely employed in exactly the same way in all instances, but rather as a process of thinking about solving a problem in which the reasoning employed must be modified to adapt to each new situation. Consequently, you would not present a main idea as a set of rules to follow, but rather as an adaptive thinking process in which the reader uses clues in the text to reason about what major point the author is making.

To summarize, expert readers routinely use during-reading strategies to regulate the ongoing process of getting meaning. They monitor emerging meaning to determine whether initial predictions were accurate, and if they were not, they use fix-it strategies to generate new predictions that fit the new information. The reasoning involved in accomplishing this regulatory function includes monitoring, accessing appropriate strategies, reasoning with the strategies, forming a new prediction, and testing the new prediction.

Post-Reading Strategies

Meaning getting is not complete when a reader finishes the last words in a text. Some of the most significant comprehension occurs after reading is completed. **Organizing strategies** include the processes of summarizing, determining the main point or theme, drawing conclusions; **evaluative strategies** include making judgments. These processes usually occur after reading is completed and so are called post-reading strategies.

Good readers use such strategies to reflect after they read. Like during-reading strategies, many of these post-reading strategies have traditionally been taught as skills, but they are actually flexible plans for constructing meaning, not proceduralized routines to be memorized. This book describes two types of post-reading strategies. The first focuses on organizing—or restructuring—text meaning. After reading, a reader may wish to summarize, clarify, or draw conclusions about an author's main idea or literary theme. The second focuses on evaluating and judging—or doing **critical reading**—about an author's message. A reader may make judgments about the credentials of an author, an author's relative use of facts, bias, and propaganda, or the validity of an author's conclusions.

When students are constantly confronted with real reading experiences, they learn why it is important to understand comprehension strategies.

To illustrate, consider the previously described selection about group courage in the face of a flood caused by rainfall. You teach students to reflect on the thematic meaning of this selection as it relates to other selections in the section on courage. A reader may wish to summarize the author's message about group courage and compare it to other kinds of courage described in earlier selections. Or a reader may wish to judge the validity of the author's argument for group efforts rather than individual efforts.

Such post-reading reflection requires strategic thinking. A reader must regulate, or be in control of, the reasoning involved in organizing an author's information or making judgments about it. This post-reading **self-regulation,** like initiating strategies and during-reading strategies, requires instruction to help students be conscious of what they are doing, why they are doing it, and how to do it.

To summarize, like all metacognitive strategies, comprehension strategies are taught to help students reason about solutions to comprehension difficulties. When students begin reading, you want them to approach it as a problem to be solved; to access and use appropriate topic, text, and purpose initiating strategies; and to make initial predictions. When students encounter comprehension difficulties during reading, you want them to access the appropriate strategies for determining author's meaning and for constructing meaning beyond what the author intended; and to use these strategies to solve any problems. When students finish reading you want them to access appropriate post-reading strategies to reflect about the text's meaning.

INSTRUCTIONAL EMPHASIS IN COMPREHENSION PROCESSES

As with other goals, instruction in comprehension processes can be discussed in terms of the literate environment (indirect instruction) and the teacher's role as a mediator (direct instruction).

The Literate Environment

Since comprehension is the heart of reading, the classroom environment should feature getting meaning from connected text. **Connected text** is any printed matter that represents a complete message being conveyed in a meaningful environment. For instance, a note the teacher writes to a student about progress in school is connected text. Similarly, written directions for how to run the classroom movie projector, invitations asking community leaders to speak to the class, poems written by students in the class, storybooks students choose from the library, classroom newspapers, comic strips, and various forms of language experience stories all are examples of connected text. The literate environment should abound with such materials.

When connected text pervades the classroom environment, students are constantly confronted with real-life reading experiences that demand comprehension, and consequently, they learn first-hand why it is important to learn comprehension strategies. This understanding is the basis for motivation: because your students understand what real reading is all about, they are willing to expend the necessary energy to learn comprehension strategies. Without these experiences, students construct alternative schemata for reading. If a classroom environment emphasizes isolated reading tasks, such as those typically found in workbooks, students will conceptualize reading as busy work. If a classroom fails to build an understanding of what reading is, students see no compelling reason why they should try to learn comprehension strategies.

Direct Teacher Guidance

Direct instruction in comprehension processes focuses on helping your students become metacognitively aware, using techniques such as the modified directed reading lesson developed in Chapter 7. Like word-level strategies, instruction in comprehension strategies focuses students on the reasoning that leads them to meaning. The idea is not to teach students to master individual strategies, but to teach them to use strategies flexibly and in combination.

In teaching students to activate background knowledge before beginning to read, organize your instruction using an MDRL. First, introduce the selection to be read, so that the strategy is presented as part of a real reading task. Then, state the purpose of the lesson—that is, how to use clues to make predictions about meaning before reading even begins. Use the selection to be read as an example along with other examples of similar text. Then, model how to use text clues and background knowledge to make initial predictions about the meaning in the text; check students' understanding of the strategy by giving them other textual examples and guiding them as they try out the strategy. Once you are reasonably sure your students understand how to use the strategy, have them read the selection and apply the strategy. Thus, students immediately apply the strategy in a real reading situation.

Follow the same format when you teach during-reading and post-reading strategies. Always introduce the strategies within the context of a real reading task so your students have a place to apply it. Mediate students' understanding about how to use the strategy by providing explicit introductions, modeling the mental processing involved, assessing their responses during the course of guided practice, and providing appropriate additional assistance as needed. Then have students apply the strategy immediately in the daily reading selection.

Role of Teacher Questioning

Comprehension questions are probably the most prevalent activity in comprehension lessons. That is, teachers have students read a selection and then ask comprehension questions about it. When your goal is to develop comprehension strategies, this practice is questionable for two reasons.

First, as noted earlier, such comprehension questions focus students on content, not on the mental processes used to acquire that content. Consequently, students do not attend to the reasoning involved in answering your questions. From your perspective, questions about content provide useful assessment data about who is comprehending and who is not, but the questions themselves do not teach students to comprehend.

Second, such comprehension questions are frequently asked before students have been given explicit instruction in how to comprehend. The point is not that you should ask no comprehension questions. That would be foolish. It is virtually impossible to conduct instruction without asking questions. Rather, you need to give students explicit instruction about how to comprehend before you ask questions to see if they can comprehend. After you model how to reason and provide graduated assistance in doing such reasoning, questions help keep students focused on the reasoning they are doing. Question asking alone, however, does not provide students with the raw materials needed to build schemata for how to comprehend.

Integration with Writing

Reading comprehension strategies can also be used in writing. If good readers initiate meaning getting by looking for clues with which to predict meaning, then good writers should provide such clues when composing messages. If good readers use text clues to fix blockages to meaning, good writers should include such clues in the text they compose. And if good readers find meaning through post-reading strategies such as organizing and evaluating, good writers should embed in the text information to assist readers in constructing such meaning.

TEACHING COMPREHENSION AT VARIOUS DEVELOPMENTAL LEVELS

Emergent Literacy Stage

Comprehension at the emergent literacy stage emphasizes listening comprehension, since students in preschool and kindergarten cannot yet read. Consequently, at the emergent literacy stage comprehension processes are taught through listening, and what is learned is later transferred when students begin reading at the initial mastery stage.

Listening comprehension is virtually the same as reading comprehension. It is enhanced when background knowledge is activated and predictions are made before beginning to listen, when sense making is monitored and breaks in meaning getting are repaired during listening, and when information is organized and judged after listening. Consequently, the thinking students do to comprehend text in listening situations serves as a useful foundation for the thinking required for reading comprehension.

At the emergent literacy stage, you should also employ language experience stories to help students make the transition from strategic listening to strategic reading. You could use a common class experience to build a story with students and use that story to illustrate how readers use initiating strategies, monitor and repair meaning as the text is processed, and finally organize and judge information in the text after reading.

Example 8.1 illustrates how to teach comprehension at the emergent literacy stage using both listening and language experiences.

EXAMPLE 8.1   Developing Comprehension Processes at the Emergent Literacy Stage

I. Initiating strategies
- A. *Activate background knowledge of topic*
  - 1. Predict content as signaled by picture and title
- B. *Activate background knowledge of text*
  - 1. Recognize story structure to predict content
- C. *Activate knowledge about author's purpose*

II. During-reading strategies
- A. *Use monitoring strategies to identify problem*
- B. *Access strategies*
  - 1. Determine author meaning — recognize details in a listening situation and make inferences about relationships when key words are stated
  - 2. Beyond the author's meaning — make inferences about relationships based on readers' background knowledge
- C. *Implement the strategy*
- D. *Verify that problem is solved*

III. Post-reading strategies
- A. *Use organizing strategies*
  - 1. Recall what is important through story structure: beginning, middle, end
- B. *Use evaluating strategies*
  - 1. Judge fantasy or reality

Linda Chang wanted to develop comprehension processes. She used the oral reading of *Swimmy* to develop three comprehension strategies: predicting content from pictures and title (initiating strategies); monitoring the accuracy of the predictions (during-reading strategies); and recalling what's important by using the story structure of beginning, middle, and end (post-reading strategies).

For the initiating strategy of predicting from the title and pictures, Ms. Chang showed the children the cover, which depicts an underwater scene, read aloud the title, *Swimmy,* and modeled for them how to predict what the story was about. She helped them by showing how she thought about things that swim under water. When Ms. Chang and the children had created their predictions, she read the book aloud showing them all the illustrations. Periodically she helped the children monitor their predictions by comparing their predictions to the actual text in order to see which ones were accurate. After the story was finished, Ms. Chang helped the children recall what was important in the story by using the story parts of beginning, middle, and end. They decided the following events were important: Swimmy finding himself alone; Swimmy swimming through the water; Swimmy finding a school of red fish; and Swimmy teaching them to swim in formation so they looked like one big fish. As the students recalled the important parts, Ms. Chang wrote them on the board. When their recall was completed, Ms. Chang and the students read this jointly constructed text.

Initial Mastery Stage

As students begin to accumulate a sight word vocabulary, you will help them make the transition from listening comprehension to reading comprehension. Show students how the thinking they do when listening to a story is essentially the same thinking they do when reading a preprimer or primer on their own. Show them how to initiate reading comprehension by activating appropriate background information and making initial predictions about the meaning of the text; show how to monitor and repair breaks during reading; and help students engage in post-reading thinking.

However, the task gradually becomes more complex at this stage. The initiating strategies expand to include simple expository text as well as narrative text; the during-reading strategies include typographic cues, such as question marks and exclamation points, which do not appear in listening situations, as well as more complex kinds of relationships, such as sequence and cause-effect; and the post-reading strategies include main-idea thinking and using certain word clues to judge author bias. Example 8.2 illustrates how to teach beginning readers to apply strategic comprehension processes at the initial mastery stage.

Expanded Fundamentals Stage

As students progress to reading third and fourth grade text, the comprehension emphasis broadens. Now you will teach students to use initiating strategies with a greater variety of text and for a greater variety and complexity of purposes. During-reading strategies focus on how to monitor and repair increasingly complex kinds of comprehension problems, such as how to use key words to identify compare-contrast relationships, how to infer such relationships when key words are not provided, and how to use background experience to make inferences beyond what the author implies. Finally, post-reading strategies focus on determining what is particularly important in the text by summarizing and by making judgments based on the author's use of **denotative** (emotionally laden) and **connotative** (neutral) language. Example 8.3 illustrates how to teach comprehension at the expanded fundamentals stage.

Application Stage

As students move into the upper grades, they spend a great deal of time working in content areas such as social studies, literature, science, and mathematics. Consequently, reading content area materials becomes very important and is reflected in the comprehension instruction provided at the application stage.

Here, comprehension strategies emphasize initiating reading in a variety of text types, repairing problems encountered in content area materials, and following up the reading with sophisticated organizational and evaluation strategies, such as drawing conclusions and determining the validity of the author's

I. Initiating strategies
 A. *Activate background knowledge of topic*
  1. Predict content as signaled by picture and title
 B. *Activate background knowledge of text*
  1. Recognize story structure and expository structure to predict content
 C. *Activate knowledge of author's purpose*
II. During-reading strategies
 A. *Use monitoring strategies to identify problem*
 B. *Access strategies*
  1. Author's meaning
   a. Recognize details
   b. Use typographic cues
   c. Recognize key words
   d. Make inferences about relationships when key words are stated
   e. Make inferences based on author's purpose
   f. Make inferences based on cause and effect, comparisons, sequence, and series
  2. Beyond the author's meaning
   a. Make inferences based on reader's background knowledge
 C. *Implement strategies*
 D. *Verify that the problem is solved*
III. Post-reading strategies
 A. *Use organizing strategies*
  1. Recall what is important using text structure
  2. Classify words and phrases
  3. Determine main ideas of expository text
 B. *Use evaluating strategies*
  1. Judge message content by author's word usage

Kelly Walters had three comprehension strategies that she wanted her first graders to learn as they listened to and read *Alexander and the Terrible, Horrible, No Good, Very Bad Day.* She wanted them to learn how to predict content using story structure knowledge (initiating strategy), how to monitor and verify the accuracy of predictions as they read (during-reading strategy), and how to organize important information by using story structure knowledge (post-reading strategy).

Ms. Walters introduced the book by telling the students that the book described a day where everything went wrong for Alexander. She asked the students to remember things that had gone wrong for them. After they had generated several instances, Ms. Walters moved to her lesson on predicting and verifying predictions using the story structure of beginning, middle, and end as cues for the predictions. Since the students already knew story parts, she taught them how to activate what they knew about the topic and to use the pictures to predict what was going to happen at the beginning, middle, and end of the book.

When the predictions were completed and grouped, the students listened to the story. Ms. Walters periodically stopped to have them verify predictions at the beginning, middle, and end of the book. When predictions were accurate, she acknowledged this and when predictions were inaccurate, she helped them as they created new predictions for each section. When the story was finished, Ms. Walters moved to the post-reading strategy of organizing what was important using their knowledge of story structure. She had the students recall events at the beginning, middle, and end as she wrote their responses on the blackboard. When the responses were completed for each section, Ms. Walters helped the students decide if each response was important or not and had them explain why. They returned to the book as necessary. The final list of important events was read and then recorded so that other students could use their list as they read about Alexander.

EXAMPLE 8.3   Developing Comprehension Processes at the Expanded Fundamentals Stage

I. Initiating strategies
  A. *Activate background knowledge of topic*
    1. Predict content as signaled by title and subtitles of text
  B. *Activate background knowledge of text*
    1. Recognize different kinds of meaning are conveyed by different types of text to predict content
  C. *Activate knowledge of author's purpose; combine with reader's purpose to predict*

II. During-reading strategies
  A. *Use monitoring strategies to identify problem*
  B. *Access strategies*
    1. Author's meaning
      a. Use key words to note sentence relationships
      b. Recognize pronoun referents
      c. Make inferences about relationships when key words are not stated
      d. Make inferences based on author's cues
    2. Beyond the author's meaning
      a. Make inferences based on reader's background knowledge
  C. *Implement strategies*
  D. *Verify that the problem is solved*

III. Post-reading strategies
  A. *Organizing strategies*
    1. Recall what is important
      a. Recognize different types of text structure (stories, articles, poems, letters)
      b. Classify sentences according to common idea or theme
      c. Determine main ideas
  B. *Evaluating strategies*
    1. Judge content of message by author's word usage—denotative and connotative words
    2. Judge content of message by completeness of content development

For his third graders who were reading the book *Spectacles,* John Gutierrez had selected the comprehension strategy of recognizing the author's purpose and combining that with the reader's purpose to predict content (initiating strategy). Since Ellen Raskin wrote *Spectacles* to show that things can be seen in two different ways, Mr. Gutierrez used her purpose to begin a unit about point of view. He told the students that they were beginning a unit that dealt with seeing things from varying points of view.

After describing why varying points of view were important, Mr. Gutierrez introduced the book *Spectacles,* telling the students why the author had written the book and that the book was about a girl who was nearsighted and had to get glasses. Taking the author's purpose and their own purpose, Mr. Gutierrez helped the students predict what the story was going to be about. After several predictions had been generated, the students read *Spectacles,* stopping periodically to verify predictions and to generate new ones (during-reading strategy).

After the story was read, the students discussed how the author uniquely showed readers that things can be seen in two different ways and how important that is for developing varying points of view. Mr. Gutierrez then used the students' new knowledge about seeing things in two ways as a basis for recognizing the point of view in *Billy Goats Gruff* and had them rewrite that story from the troll's point of view. The stories were shared and added to the class library.

EXAMPLE 8.4   Developing Comprehension Processes at the Application Stage

I. Initiating strategies
  A. *Activate background knowledge of topic*
    1. Predict content as signaled by opening and summarizing paragraphs
  B. *Activate background knowledge of text*
    1. Recognize different types of text have various text structures to predict content
  C. *Recognize reading makes most sense when author's purpose and reader's purpose coincide*
II. During-reading strategies
  A. *Use monitoring strategies to identify problem*
  B. *Access strategies*
    1. Author's meaning
      a. Use key words to note paragraph relationships
      b. Make inferences about relationships between paragraphs based on author's cues

    2. Beyond the author's meaning
      a. Make inferences based on reader's background knowledge
  C. *Implement strategies*
  D. *Verify that the problem is solved*
III. Post-reading strategies
  A. *Organizing strategies*
    1. Recall what is important
      a. Use knowledge of the different types of text structure
      b. Classify paragraphs
      c. Determine main ideas
    2. Draw conclusions
    3. Summarize content
  B. *Evaluating strategies*
    1. Judge content of text in reference to prior experience
    2. Judge author's structuring of text in reference to content

The fifth graders in Donna O'Malley's room were beginning a unit on courage in their reading group. Ms. O'Malley had selected *Julie of the Wolves* as the first selection because Julie showed great courage when she found herself alone and starving on the North Slope of Alaska. Julie established social relationships with a pack of wolves in order to survive and eventually helped the wolf pack survive. Ms. O'Malley chose the

---

position. In general, comprehension strategies taught at the application stage are more complex because the text being read is of greater variety and complexity. Also, signals provided by the author are more subtle, and the reader must be more active in inferring meaning. Example 8.4 illustrates how to teach comprehension at the application stage.

SUMMARY

Comprehension processes focus on the reasoning involved in comprehending, not on the attitudes required or the content of the message itself. The goal is to make students conscious of the reasoning employed by self-regulated readers. You want students to know how to activate background knowledge and make predictions as they begin to read; you want them to monitor their meaning getting

initiating strategy of recognizing that reading makes most sense when author's purpose and reader's purpose coincide. This fit because she wanted her students to generate characteristics of courageous people, and Jean George had written extensively about Julie's courage.

As the unit began, Ms. O'Malley established with students that a purpose for reading *Julie of the Wolves* was to discover characteristics of courageous people. She followed that with a short lesson on the effectiveness of predicting when author and reader purposes coincide. She modeled how to use the book's cover flaps, where the publisher states that courage was a major component of the book, to establish the author's purpose. The students were alerted as they read to see if they could discover more information about how their purposes and the author's purposes coincide.

Ms. O'Malley's during-reading strategies involved teaching students to make inferences based on their background knowledge. For instance, when Julie made initial contact with the wolf pack leader, he showed anger, but, rather than retreating, she moved closer and triggered acceptance by patting him under the chin. Ms. O'Malley used this instance to model for her students how to make inferences about courage based on their background. She asked her students to recall when they had been confronted by a strange, large dog that had growled or seemed angry. When several did, she asked them what they had felt or done. All said they had been scared and had run away. Ms. O'Malley then related that Julie also was scared and wanted to run away, but understood that the only way to get food from the wolf pack was to move forward to get acceptance. Julie showed courage.

For the post-reading strategy, Ms. O'Malley modeled how to draw conclusions by examining what Julie had done and deciding if Julie's behavior showed courage or not. Ms. O'Malley gradually moved from telling her students how to draw conclusions to asking them to draw their own conclusions as she supported them. This reading lesson closed when Ms. O'Malley had her students write stories about people showing courage. These stories became a book that was placed in the classroom library for other students to read as they completed units on courage.

and employ strategies if blockages to meaning occur while reading; and you want students to organize and evaluate what they read once they finish. Your role in teaching these strategies is to develop a classroom environment that emphasizes the reading of connected text and to explain to students the strategic reasoning to use when engaged in such reading. You can enhance students' learning of comprehension processes by showing them how many of the same strategies are used by good writers as they compose text. Instruction in comprehension processes begins with listening comprehension at the emergent literacy stage and progresses gradually through more and more complex processes and types of text.

SUGGESTED ADDITIONAL READING

ANGELETT, S. (1991). Encouraging students to think about what they read. *Reading Teacher,* 45(4), 288–297.

BAUMAN, J. & SCHMITT, M. (1986). The what, why, how, and when of comprehension instruction. *Reading Teacher,* 39, 640–647.

BECK, I. (1989). Reading and reasoning. *Reading Teacher,* 42(9), 676–682.

DAVIS, Z. & MCPHERSON, M. (1989). Story map instruction: A road map for reading comprehension. *Reading Teacher,* 43(3), 232–240.

DUFFY, G., ROEHLER, L., & HERRMANN, B. (1988). Modeling mental processes helps poor readers become strategic readers. *Reading Teacher,* 41(8), 762–767.

FARRAR, M. T. (1984). Why do we ask comprehension questions? A new conception of comprehension instruction. *Reading Teacher,* 37(6), 452–456.

GARNER, R. (1982). Resolving comprehension failure through text lookbacks: Direct training and practice effects among good and poor comprehenders in grades six and seven. *Reading Psychology,* 3(3), 221–231.

GORDON, C. (1985). Modeling inference awareness across the curriculum. *Journal of Reading,* 28, 444–447.

GORDON, C. J., & BRAUN, C. (1983). Using story schema as an aid to reading and writing. *Reading Teacher,* 37(2), 116–121.

HERRMANN, B. A. (1992). Teaching and assessing strategic reasoning: Dealing with the dilemmas. *Reading Teacher,* 45(6), 428–437.

KIMMEL, S., & MACGINITIE, W. (1985). Helping students revise hypotheses while reading. *Reading Teacher,* 38(8), 768–771.

MCGEA, L., & RICHGELS, D. (1985). Teaching expository text structure to elementary students. *Reading Teacher,* 38(8), 739–749.

MCINTOSH, M. (1985). What do practitioners need to know about current inference research? *Reading Teacher,* 38(8), 755–761.

MCKEOWN, M. G. (1979). Developing language awareness, or why leg was once a dirty word. *Language Arts,* 56(2), 175–180.

MOLDOFSKY, P. B. (1983). Teaching students to determine the central story problem: A practical application of schema theory. *Reading Teacher,* 36(8), 740–745.

POINDEXTER, C., & PRESCOTT, S. (1986). A technique for teaching students to draw inferences from text. *Reading Teacher,* 39, 908–911.

READENCE, J., BALDWIN, R. S., & HEAD, M. (1987). Teaching young readers to interpret metaphors. *Reading Teacher,* 40, 439–443.

REUTZEL, D. R. (1985). Story maps improve comprehension. *Reading Teacher,* 38(4), 400–404.

TAYLOR, K. (1984). Teaching summarization skills. *Journal of Reading,* 27, 389–393.

THE RESEARCH BASE

AFFLERBACH, P. (1990). The influence of prior knowledge and text genre on readers' prediction strategies. *Journal of Reading Behavior,* 22(2), 131–148.

BAKER, L., & BROWN, A. (1984). Metacognitive skills and reading. In P. D. Pearson (Ed.), *Handbook of reading research* (pp. 353–394). New York: Longman.

DUFFY, G., ROEHLER, L., & MASON, J. (1984). *Comprehension instruction: Perspectives and suggestions.* New York: Longman.

ENGLERT, C., RAPHAEL, T., ANDERSON, L., ANTHONY, H., & STEVENS, D. (1991). Making strategies and self-talk visible: Writing instruction in regular and special education classrooms. *American Educational Research Journal, 28*(2), 337–372.

GARNER, R. (1992). Metacognition and self-monitoring strategies. In J. Samuels & A. Farstrup (Eds.) *What research has to say about reading instruction,* 2nd edition (pp. 236–252). Newark, DE: International Reading Association.

LANDER, J. (1986). *Children reading and writing.* Norwood, NJ: Ablex Publishing Corporation.

PARIS, S., OKA, E., & DEBRITTO, A. (1983). Beyond decoding: Synthesis of research in reading comprehension. *Educational Leadership, 41,* 78–83.

PRESSLEY, M., GOODCHILD, F., FLEET, J., ZAJCHOWSKI, R., & EVANS, E. (1989). The challenges of classroom strategy instruction. *Elementary School Journal, 89*(3), 301–342.

PRESSLEY, M., JOHNSON, C., SYMONS, S., MCGOLDRICK, J., & KURITA, J. (1989). Strategies that improve children's memory and comprehension of text. *Elementary School Journal, 90*(1), 3–32.

TIERNEY, R., & CUNNINGHAM, J. (1984). Research on teaching reading comprehension. In P. D. Pearson (Ed.), *Handbook of reading research* (pp. 609–656). New York: Longman.

TIERNEY, R., & PEARSON, P. D. (1983). Toward a composing model of reading. *Language Arts, 60,* 568–580.

ACTIVITIES FOR REFLECTING, OBSERVING, AND TEACHING

Reflecting on Helping Students Use Comprehension Strategies

PURPOSE: As noted in the activities at the end of Chapter 6, the hardest thing about comprehension instruction is distinguishing between when you guide students to understand the content of a selection (Chapter 6) and when you are teaching students to understand the process they used to comprehend the content so that they can read and comprehend text without any guidance from you (which is the focus of this chapter). Because the difference is crucial if we are to help students become independent readers who can comprehend content without a teacher's guidance, this activity is designed to further help you make this distinction.

DIRECTIONS: When considering comprehending a text, it is usually helpful to think in terms of what one does before starting to read, what one does during reading, and what one does after getting done reading. In the section below, compare how the focus changes at the "before," "during," and "after" stages when the teacher is guiding the student's reading (or developing content goals as described in Chapter 6) and when the student is independently using strategies (has metacognitive control of the comprehension process as described in this chapter).

	What the Teacher Does If Guiding Student's Reading	What the Reader Does If Comprehending Independently
Before Reading		
During Reading		
After Reading		

Watching Others Teach Comprehension Strategies

PURPOSE: You can learn a lot by watching an experienced teacher teaching students comprehension strategies. The following activity is designed to help you set up such an observation.

DIRECTIONS: Arrange to watch a teacher of a grade level at the developmental stage you are most interested in teaching yourself. Pay particular attention to what the teacher does to develop comprehension. As you watch the teacher teach, particularly note the following:

1. At what point was the teacher teaching comprehension?

2. Was the teacher developing content goals (Chapter 6) or process goals (this chapter)?

3. What kind of comprehension strategies did the teacher teach? Initiating strategies? During-reading strategies? Post-reading strategies?

4. How did the teacher structure the lesson? Did he or she use a variation of the modified directed reading lesson? Some other technique?

5. Compare what the teacher did with the examples provided for the various developmental stages in this chapter. How do the chapter examples differ from what you observed? Why do you think they differed?

If possible, follow the observation with a discussion with the teacher. Ask for clarification regarding the above questions, particularly where you perceive that there is a difference between what is recommended in the chapter and what you observed.

Trying It Yourself: Teaching Comprehension Strategies

PURPOSE: At the end of Chapter 6, we recommended that you teach a lesson designed to guide students' comprehension of content. Now we recommend that you teach a lesson designed to help students become independently strategic in figuring out the content for themselves.

DIRECTIONS: Arrange to teach a small group of students. Get the teacher to recommend an appropriate initiating strategy, during-reading strategy or post-reading strategy (or, alternatively, use the suggestions provided in the chapter). Plan the lesson using a modified directed reading lesson format. Afterwards, ask the students questions such as the following: What was I teaching you today? When will you use it? When it is time to use it, tell me how you will do it. If their answers to these questions are different from what you expected the students would learn, reflect on what you would do differently next time to increase student understanding of what you are teaching.

9 Helping Students Study: Process Goals

GETTING READY

Studying is an important part of learning to read. It involves special kinds of reading, traditionally called study skills. However, study skills are more properly described as strategies, since students must be in metacognitive control of the mental processes involved. This chapter describes the process goals for study strategies taught at each stage of developmental reading growth in elementary school. Related writing goals are also described. Again, both what study strategies to teach and how to teach them are discussed. More detailed suggestions for teaching are described in the appropriate chapters in Part 4. Our sample teachers again provide illustrations for various levels.

FOCUS QUESTIONS

- How do study strategies differ from comprehension strategies? from content goals?

- What kinds of study strategies help students become self-regulated?

- What specific strategies are taught to help students locate information? determine reading rate? remember information? organize information? develop study habits?

- How do teachers develop student understanding of study strategies?

- How are study strategies related to writing?

- What are the curricular emphases when teaching study strategy processes at various levels of developmental reading growth?

DEFINING STUDY STRATEGIES

Very early in their school experience students learn that reading is closely associated with study. They learn that books are not only a source of pleasure, but also a source of homework. They also learn early that various kinds of text can be used to find needed information. Efficiently finding and using information from various kinds of text requires special abilities.

Study strategies, like word knowledge and comprehension strategies, are process goals because they are the means in a means-end relationship. The end goal is the effective use of textbooks and other study materials, but the means to that end are the strategies good readers use.

Distinguishing Study Strategies from Comprehension

Comprehension is constructing understanding of a given unit of text. The reader processes the text, combines the text information with prior knowledge, and reconstructs the author's message.

Study goes beyond comprehension. Although understanding is a prerequisite, students must do more than simply understand. They must efficiently locate, sort, and remember particular kinds of information, often from a variety of sources. In short, study strategies are more complex than comprehension. While students must comprehend whenever they read, study requires strategies for efficiently dealing with the demands of text. When reading a history text, students must not only comprehend, but also must know which parts of the text to read slowly and which to skim, how to organize the material for recall at a later date, and how to restructure the content for use as specified by the context of the content area of history.

Distinguishing Study Strategies from Content Goals

Study strategies are closely associated with **content area reading,** that is, the textbook reading done in association with content areas such as science, mathematics, English, and social studies. To help students understand a textbook author's message, you structure the instructional situation, as described in Chapter 6, to guide students to the desired understanding.

Study also involves locating and using information from a variety of other textual sources in order to achieve some specific goal. Therefore, study strategies go beyond content goals because they focus on textbook use and on gathering and using information from other textual sources.

To summarize, study strategies are those used by expert readers to gather and use information efficiently from a variety of text sources in order to meet the demands of study. They encompass the efficient use of all types of functional text including textbooks, dictionaries, encyclopedias, newspapers, magazines, and journals. These strategies are used in study situations in which students need to gather, organize, and remember specialized information for particular purposes.

TYPES OF STUDY STRATEGIES

Study strategies are organized into five categories, all of which are used metacognitively. You should teach students to be conscious of how to access these

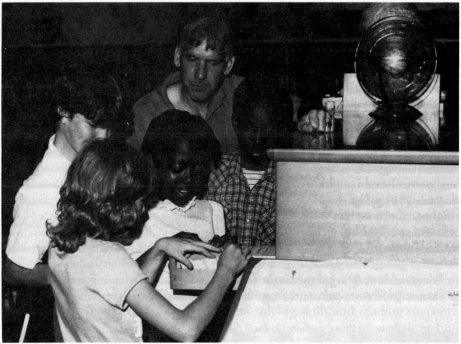

Library strategies include learning how to use card catalogs.

strategies so they can regulate their meaning getting in specific study situations.

Locational Strategies

Locational strategies, as the name implies, are strategies used to locate information. Your students may need to find specialized information in a particular type of book, periodical, or graphic reference source typically found in libraries or other public agencies. When this occurs, expert readers stop and think, "What do I know about finding such information?" You teach locational strategies to answer that question.

Locational strategies include book-part strategies, library strategies, reference-source strategies, and graphic strategies. **Book-part strategies** include learning how to find specific information in books, through efficient use of the table of contents, index, and glossary. **Library strategies** include learning to use card catalogs and the Dewey Decimal System. **Reference-source strategies** include learning how to use dictionaries, encyclopedias, atlases, and other major reference sources. **Graphic strategies** include learning how to use graphs, charts, tables, and other graphic means for displaying information. Table 9.1 pairs the source of information with the applicable strategies.

TABLE 9.1 Strategies for Locating Information

SOURCE	USING
Books	Table of contents, index, glossary, preface, footnotes
Library	Dewey Decimal System, card catalog, indexing
Reference sources	Dictionaries, encyclopedias, atlases
Graphic devices	Charts, maps, tables, figures, illustrations

Rate Strategies

Rate strategies follow logically from locational strategies because once information is located, it must be read. Good students do not read all study materials at the same rate. Instead, they read at varying rates of speed, depending upon the situation. The curricular goal here is to teach your students to ask themselves, "How fast should I read this material in order to get the information I need?" and then to show them how to vary reading rate according to the demands of the situation.

Using a variety of reading rates is not the same as speed reading. In fact, speed reading has no real place in the elementary reading curriculum because it is highly specialized and of limited use. Adjusting the rate of reading to one's purpose, however, is something all your students can learn to do, and it is applicable to many study situations. It involves teaching your students that good readers read at a very rapid **scanning** pace when previewing material or glancing through it to see if it contains the information being sought, at a rapid, **skimming** pace when looking for a key word or key idea that locates the information being sought in that particular location, and at a slow and careful pace when the reader has located the exact part of the text where specific information is located. In preparing a report on atomic energy, for instance, a student might scan a book on nuclear reactors to see if it contains relevant information, skim a particular chapter in the book to locate particular sections of interest, and then read those sections slowly.

Reading rate is one of the keys to efficient study. Instead of reading every word, expert readers scan to find potentially helpful information, skim that information to locate key words that signal discussion of the information they need, and read carefully only the text that is particularly helpful.

Remembering Strategies

Remembering strategies follow logically from rate strategies because once information has been read, students must remember it, particularly in study situations. When the need to remember information arises, your students should stop and think, "This is information that I am going to have to remember. What do I know about remembering difficult material that will help me here?"

The best-known technique for remembering what is read is SQ3R. **SQ3R** stands for the following steps: survey, question, read, recite, and review. With this system, you teach students to survey the text to be read to get the general idea of what is coming; use the headings, subheadings, and other graphic cues to predict what questions might be asked at the end of each chapter; read the text with those questions in mind; check to see if they know the answers to these questions after reading the text; and review the material for answers to any questions that they were unable to recite. This simple five-step pattern has repeatedly proven effective in improving students' retention of the material read in texts. It works well because it involves readers in establishing purposes for reading, allows them to get a feel for the text through an initial survey, encourages reading to confirm or disprove predictions embodied in the questions, and promotes the habit of checking to make sure that predictions have indeed been confirmed.

Summarizing is another good technique for remembering. Summarization requires that after reading a passage of difficult text, the reader should extract the important points and then restate the passage in terms of just those points. In doing so, students are aided in separating less important information from crucial information. Similarly, main idea strategies, in which students distinguish passage details from the gist, are helpful for remembering. Other strategies for remembering, similar to SQ3R and summarizing, are detailed in Chapter 18.

Organizing Strategies

Reading for study purposes is characterized by two kinds of difficulties: The material is often complex, and it is often necessary to collect information from more than one source. You teach **organizing strategies** when your students are faced with such difficulties and say to themselves, "How am I going to put all this information into sensible order?"

There are three major kinds of organizing strategies: note taking, outlining, and semantic maps. Note taking involves teaching students to identify both the purpose of note taking (what information is needed?) and the structure of the text (what headings, subheadings, and other devices does the author provide to help?); to use both the purpose and the text structure to identify particularly important information; and to condense relevant information into note form. It is helpful to teach your students how to use 3″ by 5″ note cards for note taking.

Outlining involves teaching students to organize their notes into a series of major headings and more detailed subheadings. You might show them how to physically group note cards in piles under each major heading and then to put the note cards in each category into the desired sequence.

Semantic mapping can be used both before and after reading to organize information. Before reading, you can put the topic for the day on the blackboard and have students tell what they know about it. As they provide concepts and ideas from their prior knowledge, organize them into categories. For instance, if the topic is Alaska, students might suggest *cold, Eskimos,* and *igloos* as ideas

they already possess about Alaska. Organize these into a semantic map with the categories *climate, people,* and *housing,* respectively. After reading, have your students contribute additional ideas and concepts that might alter the semantic map, noting for instance that parts of Alaska are relatively warm, that many different kinds of people live in Alaska, and that there are modern buildings and houses throughout Alaska. Through the use of semantic mapping, your students can organize large amounts of information.

Such organization strategies serve three purposes. First, they help students sort out complex material or combine material from several sources into a comprehensible form. Second, they help students remember important information. Finally, they help students transform what they have read into written form.

Study Habits

Study habits include a variety of abilities crucial to effective studying. One is organizing time to study. When students wonder why they are falling behind their classmates, the answer may be that their peers are making better use of their study time. Your students can learn to control this problem if you teach them to use free time efficiently, by estimating available study time, by prioritizing study assignments, and by making a "time budget" to distribute available time according to priorities.

Other important study habits include learning to follow directions and how to take tests. Students can be taught to follow directions and to be strategic when taking tests. Table 9.2 gives examples of some test-taking strategies.

To summarize, like metacognitive strategies for word recognition and vocabulary and for comprehension, study strategies are taught in a problem-solving mode. That is, readers are taught to monitor their study and to access and use strategies appropriate for solving specific problems. If the study problem is one of locating information, you want students to use locational strategies. If the problem is determining how carefully material must be read, you want students to use rate strategies. If the problem is one of recalling text information, you want students to use remembering strategies. If the problem is organizing information, you want students to use organizational strategies. If the problem is efficient study, you want students to use study-habit strategies.

INSTRUCTIONAL EMPHASIS IN STUDY STRATEGIES

As with other curricular goals, instruction in study strategies can be discussed in terms of indirect instruction in a literate environment and the more direct instruction associated with teacher mediation.

The Literate Environment

The primary function of the literate environment is to help students develop accurate conceptual understandings and positive feelings. This is a particularly

TABLE 9.2   Strategies for Taking Tests

TEST SITUATION	STRATEGY
Students psychologically freeze and forget what they know	Complete practice tests for familiarization with materials, environments, and expectations
Students start answering questions too soon	Practice looking over the test to see what is required
Students do not plan time well and end up without time to finish	Allocate a specific amount of time to teach part of the test before beginning
Students do not read the directions carefully	Teach students to read directions and to follow directions as stated
Students get stuck on one hard question and do not answer other questions	Teach students to answer questions they know first and to save the hardest questions for the end
Students skip questions they are unsure of	Teach students to make educated guesses unless there is a penalty for wrong answers
Students spend extra time on questions that have little value	Teach students to answer first those questions that have the most value
Students leave no time to check over their tests	Teach students to save the last 2 or 3 minutes to check over their tests
Students do not read multiple choice tests carefully	Teach students to read questions carefully, to find answers that are clearly wrong first, and to select the best answer from among those choices remaining
Students do not prepare themselves physically or mentally for the test	Teach students to get a good night's rest, to eat before the test, and to review before taking the test
Students do not look at corrected tests	Teach students to analyze to determine whether incorrect answers were due to misinterpreting directions, faulty time allocation, lack of information, etc. so that the same mistakes will not be repeated

difficult task when teaching study strategies because most students have negative feelings about studying.

A properly developed literate environment helps transform studying from boring work on meaningless topics into a satisfying experience involving curiosity and empowerment. To accomplish this, you must structure a classroom environment in which required topics are presented in light of your students' interests, and you must ensure that your students interact with content in meaningful and interesting ways. If the class is studying Alaska, you and your students might decide to produce travel brochures designed to entice tourists to visit Alaska, rather than simply read a textbook chapter on Alaska and then answer a few end-of-chapter questions. To produce the brochures, you would have to teach your students to locate information, how to use reading rate strategies, how to remember pertinent information, and how to organize it in preparation for writing the brochure. Hence, study strategies become part of an environment that emphasizes pursuit of an interesting and meaningful project. As a result, your students develop better concepts about study, have more positive feelings about engaging in study activities, and are better motivated.

The trick in developing a literate environment for study strategies is to make every effort to transform study content into projects meaningful to students. **Teacher-pupil planning** is often useful here. This technique calls for you to introduce new subject-matter content by talking with your students about their interests with that topic. Then use the expressed interests to develop meaningful study projects. Such planning demands extra effort from you, but the payoff in your students' motivation to study justifies it.

Direct Teacher Guidance

Whereas efforts to develop positive study environments are covert, developing study strategies is an overt process. In teaching study strategies, you focus on helping students become metacognitively aware of what the study strategies are, when it is appropriate to use each one, and the mental processes they should employ with each.

In providing such overt instruction, use the modified directed reading lesson presented in Chapter 7. Start by identifying the situation where the study strategy will be used in that day's work, and then provide explicit information about what the strategy is, when it will be used, and how to use it (including a model or demonstration). After modeling the strategy, provide students with opportunities to try out the strategy themselves, giving additional help as needed. Finally, when your students understand how to use the strategy, return to the task for the day, reminding students that they should apply the newly learned strategy in completing the task.

In the previous example about making brochures about Alaska, your students may have to read information books that contain difficult terminology. Therefore, you may decide to teach a lesson on dictionary usage so that while using the information books, students will be able to locate the meaning of difficult words. Consequently, you would introduce the lesson by referring to the difficult words students are likely to encounter in the reading they are doing in preparation for making the brochures. State that you are going to provide them with a strategy for finding out the meaning of such words, and give them explicit instructions for using the dictionary. Part of this instruction involves expressing your thought processes as you use the dictionary. Then give students the opportunity to use the dictionary to find the meaning of unknown words, and provide assistance as needed. After students have demonstrated competence with the dictionary, have them return to their reading assignments about Alaska using the dictionary as needed.

Integration with Writing

Study strategies are not limited to reading. In fact, because most study involves written assignments of some kind (reports, essays, homework), study strategies

Students learn to use the dictionary as a study strategy for finding the meaning of unknown words.

---

are as applicable to writing as to reading. Consequently, students should be taught study strategies as part of the writing curriculum as well.

In the previous example, study strategies are used both in reading about Alaska and in preparing the brochures about Alaska. Hence, study strategies can be taught in an integrated reading-writing situation.

TEACHING STUDY STRATEGIES AT VARIOUS DEVELOPMENTAL LEVELS

There is relatively little instructional emphasis on study strategies at the emergent literacy and initial mastery stages, but a progressively heavier emphasis as students move through the expanded fundamentals and application stages. This is because formal study of subject matter such as social studies and science begins to receive emphasis at about fourth grade.

Emergent Literacy Stage

There is very little emphasis on study strategies at the emergent literacy stage. Students at this level do not read and write, and their listening comprehension activities call for little subject-matter learning involving complex material or

---

EXAMPLE 9.1   Developing Study Strategies at the Emergent Literacy Stage

I. Study strategies
  A. Study habits
    1. Following simple oral directions

For study strategies, Linda Chang taught her kindergarten class how to follow oral directions. Since they had already heard the story of *Swimmy,* she used that information as the content for a lesson on following directions. First, she modeled how she successfully follows directions. Then, in small groups, each student was given a picture of Swimmy the black fish, a big fish, some red fish, and a jellyfish. Ms. Chang began with two directions, telling the children to put Swimmy at the left corner of their page on the first line and then to put the big fish next to Swimmy on the same line. She continued giving directions for two items until every member of the group was successful. The students worked in pairs checking each other's work. Ms. Chang then increased the number of directions to three and continued having children work in pairs. Toward the end of the lesson, students were asked to give three directions to the other members of the group, using the *Swimmy* characters. The lesson ended when Ms. Chang had the students review what they had learned about following directions.

---

multiple information sources. The only study strategy that receives any emphasis at this stage is learning to follow oral directions involving two or three steps. This is the beginning of instruction in following directions that increases in complexity as students move to the more demanding situations at higher grade levels. Example 9.1 illustrates how to teach following directions at the readiness stage.

Initial Mastery Stage

As with the emergent literacy stage, there is little emphasis on study strategies in first and second grade. This is because the academic efforts of students at this stage are devoted almost exclusively to learning how to read, and relatively little emphasis is placed on learning any subject matter or on associated study activities.

However, first and second grade teachers do provide initial instruction in study strategies, which forms the basis for more in-depth study at later stages. For instance, first and second grade teachers continue to provide instruction in following directions and introduce such study habits as getting proper rest in order to pursue study tasks. Additionally, students at this level are introduced to locational skills through picture dictionaries; they are taught simplified versions of SQ3R to help them remember certain kinds of information; and they use simple semantic maps to organize information. These efforts are introductory in nature, however, because in the absence of heavy subject-matter demands in first and second grade, there is relatively little call for study strategies. Example 9.2 illustrates how to study strategies at the initial mastery stage.

EXAMPLE 9.2 Developing Study Strategies at the Initial Mastery Stage

I. Study strategies
   A. *Study habits*
      1. Follow directions
      2. Proper rest for academic work
   B. *Locational strategies*
      1. Picture dictionaries
   C. *Remembering strategies*
      1. Simple SQ3R
   D. *Organizing strategies*
      1. Simple semantic maps

A group of first graders eagerly gathered around Kelly Walters for their reading class. Earlier she had asked them to remember what happened to Alexander in *Alexander and the Terrible, Horrible, No Good, Very Bad Day* and had told them they would use what they remembered in their reading lesson. Ms. Walters planned to use what they remembered to teach them how to follow directions. Each student was given a set of cards with each card having one event from the story about Alexander printed on it (going to the dentist, getting shoes, seeing Dad, riding in the car, etc.). After modeling how to follow directions and reading the phrases aloud, Ms. Walters began with two directions that required students to put the "seeing Dad" card first and the "riding in the car" card second. When the students were easily handling two directions, she began giving them three directions. The students worked in pairs, checking to see if the cards were placed in the order given by the teacher. The lesson ended when the students reviewed what they had learned about following directions.

Expanded Fundamentals Stage

By grades 3 and 4, instruction in study strategies noticeably increases. Students encounter their first subject matter, such as social studies and science, and are first assigned to read textbooks that typically accompany the study of these subjects. As subject-matter instruction increases, the need for study strategies becomes apparent, and more and more instructional time is devoted to it.

Students at the expanded fundamentals stage receive serious instruction in locational strategies, including use of the library, book parts, and dictionaries and encyclopedias, as well as interpretation of simple graphs and charts. Students are taught to make initial adjustments in reading rate, to use SQ3R and summarizing techniques to remember information, and to increase their use of both semantic maps and techniques for following directions. Example 9.3 illustrates how to teach study strategies at the expanded fundamentals stage.

Application Stage

The heaviest emphasis on study strategies occurs in the upper grades. This is because in grades 5 through 8 the instructional emphasis shifts from learning how to read to learning through reading. At the upper grades, teachers expect students to already know the rudiments of how to read so they devote much of their instructional effort to the more specialized demands of study. Because

EXAMPLE 9.3   Developing Study Strategies at the Expanded Fundamentals Stage

I. Study strategies
  A. *Locational strategies*
    1. Use the library card catalog to locate books by title or author
    2. Use a book's table of contents and glossary to locate information
    3. Use a dictionary to find word meanings
    4. Use simple bar and line graphs to gain meaning

  B. *Rate strategies*
    1. Use a slow pace for careful reading
    2. Use a fast pace for skimming
  C. *Remembering strategies*
    1. Summarize
  D. *Organizing strategies*
    1. Develop semantic maps
  E. *Study habits*
    1. Follow written directions involving three or more parts

In John Gutierrez's third grade class, the students read *Spectacles* as part of a unit on the care of eyes. Mr. Gutierrez decided to have the students organize the information on eye care by creating a semantic map. After reading the book, students listed all the things they remembered about eye care. Since *Spectacles* describes the sequence of getting glasses (recognizing a problem, visiting the eye doctor, visiting the optician, selecting frames, wearing glasses, correcting the problem), Mr. Gutierrez used sequence as the way to organize the semantic map. As a group, the students classified the events under what happened first, second, third, and so forth as Mr. Gutierrez completed a semantic map on the board. Multiple copies of the semantic map were made, and it became a source of information as students completed the unit on eye care.

most middle schools and junior high schools are departmentalized by subject matter, students are taught study strategies in the context of their social studies, science, English, and math classes.

The strategies also become more complex at this stage. Study habits no longer emphasize following directions, but focus on helping students organize study time and take tests; locational strategies move into indexing, the thesaurus, atlases, and complex graphic material; reading rate breaks down fast reading into skimming and scanning; and organizing is broadened to include heavy emphasis on note taking and outlining. Example 9.4 illustrates how to teach study strategies at the application stage.

SUMMARY

Although study strategies are based in comprehension processes and are used in situations where the focus is text content, they are different from both comprehension processes and content goals. This is because study strategies go beyond the construction of meaning to focus on how to deal efficiently with the demands of study. The intent is to help students become metacognitive about study strategies so they can be in control of the studying they are faced with. Five kinds

EXAMPLE 9.4   Developing Study Strategies at the Application Stage

I. Study strategies

   A. *Locational strategies*
     1. Use a book's table of contents, glossary, and index to locate information
     2. Use library card catalogs and the Dewey Decimal System to locate information
     3. Use dictionaries, encyclopedias, atlases, thesauri, etc. to locate information
     4. Use graphs, charts, tables, etc. to locate information
   B. *Rate strategies*
     1. Scanning pace
     2. Skimming pace
     3. Careful slow pace
   C. *Remembering strategies*
     1. SQ3R—survey, question, read, recite, and review (and variations of this technique)
     2. Summarizing
   D. *Organizing strategies*
     1. Note taking
     2. Outlining
     3. Semantic maps
   E. *Study habits*
     1. Organizing time
     2. Test taking

The students in Donna O'Malley's fifth grade class were well into their unit on courage. Because they were very excited by the unit and wanted to find out more about courage, she taught them study strategies they could use to find more information on their own. For locational strategies, she taught them how to use the subject index of the card catalog in the library and gave them opportunities to use it during reading time and free time in order to find more information on courage. For rate strategies, Ms. O'Malley taught her students how to scan so they wouldn't have to read every word they found about courage. When the students knew how to scan, they could more easily decide if the information they found was suited to their purposes. For remembering strategies, the students learned how to summarize. First Ms. O'Malley modeled summarizing; then the students practiced summarizing as they collected information on courage. For organizing strategies, Ms. O'Malley taught her students how to take notes in which they primarily recorded summaries in phrase form. The students used their summarizing strategies and note-taking strategies as they collected information about courage.

When the students showed signs that they were ready to move to the next section of the unit, Ms. O'Malley helped them generate a lengthy list of the information they had collected about courage. Because the students knew how to group and classify, they created a semantic map from this list. Small groups of students then chose the part of the semantic map about which they had gathered information and decided how to present it to the rest of the class. Some students wrote stories like *Julie of the Wolves,* while others created plays and others wrote factual articles. The unit culminated with a "courage seminar" for the principal and parents during which the students shared their knowledge about courage.

of study strategies help students become more efficient about study demands: strategies for locating information, for determining rate, for remembering information, for organizing information, and for using helpful study habits. Your role is to create an environment where study is meaningfully employed and to explain to students the reasoning involved when using study strategies in those situations, both in reading and in writing. Instruction in study strategies receives relatively little emphasis at the early developmental stages, but gradually increases as students encounter more and more complex text in the upper grades.

SUGGESTION ADDITIONAL READING

BEAN, T., SINGER, H., & COWAN, S. (1985). Analogical study guides: Improving comprehension in science. *Journal of Reading, 29,* 246–250.

BROMLEY, K. D. (1985). Precise writing and outlining enhance content learning. *Reading Teacher, 38*(4), 406–411.

FINLEY, C., & SEATON, M. (1987). Using text patterns and question prediction to study for tests. *Journal of Reading, 31,* 124–132.

LANGER, J. (1986). Learning through writing: Study skills in the content areas. *Journal of Reading, 29,* 400–406.

MUIR, S. (1985). Understanding and improving students' map reading skills. *Elementary School Journal, 86,* 207–216.

REINKING, D. (1986). Integrating graphic aids into content area instruction: The graphic information lesson. *Journal of Reading, 28,* 136–143.

REINKING, D., HAYES, D., & MCENEANEY, J. (1988). Good and poor readers' use of explicitly cued graphic aids. *Journal of Reading Behavior, 20*(3), 229–248.

ROGERS, D. G. (1984). Assessing study skills. *Journal of Reading, 27*(4), 346–354.

SIMPSON, M. (1984). The status of study strategy instruction: Implications for classroom teachers. *Journal of Reading, 28,* 136–143.

STEWARD, O., & GREEN, D. S. (1983). Test-taking skills for standardized test of reading. *Reading Teacher, 36*(7), 634–638.

TOWNSEND, M. & CLARIHEW, A. (1989). Facilitating children's comprehension through the use of advance organizers. *Journal of Reading Behavior, 21*(1), 15–35.

WILHITE, S. (1988). Reading for a multiple-choice test: Headings as schema activators. *Journal of Reading Behavior, 20*(3), 215–228.

WRIGHTS, J. P., & ANDEREASEN, N. L. (1980). Practice in using location skills in a content area. *Reading Teacher, 34*(2), 184–186.

THE RESEARCH BASE

ANDERSON, T. H., & ARMBRUSTER, B. B. (1984). Studying. In P. D. Pearson (Ed.), *Handbook of reading research.* New York: Longman.

BEACH, R., & APPLEMAN, D. (1984). Reading strategies for expository and literary text types. In A. Purves & O. Niles (Eds.), *Becoming a reader in a complex society.* Eighty-third Yearbook of the National Society for the Study of Education (Part 1). Chicago: University of Chicago Press.

ACTIVITIES FOR REFLECTING, OBSERVING, AND TEACHING

Reflecting on Helping Students Study

PURPOSE: As is the case with all reading instruction, the key to effective instruction is a meaningful reason for doing the reading in the first place. This is no less true for study strategies. To be learned effectively, they must be learned in a situation where it makes sense to use the strategies. This activity is designed to help you understand the relationship between various kinds of study strategies and sensible situations in which to learn those strategies.

DIRECTIONS: For each of the study strategies listed below, describe a sensible—or authentic—situation in which one would be called on to genuinely use the strategy.

Locational strategies—

Rate strategies—

Remembering strategies—

Organizing strategies—

Study Habits—

Watching Others Teach Study Strategies

PURPOSE: You will better understand how to teach study strategies yourself if you have a chance to interact with a teacher you observe teaching study strategies. This activity provides you a structure for such an observation.

DIRECTIONS: Arrange to observe a teacher teaching study strategies. Note particularly the relationship between the environment of the classroom, the genuineness of the reason for learning study strategies in the first place, and the students' enthusiasm for the lesson. Note also the way the teacher structures the lesson itself. Is a modified directed reading lesson format used? Some other format? Is there any relationship between the examples provided in the chapter for the various developmental stages and what you see the teacher doing? If possible, talk to the teacher following the lesson and ask questions regarding the differences between what you saw being done and what the content of this chapter led you to believe you should have seen.

Trying It Yourself: Teaching Study Strategies

PURPOSE: While there is some similarity between teaching study strategies and teaching other process goals (such as word strategies and comprehension strategies), you will understand better how to teach study strategies if you actually get experience trying to teach them. This activity suggests what you should do if you get such a chance.

DIRECTIONS: Arrange for a small group of students, preferably at a developmental stage similar to the age you hope to teach. Plan and teach a lesson. Keep two points especially in mind. First, think carefully about how you can situate the lesson so that there is an authentic reason for learning the strategy; second, try to use a modified directed reading lesson format in planning the lesson.

Part 3

Getting Organized For Instruction

The information about what to teach provided in the previous chapters is an important foundation for reading instruction. However, you must also know how to organize for instruction. That is, you must know how to arrange your classroom environment to promote literacy, how to assess, how to group, how to adapt basal textbook prescriptions, and how to manage students and instruction. The chapters in this section provide that information.

10 How to Establish a Literate Environment: The Key to Whole Language Instruction

GETTING READY

What your students think and feel about reading depends on the environment in which they learn to read. Different concepts develop depending on whether the environment you create emphasizes nonliterate tasks or whole language activities involving books, libraries, discussion, and writing.

This chapter describes how to promote accurate concepts about reading by establishing a literate environment in the classroom. Creating such an environment, which emphasizes the pursuit of literate activities, is a fundamental part of organizing for instruction that leads to optimum learning.

FOCUS QUESTIONS

- Why is a literate environment necessary?

- What does the physical environment consist of?

- What does the intellectual environment consist of?

- What does the social-emotional environment consist of?

- How does the literacy cycle work?

- How do I get ready to use the literate environment for instruction?

IMPORTANCE OF A CONCEPTUAL FOUNDATION

Reading cannot be taught in isolation. It should occur with discussion and writing. The instructional environment must provide a supportive conceptual foundation for what reading is and for what good readers do by emphasizing the pursuit of literate activities.

What happens if reading is taught in an environment that does not emphasize literate activities? Consider the experience of one teacher. A new student came to her fifth grade class from a large-city school district where heavy emphasis was placed on mastering long lists of skills and in which instruction consisted of following the teacher's directions. The day the new boy arrived, the teacher was confronted with a negative attitude.

T: I'm going to explain how to use a strategy to solve a problem encountered when reading.

S: How many of these dumb things do I have to learn?

T: Only as many as you need to make sense out of what you read.

S: And you call yourself a teacher?

It is clear that students' understandings about reading are a product of the interpretation they make of their environment. The student in this example interpreted his previous school environment to mean that reading is learning a list of skills dictated by the teacher. He had no idea that reading is a meaning-getting process or that making sense of text depends on the reader's ability to impose meaning on it. He carried this concept from his former school into the new classroom. If the old understandings remain unchanged, no amount of explicit teacher explanations about strategy use will work, because the boy will continue to try to make the new teacher's explanations fit his old understandings of skills and following teacher directions.

Another teacher related that she was having trouble getting her fourth grade students to use fix-it strategies because they refused to admit they had problems with reading. When her students encountered an unknown word or an unfamiliar idea, they tried to maintain an illusion of fluency by bluffing their way through it. It is not hard to understand why they did this. Their first, second, and third grade instruction had emphasized fluency, accuracy, and oral round-robin reading, and their former teachers had signalled to them that not knowing all the words or not instantly answering all the comprehension questions was unacceptable. These teachers conveyed the message that reading is knowing words and answers instantly, not that reading involves reasoning. Consequently, when these students got to fourth grade, they operated on the concepts learned from earlier teachers. If these old concepts remain unchanged, these students will continue to try to make their fourth grade teacher's instruction fit their old concept that reading is error-free fluency.

In both cases, the new teacher's success depends on changing students' concepts about reading and about what good readers do and how that all fits into writing and talking. That is, the teacher must build an instructional foundation that causes students to think differently. A literate environment in the classroom is a major force in building desired conceptual understandings about reading.

PURPOSE OF A LITERATE ENVIRONMENT

In a literate environment, the most visible classroom activities illustrate, in an atmosphere of love and fun, how language is used for real purposes. For instance, there is an emphasis on free-choice reading and writing; on student authorship; on various kinds of writing for communicating real and important messages; on projects that involve reading directions and collecting, analyzing and comparing information; on a variety of different kinds of text, from newspapers and catalogs to student-written books where decision-making, drafting, reflecting And discussions are encouraged; on the teacher's own engagement in reading and writing activities; and on the sharing of enjoyable and functional literacy events. Although the more traditional tasks associated with school are also evident, the emphasis is on authentic language, and the classroom reflects the flair and excitement that comes with real language use. The teacher's intent is to provide daily evidence that reading is a meaning-getting process and that what we are trying to learn during reading class is to send and receive real messages. When provided with such evidence, students become aware of why they are learning what they are learning about reading. In short, the reading instruction becomes meaningful, and students gradually build accurate concepts that provide a foundation for instruction. In contrast, if the classroom environment emphasizes nonliterate tasks, such as isolated work sheets, memorized rules, procedures, and endless skill tests, students tend to conclude that the name of the reading game is to "get done," and reading instruction is based on inaccurate concepts.

WHAT A LITERATE ENVIRONMENT LOOKS LIKE

A literate environment should provide multiple opportunities for a wide variety of writing, for interacting with books, and for student talk. Opportunities for writing include choice of topics and issues; the use of home, school, and book experiences; journals; reports; story mapping. Opportunities for reading include books read aloud and discussed, independent reading of books and other printed materials, small group discussion of topics and issues in books, and literature across all subject areas. Opportunities to talk include collaborative activities, cooperative activities, choice of topics, book clubs, and drama activities.

In a literate environment, the classroom should emphasize whole language. There should be many examples of literacy and language in action—real language and real literacy. Instead of the traditional situation in which a teacher talks and everyone else is quiet, the literate environment encourages various kinds of oral and written student communication. Instead of limiting written material to textbooks, many other kinds of printed materials are used as well, including trade books, magazines, comic books, catalogs, recipes, and newspapers. Writing is not taught as a separate subject with an emphasis on neatness and accuracy of script, but is integrated into reading activities along with speaking and listening.

In a global sense, then, a literate environment provides numerous opportunities for students to encounter and participate in real language and literacy experiences, thereby increasing the chances they will develop accurate concepts about reading and positive feelings for it. Teachers deliberately create these opportunities.

Consider seatwork and how it can be changed to match the characteristics of a literate environment. In many classrooms it is not unusual to see students sitting at desks completing piles of ditto and practice sheets geared to habituate isolated skills and bits of knowledge. Communication is at a minimum, and the emphasis is on busy work. In contrast, in a literate environment seatwork might include independent reading for information or pleasure or journal writing for reflective or expressive purposes. Seatwork is often done in pairs or small groups rather than individually, and it includes shared oral reading, think-aloud activities to develop reasoning abilities, peer tutoring, interviews, and author's chair activities in which student authors are interviewed about their creativity and craftsmanship. Small-group activities include collaborative group assessment of stories and articles, creative drama development, teacher-made games for prac-

Teachers should provide daily evidence that reading class teaches about receiving and sending oral messages.

ticing strategies and skills, and cooperative group discussions of other content areas. All of these examples of seatwork reflect literate activity and would be part of a literate environment.

A classroom environment is what the teacher makes it. It *is* possible to create alternatives to traditional classroom environments so that students build accurate conceptual foundations about what reading is and what it is used for.

COMPONENTS OF A LITERATE ENVIRONMENT

You create a literate environment by orchestrating physical, intellectual, and social-emotional environments. The physical environment refers to things physically evident in the classroom; the intellectual environment consists of mental challenge; and the social-emotional environment encourages socialization with language. Use these environments to create an atmosphere in which meaningful language becomes an integral part of daily activities.

Physical Environment

To establish a physical environment conducive to literacy, print must be everywhere. In most areas where Americans live, print guides and challenges our everyday lives. A trip to the store is guided by stop signs, yield signs, walk and don't walk signs. Printed sales slips record our purchases, and we keep track of them in checkbooks. Billboards and written advertisements challenge and entice us to try certain products. Consumer magazines assist us as we attempt to select the best products. Editorials persuade us to consider a certain point of view, and books and magazines provide challenges, enticements, and entertainment.

You should create a similar environment in your classroom by displaying print prominently and using it in a variety of ways. Display classroom rules, directions, and procedures in print. Encourage your students to verify uncertainties by referring to a printed reference. Encourage recreational activities, such as free reading, choral reading, sharing of poetry, etc., and encourage sharing of reference work, as when students turn to a recipe book for a class cooking project or to directions for assembling something the class has ordered. Display printed language that issues challenges to the students; and display thought-provoking questions around the room on bulletin boards, chalkboards, and display tables with printed answers to the questions placed close by or with written directions for where to find the answers attached to the questions.

Draw your students' attention to the integrated nature of language use, to the way all the language modes are used for communication. Your students will learn what you emphasize; if you talk about the integrated nature of language, your students will become aware of it. Consequently, your physical environment should include not only the prominent display of print but also tangible evidence of the integrated nature of print and its relationship with other language modes.

Intellectual Environment

You cannot base a literate environment on physical environment alone; an intellectual environment must accompany it. You orchestrate the intellectual environment by creating challenges. This is done by setting expectations, by modeling, and by capitalizing on your students' interests and motivation.

Expectations   Challenges always involve the possibility of failure; the trick is to choose the right challenge. Part of choosing the right challenge lies with the concept of **expectations.**

The expectations of those around us influence how we view ourselves. Consequently, the expectations you communicate to your students can lead them to believe that they can become literate. Do your words and actions convey negative feelings about risk taking, or do they convey trust and the feeling that it is okay to fail when trying something new because we can learn from our mistakes? Do your words imply that only perfection is acceptable, or do you value ever closer approximations as students move toward a final goal? You should set the expectations that all your students can learn, that learning takes time, that failures and mistakes are inevitable and no reason to quit. By setting positive expectations, you make it easier for your students to accept challenges and to persevere in completing them.

We communicate expectations about language as well as about people. For instance, in talking with your students, you establish expectations about the integrated nature of language by ensuring that what is written will be read by someone; by emphasizing that language is a tool for conveying information, ideas, and experiences; and by making sure reading is seen as one of the four language modes, not as an isolated skill.

Modeling   Modeling, a powerful tool for learning, influences us at all levels of development. At a very early age, we watch others and then do what we see them doing. Much of our early learning comes from emulating a model, and you can use this phenomenon to develop a strong intellectual environment. Modeling can be simply doing the reading of books, talking aloud when we discuss how we use reading to understand others, or thinking aloud when we explain our reasoning as we communicate in writing (with the principal's office, with other teachers, and with the parents). Make an effort to model all possible uses of the written word.

Interests   Student interests are the areas of knowledge your students are curious about and want to explore. Topics such as dinosaurs, tornadoes, vampire bats, horses, and unexplained events fall into this category for many children. When you want your students to use language (especially reading), high-interest topics such as these can be used to create challenges they are willing to pursue.

One strategy is to have your students themselves become resident experts on topics of interest to them. Each student selects an interest area, such as whales, doll making, or computers, and becomes the class expert through ex-

Teachers model recreational reading as part of the intellectual environment.

tensive reading. You then direct all questions on the topic to that student. This is also an excellent way to illustrate the integrated nature of language, since all four language modes are typically used when the resident experts are consulted.

Internal Motivators Most students possess a set of internal motivators that, when activated by well-chosen activities, produce a positive attitude toward the activity and result in higher achievement.

The first internal motivator is choice. Whenever students are provided choice during activities, motivation is activated. You are employing choice when you include the selection of two or three activities or topics for your students to choose from, the selection of the language mode to use (listen or read, speak or write), and the selection of the time necessary to complete the activities.

A second internal motivator is the opportunity to act like an adult. Most students enjoy opportunities to become the teacher, whether it is with pairs of students, a small group of students, or an entire class of students. You can add this internal motivator to many different types of activities.

A third internal motivator is the opportunity to alter language. Activities such as creating new definitions for words (*illegal* is a sick bird; *bulldozer* is a sleeping bovine) are helpful; students may also create new words for definitions (a very fast car is a *zoommobile;* an awesome football team is the *terror machine*).

Another internal motivator is the opportunity to create language. You can do this by having your students create poems, stories, or articles. A sixth grade student created the following story patterned after Remy Charlip's *Fortunately*.

Fortunately I had a friend.

Unfortunately he died.

Fortunately there was a funeral.

Unfortunately it was sad.

Fortunately there were flowers.

Unfortunately I wish there were more.

Fortunately everyone was there.

Fortunately so was I.

Fortunately I want to be just like him.

A second grade student created the following paragraph as part of an activity that encouraged him to create language.

All about Computers

I will answer five questions about computers.

What are the five main parts of a computer? The five main parts of a computer are the control unit, the arithmetic unit, memory devices, input devices, and output devices.

Where did the word computer get its name? The computer got its name from compute.

Why do computers punch holes? The holes are for computers to read.

What does COBOL stand for? COBOL stands for common business oriented language.

Is there any such thing as a computer language? Yes, COBOL is a computer language.

The main idea is about computers, how come they punch holes, what the five main parts of a computer are, and what COBOL stands for.

Whenever you activate these internal motivators, you increase the possibility of student engagement and success.

One example of how the intellectual environment can be orchestrated using expectations, modeling, interests, and motivation is a technique called un-interrupted sustained silent reading (USSR). USSR is a good example of indirect instruction designed to develop accurate concepts and positive feelings about reading. The technique is deceptively simple: you and your students read books of their choice individually for sustained periods of time each day. The purpose is to get your students hooked on reading and to offer them sustained opportunities to practice real reading. It works because you set an expectation that all students will read, you model reading and students emulate you, you account for the interest of every student through individual choice of books, and you account for motivation by allowing your students choice of what to read, how much to read, and how to follow up on the reading. The steps in establishing USSR in the classroom are listed in Figure 10.1. When used well, USSR can lead to other activities which promote literacy, such as drama, book clubs, book exchanges, and so on.

Social-Emotional Environment

Literacy and the social-emotional environment in which literacy occurs are closely related. Literacy is the communication of ideas and, as such, is a social event influenced by the emotions of the communication. Consequently, you should orchestrate social-emotional factors when building a literate environment. These factors include social interactions and collaborative sharing.

Social Interactions   The quality of the social interactions accompanying reading activities influences your students' feelings and concepts about reading. When your students discuss a book together (such as Sendak's *Where the Wild Things Are* or White's *Charlotte's Web*), they not only have the opportunity to express

---

FIGURE 10.1   Establishing USSR in Classrooms

Step 1	Establish a spot in the room for a room library.
Step 2	Choose three to five books per student.
Step 3	Select books that range in topic and difficulty.
Step 4	Include magazines, newspapers, comics, and catalogs.
Step 5	Have each student choose something to read.
Step 6	Keep the first session only 5 minutes long (or less).
Step 7	Increase each succeeding session by 1 minute until the desired length of time is attained.
Step 8	Periodically change the books, usually every month or so.
Step 9	Have students keep some sort of record of what they are reading, but do not give grades or establish competitions for the most books read.
Step 10	Periodically have sessions with your students to share what they've read and to talk about the nature of reading. Keep these sessions very informal.

their own concepts and feelings but to hear others expressing theirs. As a result of this social interaction, they modify their own feelings and concepts about reading. Social interactions help promote the understanding that reading is communication and that communication brings satisfaction.

Collaborative Sharing   Collaborative sharing is a specialized type of communication that assists in developing positive attitudes about reading. In **collaborative sharing**, you assign each member of the group a responsibility. One student is the facilitator, another the recorder, another the researcher, and so on. Group size is determined by the number of responsibilities; the usual number is three or four. The facilitator keeps the group on task and makes certain everyone participates; the recorder keeps a written record of the interaction; and the researcher goes back to the original source of the information when needed. If any group member has difficulty, all group members help. Since everyone has a responsible role to play within the group, social interactions bring high status to everyone, not just to those who already enjoy it. When you arrange your environment to include such sharing, the high status felt by all students increases the feeling that reading is satisfying while also enriching the concept that reading, writing, talking, and listening are all elements of communication.

STRUCTURING A LITERATE ENVIRONMENT

The development of a literate environment needs a structure you can count on as you make ongoing decisions about students and their learning. Since most of your cognitive energy will be involved in these ongoing decisions, a structure which you and your students understand and can use is critical. A **literacy cycle** is such a structure.

The literacy cycle provides a support for implementing and using literacy activities. Unlike the basal programs which generally provide step-by-step directions for activities that often remove ongoing decision making for teachers, the literacy cycle provides a frame which enhances decision making. Since one of the goals of this book is to develop teachers who make and carry out ongoing instructional decisions, the literacy cycle becomes a powerful tool.

Within the literacy cycle (see Figure 10.2), students are continually reading, writing, and discussing all subject areas. These activities may be independent of the teacher or teacher directed. In either case, students are provided with opportunities to become literate and are helped as they do so.

Students usually enter the literacy cycle where guided reading and writing occur. As they enter, they bring with them their life experiences, their school experiences, and their current discourse experiences which reflect their classroom community, their school community, their home community, their neighborhood community, etc. As they progress through the literacy cycle, students need to activate and use their past experiences as they create new experiences.

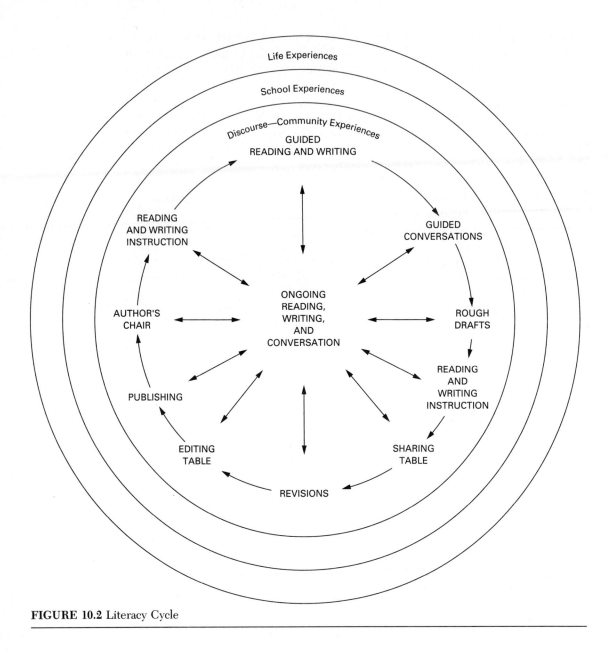

FIGURE 10.2 Literacy Cycle

Guided reading and writing are usually embedded in units which center around themes or topics (see Chapter 14). Examples of topics include subject matter areas such as ecology or friendship, a particular author such as Judy Blume or Maurice Sendak, or a particular book such as *A Thousand Cranes* or *Julie and the Wolves*; examples of themes include "The Uses and Value of Garbage," "Saving the Rhinos," or "The Reciprocal Nature of Friendship."

As students move from guided reading and writing to guided instructional conversations about that reading and writing, they need many opportunities to receive information through listening, reading, and observing. They also need opportunities to express their ideas and feelings through speaking, writing, and doing. These activities set the stage for instructional conversations where students use their strategies of questioning, predicting, verifying, challenging, problem framing, and problem solving. Since most students have been participating in conversations most of their lives, this structure is familiar and comfortable.

Instructional conversations lead to opportunities for rough drafts, the first attempts at putting on paper the information for others to read. The main outcome of rough drafts is to get ideas on paper. Mechanics such as spelling and grammar are not a concern at this time.

As the students are involved in literacy activities and conversations, you, as the teacher, should be observing and assessing students' strengths and areas of needed growth. This information becomes the basis for reading and writing instruction that includes concept and positive response development, routine skills, metacognitive strategies, and recreational and functional text capabilities. It should be noted that reading and writing instruction occurs here and at a point further in the literacy cycle for convenience sake. This type of instruction can be inserted at any point that makes sense to you. The important component is to have assessment information to use as the basis for instructional planning and implementation.

Once rough drafts are started, students need help with their rough drafts. Their difficulty may be putting ideas into a coherent sequence or it may be getting ideas in the first place. In any case, a sharing table is the place to give and receive help. Students talk with one another with excitement about their rough drafts and their problems with their rough drafts, and help each other with possible ideas and resolutions. The teacher can be heavily involved, somewhat involved, or not at all.

After the sharing table, rough drafts need to be revised. Students need to question their writings. They can question themselves or have others question them as they prepare to do a first revision. These questions can include ones like: Did I get said what I wanted to say? Will the reader understand my message? Do I have a good ending?

When second drafts are completed, they are taken to an editing table where current drafts are critiqued for content and mechanics. A procedure for doing this can be developed where questions like the following are included: "Does the story have a beginning, middle, and end?" "Does the article have an opening where what will be discussed is presented and a closing where the content is summarized?" "Are the describing words appropriate?" If the story or article is going to be published, the questions might be, "Is the spelling appropriate?" "Is the grammar correct?" "Are the sentences appropriately started and ended?"

The person or people in charge of the editing table can be students in the class, older students, volunteer parents, teacher aides, or teachers. Whoever the helpers at the editing table are, their role is one of helping authors critique their writing for content, coherence, and mechanics appropriate for the grade level and type of writing.

After the editing table, students prepare their writing for publication. Illustrations, diagrams, and figures are added as authors put their work into final form. Books, magazines, and newspapers are created for others to read. The published forms can be individually or group authored.

An author's chair is one way to share writings with members of the class, members of other classes, parents, friends, and neighbors. It signifies that something special has been created and is worthy of being heard by others. An author's chair is usually a designated place in a classroom with its own set of procedures for use.

As teacher, you may complete the literacy cycle with another set of activities for reading and writing instruction. It is important to note that students may stay at any point for varying amounts of time and return to previous points as needed while they are reading and writing. The literacy cycle is not a lock-step procedure.

The final step in the literacy cycle is connecting the reading, writing, and conversation that occurs to ongoing reading, writing, and conversation in other in-school and out-of-school activities. The purpose of literacy and conversation activities is to increase world knowledge, help develop positive attitudes, and promote the acquisition of routine skills and metacognitive strategies.

CREATING A LITERATE ENVIRONMENT

The planning of a literate environment starts with the three goals of reading instruction developed in Chapter 3. You first decide what curricular goals to work toward, then use the literacy cycle to build a literate environment designed to support these goals. Use the following seven-part guide to build a literate environment.

1. *Decide on the goals you wish to develop.* Attitude goals are best developed through activities associated with the literate environment. For these goals, the environment plays the dominant role, whereas for process and content goals, the teacher plays the dominant role. Select the curriculum goals you wish to achieve with your class (see Chapter 3). At the readiness and initial mastery stages, you might select feelings such as "reading satisfies the need to know" or concepts such as "reading is for information." At the expanded fundamentals and application stages, you might select feelings such as "reading helps you feel good about yourself and others" and concepts such as "reading is a tool that can clarify knowledge, feelings, and attitudes." The curriculum goals you select depend on the development stage and the needs of the students. However, you must select the curriculum goals before establishing activities to develop those goals.

2. *Decide which components you want in the literacy cycle.* We know that the age of the students partially determines which components to have in the literacy cycle. Primary grade students may not revise their writings. Older stu-

dents may revise more than twice. You need to decide how the components will be placed. Where do you want to provide instructional opportunities for strategy and skill instruction? How often do you want to provide instructional opportunities for strategies and skills? The components you select and the order of those components depend upon the developmental stages and needs of your students.

3. *Allocate sufficient time for instruction.* We know that time is connected to learning; that is, the more time given to a goal, the more that is learned. Similarly, the less time allocated, the less that is learned. Activities in the literate environment must be allocated sufficient time if the goals are to be achieved.

4. *Employ indirect instruction.* Organize activities such as learning centers, classroom libraries, and visual displays to indirectly lead your students to achievement of the goals.

5. *Orchestrate the physical, intellectual, and social-emotional environments to create desired conditions.*

Physical environment: At the readiness and initial mastery stages, the following examples illustrate what could be done: Install a cooking center or a science center with written directions; prominently display books that provide either information or enjoyment in the classroom library; title a bulletin board "the wonders of the animal world" and post pictures, with questions to be answered in print, of such wonders as flying squirrels or the 16-foot white shark. At the expanded fundamentals and application stages, activities could include the following: Install a science center or an anthropological center involving a dig; develop a time capsule; prominently display books that provide additional information on digs or time capsules in the classroom library; post a bulletin board with pictures of the products of a dig; develop the progress of the dig in a time line or chart. The range and variety of goal-directed activities is limitless.

Intellectual environment: At the readiness and initial mastery stages, similarly develop elements of the intellectual environment (expectations, modeling, interests, and motivation) in several ways. In the cooking and science centers, set the expectation that all students will use them; model the desired outcome; use the interests of specific students (such as one student's interest in octopuses or another's interest in kangaroos) as topics in the science center; use pictures to stimulate motivation. At the expanded fundamentals and application stages, employ similar procedures. Set the expectation that all students will be involved in the anthropological center, that the student experts are ready to be called on for help, that any developing interest in digs or other related activities will be included, that new experts might emerge, and that the teacher will model the desired outcomes.

Social-emotional environment: Social interactions and collaborative sharing support the goals selected. At the readiness and initial mastery stage, allocate time for informal social interactions about the work in the center. Establish collaborative endeavors for more formal interactions among students, in which you predetermine the tasks and outcomes, but the groups implement them. At the expanded fundamentals and application stages, allocate time for informal social

A rich literate environment encourages students to accomplish goals independently through indirect instruction.

interactions about the anthropological center and keep formal social interactions in the collaborative groups.

6. *Match groupings to specific activities and goals.* During indirect instruction in the literate environment, students normally work in small groups or as individuals. At times, however, you may wish to explain certain procedures to the whole class. Some groupings may be formally established by you, as for collaborative groups, but many will be informal.

7. *Monitor activities in terms of desired goals.* Once the literate environment has been planned and is operating, you monitor its effectiveness. Activities that do not lead to the desired goal can be dropped, and more effective activities can be substituted.

SUMMARY

It is crucial that you create a literate environment in your classroom if you want your students to develop accurate concepts about reading and what it is for. Students can develop such concepts only if they participate in experiences that represent what literate people actually do with reading. Your role in creating a literate environment is primarily one of providing activities for students to pursue. One way to think about creating such an environment is in terms of what is physically present in the classroom to stimulate literate activities, whether intellectual challenges and expectations you set encourage pursuit of literate activities, and whether the social-emotional climate of the classroom promotes literate activity. The literacy cycle can provide the structure.

SUGGESTED ADDITIONAL READING

ALLINGTON, R. (1977). If they don't read much, how are they ever gonna get good? *Journal of Reading, 21,* 57–61.

BERGLUND, R. L., & JOHNS, J. L. (1983). A printer on uninterrupted sustained silent reading. *Reading Teacher, 36*(6), 534–539.

BOODT, G. M. (1982). Up! up! and away! writing poetry in the reading class. *Language Arts, 59*(3), 239–244.

CHRISTIE, J. (1990). Dramatic play: A context for meaningful engagements. *Reading Teacher, 43*(3), 542–545.

COODY, B., & NELSON, D. (1982). *Successful activities for enriching the language arts.* Belmont, CA: Wadsworth.

CUNNINGHAM, P., ARTHUR, S., & CUNNINGHAM, J. (1977). *Classroom reading instruction.* Lexington, MA: D.C. Heath and Company.

DEFORD, D. E. (1984). Classroom contexts for literacy learning. In T. Raphael (Ed.), *Contexts of school-based literacy* (pp. 163–180). New York: Random House.

DUFFY, G. G. (1967). Developing the reading habit. *Reading Teacher, 21,* 253–256.

EVANS, H. M., & TOWNER, J. C. (1975). Sustained silent reading: Does it increase skills? *Reading Teacher, 29,* 155–156.

GENTILE, L. M., & MCMILLAN, M. M. (1978). Humor and reading program. *Journal of Reading, 21*(4), 343–349.

HAMILTON, S. F. (1983). Socialization for learning: Insights from ecological research in classrooms. *Reading Teacher, 37*(2), 150–156.

HARSTE, J., SHORT, K., & BURKE, C. (1988). *Creating classrooms for authors: The reading-writing connection.* Portsmouth, NH: Heinemann.

HOLBROOK, H. T. (1982). Motivating reluctant readers: A gentle push. *Language Arts, 59*(4), 385–390.

HUBBARD, R. (1985). Second graders answer the question "Why publish?" *Reading Teacher, 38*(7), 658–662.

JANNEY, K. P. (1980). Introducing oral interpretation in elementary school. *Reading Teacher, 33,* 544–547.

LANGER, J. A. (1982). Reading, thinking, writing and teaching. *Language Arts, 59*(4), 336–341.

LEVINE, S. (1984). USSR: A necessary component in teaching reading. *Journal of Reading, 28,* 394–400.

MANNA, A. L. (1984). Making language come alive through reading plays. *Reading Teacher, 37*(8), 712–717.

MARTIN, C. E., CRAMOND, B., & SAFTER, T. (1982). Developing creativity through the reading program. *Reading Teacher, 35*(5), 568–572.

MCCRACKEN, R. A., & MCCRACKEN, J. J. (1978). Modeling is the key to sustained silent reading. *Reading Teacher, 31*(4), 406–408.

MENDOZA, A. (1985). Reading to children: Their preferences. *Reading Teacher, 38*(6), 522–527.

MICHENER, D. (1988). Test your reading aloud I.Q. *Reading Teacher, 42*(2), 118–121.

MIKKELSEN, N. (1982). Celebrating children's books throughout the year. *Reading Teacher, 35*, 790–795.

MILLER, G. M., & MASON, G. E. (1983). Dramatic improvisation: Risk-free role playing for improving reading performance. *Reading Teacher, 37*(2), 128–131.

MOORE, J. C., JONES, C. J., & MILLER, D. C. (1980). What we know after a decade of sustained silent reading. *Reading Teacher, 33*(4), 445–450.

MORROW, L., & RAND, M. (1991). Promoting literacy during play by designing early childhood classroom environment. *Reading Teacher, 44*(6), 396–402.

NESSEL, D. D. (1985). Storytelling in the reading program. *Reading Teacher, 38*(4), 378–381.

NEUMAN, S., & ROSKOS, K. (1990). Play, print and purpose: Enriching play environments for literacy development. *Reading Teacher, 44*(3), 214–221.

RASINSKI, T., & NATHENSON-MEJIA, S. (1987). Commentary: Learning to read, learning community: Considerations of the social contexts for literacy instruction. *Reading Teacher, 41*, 260–265.

SEAVER, J. T., & BOTEL, M. (1983). A first-grade teacher teaches reading, writing, and oral communication across the curriculum. *Reading Teacher, 36*(7), 656–664.

SIDES, N. K. (1982). Story time is not enough. *Reading Teacher, 36*(3), 280–283.

SMITH, C. (1989). Reading aloud: An experience for sharing. *Reading Teacher, 42*(4), 320.

STRICKLAND, D., & MORROW, L. (1988). Creating a print-rich environment. *Reading Teacher, 42*(2), 156–157.

WAGNER, B. J. (1979). Using drama to create an environment for language development. *Language Arts, 56*(3), 268–274.

WETZEL, N. R., DAVIS, L., & JAMSA, E. (1983). Young authors conference. *Reading Teacher, 36*(6), 530–533.

WHITE, J., VAUGHN, J., & RORIE, I. (1986). Picture of a classroom where reading is for real. *Reading Teacher, 40*, 84–87.

WINOGRAD, P., & SMITH, L. (1987). Improving the climate for reading comprehension instruction. *Reading Teacher, 41*, 304–310.

THE RESEARCH BASE

DUFFY, G., & ROEHLER, L. (1987). Building a foundation for strategic reading. *California Reader, 20*(2), 6–10.

EVANS, H., & TOWNER, J. (1975). Sustained silent reading: Does it increase skills? *Reading Teacher, 29*, 155–156.

FADER, D., & MCNEIL, E. (1968). *Hooked on books: Program and proof.* New York: Berkeley.

HOLDAWAY, D. (1979). *The foundations of literacy.* Sydney, Australia: Ashton Scholastic.

JONES, J. (1977) Children's concepts of reading and their reading achievement. *Journal of Reading Behavior, 4,* 56–57.

ROEHLER, L. (1991, December). *Increasing learning for understanding for elementary at-risk ESL students.* Paper presented at the National Reading Conference, Palm Springs, CA.

THOMAS, J. (1975). *Learning centers: Opening up the classroom.* Boston: Holbrook.

ACTIVITIES FOR REFLECTING, OBSERVING, AND TEACHING

Reflecting on the Literate Environment

PURPOSE: Establishment of a literate environment is a crucial foundation for your instructional program. It sets the flavor and tone of instruction, and plays a crucial role in the development of student conceptions of what literacy is and its functions. The purpose of this activity is to help you think about the impact of a literate environment.

DIRECTIONS: Think about the grade level you hope to teach. For that grade level, consider the following:

What do you think are the crucial conceptual understandings students should develop about literacy at that grade level? _____

_____

_____

What kinds of experiences must children of that age have in order to build such conceptions? List the kinds of experiences which would result in such conceptual understandings. _____

_____

_____

What could you have going on in your classroom which would involve your students in such experiences? _____

_____

_____

Watching Others Provide a Literate Environment

PURPOSE: If you can watch another teacher establish and use a literate environment as part of his or her instructional program, you will be in a better position to do so yourself. This activity is designed to help you structure such an opportunity.

DIRECTIONS: Arrange to visit a classroom at a grade level similar to the one you wish to teach. As you watch that teacher work, note the following:

Does the physical environment provide opportunities for students to engage in experiences which promote accurate conceptions about literacy? What are they?

Does the intellectual environment of the classroom encourage experiences which promote accurate conceptions of literacy? Cite some of these.

Does the social-emotional environment of the classroom encourage experiences which promote accurate conceptions of literacy? Cite some of these.

Do you see evidences of a literacy cycle at work? Describe what you see.

Trying It Yourself

PURPOSE: Establishing and maintaining a literate environment is a complex, multi-faceted activity. Until you have your own classroom, it is unlikely that you would have the opportunity to orchestrate all the features of a literate environment. However, you can experience providing children with short-term experiences designed to promote accurate conceptions about literacy. This activity is designed to help you do so.

DIRECTIONS: Arrange an opportunity to work briefly with a small group of children in a classroom. During that time, engage them in an experience designed to promote a particular conception about literacy. For instance, you might read them a story or poem, or bake cookies with them using a recipe, or have them write letters to your hospitalized mother, or some other activity which gives them experience with real literacy. Following the activity, interview a small sample of the group to determine whether the experience helped them understand literacy better. For instance, ask questions such as, "What did you learn today about reading (or writing)?" and "How is what we did today like what people really do?"

11 | Assessing Students During Classroom Interactions

GETTING READY

What your students learn depends on your capabilities for assessing their individual strengths in the outcome areas of attitude, content, and process. Then you need to use that knowledge to create instructional opportunities for more learning to occur. This chapter describes how you can organize to assess the strengths of your students and keep track of their growth for reporting to parents, administrators, other teachers, and community members.

FOCUS QUESTIONS

- Why are there individual differences in student learning?
- What are the guidelines for classroom literacy assessment?
- What is the value of portfolios?
- How are portfolios organized?
- How is individual student growth reported?

CHANGES IN LITERACY ASSESSMENT

Assessment of classroom literacy is changing. In the past, students took separate standardized tests for reading and writing. For reading, students responded to isolated items and short paragraphs. For writing, students responded to requests to write about a specified topic. The tests were scored, students were compared, and judgments were made about the quality of teaching and learning. There was little consideration given to the strengths of the individual students, other performances of the students not measured on the test, or the context of the learning situation. It was assumed that single tests were appropriate for all purposes;

that special times for tests were needed; that reading and writing should be assessed separately; that assessment with one type of text would signal performance for all types of texts; and that assessment of enjoyment, empowerment, self-responsibility, and self-assessment was unimportant.

Now, however, classroom literacy assessment needs to reflect the complexities of changing literacy programs found in the classroom. Students use various combinations of reading, writing, and oral language. They read and write about ideas and experiences. They write classroom books and then read about each other's ideas and experiences. They talk about their ideas and experiences, and then write and read about them. Assessment practices need to capture these complexities.

This chapter will help you prepare for the complexities associated with classroom literacy assessment.

CONDITIONS THAT RESULT IN INDIVIDUAL DIFFERENCES

In order to assess the strengths and needed areas of growth of your students, you need to understand individual differences and why they occur. To some degree, individual differences can be attributed to varying quality of instruction. That is, students may not be growing because they received poor instruction. However, even when instruction is excellent, differences in student progress occur.

Aptitude for Verbal Learning

One of the influences on student ability to understand and respond to instruction is aptitude for **verbal learning.** Some of your students have an aptitude for reading. Just as some people have an aptitude for mechanics or mathematics or poetry writing and others do not, some people have more aptitude for learning to read than others. There is nothing wrong with either the fast developers or the slow developers; they are just different.

Background experience influences verbal learning and, ultimately, reading development. Some of your students come to school with rich experiences which enhance verbal learning. They have been to many different places, they have had a variety of vicarious experiences through the media, they have encountered many different ideas and concepts, their oral vocabulary is rich and varied, and their families value accepted school behavior. Conversely, other students have seldom been outside their immediate neighborhood, they have had limited vicarious experiences that relate to school, their oral vocabulary is limited, and their family values may be different than accepted school behavior. Since reading involves constructing meaning using prior knowledge and text information, students with rich background experiences that are valued in school can be expected to construct meaning easier and progress faster than students whose background experience is not valued in school.

Similarly, culture and cultural variations influence students' aptitude for learning to read. Our society includes children from various cultural backgrounds, various economic groups, various ethnic groups, and various locations such as small town, rural, and urban. They must all learn side by side. Even when language is no problem, traditions and expectations for how to do things vary in cultures. The ways of one culture are not better than the ways of another; they are just different.

Students whose cultural traditions match the expectations of schools have less trouble adapting to the materials, rules, and teachers because of background familiarity with the way things are done. The expectations associated with school materials, rules, and teacher attitudes may be new to students from certain

Children from homes where reading is valued and practiced naturally progress faster in school settings.

cultures. For example, Oriental cultures highly respect teachers, and teacher-student interactions are usually formal. Consequently, Oriental students generally do well in school, but some of them may have difficulty adjusting to the more informal teacher-student interactions typically found in American schools. These cultural differences may affect verbal learning and, ultimately, progress in learning to read.

Language variations of several kinds influence students' verbal learning. For instance, in many American schools some students are having difficulty with English since they speak another language at home. These students generally move more slowly through the developmental stages. Similarly, some students have dialects that differ greatly from the dialect used for instruction, which could impede students' movement through the developmental stages.

Differences in reading progress are found in all classrooms and may stem from factors that influence students' verbal learning. You will see such differences in every class you teach. You should take them into account to understand why some students are learning more quickly than others.

Perseverance

Verbal learning problems account for some differences in the rate of reading progress, but they do not account for all. **Perseverance** also explains some differences in the rate of reading growth. Three conditions affect perseverance: **expectations, self-concept,** and **motivation.**

Expectation is the most influential condition. Children from homes where reading and learning are valued tend to have positive expectations about these activities. Because important people in their lives expect them to learn to read, they learn to read. This phenomenon is called a self-fulfilling prophecy because humans tend to fulfill the expectations set for them.

Teachers' expectations can be quite subtly communicated. For instance, by regularly calling on certain students more than others, by regularly providing feedback for some students more than others, and by setting slightly higher academic standards for some students than for others, teachers create an expectation that certain students are smarter and more capable of learning than others.

Communicating expectations can be insidious; you can communicate negative or positive expectations without knowing you are doing so. For instance, you may unconsciously work harder with students of one gender, thereby setting more positive expectations for the favored group and less positive expectations for the other. Such positive and negative expectations influence your students' perseverance and, ultimately, their rate of learning to read. Students for whom positive expectations are set tend to persevere and learn to read faster than those for whom negative expectations are set.

Self-concept is closely related to expectations; it refers to the image that people hold of themselves. If a student has a positive self-image, the chances for normal developmental reading growth are favorable; if a student has a negative

Individual aptitude and perserverance influence rate of reading growth.

self-image, the chances for normal reading progress are less favorable. People's positive and negative self-images are closely related to expectation because we develop our self-images from our perceptions of what other people think of us. If you set high expectations for your students, they tend to develop positive self-images. If you set low expectations for your students, or expect them to be ineffective or unimportant, they tend to develop less positive self-images. The more positive a self-image, the more confidence there will be in approaching difficult tasks such as learning to read. Hence, positive self-images help students persevere.

Connected to self-images is the **self-efficacy** or "I-can-do" attitude. Students who have positive self images and understand that they are capable of performing school tasks generally do better in school. This "I-can-do" attitude helps students become self-reliant, independent readers and users of language.

Motivation is another major influence on your students' ability to persevere. As noted in Chapter 4, motivation is influenced by both whether the student values what is being learned and whether it can be learned relatively easily. Your students will value what they learn when you present content meaningfully, usually through integration within and across lessons. Your students' success in learning, however, depends on whether you assign tasks slightly above their performance level. That is, students who are given reading tasks where they are challenged yet can succeed are motivated, and they persevere in the task; students who are given tasks which are very difficult for them become discouraged and unmotivated, and they do not persevere during instruction.

To summarize, a student's rate of progress throughout school is greatly influenced by both perseverance and aptitude for verbal learning. Both are necessary for learning to read. Since your students possess different amounts of aptitude for verbal learning and perseverance, you can expect them to progress in reading at different rates of speed, even if your instruction is excellent.

GUIDELINES FOR CLASSROOM LITERACY ASSESSMENT

Literacy assessment is no longer viewed from a deficit-model standpoint where the goal is to find out what students lack and then teach to fill in that hole. Instead, the goal is to find out what students know and build on that knowledge. Find out about their strengths, their interests, and their talents. Guidelines for doing this type of assessment fall into the three categories: students, the teacher's role, and assessment practices.

Students

Within this category, there are two guidelines. First and foremost, students are viewed as individuals living and operating within groups. All students have strengths and areas of needed growth, both within themselves and as a part of a group. The goal is to start with the students' strengths and provide opportunities for them to grow in needed literacy areas of attitude, content, and process outcomes. It is a difficult task to view students as unique individuals within groups moving toward expertise in reading and writing. Forms of **authentic assessment** must take place in the context of the learning process. Both the learning and the situation in which the students are assessed must be considered. Thus individual and group measures of growth need to be distinguished in order to become powerful tools to help improve teaching and learning.

Second, your students should be active participants in your assessment program. When the emphasis is on what has been learned and what needs to be learned next, students can play a critical role in their learning. Their self assessments of their own past and anticipated growth provide valuable information for you as the teacher. It also gives students equal status in their learning process, increases self efficacy, and enhances feelings of empowerment, providing students opportunities to improve their learning.

Teacher's Role

The teacher's role is one of making decisions about assessment. When you assess students' differences, you start with the understanding that they already have knowledge in the areas of attitude, content, and process outcomes that were specified in Chapter 2. Your task is to find out where they are and then keep track of their growth. If students are developing accurate concepts of what reading is and responding positively to reading (attitude goals), are getting content meaning from functional or recreational text (content goals), and are understanding how reading works (process goals), then they are growing toward literacy. If students are not moving in one or more of these categories, an instructional problem exists. You as the teacher have expertise in assessment, and you will be able to convey to parents, administrators, community members, and other teachers how your students are growing in the literacy areas. You are in a position to provide a complex picture of the students' knowledge. You will be able to understand how they learn in groups. You will be able to understand the contexts. You will be able to gain this knowledge in first-hand situations. You will then be able to take the results of these classroom assessment devices, add in standardized

Students should participate in assessing their own reading and writing.

test scores, recognize patterns of growth and areas where you need to provide learning opportunities, and use that knowledge as you plan.

Assessment Practices

Four guidelines are important in assessment practices. First, you should use assessment procedures that reflect what the students are learning and doing in reading and writing. When assessment procedures don't reflect what is happening in the classroom, teaching and learning often become redirected toward the expected answers of the test. When this occurs, learning generally lessens and often becomes a chore that has little usefulness for the students. Multiple indicators of learning students' attitudes and process and content outcomes are vital. Authentic forms of assessment reflect relevant, real world applications. Worthwhile tasks empower students.

Second, classroom literacy assessment needs to be continuous and inseparable from instruction. Authentic assessment is evaluated in terms of whether it improves instruction. Most forms of assessment should be integral components of the instructional day. While it is difficult to tie standardized tests into your ongoing instruction, you should at least use the results as you make decisions about teaching and learning for your students. As you organize the instructional day, you may decide to have specified times for assessment or you may fit them in as appropriate. It is your decision according to what makes most sense to you. Since authentic assessment is instructionally relevant and relates to tasks that are meaningful to students, an assessment form is only as authentic as the tasks these students are being tested on.

Third, your program should have assessment procedures that clearly and accurately describe how students have grown on a variety of measures over time. You want to be able to provide information about the progress of your students, their achievements, their efforts, their attitudes, and their knowledge of how reading and writing work.

Fourth, adequate record-keeping devices are essential when the complexities of classroom assessment are acknowledged and used for teaching and learning purposes. Students, parents, administrators, and teachers need to know where individual students are in their growth toward literacy understanding. Additionally, administrators and teachers also need to know where groups of students are in their growth toward literacy. Finally, teachers need to know where students are in their growth in group interactions. The complexities of the classroom make it impossible to keep all that information organized in a casual manner. Effective and efficient record-keeping devices help you to keep track and organize student growth individually and in groups. Record-keeping devices will help you, your students, administrators, and community members understand the growth that is occurring.

The guidelines within the categories of students, the teacher's role, and assessment practices should help you select and implement good assessment techniques like portfolios.

ASSESSING THROUGH PORTFOLIOS

Portfolios are an effective way for you to assess student growth. They contain systematic collections of students' continual growth. Portfolio artifacts include evidence about a student's attitudes about reading, including their conceptual understandings about reading, their strategic processes and routine skills, and their content knowledge. Because you need to (a) identify where students are in their growth toward literacy, (b) predict future growth of your students, (c) assess the results of your teaching, and (d) account for individual growth and group growth within the three outcomes of attitude, content and process, the evidence in portfolios should include reflections of the students' activities, the processes students use during the activities, and the learning that results from the activities. One form of a reading record for portfolios is found in Figure 11.1. A structure for writing outcomes is also important and can be adapted from the reading form.

The three major outcomes presented in Chapter 2 provide the frame for the reading portfolio. Attitude outcomes have two subgoals, the development of positive attitudes toward reading and writing and the development of conceptual

FIGURE 11.1   Portfolio Reading Record

Name _____

	ATTITUDES		CONTENT		PROCESSES	
Date	Posit. Resp.	Concept. Underst.	Recreat. Text	Funct. Text	Strat. Proc.	Routine Skills
1/6/92	o	Jack chose to read *Feathers for Lunch* during choice time.			c	Jack summarized the story and generated two questions about birds. Questions in folder.
	c	During a conference, Jack explained how reading this was a way to gain information. Observation and conference notes are included in folder.				
1/10/92			o	Jack read his authored book on friendship to Nika, Finnan, and Diane.	o	Jack's reading was fluent and included intonations. He explained his illustrations.
					o	He pronounced all words, stopped at periods, and signaled question marks with his voice.

KEY: o = observation; c = conference; p = performance results

understandings. Within positive attitudes, students need enthusiasm about reading and writing and they need self efficacy or an "I-can-do" attitude. Enthusiasm and self-efficacy growth both need to be measured and tracked.

Evidence about positive attitudes includes records of smiles and other signs of pleasure when reading opportunities are provided. It also includes records of students' favorite stories and poems, favorite ways to communicate, and favorite ways to solve problems.

Conceptual understandings, the broad understandings that students develop for reading, writing, and oral language, include the development of dispositions such as "reading is a tool," "reading solves problems," "reading is a way to gain information," "reading satisfies curiosity," or "reading is a way to get rid of boredom." Evidence about conceptual understandings includes records of problem framing and solving, communication with others, and the carrying out of projects that are integrated across the curriculum.

Content outcomes also have two subgoals. These include the development of content knowledge from recreational text and the development of knowledge from functional text. Within each of these two areas, students should move toward expertise. Evidence of content learning includes records of content understanding from texts, student-authored articles and stories about specific content, semantic maps of specific content, and questions posed and answered about specific content.

Finally, process outcomes have two subgoals, the development of routine skills and the development of metacognitive strategies. Within the routine skills area, students should move toward expertise in language conventions and linguistic units. Evidence of gaining routine skills includes records of vocabulary words, uses of punctuation when reading and writing, and letter naming. Within the metacognitive strategies area, students should move toward expertise in reading for initiating strategies, during-reading strategies, post-reading strategies, and study strategies. Evidence of strategic processes include records of students' predicting before reading, monitoring understanding while reading, organizing and remembering information after reading, and their uses of study strategies in all content areas.

In summary, portfolios are effective ways to assess student learning. The attitude, processes, and content outcomes provide the overall frame. The next step is to organize the portfolios.

ORGANIZING PORTFOLIOS

Broad categories for organizing portfolios include a way to store evidence of the ongoing and periodic assessment devices for growth. Within these categories, individual teachers create their own structures according to their needs, their students' needs, and the context of the classroom. A variety of evidence is critical. It is also important that your portfolio be structured in ways that allow you easily to use all types of information for a variety of purposes. An overall structure for organizing portfolio assessment is provided in Figure 11.2.

FIGURE 11.2 Structure for Assessing Reading Expertise

Student's name _____

Student's age and grade _____

Student's expected reading progress _____
Comments should be added in the space provided.

YES	NO	Performance associated with expectations for that age and grade	How to find data to answer questions
		I. ATTITUDE GOALS	
		A. Conceptual understandings	
____	____	Understands that reading is meaning getting?	Conference with student. Observe how student makes use of reading.
____	____	Has a rich concept of the function of reading?	Same as above.
		B. Positive response	
____	____	Has positive feelings about reading?	Conference with student. Observe student during free time, reading times, etc.
____	____	Likes to read?	Observe student's response to various kinds of reading situations.
		II. PROCESS GOALS	
		A. Routine skills	
		1. Language conventions	
____	____	Routinely uses language conventions such as left-to-right directions?	Conference with student. Observe how student moves eyes across a page of text.
		2. Linguistic units	
____	____	Knows most words instantly?	Listen to student read text at grade level. Are most of the words recognized instantly?
____	____	Has meaning for words met in reading?	Select words from text materials and ask student to use them in conversation.

FIGURE 11.2 (continued)

B.   Metacognitive strategies

1.   Initiating strategies

_____ _____   Uses knowledge of topic to predict meaning? Give student several reading tasks and ask student to tell how meaning is obtained and how words, topic, purpose, and text structure are used to predict.

_____ _____   Uses knowledge of author's purpose to predict meaning?   Ask student to state predictions and how these predictions were decided.

_____ _____   Uses knowledge of text structure to predict meaning?   Same as above.

2.   During-reading strategies

_____ _____   Reads with fluency?   Listen to student read and note number of hesitations, repetitions, etc.

Analyzes unknown words:

_____ _____   ● Using context clues?   Give student texts that can be read but have words missing. Are the missing words correctly predicted?

_____ _____   ● Using structural analysis?   Give student texts that have affixes. Are the words correctly identified?

_____ _____   ● Using phonics?   Give student nonsense words containing phonic elements that should be known at that level and embedded in text. Are the words correctly pronounced?

_____ _____   Generates new predictions?   Give student passages to read that are somewhat difficult and have student read them out loud. When student encounters difficulty, observe whether student looks back and starts over with a new prediction.

_____ _____   Constructs meaning using typographic cues:

_____ _____   ● Using roots and affixes?   Give student affixed words and have student explain how the meaning of the root word was changed.

_____ _____   ● Using key words?   Give student a grade level paragraph with relationships signaled by key words and ask student to talk about the relationships.

_____ _____   ● Using context?   Give student grade-level sentences within text that has one unknown word and ask student to predict what the unknown word means.

FIGURE 11.2 (continued)

___ ___		Analyzes text and text structure?	Give student samples of text and ask student to tell you what clues they offer for meaning.
___ ___		Matches author's purpose with reader's purpose?	Give student sample of text and ask student to identify author's purpose, student's own purpose, and how these relate to meaning getting.
	3.	Post-reading strategies	
___ ___		Constructs meaning by classifying?	Give student a list of grade level words drawn from a passage and have student classify them into categories and label them.
___ ___		Infers from gist?	Have student read a grade level text and ask questions that require inference from gist.
___ ___		Draws conclusions?	Have student read a grade level text and ask questions that require drawing conclusions.
___ ___		Makes judgments?	Have student read a grade level text and ask questions that require making judgments.
	III.	CONTENT GOALS	
	A.	FUNCTIONAL TEXT	
___ ___		Reads and understands expository text?	Give student samples of functional text and check understanding by having student summarize and/or answer questions about text content.
___ ___		Reads and understands specialized kinds of functional text (recipes, application forms, etc.)?	Same as above
	B.	RECREATIONAL TEXT	
___ ___		Reads and understands narrative text?	Give student samples of narrative text and check understanding by having student summarize and/or answer questions about text content.
___ ___		Reads and understands poems?	Same as above, but with poetry.
___ ___		Reads and understands specialized kinds of narratives (fantasy, folk literature, etc.)?	Same as above, but with a specialized narrative.

Ongoing Assessment Devices

Within the complex classroom community, you need to keep track of the multiple indicators of growth and the difficulties of individuals and groups of students. This assessment responsibility can be overwhelming. One way to deal with this complexity is to use three types of assessment devices: observations, conferences, and collections of performance results. Materials you will need to collect this material are provided in Figure 11.3.

Observations

You can assess your students as they think and perform in your classroom by observing them and noting where they are growing and how they are growing,

Conferences are a valuable assessment tool because they allow students to display their thinking.

FIGURE 11.3 Material Needed to Collect Assessment Data about Reading

I. Attitude goals
- A. Conference questions
- B. Check list for observing students
- C. Interest inventory and other forms students can discuss and complete

II. Content goals
- A. Functional text
  1. Various kinds of functional text appropriate for students' stage of developmental reading growth
  2. Questions designed to determine students' comprehension of the particular kind of text
- B. Recreational text
  1. Various kinds of recreational text appropriate for students' stage of developmental reading growth
  2. Questions designed to determine students' comprehension of the particular kind of text.

III. Process goals
- A. Routine skills
  1. Linguistic units
     - a. Work recognition
       - (1) List of high utility words
       - (2) Stories for oral reading
     - b. Vocabulary: list of words from the texts that may be unknown
  2. Language conventions
     - a. Sample of various types of text
     - b. Conference questions designed to get students to talk out loud about what they are doing
     - c. Observations of their use of language conventions
- B. Metacognitive strategies
  1. Sample stories for students to read
  2. Conference questions to use with these paragraphs to get students to talk out loud about what they do before reading, during reading, and after reading
  3. Materials for assessing specific strategies
     - a. Stories with sentences in which unidentified words are signaled by various context clues
     - b. Stories with sentences in which unidentified words are signaled by structural analysis
     - c. Stories with nonsense words containing phonic elements to be assessed
     - d. Stories with sentences and paragraphs that cause blockages and in which there are syntactic and semantic cues for removing the blockage
     - e. Stories with sentences and paragraphs containing explicit syntactic cues (typographic cues, structural units, and key words) and semantic clues (context)
     - f. Samples of various types of text
  4. Conference questions designed to get students to talk out loud about how they use their prior knowledge to get meaning, how they make sense of the content, and how they organize for remembering the content

as well as any difficulties they are having. This assessment device is useful because students are involved in ongoing literacy activities, so assessment is part of instruction. The guideline that students should participate in their own self assessment is difficult to accommodate during observations. Since students are fully engaged in the classroom activities, reflections on the activities should occur at a later time. During observations, it is important to note which students seem to be using strategies and routine skills as they gain content knowledge and which ones are not. It is also important to be aware of which students have positive responses about reading, which ones are showing an "I-can-do" attitude, and which ones are developing conceptual understandings appropriate for their developmental level. Growth in content knowledge should be noted, too. Likewise, you need to know which students are not showing growth. All this information becomes important when you have time to reflect and examine student growth, plan your next set of lessons, or prepare reports about student growth. Figure 11.4 shows one way to keep track of students through observation.

Observing individual student growth is important, but observing group growth is also important. You want to know which groups are working well and

---

FIGURE 11.4 Observation Form For Individual Students

Name _____

Date _____

Outcome for learning activity:

— to research, develop, and present self-selected information in a report on whales to class members.

Student performance:

— Max moved through the reading and writing process. He organized thoughts on paper, wrote rough drafts, revised, and wrote a final copy. His presentation on the body parts of whales was clear. He used visuals to illustrate how the "melon" amplifies sound. He used self-generated questions as a way to guide listener learning.

Attitude during learning:

— Max enjoys all aspects of the literacy cycle and feels confident about his abilities. He is very enthusiastic and has a positive attitude about learning. Max said reading is a lot of fun, and he likes it a lot because you get to learn new things. Max said reading makes him feel good!

Evidence of growth:

— During reading, Max used context clues to figure out unknown words. He has also developed a strong understanding of post-reading strategies of organizing. He created a semantic map (found in portfolio) to help him organize his information.

Needed areas of growth:

— Max needs to develop summarizing strategies. He sometimes has difficulty being a learner when the teacher is a peer.

why. You also want to know which groups aren't working well and why. The form shown in Figure 11.4 can be modified for group observations.

Conferences

Conferences are another way to explore the growth that individual students have made in a more concentrated way. Students have your individual attention. Students have opportunities through conversations often connected to performances to show you what they know and can do, that they are aware of how to think and perform, and that they understand how content skills and strategies are useful. They can also show you the breadth of their conceptual understandings as you carry on conversations with them.

Conferences are valuable because you gain information that you can't get anywhere else. During conversations, students often display their thinking. The complexities of the classroom usually work against opportunities to see students' line of reasoning on a regular basis. However, conferences provide that opportunity. The difficulty with conferences is that they take time and have to be carefully scheduled into the teaching day.

Conferences can also be used as opportunities for students to gradually take responsibility and, therefore, become responsible for their learning. Within their learning, they can begin to self assess. They can determine what they are learning, what they think they need next, and how they think they can best learn what is needed. Figure 11.5 illustrates a series of conversation starters that could be used during a reading conference.

FIGURE 11.5   Conference Conversation Starters

Attitude Outcomes
1. Think about your time reading in this classroom. Talk about what you like to do. Tell me why.

2. Think about reading. Tell me what you think reading is.

Content Outcomes
1. Think about reading for science or social studies class. Tell me how you prepare to read assignments in these classes. Tell me what you do after you finish reading.

2. Think about reading for fun. Talk about what you do before and after you read.

Process Outcomes
Think about a homework assignment. Talk about what you do before you start reading... while you are reading... after you read.

Collections of performance results

Students are constantly showing the results of their learning during the class-room day as they read, write, talk, and complete activities. These results may be noted from answers given during discussions around the themes and contents of shared books. They may be noted in discussions around newspaper articles and editorials. Your students can read aloud and then respond to what they understood from that reading. You need to record these efforts. Oral performance results can be taped, you or another adult can record the students' responses, or they can record their responses later in journal entries. Copies of written responses can be added to the portfolios.

Most of the guidelines are accommodated during this assessment device. Evidence of growth occurs as students live and operate within groups in the classroom. Students are active participants in their learning, with journal entries providing opportunities for self-assessment. If the learning tasks are authentic,

---

FIGURE 11.6   Reading Portfolio Assessment

Circle the number that best reflects student growth. Comments should be added in the space provided.

Developmental level _____   Name _____

	A lot Growth	Some Grth.	Little Growth	No Grth.

Attitude Outcomes
1. Accurate concepts of reading
2. Positive feelings toward reading

Content Outcomes
1. Reads and understands expository text
2. Reads and understands narratives

Process Outcomes
1. Uses routine skills when reading
2. Uses metacognitive strategies
   when reading

Overall Growth:

Areas of Strength:

Needed Growth Areas:

FIGURE 11.7   Sample Reporting Device

Student Literacy Report—Grade 2

Student name:_____   Teacher: <u>Danise Cantloan</u>

Units of study: Native American Indians (10–1–92 to 12–20–92), Settlers (1–6–92 to 2–14–92), England (2–17–92 to present)

Key: The lists in the boxes below indicate the dispositions, strategies, and world knowledge your child has worked on during the literacy cycle (reading, writing, listening, and speaking). Comments below elaborate.

COMMUNICATION GOALS	MARKING PERIOD I November 1991	MARKING PERIOD II March 1992	MARKING PERIOD III June 1992
Attitude	• Conceptual understanding about literacy • Feels good about self as a reader • Enthusiasm for learning • Self-motivated to learn • Positive attitude about literacy	• Conceptual understanding about literacy • Feels good about self as a reader • Enthusiasm for learning • Self-motivated to learn • Positive attitude about literacy	
Process	Writing strategies: • Prewrite (thinking, planning, organizing) • Draft (sense-making, writing) • Final copy (editing, revising) Reading strategies: • Pre-reading (predicting, using text, topic, and purpose) • During reading (sense-making, comprehending, word recognizing) • Post-reading (reflecting, evaluating)	Writing strategies • Prewrite (thinking, planning, organizing) • Draft (sense-making, writing) • Final copy (editing, revising) Reading strategies: • Pre-reading (predicting, using text, topic, and purpose) • During reading (sense-making, comprehending, word recognizing) • Post-reading (reflecting, evaluating)	
Content	Narrative text: • Poetry • Friendship story • Native American legend Expository text: • Research paper	Narrative text: • Legend • Poetry • Tall tale Expository: • Research paper • Explanation paper • Pen-pal letter	

FIGURE 11.7 (continued)

COMMENTS, February, 1992

Tico continues to have a positive attitude toward literacy and learning and shows growth in all four areas of literacy: reading, writing, speaking, and listening. He is a frequent contributor to our discussions. I think one of his frustrations is that he has so much to say and we don't get to all of his ideas. He listens well to others students' comments. Tico is a great teacher! He is self-motivated about learning new things. Tico is responsible for his own learning. He really enjoys researching an idea and presenting it to the class. He is very comfortable expressing his thoughts. Tico has a strong understanding about the relationship between reading and writing. He said you need to know how to read because "if you can read it, you can write it. Also, if you can't read, you can't write." He reads to help with homework and for fun. Tico enjoys reading before bedtime and at Book Time. He likes to read encyclopedias and magazines he gets through the mail.

Before reading a story, Tico makes predictions by looking at the book cover. He said "predictions change as you read more of the story." During reading, when he comes across an unknown word, he "tries to sound it out, look it up in the dictionary, use context clues, or look at the prefix/suffix." He said, "Figuring out unknown words is like a prediction, because you are not quite sure until you read another sentence." Tico's post-reading strategies include thinking back on the book. He said he writes things down that he learned at home. He often thinks about reading another book by the same author if he enjoyed the first book. Tico also mentioned one of the most important things about reading is that, "It is nice to know what happened when you're done."

Tico has written a variety of genres. He's participated in the writing process with Native American legends, explanation papers, tall tales, research papers, poetry, and pen-pal letters. He enjoys writing and often writes during his free time. He takes his time when composing and is very reflective. Tico's writing is often succinct, but always makes sense. He uses his daily journal to record thoughts, write stories, or provide directions on how to play a game. He was very creative in his Inventions Book, which is what we have learned about in science. In his Literature Log, "A Lion to Guard Us," Tico expressed his ideas, feelings, and thoughts well.

---

then the records of performance results will be reflections of authenticity. This type of assessment device is closely connected to instruction, includes a variety of measures, and fits easily into the portfolio structures.

To make decisions about where a student is in moving toward literacy, you use knowledge about the goals of reading and knowledge about what constitutes reasonable progress for the student's age. You can modify the check list shown in Figure 11.2 to fit each level and then use it as an initial tool in deciding where an individual student is. For each student check *yes* or *no* in the left-hand column for evidence of understanding at a particular level, making the necessary decision on the basis of data-collection techniques such as those listed in the right-hand column. If you check *yes* at a particular level, a student can be said to have understandings for that outcome at that level.

Periodic Portfolio Growth Conferences

As a classroom teacher, you need not only collect evidence of learning, you also need to periodically assess individual student growth. Portfolio growth

---

FIGURE 11.8   Semester Report (From Your Child's Perspective)

Dear __Mom and Dad__

I want to let you know how I am doing at school. Some things I enjoy doing at school are learning about how other kids think. Because other kids have good ideas, too. It's nice to listen to other people's ideas.

Some things I feel like I'm getting better at in school are __learning to read better and faster.__

I need to practice __listening at group. My friends and I distract each other.__

I am having a hard time with __nothing. I like everything.__

The best thing about school for me is __just what we're supposed to be.__

One thing I would like to change is __more time to eat. Lunch is too short.__

Love, __Tico__

- - - - - - - - - - - - - - - - - - - -

(Please detach and return to school.)

Parent's comments: *We are so pleased that Tico is excelling at school. He looks forward to sharing what he's learned and is very pleased at the "end results" (journals, etc.) that he can bring home.*

What evidence of learning are you seeing at home? *Tico is very content and self-confident with the new things he's learning. He likes to share what he knows with us and likes to "teach" us, too. He enjoys trying to teach his brother, too (if he's in the mood to listen).*

What information does your child share with you about our studies? *He talks about the settlers—what they used to do and how they lived. He was very excited about the "peace" quilt and could hardly wait to design and make it.*

What information would be helpful for the teacher to share with you about your child? *We very much look forward to and learn from the "Let's Communicate" folder that goes back and forth between us. The updates from Ms. Cantlon are always informative and helpful.*

Parent's signature

---

conferences can serve this purpose. The procedures for ongoing conferences described earlier in the chapter are again useful. Remember, collaborative assessment strengthens the bond between students and teachers. Figure 11.5 can be used to help structure a portfolio growth conference. The major divisions are attitude, content, and process outcomes. Specific questions will vary according to a student's age and level. Since you also need to know what and how groups of students are learning in your classroom, you need a way to summarize portfolio data. Such a summary will be helpful during unit planning and for reporting to parents and community members. The format in Figure 11.6 can be modified to meet this need.

REPORTING INDIVIDUAL GROWTH

It is important for parents, administrators, and community members to understand your approach to assessment and the areas in which your students are growing. The reporting devices that you use and the content you put in those devices will convey both these messages. Figure 11.7 shows the reporting device of literacy growth for one second grade teacher. It can be modified to fit any grade level.

At the top, the specific units of study and the dates of the unit are listed. The remainder of the report lists specific growth areas for each student for each marking period. The noted specific areas of growth are accompanied by a narrative that elaborates on each child's growth. The first paragraph describes attitude growth, the second paragraph describes process growth, and the third paragraphs describes content growth.

In efforts to report growth of students, it is important that they are aware of their own growth. They need to make self assessments. This process helps them to become aware of their specific growth. Figure 11.8 shows on type of self assessment for second graders. The students reflect on their growth for the semester and respond to specific questions that were posed by the teacher. The report is taken home and read by parents or other caretakers. The parents or caretakers respond to specific questions which are then returned to the teacher. The end result is an interactive communication system about the growth of children that involves the children, the caretakers, and the teachers.

SUMMARY

Assessing students during classroom interactions is a crucial component of effective reading instruction. Guidelines for this type of assessment provide help when creating portfolios, one way to store and keep track of student strengths and growth. Portfolios then provide specific data for reporting to parents, administrators, and community members.

SUGGESTED ADDITIONAL READING

AU, K., SCHEU, J., KAWAKAMI, A., & HERMAN, P. (1990). Assessment and accountability in a whole literacy curriculum. *Reading Teacher, 43*(3), 574–578.

BAUMANN, J. F., & STEVENSON, J. A. (1982). Understanding standardized reading achievement test scores. *Reading Teacher, 35*(6), 648–654.

BAUMANN, J. F., & STEVENSON, J. A. (1982). Using scores from standardized reading achievement test. *Reading Teacher, 35*(5), 528–532.

BLACK, J. K. (1980). Those "mistakes" tell us a lot. *Language Arts, 57*(5), 508–513.

BRECHT, R. D. (1977). Testing format and instructional level with the informal reading inventory. *Reading Teacher, 31*(1), 57–59.

BRISTOW, P. S., PIKULSKI, J. J., & PELOSI, P. L. (1983). A comparison of five estimates of reading instructional level. *Reading Teacher, 37*(3), 273–280.

CALDWELL, J. (1985). A new look at the old informal reading inventory. *Reading Teacher, 39,* 168–173.

CAMBOURNE, B., & TURBILL, J. (1990). Assessment in whole language classrooms: Theory into practice. *Elementary School Journal, 90*(3), 338–349.

CARNEY, J., & CIOFFI, G. (1990). Extending traditional diagnosis: The dynamic assessment of reading abilities. *Reading Psychology, 11*(3), 177–192.

DAVEY, B. (1989). Assessing comprehension: Selected interactions of task and reader. *Reading Teacher, 42*(9), 694–697.

FLOOD, J. & LAPP, D. (1989). Reporting reading progress: A comparison portfolio for parents. *Reading Teacher, 42*(7), 508–514.

HU-PEI AU, K. (1977). Analyzing oral reading error to improve instruction. *Reading Teacher* 38, 168–173.

JETT-SIMPSON, M. (1990). *Toward an ecological assessment of reading progress.* Newark, DE: International Reading Association.

JOHNSON, M. S., & KRESS, R. A. (1965). *Informal reading inventories.* Newark, DE: International Reading Association.

JOHNSTON, P. (1992). *Constructive evaluation of literacy activity.* New York: Longman.

JONGSMA, K. (1991). Rethinking grading practices. *Reading Teacher, 45*(4), 318–319.

LANG, J. B. (1976). Self-concept and reading achievement: An annotated bibliography. *Reading Teacher, 29*(8), 787–793.

MARSHALL, N. (1983). Using story grammar to assess reading comprehension. *Reading Teacher, 36*(7), 616–620.

MCKENNA, M. C. (1983). Informal reading inventories: A review of the issues. *Reading Teacher, 36*(7), 670–679.

MURPHY, S. & SMITH, M. (1991). *Writing Portfolios.* Markhem, Ontario: Pippin.

OLSON, M. (1991). Portfolios: Education tools. *Reading Psychology, 12*(1), 73–80.

OMOTOSO, S. O.,& LAMME, L. L. (1979). Using wordless picture books to assess cross-cultural differences in seven-year-olds. *Reading Teacher, 32*(4), 414–419.

PFLAUM, S. W. (1979). Diagnosis of oral reading. *Reading Teacher, 33*(3), 279–284.

PIKULSKI, J. (1989). The assessment of reading: A time for change? *Reading Teacher, 43*(1), 80–81.

RODERICK, J. (1991). *Context-responsive approaches to assessing children's language.* Urbana, IL: National Conference on Research in English.

ROSER, N., & HOLMES, B. (1987). Five ways to assess readers' prior knowledge. *Reading Teacher, 40,* 646–649.

SCHELL, L. (1988). Dilemmas in assessing reading comprehension. *Reading Teacher, 42*(1), 12–16.

SCHMITT, M. (1990). A questionnaire to measure children's awareness of strategic reading processes. *Reading Teacher, 43*(7), 454–461.

TEALE, W. (1988). Developmentally appropriate assessment of reading and writing on the early childhood classroom. *Elementary School Journal, 89*(2), 174–183.

TIERNEY, R., CARTER, M., & DESAI, L. (1991). *Portfolio assessment in the reading-writing classroom.* Norwood, MA: Christopher-Gorden.

VALENCIA, S. (1990). Alternative assessment: Separating the wheat from the chaff. *Reading Teacher, 44*(1), 60–61.

VALENCIA, S. . (1990). A portfolio approach to classroom reading assessment: The whys, whats, and hows. *Reading Teacher, 43*(4), 338–340.

VALENCIA, S., & PEARSON, P. D.   (1987) Reading Assessment: Time for a change. *Reading Teacher, 40*, 726–733.

WADE, S.   (1990). Using think aloud to assess comprehension. *Reading Teacher, 43*(7), 442–451.

WINOGRAD, P., PARIS, S., & BRIDGE, C.   (1991). Improving the assessment of literacy. *Reading Teacher, 45*(2), 108–117.

WIXSON, K. K., ET AL.   (1984). An interview for assessing students' perceptions of classroom reading tasks. *Reading Teacher, 37*(4), 346–352.

WOOD, K.   (1988). Techniques for assessing students' potential for learning. *Reading Teacher, 41*, 440-447.

WULZ, S. V.   (1979). Comprehension testing: Functions and procedures. *Reading Teacher, 33*(3), 295–299.

THE RESEARCH BASE

CALFEE, R., & HIEBERT, E.   (1991). Classroom assessment of reading. In R. Barr, M. Kamil, P. Mosenthal, & P. D. Pearson (Eds.), *Handbook of reading research, volume II.* (pp. 281–309). New York: Longman.

COLE, N.   (1990). Conceptions of educational achievement. *Educational Researcher, 19*(3), 2–7.

CROOKS, T.   (1988). The impact of classroom evaluation practices on students. *Review of Educational Research, 58*(4), 438–481.

FARR, R.   (1969). *Reading: What can be measured?* Newark, DE: International Reading Association.

HIEBERT, E., & CALFEE, R.   (1992). Assessing literacy: From standardized tests to portfolios and performances. In J. Samuels & A. Farstrup (Eds.), *What research has to say about reading instruction*, 2nd ed. (pp. 70–100). Newark, DE: International Reading Association.

HOGE, R., & COLADARCI, T.   (1989). Teacher-based judgments of academic achievement: A review of literature. *Review of Educational Research, 59*(3), 297–314.

JOHNSTON, P.   (1983). *Reading comprehension assessment: A cognitive basis.* Newark, DE: International Reading Association.

JOHNSTON, P.   (1984). Assessment in reading. In P. D. Pearson (Ed.), *Handbook of reading research* (pp. 147–184). New York: Longman.

MILLER, S., & YOAKUM, N.   (1991). Asking students about the nature of their reading difficulties. *Journal of Reading Behavior, 23*(4), 465–486.

NICKERSON, R.   (1989). New directions for educational assessment. *Educational Researcher, 18*(9), 3–7.

OLSON, M., YOCHUM, N., & MILLER, S.   (1990). Classroom reading assessment: Using students' perceptions. *Reading Psychology, 11*(2), 159–165.

WIXSON, K., & LIPSON, M.   (1986). Reading (dis)ability: An interaction and perspective. In T. Raphael (Ed.), *Contexts of school-based literacy* (pp. 131–148). New York: Random House.

ACTIVITIES FOR REFLECTING, OBSERVING, AND TEACHING

Reflecting on Student Assessment

PURPOSE: The important component for this chapter is the creation of assessment procedures that are embedded into ongoing classroom activities. This requires a way to keep track of students' learning and growth. These activities are designed to help you do this.

Task One

DIRECTIONS: Develop a portfolio for a given student at a selected developmental stage. The example in Figure 11.2 can be used as a beginning model. For each of the three outcomes and their two subgoals, select appropriate student learning measures.

Task Two

DIRECTIONS: Modify your portfolio assessment for one student to an assessment of learning for a group of students.

Watching Others Assess Student Learning

PURPOSE: You can gain a lot of information by watching teachers assess during instructional activities and talking with them afterwards about your observations. This activity is designed to help you do this.

DIRECTIONS: Arrange to watch an elementary teacher teach reading. Before observing, review the growth measures provided in this chapter. During the observation, note whether the teacher keeps a written record of student growth. Ask if you can see the written record and use it as a basis for talking about student learning. If no written records are kept, invite the teacher to talk with you about the learning of individual students and groups of students that occurred. Talk about your feelings and ideas as you converse with the teacher.

Trying it Yourself: Assessing Student Learning

PURPOSE: Learning how to assess learning is difficult to do if you never have an opportunity to try it yourself. Arrange an opportunity to assess a student's or group of students' learning.

DIRECTIONS: In planning this activity, decide whether to assess one student or several students' learning. Then think about the outcome(s) you want to assess. Talk to the teacher about strengths, needed areas of growth, and interests of the student(s) selected for assessment. Using that information and the suggestions in this chapter, plan an assessment activity. After the assessment has occurred, write a brief report about the learning levels of the student(s). Discuss this report with the classroom teacher.

Grouping: Whole, Collaborative, and Reading Level

12

GETTING READY

One of the things that makes reading difficult to teach is the fact that students in one class can represent several levels of developmental reading growth, background experiences, cultures, motivation, and interests. To deal with individual differences, reading groups are sometimes formed so that students with similar needs are taught together. In this chapter we recommend three types of groups and describe them.

FOCUS QUESTIONS

- Why are reading groups desirable?

- What characteristics distinguish whole groups?

- What characteristics distinguish collaborative groups?

- What characteristics distinguish reading level groups?

- How do you decide what students to assign to a collaborative group?

- How do you decide what students to assign to a reading level group?

PURPOSE OF READING GROUPS

Some reading instruction occurs in large group settings. However, small reading groups are found in virtually all elementary classrooms because students vary so much in their reading levels. In a third grade class with 24 students, for instance, reading levels will normally range from beginning reading (about first grade) to upper grade reading (about sixth grade). If you try to teach all 24 children in one large group, advanced readers will get bored and lose interest, while low-aptitude readers will get frustrated and lose interest. When students are grouped by level, however, each group receives instruction at an appropriate level.

KINDS OF READING GROUPS

Many classrooms have only one kind of reading group—the traditional basal textbook ability group formed on the basis of reading level. There is a serious weakness in this practice. While basal textbooks are helpful in developing process and content goals, they are less helpful in developing attitude goals. Hence, when you have only reading level groups, the instructional emphasis tends to be on the former, to the neglect of the latter.

This problem can be eased by thinking in terms of three kinds of groups. Just as a literate classroom environment must have a variety of activities reflecting the three goals of reading instruction, grouping patterns must match various goals. We suggest three kinds of grouping practices—**whole group, collaborative**, and **reading level**—with the teacher making the decision as to when each grouping pattern will be used and what specific goal is to be achieved.

Whole groups are just what the name says—all the students are taught in a single group. There are two major advantages in doing whole group instruction: first, it cuts down on the teacher's work load because one need only prepare for one lesson rather than preparing lessons for each of several small groups and, second, it builds a sense of community in the classroom. The second reason is by far the most important reason for doing whole-group instruction. A major disadvantage of any kind of grouping is that it sets students apart from each other and creates artificial barriers and, on some occasions, sets up a kind of elitism which is destructive to good learning. For instance, when ability groups are used, the students in the top group often feel elite, while the students in the low group feel dumb. Whole group instruction, in contrast, creates quite a different feeling—a feeling that we are all part of a community striving to achieve certain goals together. The expectation is that the low-level readers will do many of the same tasks as the high-ability students—and because that expectation is set, students tend to achieve at that level. The result is often better achievement for all students.

This is not to imply that you would necessarily use whole-group instruction all the time. In fact, most teachers choose to use whole-group instruction some of the time and choose to use collaborative or reading level groups at other times. The important thing is for the teacher to think carefully about the instructional goal and then to choose a form of grouping which will promote acquisition of that goal. For instance, a teacher will choose to use whole-group instruction when the goal is to develop a sense of esprit and togetherness in the class. Consequently, teachers begin most unit activities with whole group instruction, which gets all the students involved in the topic or theme to be pursued and ensures that they will all have a stake in accomplishing the unit goal. Similarly, teachers tend to use whole-group instruction to build positive feelings about reading and writing and to teach lessons designed to build important concepts about reading and writing. For instance, a teacher may use whole-group instruction to teach a lesson on what it means to be generally strategic when beginning to read a text, but would then use a collaborative group when students were actually using a text to get specific information and would organize the class into reading level groups to help students who were having difficulties using specific kinds of strategies.

Collaborative groups are temporary groups. They are heterogeneous in that three to four children of varying abilities work together on a particular project. For purposes of reading instruction, collaborative group projects are usually directed toward attitude goals. For instance, you may form temporary collaborative groups to create language experience stories; to read and discuss certain kinds of books; to discuss themes and issues relating to outside reading; to organize and prepare presentations to the rest of the class or to other classes; to produce various kinds of text, such as poetry, drama, letters to the editor, and essays; to follow written directions, such as recipes; and to engage in a variety of other activities that result in positive responses and conceptual understanding of reading. The group members normally divide up the work according to their particular strengths. Seldom do all the group members perform the same functions or do the same reading. Such grouping is sometimes called **cooperative grouping** because all group members contribute to the completion of the activity.

Reading level groups, in contrast, are homogenous groups in which four to eight students are grouped together because they are all working at the same reading level. Consequently, you can give them all the same written material in the expectation that all will be able to read it and perform the required tasks. In contrast to collaborative groups in which each participant contributes to a group goal by performing a different task, reading level groups require each member of the group to perform the same tasks to ensure that everyone achieves certain goals. For instance, you may teach how stories are structured to a reading level group, so all your students in that group can use this as a strategy to predict meaning; or you may demonstrate a study guide to the same group, which will help them locate and comprehend salient information in a selection they will read together.

All three groups are important. Whole and collaborative groups provide opportunities for students to develop the attitude goals of reading, while reading level groups permit teachers to show how reading works and how to understand the messages in texts. The greatest benefit of using all three kinds of groups may lie with the potential for neutralizing negative expectations. One of the persistent problems in grouping only by reading level is that negative expectations are communicated to students in the low group. Low-group students are publicly labeled dummies. No matter what you say to soften this label, the fact remains that the students are in the lowest reading group and everyone knows it. These negative expectations are neutralized somewhat if whole groups and collaborative groups also exist. In collaborative groups each student is a worthwhile contributor to a heterogeneous group, and consequently, morale and perseverance are maintained.

INFORMATION NEEDED TO FORM READING GROUPS

Having various kinds of reading groups means that you must decide how to assign students to each kind of group. The following section describes the information needed to make such decisions. What you learned in Chapter 11 about assessment is also relevant here.

Collecting Information to Form Whole Groups

As noted in the following sections, teachers must collect information about students in order to assign them to collaborative or reading level groups. For instance, to ensure smoothly functioning collaborative groups, it is wise to collect information about which students work best together; to ensure effective reading

Collaborative groups help to develop attitude goals.

level groups, it is wise to collect information which allows you to be precise in grouping together students with like strengths and needs.

Whole-group instruction does not require the same kind of student information collection. The whole class is to be the group, so there is no need to focus on specific individuals for the specific task. Information already known about individuals is normally used as decisions are made.

However, that does not mean that teachers do not collect information before initiating whole-group instruction. To the contrary, while teachers do not collect new information about individual students, they do collect information about the overall morale of the group. For instance, when teachers detect a sense of discrimination between high reading level students and low reading level students or when low reading level students begin feeling like they are dumb, it is time for the teacher to do more whole-group instruction, which is designed to bring all the students together in pursuit of a common goal. Similarly, when the feeling in the class is not one of "family" and "community" spirit, it may be time for the teacher to plan a whole group activity which will bring students together.

In sum, while whole-group instruction may not call for information collection about individuals, it nevertheless demands that teachers collect information. In this case, however, the information focuses on the spirit of the group as a whole. And the teacher's decision revolves around how to create in the class the communal spirit and high expectations which promote good learning.

Collecting Information to Form Collaborative Groups

A collaborative group must work together to accomplish a goal using student differences. This means that you must avoid assigned existing cliques of children to the same collaborative groups simply because they know how to get a job done. To form collaborative groups, you collect information about students' interests, about their ability to get along with others, and about the current social relationships in the classroom. There are several ways to do this.

The most useful is daily observation. Much can be learned about your students simply by watching what they do and say in a variety of situations. Whom do they talk to? Who talks to them? Who are the leaders and who are the followers? Who is being picked on? What interests, strengths, and needs do various children display?

Another useful technique is to use a questionnaire to solicit your students' interests and attitudes. You can administer it in interview form in kindergarten and the primary grades and in its written form with more mature students. Such questionnaires should be simple and easy to complete. For instance, sentence completion tasks such as the following are useful:

My idea of a good time is _____

The smartest person in the class is _____

I like _____ because _____

_____

Another simple technique is to give your students a list of statements and ask them whether these are true or false about themselves:

I think most of the kids in school like me.

I get nervous when I have to talk in front of the class.

Another useful technique is to talk to each student. You can engage a student in conversation while supervising recess or while waiting to go to lunch. Such conversations, because they are so informal and nonthreatening, can yield valuable information.

A sociogram is often a useful indicator of the social relationships in the classroom. A sociogram is administered by asking students to list the three children in the class that they would most and least want to be with in a group. As shown in Figure 12.1, the results can be plotted to graphically display who the popular children are, who the isolates are, and where the cliques exist. You can use such information when forming collaborative groups to help decide where to place the isolates, whether to split up a clique, and how to separate class leaders. Sociogram data are useful in making a variety of grouping decisions.

There is no totally systematic way to form collaborative groups. However, because group composition changes from activity to activity, it is a decision that you must make frequently. Your decisions will be better if you base them on information you have gathered about your students, their preferences, their own perceptions about themselves, and the way other students view them.

Collecting Information to Form Reading Level Groups

Since ability groups are composed of students with similar reading levels, you collect information about student ability. The question is, "What reading level?"

Traditionally, teachers have assessed reading levels by asking students to read aloud progressively more difficult paragraphs and to respond to a series of questions about the content of those paragraphs. To determine if a student has a third grade reading level, for instance, the teacher would make an oral reading assignment from a third grade book and then ask questions about the paragraph's content. If the student is 99 percent fluent in identifying words in the text and 90 percent accurate in answering questions about the passage, that level of text is considered to be the student's **independent reading level;** that is, the child can read material from that level without assistance from the teacher or another adult. If the student reads with 95 to 99 percent word recognition and 75 to 90 percent accuracy in comprehension, that level of text is considered the student's **instructional reading level;** that is, material from that level can be read by the student with some assistance from the teacher. If the student

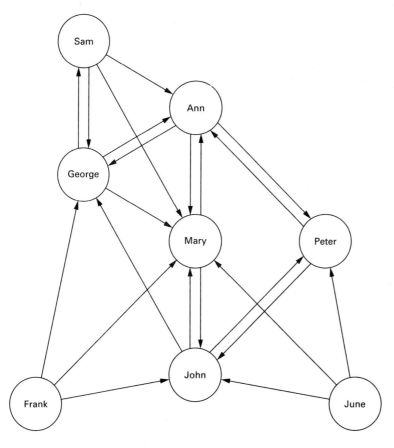

Class leader: Mary
Clique: Mary, John, Peter, and Ann
Isolates: Frank and June

FIGURE 12.1 Sample Results of a Sociogram

reads the material with less than 95 percent fluency in word recognition or less than 75 percent accuracy in comprehension, the material is considered to be the student's **frustration reading level;** that is, such material is too difficult for the child to read under any circumstances.

It is important to keep students' motivation in mind when placing them in reading groups. If you place students in groups in which the reading tasks are at their frustration reading level, they will be unmotivated and they will not persevere in the task of learning to read. Similarly, if you place them in groups in which the reading tasks are at their independent reading level, they will not learn new things because they know everything at that level. If, however, you place them at their instructional reading levels, they benefit from an appropriate blend of new information and challenge.

While it is comforting to have such quantitative guidelines for determining reading levels, current knowledge about how reading works suggests that using this technique alone may not be completely adequate. A student's reading level is not entirely revealed by number of words identified and the number of the questions answered in a sample of graded text. Whether students can read a passage or not depends first on their prior knowledge—on whether they have a schematic structure for the topic being discussed. In other words, an individual's reading level in a particular text depends on the topic being discussed. A selection on one topic from a typical third grade book may be easy for one student because of familiarity with that topic, while another student in the same reading group may find it quite difficult due to lack of background about the topic. In addition, factors such as syntax and special vocabulary can affect text difficulty. Consequently, if the practice of establishing independent, instructional, and frustration reading levels implies a single, static reading level for each child, it is misleading.

In view of the above, how do you assign students to the "proper" text in a basal series when each level consists of a variety of selections, some of which may reflect a student's background experience and some of which may not? This is a classic example of a teaching dilemma. As with all dilemmas, there is no single right answer; instead, you must use available information to make the best decisions possible and, when additional information becomes available, remain flexible enough to modify your decision.

A good practice when beginning the school year is to listen to each student read passages selected at random from various levels of a basal text series as previously described. If you are teaching third grade, for instance, ask your students to read samples of basal text from the first, second, third, and fourth level books. As students read, note any breaks in fluency: Note any places where the student's intonation pattern does not match the meaning of the text; where words are miscalled or omitted, where words are inserted or substituted; where words are repeated or identified incorrectly and then corrected; where noticeable hesitations are made before words; where the pattern does not match the meaning of the text; where punctuation is ignored; and where any other indications of nonfluent reading occur. You should note particularly breaks in fluency that alter the meaning of the text and remain uncorrected by the student, because such breaks suggest that the student is not self-monitoring the meaning-getting process. After oral reading is completed, assess comprehension by having the student first retell or summarize what the selection is about. If important meaning relationships are omitted, probe with questions designed to assess the student's comprehension of that particular relationship. After the student reads successively more difficult passages, examine the student's performance pattern across the various passages. Using the criteria for independent, instructional, and frustration levels as a guide (but not as an iron-clad rule), ask and answer questions such as the following.

- What passages did the student read with no apparent difficulty?

- In what passage did the student first begin to show some frustration?

- At what point did the reading become clearly frustrating for the student?

- On the basis of the student's reading performance across these paragraphs, what basal text seems to be comfortable—not too frustrating and not too easy?

It is sometimes difficult to decide on initial student placements in a basal text despite having listened to each student read. In such cases, check other data sources. The previous year's teacher can tell you what level text the student was in before, and you can look in the student's cumulative record folder for recommendations from other teachers and for the results of other tests.

If placement is still difficult, it is best to follow the rule, "When in doubt, go low." If you cannot decide between placement in a second or third level book, it is probably best to begin with the second level book. By doing so, you protect students' self-concepts. If you start high and later on move students to a lower group, they are bound to feel discouraged, and it can cast a pall on their motivation for the rest of the year. If you begin by making the lower of the two placements and later assign students to the higher level, they will be encouraged and motivated.

The assessment task is not over when you assign students to groups, however. As noted before, reading level is not static, and you must continue to collect and act upon fresh information. Because the level of difficulty in a basal text selection depends partly on a student's background experience regarding the topic, you must make adjustments for individual students despite the fact that all the students are supposedly at a particular reading level. A selection on sheepherding in the Rocky Mountains will be easier for students who have some prior knowledge about sheep, sheepherding, or the Rocky Mountains. In this sense, the students in a group are never reading at the same reading level. Consequently, you must continually monitor students' prior knowledge to ensure a match between student and text.

MONITORING STUDENT PROGRESS IN GROUPS

Although students are assigned to a reading level group, they do not necessarily stay in it all year. Depending on their progress, individual students may be moved to a higher or a lower level. To make decisions about when to move a student to another group, you should regularly collect information about his or her progress in the three major goals of reading instruction.

Collecting Data about Attitude Goals

To monitor your students' conceptual understanding of reading, conduct interviews, and ask questions such as, "What is reading? Why do people read? What is the purpose of reading?" and "Where did the writing on the page come from?"

Observe how your students use reading: Do they read to solve problems or for pleasure? Do they treat reading as a communication process? Do they understand the relationship between reading and the other language modes, particularly writing? Then compare the information you obtain from these observations and interviews to the typical curricula found at the various stages of developmental reading growth to determine which concepts must yet be developed (use the examples in Chapter 5 to help you).

Use similar techniques to monitor your students' responses to reading. In interviews ask your students what feelings they experience when reading, what they appreciate about reading, how often they read, what their favorite book is and why, and so on. Observe whether your students choose to read during leisure time, whether they respond emotionally to what is read, whether they seem to value what has been read, and so on. Again, compare the information you obtain to the attitude goals listed in Chapter 5 for the various stages of developmental reading growth. By comparing your data about your students' attitudes with the expectations for each stage of growth, you can determine which feelings and concepts must yet be developed.

Collecting Data about Process Goals

Process goals are divided into routine skills and metacognitive strategies.

Collecting Information on Routine Skills   Routine skills focus on the language conventions and linguistic units that are used identically on every occasion. As such, routine skills are automatic responses requiring little conscious reasoning. Good examples are moving across the page in a left-to-right progression (a language convention) and word knowledge (a linguistic unit).

To assess language conventions such as left-to-right progression, observe your students' eye movements as they read. While no reader, no matter how expert, moves his or her eye steadily across a page without any regression at all, good readers do process text in a left-to-right progression. You can assess student use of this convention by watching eye movements or, in the case of very young readers, the movement of the finger being used to keep their place in the text. If the movement is in a generally consistent left-to-right order, students can be said to be employing this language convention.

The task of assessing linguistic units is more complex because there are more things to consider. For instance, in the case of words, you need to determine two things. First, you need to know what printed words can be identified, since individual words must be recognized in order to predict meaning. This can be determined by having students read a sample of text at the appropriate reading level and noting all the words that are not recognized, are miscalled, or cause the student to break the fluency of reading. Another technique is to use a graded list of words. Put each word on a card and flash these to the student one at a time. Those the student identifies instantly are sight words; those that cause hesitation or cannot be identified must be learned. For a student who is at the emerging

To make decisions about when to change a student's reading group, teachers routinely collect data about the student's progress.

literacy level, the same technique can be used to determine how many alphabet letters are known (since, at the emerging literacy level, the students have not yet learned many words).

The second thing you need to find out about students' word knowledge is their understanding of the meaning of words encountered in text. To gather this information, first pronounce the word and then ask the student to use the word aloud in a sentence. If the word is correctly used, the student knows the meaning of the word in that context. By identifying what words the student does not know (that is, words that are not recognized in print or for which the student has no meaning), you know which words to teach for sight recognition and which to teach for meaning.

Collecting Information on Metacognitive Strategies   What you are looking for in assessing metacognitive strategies is students' reasoning about how they get meaning as they begin to read, what they do during reading when something goes wrong, and how they reflect on what they read after reading. While your students will not talk about processes like you do, their self-reports reveal whether they have an understanding of how to use knowledge about how the reading system works. For instance, you can ask students as they begin to read, "What are you thinking right now? What is it you are trying to do?" Also, after reading, when students are trying to draw conclusions or to determine the theme, you can ask, "How are you trying to figure this out? What are you thinking in order to figure this out?" Students' self-reports about their thinking provide the window into the mind that allows you to decide whether or not students are metacognitive about the strategies they employ.

To illustrate more fully, consider how you can assess your students' use of fix-it strategies during reading. When a reader's predictions about text meaning are confirmed, the text processing continues smoothly. However, when the predictions are not confirmed, the reader stops and says, "Oh, oh, this doesn't make sense" or "Oh, oh, something's wrong here." At this point, the reader must become strategic. That is, the source of the difficulty must be located and an appropriate strategy applied to fix the blockage so that text processing can proceed. To monitor whether students use fix-it strategies, you can listen to their oral reading. When a blockage is encountered, ask students to talk out loud about fixing the blockage. In the course of this assessment, you are trying to answer four questions:

1. Does the reader recognize when a blockage to meaning occurs and stop to figure out what is wrong?

2. Once recognized, can the reader determine the source of the difficulty?

3. Can the reader identify the source of difficulty as one that can be fixed by reference to what is right there on the page? through search and think? or on his or her own?

4. Once the source of the difficulty has been located, can the reader apply an appropriate fix-it strategy? For instance, if the source of difficulty is a word unrecognized in print, can the reader retrieve a context strategy, a structural analysis strategy, or a phonics strategy to analyze and identify the word? Such assessment helps you determine the reader's ability to monitor his or her reading performance and to retrieve and apply fix-it strategies as needed. As a result, you can decide whether you need to emphasize strategies and, if so, which ones.

If enough text is read, students will eventually encounter a variety of blockages which, in turn, will allow you to observe their repertoire of fix-it strategies. However, this is a time-consuming procedure and, for assessment purposes, it is sometimes more efficient to assess strategy usage in more isolated tasks.

For instance, if you want to determine whether your students have strategies for decoding words not recognized in print, you can build brief assessments that check each of the three ways (context clues, structural analysis, and phonics) of analyzing unknown words. To determine whether your students can analyze using context clues, give them sentences with missing words and ask them to predict the missing word; to determine whether they can analyze using structural analysis, give them unrecognized words that can be identified through known prefixes and suffixes; to determine whether they can analyze using phonics, give them nonsense words containing known phonic elements and ask them to pronounce them. In each case, you should have the students talk out loud about their analysis so you can determine whether or not a strategy is being appropriately applied.

You can also build informal assessments to determine whether students are metacognitive about comprehension. For instance, you can create examples that are similar to the passage about *rotation* in Chapter 3, in which you deliberately cause a certain prediction to be made initially, knowing that students will change it as they read further. Ask students to read a text orally, noting whether they look back when the blockage is encountered. Since you have intentionally included syntactic and semantic cues that can be reexamined during the look back, ask students to explain what cues are being used and how the predictions are being made. This technique gives you another check on students' overall awareness of their need to monitor meaning getting and gives you insight into their use of syntactic and semantic cues.

You can also create informal devices to assess students' ability to get and to go beyond the author's meaning. For instance, you can ask a student to read a sentence such as the following one:

> After the dance, I was unable to smile because Mary, who *was* my friend, played a despicable trick on me.

A variety of strategies are useful for getting the author's meaning in this sentence. Readers can use the comma after *dance* and commas setting off the phrase "who *was* my friend," as well as the italicized *was* to figure out what the sentence means. The meaning of the verb *unable* can be figured out from its root and prefix; and the words *after* and *because* are key words, the former because it signals a chronological relationship and the latter because it signals a cause-effect relationship. The meaning of *despicable* can be figured out using other words in the sentence. By asking students to explain how they get meaning from sentences such as this, you can assess their use of various kinds of strategies. Similarly, you can provide samples of various kinds of text and have students talk out loud about how they used their experience to get the author's meaning. For instance, a paragraph such as the following might be used:

> The camel and his driver were stumbling across the desert. They had not seen an oasis for days. The sun was low on the horizon on the fourteenth day when the driver croaked, "I see one." But he really didn't. It was just a mirage.

After this is read, ask a classification question such as: "Into what category would you put the words *camel, desert, oasis,* and *mirage?*" A question designed to elicit inference from gist might be: "Why did the driver want to find an oasis?" A question designed to elicit inference based on relationships might be: "At what time of day did the driver think he saw an oasis?" A post-reading question requiring the drawing of a conclusion might be: "What caused the driver to think he saw an oasis?" Finally, to determine the ability to make judgments, you might ask: "What do you think the driver could have done to prevent this situation from happening?"

To find out whether students can go beyond the author's meaning, you must ask questions that require them to create meaning beyond what the author intended to communicate. For instance, for the sentence about the dance you might ask students how people ought to respond when friends play tricks on them, and for the paragraph about traveling in the desert you might ask students whether mirages are real or imagined or to judge whether a word such as *stumbling* is an accurate descriptor for what camels are likely to do. By listening to students' answers to these questions and to their explanations of how they figured out the answers, you can assess whether they possess strategies for going beyond an author's meaning.

Collecting Information about Content Goals

To assess your students' ability to understand various kinds of text, you need to listen to them read functional and recreational text appropriate for their developmental level. In third grade, for instance, you might listen to students read expository materials such as social studies texts, directions for games, sections of the newspaper, and simple encyclopedia entries, and you might listen to them read narrative text such as children's realistic fiction, narrative poetry, fantasy, and fables.

To assess your student's comprehension of functional and recreational texts, follow the same procedure described earlier for determining comprehension of graded oral reading paragraphs. First, give your students an opportunity to retell or summarize the selection; then ask specific questions about the facts, concepts, or relationships that were omitted in the retelling. If your students demonstrate understanding of the various types of expository and narrative text typically found at that level, they are "healthy" regarding the content goal. If comprehension gaps are found in the reading of certain types of text, instructional assistance must be provided. Use the examples provided in Chapter 6 to compare your students' performance with the normal developmental progression.

SUMMARY

Grouping is useful because it helps you deal with the wide variety of levels found in virtually all classrooms. Differences occur in students' verbal learning and perseverance, which, in turn, cause students to move through the developmental stages of reading growth at varying rates of speed. Whole group instruction should be frequently used because it cultivates a sense of unity, esprit, and community. Teachers provide for student differences by using reading level groups, in which students are grouped by level to perform the task being learned, and collaborative groups, in which students are grouped heterogeneously to work together temporarily on a specific task. Generally, collaborative groups are used when teaching attitude goals; reading level groups are used when teaching process goals and content goals. To form groups, you must collect appropriate information on your students. Collaborative groups, for instance, require data on which students work well together; reading level groups require information on each student's level of performance on the task to be taught. Once groups are formed, you should be prepared to continue collecting information on students' attitudes, processes, and abilities to understand content, which will change as the year progresses.

SUGGESTED ADDITIONAL READING

BERGHOFF, B., & EGAWA, K. (1991). No more "rocks": Grouping to give students control of their learning. *Reading Teacher, 44*(8), 536–541.

CAIRNEY, T., & LANGBIEN, S. (1989). Building communities of readers and writers. *Reading Teacher, 42*(8), 560–567.

FORELL, E. (1987). The case for conservative readers placement. *Reading Teacher, 41,* 857–862.

HALLER, E., & WATERMAN, M. (1985). The criteria of reading group assignments. *Reading Teacher, 38*(8), 772–781.

HARP, B. (1989). "What do we know now about ability grouping?" *Reading Teacher, 42*(6), 430–431.

JONGSMA, K. (1990). Making decisions about grouping with basals. *Reading Teacher, 44*(1), 80–81.

KEEGAN, S., & SHRAKE, K. (1991). Literature study groups: An alternative to ability grouping. *Reading Teacher, 44*(8), 542–547.

STRICKLAND, D., MORROW, L., & PELOVITZ, T. (1991). Cooperative, collaborative learning for children and teachers. *Reading Teacher, 44*(8), 600–602.

TOPPING, K. (1989). Peer tutoring and paired reading: Combining two powerful techniques. *Reading Teacher, 42*(7), 488–494.

WESSON, C., VIERTHALER, J., & HAUBRICH, P. (1989). An efficient technique for establishing reading groups. *Reading Teacher, 42*(7), 466-469.

THE RESEARCH BASE

BARR, R., & DREEBAN, R. (1991). Grouping students for reading instruction. In R. Barr, M. Kamil, P. Mosenthal, & P. D. Pearson (Eds.), *Handbook of reading research, volume II* (pp. 885–910). New York: Longman.

DIPARDO, A., & FREEDMAN, S. (1988). Peer response groups in the writing classroom: Theoretic foundations and new directions. *Review of Educational Research, 58 (2),* 119–149.

O'DONNELL, A., DANSEREAU, D., ROCKLIN, T., HYTHECKER, V., YOUNG, M., HALL, R., SKAGGS, L., & LAMBIOTTE, J. (1988). Promoting functional literacy through cooperative learning. *Journal of Reading Behavior, 20*(4), 339–355.

ROSS, J. (1988). Improving social-environmental studies problem-solving through cooperative learning. *American Educational Research Journal, 25*(4), 573–591.

ACTIVITIES FOR REFLECTING, OBSERVING, AND TEACHING

Reflecting on Grouping

PURPOSE: Grouping is a matter of decision making. That is, the teacher must determine when to use one kind of group and when to use another. The purpose of this activity is to help you decide when to use one form of grouping and when to use another.

DIRECTION: Think about the grade level you hope to teach. Then, for each form of grouping listed below, imagine a situation in which you would try to use whole-group instruction, collaborative groups, or reading level groups.

I would use whole-group instruction when _____

_____

_____

I would use collaborative grouping when _____

_____

_____

I would use reading level groups when _____

_____

_____

Watching Others Work With Groups

PURPOSE: Your understanding of grouping and the decisions that go into deciding to use one group or another will be enhanced if you have the opportunity to observe a teacher using various kinds of grouping patterns. This activity is designed to help you structure such an observation if you have the opportunity to do it.

DIRECTIONS: Since it is unlikely that a teacher would use several different forms of grouping in the same day, it is necessary that you plan to observe over a period of several days. During that period, watch how the teacher groups students for different activities. An important part of this observation will be your discussion with the teacher following your observation since you will want to find out how the teacher decided to use one form of grouping at one time and another form of grouping at another time. Make the discussion as conversational as possible.

Trying It Yourself

PURPOSE: Your understanding of the decisions which go into grouping will be complete once you have engaged in such decision making yourself. The purpose of this activity, therefore, is to give you an opportunity to engage in this decision making. It is important to note here that this activity does not mean that you *manage* a group yourself. Rather, the focus is on making the decisions about what kind of grouping to employ.

DIRECTIONS: Arrange to work with a classroom teacher as he or she plans for future instruction. As you and the teacher talk through the instructional objectives and the information regarding the group and individuals within the group, make recommendations regarding what kind of grouping might be used with different instructional activities. Ask the teacher to critique your decisions.

13 How to Modify Basal Text Prescriptions

GETTING READY

Once you form your reading groups, instruction can begin. It is at this point that you turn to basal reading textbooks. What you do with the basal—whether you make professional adaptations or simply follow prescriptions like a technician— is especially important. This chapter describes how it is possible to modify basal text prescriptions, thereby remaining in control of your own instruction.

FOCUS QUESTIONS

- What are the strengths and weaknesses of the basal reading textbook?

- How can you modify basal text grouping patterns?

- How can you modify basal text units?

- How can you modify basal text lessons?

- How can you modify basal text seatwork?

STRENGTHS AND WEAKNESSES OF BASALS

This chapter helps you avoid teaching like a technician by showing you how to organize your time so that the three major sub-goals of reading can be accomplished despite the constraints posed by basal textbooks. You must first have a literate environment in place, as described in Chapter 10. Then you must know what the strengths and shortcomings of basal texts are and how to compensate for these shortcomings while capitalizing on the strengths. This chapter provides a plan for doing so.

As noted in Part 1, the basal textbook has many appealing characteristics. Its sequential lessons provide a structured progression in which the gradually increasing difficulty of each level expedites the process of grouping students according to ability; the prescriptions in the teacher's guide provide valuable suggestions for teaching; the reading selections are written to appeal to students at that level; and the accompanying workbook practice pages provide numerous activities to keep students occupied. The overall impression is that an entire reading program is contained right there in the materials, and that all a busy teacher has to do is follow the prescriptions to ensure that students achieve all the goals of reading. It seems to be so, but it is not. Despite appearances, the comprehensiveness of the basal program is an illusion. There are three reasons for this.

Basals Deemphasize Attitude Goals   Although basal texts prescribe many different kinds of activities, they do not give equal treatment to the three reading goals. While most basal text programs discuss the need for developing concepts and positive responses to reading, they actually allocate very little instructional time to this goal. They may suggest activities, but they provide little to help teachers incorporate these suggestions into the busy school day. Even when the basal contains good suggestions about developing attitude goals, it gives other tasks priority, leaving little time for attitude development. For instance, most basals place more emphasis on reading the selections (content goals) and on completing skill activities (process goals) than on attitude goals.

Basals Emphasize Skills, Not Strategies   At first glance, the basal seems to place heavy emphasis on process goals. There are many suggestions in the teacher's guide for developing skills, but most basals emphasize mastery and automaticity, not strategy.

Some of the newer basals use the term *strategy* frequently in their promotional material and, of those, some do include genuine strategies in their suggestions to teachers. However, you must look closely at what they are prescribing to determine whether the suggested instruction will really help students learn to be strategic. For instance, few of the basals which claim to promote strategic reading actually help students understand when the strategy would be useful in reading text, what situation might occur when reading which would be a sensible place to use the strategy, specific information about how to use the strategy thoughtfully rather than procedurally, or what mental processing to engage in when applying the strategy in real situations. In short, even in basals which are promoted as programs which emphasize strategic reading, neither knowledge about how reading works nor how strategies can be applied thoughtfully and adaptively receives much emphasis.

This is particularly evident when one examines the workbook accompanying basal textbooks. Seldom do workbook exercises provide opportunities for students to be strategic in the sense of being thoughtful, of using reason, of being flexible, and of constructing meaning. Instead, workbook pages require answer accuracy, short answers, memory, and uniformity.

The tendency to emphasize skills instead of strategies extends even to writing. In most basal programs, writing is a process of filling in the blanks on worksheets. Genuine composing of text is deemphasized. The most bizarre example of this tendency is the basal program that proclaimed that it promoted student writing of journals. However, the journal was a workbook, and the task was not student-generated writing but fill-in-the-blank activities!

Basals Emphasize Content, Not Process   Basal texts emphasize content goals. The focus is on the story, not the process used to comprehend the story. The lesson begins with an introduction to the story, a discussion of new vocabulary words, the establishment of purpose-setting questions, and the assignment of the pages to be read. No mention is made of how the reading system works or of how to get meaning from the text; instead, teachers provide students with background and a "mind set" about the content of the selection. After students read the story, the teacher usually quizzes the students in a question-and-answer period. Because these questions focus on what happened in the story, the teacher is checking the students' understanding of the story content, not their understanding of how the reading system helped them get meaning from the text or how strategies were applied when meaning broke down.

Many of the suggested instructional activities in basals are directed at answers to comprehension questions. However, the answers are isolated from the process one uses to get the answer. Consider the order in which basal lessons are typically organized. The first step is to teach the story selection; the second step is to teach the several skills or strategies recommended in that section of the teacher's guide, usually by assigning workbook pages. Seldom is there an explicit connection between the story selection and the skills or strategies to be taught. In fact, skills and strategies are typically taught only in the context of the workbook; seldom are they connected to the reading selection in the basal text.

A more logical instruction system would be to connect targeted skills and strategies to the reading selection. As part of the preparation for reading the story selection, for instance, you could recast a skill as a strategy as described in Chapter 8 and teach it in the expectation that it will be used immediately when reading the story. In that way, you provide students with a rationale for why the strategy is being taught, illustrate how it can be used strategically in reading the story, and get students to apply it as they read the story. The emphasis is on application, not learning in isolation, so rather than having skills and strategies isolated to the workbook pages, you show that they are tools for immediate application in real text.

Thus, while you may sometimes get the impression that basal textbooks are complete reading programs, this is not really the case. If you simply follow prescriptions of the basal program, you end up emphasizing the content of reading selections and skill practice unrelated to the selections. You do not get to put much emphasis on attitude goals (even though these may be recommended by the basal teacher's guide) or on direct explanation of how the reading system works.

MODIFYING BASAL TEXT READING GROUPS

Teachers who rely on the basal textbook generally conduct reading instruction in small ability groups. Some goals are better taught in whole-group situations, however. This is the first way in which you can modify basal textbook prescriptions.

The development of accurate concepts and positive responses associated with attitude goals is particularly applicable to whole-group instruction. You can do language-experience activities with the entire class, especially when the whole class has participated in a field trip, a school assembly, or other special event. The special event provides the stimulus for creating a written message. In creating this message, you develop concepts about the message-sending properties of reading, the author-reader relationship, the similarity between constructing meaning when reading and composing meaning when writing, and so on. Similarly, you can have book-sharing activities involving the entire class. During such sessions, you can develop positive attitudes toward reading by modeling, by pointing out how certain books stimulate particular emotional responses, by noting students who are particularly appreciative of literature, and so on.

You will also find whole-group instruction useful for developing certain process goals. You can teach mini-lessons about how the reading system works: Whenever there is a spare 5 minutes between activities, show students how knowledge about the reading process can help them determine the author's intended meaning. Or use such times to let students show how they constructed meaning in their own reading, or allow students to work together to resolve conflicts about the meaning of particular text passages. Finally, there are times during the school day when you may want the whole class to read the same piece of text, thereby developing content goals in a large group.

There are several advantages to such whole-group instruction. First, it moves reading outside the context of the basal textbook. In doing so, you help students learn that reading fits into virtually all situations. Second, whole-group instruction provides the opportunity for students of varying ability levels to contribute. In contrast to small reading groups, which tend to foster elitism because they are formed on the basis of ability, group instruction puts good and poor readers together. Finally, you will often find whole-group instruction to be a relaxing change of pace from the routine of daily reading groups. You can manage large groups more easily because all students are working on a single task rather than some working with you and others working independently at their seats.

Because basal text grouping patterns dominate programs in today's class-rooms, teachers sometimes overlook the potential of whole-group instruction for developing important reading goals. To ensure a broad and comprehensive pro-gram, however, you should use large groups to develop goals basal textbooks tend not to emphasize.

MODIFYING BASAL TEXT UNITS

A "unit" in most basal textbooks is comprised of several selections grouped to-gether in the book. These groupings often reflect a content theme. For instance, a basal text may have units of five stories each, with the theme of the first unit being courage, the second sports, and so on. Although the length of units and the way they are tied together vary from one basal text series to another, virtually all basals group selections into units.

Each lesson in a unit typically includes a selection to be read and skills or strategies to be taught. In most basals, the selection is taught first, followed by the skill or strategy. This tends to isolate the skill or strategy from the selection. You can rectify this by reorganizing the instructional sequence so that the skill or strategy is taught before reading the selection. In this way, the skill or strategy can be used when reading the story.

Accomplishing this reorganization is a two-step process. First, you must survey the basal prescriptions for the whole unit, reorganize these prescriptions according to the three major goals of reading, and identify which specific skill or strategy prescription goes with which goal. Second, you must decide which skill or strategy to teach with each story.

The first step is necessary because there is seldom any clear relationship among the skills or strategies taught in a particular unit and what is needed to read the selections. A phonics skill on the initial *ch* digraph may be presented in the same unit with a skill on predicting outcomes. Not only are these skills not related in any obvious way, but also the basal selections in the unit do not have any unknown *ch* words or call for predicting outcomes. In short, there is seldom a compelling reason to learn the skill or strategy.

To impose a more sensible organization on the unit, we recommend you list all the goals the basal prescribes for the unit, organize these into the three major reading goals, delete prescriptions that ought not to be taught or that do not relate to the three major goals, and add any other needed goals that the basal text may have neglected. After you have categorized all the prescribed and additional skills and strategies by goal, group together the items that go together. For instance, in the category of process goals, you would group all the routine skills together, all the initiating strategies together, all the during-reading strategies together, and all the post-reading strategies together. When you finish this categorizing, you know precisely what to teach in each of the three major goal categories and, within each category, you have lists of specific curricular

Large-group reading instruction provides the opportunity for students of varying ability groups to work together.

tasks that go together. You can then state these as objectives (see Chapter 14). Figure 13.1 illustrates the steps in accomplishing such a reorganization of basal content.

Once you have identified the objectives to be taught in a basal unit, you must decide which objective goes with which selection. This often means you

---

FIGURE 13.1   Steps in Reorganizing Basal Text Prescriptions

Step 1	List of the objectives prescribed by the basal.
Step 2	Group these objectives into three categories according to the three major reading goals (attitude, process, content).
Step 3	Delete objectives that do not reflect any of the three major goals.
Step 4	Add any objectives that the basal fails to prescribe.
Step 5	For each of the three categories, group together similar objectives (put all phonics objectives together, all comprehension strategies together, etc.).
Step 6	Examine the lists and state an objective for each task. These are your objectives for the unit.

---

must move a skill or strategy from its place in the basal and teach it with a different story. For instance, it is not unusual for a basal textbook to prescribe a lesson on figuring out word meaning through the use of prefixes without having any prefixed words in the accompanying selection. Consequently, you cannot use that particular selection as a place to apply what was learned about prefixes, so you must move the prefix lesson to another place in the unit where there *is* a selection containing prefixed words. By matching objectives and selections, you ensure that goals will be taught in the context of their application in real reading rather than in isolation. This adds a dimension of meaningfulness, makes the instruction sensible, and, consequently, helps motivate your students.

MODIFYING BASAL TEXT LESSONS

Once you have organized a unit of instruction so that specific objectives are matched to specific selections, you are ready to organize individual lessons. The first step is to decide whether you are trying to achieve a content goal, a process goal, or an attitude goal, since each one has its own organizational scheme. Because you normally use indirect instruction with language experience and personalized reading to develop attitude goals, you generally limit your use of the basal to achieving content and process goals.

A Content Lesson Format   If you decide to have students focus on the content of the selection, you organize the lesson using the six steps of the directed reading lesson: Introduce the story by activating appropriate background experience and introducing the new vocabulary words; set purposes for reading the selection; have students orally or silently read the selection; discuss the selection with students in terms of the set purposes; teach the prescribed skills; and bring the lesson to a close by summarizing the content or by involving students in an enriching activity. Throughout, your focus is on developing understanding of the content of the selection.

A Process Lesson Format   If your objective is to develop a process goal, an eight step modification of the DRL sequence, called the modified directed reading lesson, is used: Introduce the selection and cite how it is an example of a place to use the strategy to be learned; introduce the strategy to be learned; model how to do the thinking associated with the strategy; mediate students' acquisition; set purposes for reading the selection with an emphasis on applying the strategy that was learned; have students orally or silently read the selection; discuss the content of the selection and how students used the strategy while reading the selection; and bring the lesson to a close. Throughout, you focus on developing understanding of a process goal and its application to content. This is in contrast to the DRL, which focuses on developing understanding of what went on in the

FIGURE 13.2 Two Forms of the Directed Reading Lesson

Standard DRL (content lesson format)	Modified DRL (process lesson format)
Step 1 Introduce the selection (activate schemata and special vocabulary).	**Step 1** Introduce the selection as a focus for a strategy to be learned.
	Step 2 Introduce the knowledge or strategy to be taught.
	Step 3 Model how to use the knowledge or strategy.
	Step 4 Mediate student acquisition of the knowledge or strategy.
Step 2 Set purposes for reading the selection (for content understanding only).	**Step 5** Set purposes for reading the selection (include application of the knowledge or strategy as well as understanding the content).
Step 3 Have students orally or silently read the selection.	**Step 6** Have students orally or silently read the selection.
Step 4 Discuss the selection (for content understanding only).	**Step 7** Discuss the selection both in terms of the content and in terms of application of the knowledge or strategy.
Step 5 Teach the skills.	
Step 6 Bring closure to the lesson (by summarizing content only).	**Step 8** Bring closure to the lesson by summarizing both the content and the use of the knowledge or strategy.

selection in isolation from process; the MDRL focuses on making connections between how students make sense of text and how they apply that understanding in the story.

Using the Two Formats   Figure 13.2 illustrates the similarities and differences in the two forms of the directed reading lesson. Both lesson sequences are examples of direct instruction. You decide at the outset (by reference to the unit plan) what process or content goal to teach with a particular basal selection. You use a DRL format to directly assist your students if content is the goal or an MDRL format to directly assist your students if process is the goal. It is as if you are saying:

> I know something about what is to be learned here, and I'm going to share it with you so you can learn it. I'm not going to keep secret what I know about it, nor am I going

to make you figure it out by yourself as we go along. Instead, I'm going to make it as clear as possible so you can put it to work in this story and in other things that you read.

Both lesson plans require you to make decisions. If the intent is to develop a content goal, you must decide how to guide your students in activating appropriate background experience, on how to develop meaning for new words, and on how to ensure that the content is understood. To make these decisions, use your understanding of how readers tap into various knowledge sources to comprehend: knowledge of words, of topic, of purpose, and of text structure. You introduce vocabulary, tell your students what the topic of the story or selection is, state the author's purpose in writing it, and cue students to distinctive features of the text structure. Your intent is to help students activate their prior knowledge and to make initial predictions about meaning based on what they know about the topic, author purpose, and cues provided in the text structure (such as titles, subtitles, headings, illustrations, etc.). By getting students to activate appropriate knowledge and to predict on the basis of that knowledge, you get them ready to comprehend the content of the selection. Consequently, in planning the DRL you guide students regarding the words, the topic, the purpose, and the text structure.

Your decisions are somewhat different when you are developing process goals. Despite the fact that the first step in both types of lesson is nearly identical, in process lessons the intent is to identify a need for the strategy or skill being taught by establishing that it will be used in that selection. In the second step, you make a brief statement, which answers three important questions for the students: What skill or strategy will they be learning? Where will they use the skill or strategy? (In this case, state exactly where they will use the skill or strategy in the basal selection they are about to read, as well as other similar but more removed situations where they could use it in the future.) What must they pay attention to in order to learn the skill or strategy? Answers to these three questions are keys to the learning objective, and one of your most important instructional tasks is to get your students to attend to the specific keys so they can learn easily and well. This step in the MDRL, then, is a brief but explicit statement that lets students tune in to the skill or strategy to be learned.

The third step is to model the skill or strategy being taught. You say, "Here, let me show you how it's done." Then, using a sample piece of text from the basal selection or one similar to the basal selection, you explain the thinking you do in using the skill or strategy. Your modeling gives your students information they need to use the skill or strategy themselves. Consequently, you do not omit or gloss over the steps. However, no matter how explicitly and thoroughly you model, your students must be given opportunities to try out the skill or strategy and to adapt it to their own mental processing. Consequently, the fourth step is for you to provide additional text passages similar to those used for modeling

In teaching content goals, teachers stress students' understanding of topic, purpose, and text structure.

and to tell your students, "Do as I did." In short, students follow your model in explaining how they use the skill or strategy. At first, you provide lots of support in the form of cues and directives, but gradually you remove such aids as students adapt and personalize the use of the skill or strategy. This is a critical stage in the instructional sequence since it is your students' responses at this stage that reveal misunderstandings about how the skill or strategy works. If misunderstandings become evident, you must spontaneously provide explanations to eliminate the confusion and put the student back on the right track. That is why this step is called "mediating student acquisition"—you form a connecting bridge between the student and the goal. Whether students learn to use the skill or strategy often depends upon your sensitivity in performing this mediational or bridging role.

Once students understand how to use the knowledge or strategy, go to the fifth step and assign the basal selection for practice. You set two purposes for reading the basal selection: Give your students content purposes associated with getting the meaning in the text and ask them to apply to the selection the skill or strategy they have learned. In the sixth step, have students begin reading the selection together, usually silently but sometimes orally (especially in the primary grades). After they have read the selection, guide the seventh step, the discussion, talking with students about the content of the story and about how they applied the newly taught skill or strategy. Finally, in the eighth step you close the lesson by summarizing both the content of the selection and the process that was taught.

Ultimately, of course, you must ensure that students apply the skill or strategy in settings outside the basal textbook. Your real purpose in teaching reading is to help students become independent readers of real-world materials. This purpose cannot be adequately achieved if students think reading strategies are only used in basal textbooks. Consequently, your task is not done until students can apply the knowledge or strategy in natural or "outside-of-school" text. Details for planning and teaching DRL and MDRL lessons are provided in Chapter 14.

MODIFYING BASAL TEXT SEATWORK

Seatwork in most classrooms consists of work sheets. Students are given workbooks, ditto sheets, or practice sheets supplied by the basal text publisher or the publisher of supplementary materials. In most classrooms, students' seatwork time is longer than the time they spend in the reading group. Consequently, even if you provide excellent instruction for 20 minutes in a reading group, what your students do in the 40-minute seatwork time is likely to have even greater impact. If your students spend more time on practice sheets than on reading text, they will most likely conclude that reading is more like work sheets than like books.

To combat this interpretation, you must use alternative kinds of seatwork. You should supplement the usual drill and practice kind of seatwork with activities such as the following: free reading of self-selected books, journal writing, illustrating language-experience stories, paired oral reading, games, listening activities, creative drama, letter writing, gathering information from outside reading sources, and others. The point is that you are not limited to using only the seatwork provided by the basal; in fact, you must be creative enough to initiate alternative seatwork if your students are to conclude that reading is a meaningful activity.

SUMMARY

Basal textbooks are useful as tools to help you organize your reading instruction. However, they also have many serious weaknesses, particularly in the way they develop attitude and process goals. Consequently, as a professional decision maker, you must modify basal text prescriptions to capitalize on their strengths while minimizing their weaknesses. You can do so by using large groups and collaborative groups as well as the ability groups prescribed by the basal; by modifying the sequence of basal text units to ensure that skills and strategies are taught with reading selections that call for the use of the skill or strategy; by modifying the basal lesson sequence so that the skill or strategy is taught before it is to be applied in the story; and by employing seatwork that is more representative of what literate people do than the typical basal text seatwork.

SUGGESTED ADDITIONAL READING

BAUMANN, J. F. (1984). How to expand a basal reader program. *Reading Teacher, 37*(7), 604–607.

BLANTON, W., MOORMAN, G., & WOOD, K. (1986). A model of direct instruction applied to the basal skills lesson. *Reading Teacher, 40,* 299–305.

CHARNOCK, J. (1977). An alternative to the DRA. *Reading Teacher, 31*(3), 269–271.

GOURLEY, J. W. (1978). This basal is easy to read—or is it? *Reading Teacher, 32*(2), 174–182.

GREEN-WILDER, J., & KINGSTON, A. (1986). The depiction of reading in five popular basal series. *Reading Teacher, 39,* 399–402.

MCCALLUM, R. (1989). Don't throw the basals out with the bath water. *Reading Teacher, 43*(3), 204–207.

MOORE, S., & MOORE, D. (1989). How to choose and use basal readers—if you really want them. *Reading Teacher, 43*(3), 252–253.

PIERONEK, F. T. (1980). Do basal readers reflect the interests of intermediate students? *Reading Teacher, 33*(4), 408–415.

REUTZEL, D. R. (1985). Reconciling scheme theory and the basal reading lesson. *Reading Teacher, 39,* 194–197.

SCHMITT, M., & BAUMANN, J. (1986). How to incorporate comprehension monitoring strategies into basal reader instruction. *Reading Teacher 40,* 28–31.

SWABY, B. (1982). Varying the ways you teach reading with basal stories. *Reading Teacher, 35*(6), 676–680.

THE RESEARCH BASE

DOLE, J., ROGERS, T., & OSBORN, J. (1987). Improving the selection of basal reading programs: A report of the Textbook Adoption Guidelines Project. *Elementary School Journal, 87*(3), 283–298.

DUFFY, G., ROEHLER, L., & PUTNAM, J. (1987). Putting the teacher in control. Basal reading textbooks and instructional decision making. *Elementary School Journal, 87,* 357–366.

DURKIN D. (1981). Reading comprehension instruction in five basal reading series. *Reading Research Quarterly, 16,* 515–544.

SHANNON, P. (1983). The use of commercial reading materials in American elementary schools. *Reading Research Quarterly, 19,* 68–85.

ACTIVITIES FOR REFLECTING, OBSERVING, AND TEACHING

Reflecting on How to Modify Basal Prescriptions

PURPOSE: In order to understand how to modify basal text prescriptions, you must first examine basals to see what they contain. Specifically, you must examine specific basals to determine whether, as suggested in this chapter, basals really do deemphasize attitude goals, strategies, and process. This activity is designed to help you do that.

DIRECTIONS: Select a basal textbook at the level you intend to teach. Pick out a unit or lesson at random, and examine the directions in the teacher's guide for that unit or lesson. Then answer the questions posed below.

The emphasis on attitude goals: What evidence do you find in the unit or lesson regarding emphasis on attitude goals? What proportion of the lesson or unit prescriptions are directed toward development of attitude goals?

The emphasis on strategies: What evidence is there that strategies are taught in the lesson or unit? If the term "strategies" is used, look to see if the prescriptions and workbook activities promote reasoning, adaptive construction of meaning and flexibility or whether, instead, strategies are taught basically the same as skills.

The emphasis on process: What is the relative emphasis in the unit or lesson on story content and the process used to comprehend the story? Are most of the suggested questions designed to determine whether students understood the story? Or are the questions designed to determine whether students understood how they comprehended?

Watching Others Modify Basal Text Prescriptions

PURPOSE: Once you understand what basals tend to emphasize and the need to modify their prescriptions, you are faced with the task of accomplishing such modification. Because it is a complicated task, it is helpful if you can enlist the aid of a teacher. This activity is designed to help you structure such an activity.

DIRECTIONS: See if you can enlist a teacher who would be willing to let you sit with him or her while planning a basal text unit or lesson. Get the teacher to talk out loud about his or her thinking in planning the lesson or unit. Note what adaptations of basal text prescriptions the teacher makes. Compare the adaptations the teacher makes with those recommended in this chapter, and probe the teacher about the differences you note.

Trying It Yourself

PURPOSE: Ultimately, you will not be able to use a basal textbook well unless you can independently modify the prescriptions of the teacher's guide. This activity is designed to help you do that.

DIRECTIONS: Select a basal text unit at a grade level near the one you want to teach. Follow the steps in Figure 13.1 to determine the objectives for the unit.

Then break down the unit objectives into lessons. For each lesson, specify whether you are developing an attitude goal, a process goal, or a content goal. For each, describe the kind of lesson format you would use. Figure 13.2 will be helpful for process and content goals.

Finally, consider what kind of seatwork you would use during the unit.

14 How to Plan and Teach Lessons and Units

GETTING READY

Getting organized for reading instruction involves many tasks. You must organize a literate environment, collect and organize data, form reading groups,
and establish control over the basal reading textbook. Of all the organizing you
do, however, planning is particularly crucial. This chapter describes how you
can organize reading lessons and reading units using both indirect and direct
instruction.

FOCUS QUESTIONS

- Why are instructional objectives so important?

- What is the purpose of each of the three parts of an instructional objective?

- Why are units important in organizing instruction?

- Why are lessons important in organizing instruction?

- What are the decisions you must make to plan indirect lessons?

- What are the decisions you must make to plan direct lessons?

- What is the purpose of a task analysis?

- Why must teachers consider the subtleties of instruction as well as the
lesson format?

OBJECTIVES: THE CORNERSTONE OF PLANNING

When teachers are asked what task requires most of their time, they often
respond with "planning." Planning of individual lessons and units requires your
attention and effort all year long. It is crucial because it directly affects the
quality of instruction.

Regardless of whether you plan lessons and units using indirect or direct instruction, the most important thing you can do is clearly state your objectives. For instance, you should know precisely what attitude, process, or content goals you are trying to achieve. When you do, your lessons have a focus. You know what you are trying to accomplish and, because you do, your students are better able to accomplish this objective. Consequently, for any lesson you teach, you should always be able to answer the questions: "Why am I doing this? What is the goal I am after? What should my students be doing differently after this lesson?"

Stating Objectives

A good instructional objective is a carefully structured statement. It has three parts, which are described in the following sections.

Student Performance   The first and most important part of an objective is a description of what students will be able to do after successful instruction. If you are teaching an attitude goal such as appreciation of free verse poetry, you might want your students to voluntarily select free verse poems for sharing with the class, something they do not now do. The objective might be, "The student will voluntarily select free verse poems to share with the class." If you are teaching a process goal such as the use of prefixes to figure out the meaning of unknown words, you might want students to tell you both the meaning of the unknown prefixed word and the process used to figure out its meaning. So the objective might be, "The student will state the meaning of previously unknown prefixed words and the thinking used to determine the meaning." If you are teaching a content goal such as reading a history chapter for information about the causes of the Civil War, the objective might be, "The student will read the chapter and state the three causes of the Civil War cited by the author." In each case, you create a descriptive statement of what students should be able to do after instruction. The targeted student behavior must be observable so that after the lesson you can determine whether or not your students are doing what you intended.

The Situation   The second part of a good instructional objective specifies the situation where what is learned will be used. In reading, this means you must specify a real reading situation, since you want students to use what you teach when they are reading on their own. The real reading situation for the poetry objective is when students have the opportunity to voluntarily select poems to share with the class. Consequently, when you add the situation to your objective, the following statement of desired student behavior results: "Given a display of free verse poetry in the classroom, the student will voluntarily select free verse poems to share with the class." You are saying that the situation where the intended learning will be observed will be when students voluntarily read free verse poetry during class from the display provided. If, however, you want students to read free verse poetry during free time at home, then you must specify home reading as the situation that best indicates an appreciation of free verse poetry.

In a prefix lesson, you might want students to use prefixes to figure out the meaning of unknown words when reading books of their choice. Consequently, the situational part of your objective might be: "Given self-selected texts in which unknown prefixed words are encountered, the student will state the meaning of the unknown words and the thinking used to determine the meanings." Here you are saying that it is not good enough that students use prefix knowledge on workbook pages or ditto sheets; you must see them using the strategy with self-selected text to be satisfied that the desired learning has occurred.

In a lesson on the causes of the Civil War, you might amend your objective to read, "Given the history textbook and a study guide that helps locate passages about the causes of the Civil War, the student will read the chapter and state three causes of the Civil War cited by the author." Here you are saying that the desired learning should occur when students are asked to read the textbook.

The Criterion The third part of a good instructional objective is a statement of how well or how often students have to do a task for you to accept it as learned. In the case of appreciating free verse poetry, you might be satisfied with one reading of free verse. Consequently, the objective could be stated as follows: "Given a display of free verse poetry in the classroom, the student will voluntarily select at least one free verse poem to share with the class." In the case of the prefix strategy, you would not usually feel comfortable with only a single completion. Therefore, the objective might be stated: "Given self-selected text in which unknown prefixed words are encountered, the student will state the meaning of the words and the thinking used to determine the meanings on at least five occasions." For the content objective, you may decide that since a study guide has been provided the student should identify all three causes. Consequently, the objective might be stated: "Given the history text-book and a study guide that helps locate the passages dealing with the causes of the Civil War, the student will correctly state the three causes cited by the author."

To summarize, the hallmark of effective instruction is your awareness of the goal you are seeking. Specifically, the goal or objective focuses the unit or lesson, both for you and for your students. The best way to specify the goal is to state what you want students to be able to do, the situation in which it should be done, and the criterion that will make you confident that it has really been learned. With objectives clearly stated, a unit or lesson is off to a good start.

IMPORTANT ASPECTS OF UNIT PLANNING

Instructional units serve one primary purpose: to bring meaningful cohesion to a series of lessons. To achieve this function, two major conditions must be met.

First, the unit must be based on a problem. That is, the series of lessons and activities which comprise the unit are tied together by the fact that the students are solving a problem that is important to them. The problem is genuine in itself and, because it is, the activities students complete in solving the problem are examples of authentic literate activity. That is, students use language and higher-order thinking in the service of solving the real problem they face. It is the main way in which learning is situated (see Chapter 4)—that is, it is through a unit that teachers are able to put students in a situation where they are immediately using what they are learning about reading and writing in completing an authentic task.

Second, a unit brings cohesion to instruction by being directed toward a culminating activity. That is, the problem must be solved, and the culminating activity is where the resolution is played out. Often this takes the form of a project of some kind. That is, the problem which organizes the unit evolves into a project. Completion of the project means the problem has been resolved. Hence, the completion of the project culminates the problem solving activity, and marks the end of the unit.

Consider the following examples of units. In a first grade, students were concerned about saving the whales. The problem was to determine what they could do to save the whales. This problem evolved into a project: they decided to write letters to President Bush demanding legislation to protect the whales. The culminating activity to the unit was the mailing of the letters. In a third grade, students wanted to participate in a Young Authors Conference, but the problem was that they did not know what to write about. This problem evolved into a project: they all decided to write mystery stories. The culminating activity was the presentation of the mystery stories at the Young Authors Conference. In a fifth grade, students were studying about the Renaissance in social studies. They wanted to have a "Renaissance Fair" involving the whole school, but they did not know how to get the primary grades involved. The problem was how to make the Renaissance sensible to primary grade students. This problem evolved into a project: they decided to have their Fair revolve around a series of displays about famous people who lived during the Renaissance. The culminating activity was the presentation of the displays to all the students in the school, including the primary grade students. In the seventh grade, students could not understand how different people could interpret the same event in dramatically different ways. The problem was to understand "truth" and whether truth is different for different people. The project was to collect examples from their own lives of people interpreting the same event in different ways. The culminating activity was the sharing of their observations.

So, where does reading and learning how to read happen in a unit? They happen as natural events in the process of completing the project. That is, the problem and associated project represent questions to be answered; to answer these questions, students read; in order to read, students must learn concepts, strategies, and skills. In the above first grade unit, for instance, students read books about whales in order to learn about the problem and, in the process of reading whale books, learned certain concepts, skills, and strategies about reading; in the third grade unit on the Young Authors Conference, students read mysteries in order to learn about different kinds of mysteries they could write and, in the process of reading the mysteries, they needed to learn certain concepts, skills, and strategies to read those mysteries; in the fifth grade Renaissance unit, students read many different things about the Renaissance and about famous Renaissance people and, in the process, they needed to learn concepts, skills, and strategies needed to read those materials; and in the seventh grade unit on truth, students read many different literature selections in their exploration of truth and, in the process, they needed to learn concepts, skills, and strategies required for reading those pieces of literature.

The advantage of all this is that, in completing the unit, students are engaged in genuinely authentic activity in which problem identification and resolution are central to the process and in which reading and writing are instrumental in achieving the goals. If we truly believe that we want our students to be "problem solvers," we must give them opportunities to identify and resolve problems. And if we truly believe that reading and writing are genuinely useful ways to gain control of our destiny, then we must give students opportunities to use reading and writing in this way. Consequently, in such units, problem solving, reading, and writing are not artificial "school" activities; they are real. In contrast to traditional school activity where problem solving skills and reading concepts, skills, and strategies are learned "because they may help me when I grow up," in a unit, problem solving and reading concepts, skills, and strategies take on

---

FIGURE 14.1   Unit Plan Format

---

1. **Goals and objectives**
   - What attitude, process, and content goals and objectives are students to learn during the unit?

2. **Problem or theme**
   - What problem or theme will capture students' interests and impose unity on the series of lessons?

3. **Introduction and motivation**
   - How will the purpose of the unit be presented?
   - How will students be motivated?

4. **Unit schedule**
   - How many days will the unit take?
   - What will be achieved each day?

5. **Culminating activity**
   - How will the unit be ended?
   - What will be done to bring closure and a sense of wholeness to the unit?

6. **Evaluation**
   - How will you determine whether the goals and objectives were achieved?

---

a practical immediacy because they are used immediately in the pursuit of an authentic task. As a result, students are motivated, and they learn better.

A variation on the same idea can be accomplished by thinking in terms of themes rather than problems. For instance, if your students are interested in animals, you might establish an animal theme and swing all the reading and writing you do in class around that theme; if your students are interested in building something, you can establish a theme about building. Themes, like problems, help tie together a series of lessons and are also often useful in integrating content from a variety of subject-matter areas. The major weakness in using themes, however, is that the problem focus is sometimes lost and, with it, the opportunity for students to engage in problem identification and resolution.

To plan a unit, it is useful to follow a format such as that shown in Figure 14.1. Before planning individual lessons, develop the overall unit plan. After the unit is planned, plan individual lessons for each separate day.

The elements of unit planning described here should be combined with the modifications of basal units as described in Chapter 13. That is, imposing theme and culminating activity as described here is combined with reorganizing basal prescriptions as described earlier. The two result in clearly organized goals and objectives (from modifying the basal) and motivated students (from being taught within the context of a theme and a culminating activity).

LESSON PLANNING USING INDIRECT INSTRUCTION

In indirect instruction, you structure the environment and assign activities for students to interpret in ways that lead them to specific goals. Your role tends to be less intrusive than in direct instruction, and the activities you assign to your students take priority. Hence, the lesson planning format for indirect instruction revolves around an activity.

Ultimately, when students are engaged in indirect instruction they work independently with little assistance from you. However, as noted in Chapter 4, instruction can be thought of as a continuum from direct to indirect. At the extreme, indirect instruction means no intervention from you at all. However, there are many times (especially when activities are being introduced) when instruction is indirect because your students learn some goals incidentally, but direction from you is nevertheless evident. This type of lesson is described here.

There are three major steps in the planning format for indirect instruction. First, involve students in an activity. Usually, this activity is associated with the literate environment, but it is chosen because of its potential for leading students to the specific goal identified in the objective. Second, discuss the activity with students. This discussion focuses students' attention on the desired goal, although you refrain from being overly directive. Finally, involve students in a second activity. This follow-up activity is related to the first one and gives students the opportunity to further develop what was the focus of the discussion.

This three-step format—activity-discussion-activity—is typical of many lessons based on indirect instruction. For instance, you can use uninterrupted sustained silent reading to develop positive attitudes toward reading and the concept that reading is enjoyable and rewarding. During the course of a week or more, the USSR activity often follows the three-step format: The activity is the reading; periodically you hold informal discussions with your students about the books they or you are reading, with the intent of focusing them on positive responses and on the concept that reading is enjoyable and rewarding; and after the discussion, your students return to the reading activity.

Similarly, the typical language experience lesson is often organized around the three-step format. You may want to develop the twin concepts that reading and writing are related and written text conveys an author's message. To do so, you organize the first activity, a field trip to the fire station (perhaps in conjunction with a social studies unit on community helpers). On returning from the field trip, you discuss with your students the desirability of thanking the firemen for their help, shaping the discussion so students understand that their message can be effectively communicated through writing. You then move to the next activity, in which your students dictate a note of thanks, which you record on a sheet of language experience paper and then send to the firemen. Again,

Although indirect instruction often looks spontaneous, it is actually carefully planned.

the three-step format of activity-discussion-activity has guided your organization of indirect instruction.

Analyzing Planning Decisions

Indirect instruction is deceptive. It often looks spontaneous and inventive. Teachers who use indirect instruction well are often labeled creative, meaning that others admire their ability to be so innovative on the spur of the moment. However, most good indirect instruction is not entirely spontaneous; it is planned. There is creativity, but it is found not in the teacher's ability to think on the spot so much as in his or her ability to make plans. To illustrate the kinds of planning decisions that must be made, let's examine a sample lesson that has some characteristics of indirect instruction. The steps are outlined in Figure 14.2.

Assume you are teaching a second grade class. You have observed that students in this class do not make predictions using text structure and that they have difficulty seeing the relationship between reading and writing. You want to change this situation by teaching story structure. The common **story structure** consists of an introduction that includes setting, main character, problem, events related to the problem, and resolution of the problem.

Your first decision is to make instruction more indirect than direct because the goals you are after are conceptual and are best achieved through environmental experiences. Also, you are influenced by the fact that almost all the students in the class need to achieve these conceptual goals, so you use a large-group setting. Because you want your students to have experiences that cause them to associate reading with predicting and with writing, and because large-group instruction seems most efficient, you think more in terms of indirect instruction than direct instruction.

Your second decision involves translating the goals into an objective. You want students to understand that reading stories involves predicting based on typical story structure and that reading and writing are related. You translate these goals into observable student behaviors that can be stated as objectives. If you could observe your students writing a story in which they used story

---

FIGURE 14.2 Decisions to Make in Planning Indirect Instruction

1. Decide to be more indirect than direct in achieving the outcome.
2. Specify the goal or objective.
3. Decide upon the three-part format of activity-discussion-activity.
4. Decide what you will say or do to facilitate the goal at each of the three major points of the lesson.
5. Assess your success in achieving the desired goal.

structure to create the meaning, this would be evidence that both goals were being achieved. Therefore, you state the objective as follows:

"Given the opportunity to write a story, students will write their own story using a story structure similar to the story the teacher read to them." The story writing is the behavior reflecting the targeted goals; the situation is that it should be modeled on the story that was read to them; and the criterion implied is that writing a single story will be an indication that learning has occurred.

Your third decision is to identify what happens at each step of the three-step format. The first step, the activity, is to read your students a story that uses a common story structure. The second step is to discuss with your students the various parts of the story structure and how they can use these parts to predict meaning and how, if the reader uses structure to predict meaning, the writer can use it to build meaning. The last step is another activity in which your students use the first story as a model to create a new story.

Fourth, you face a series of decisions about each of the three steps of the lesson. Step 1 involves selecting an appropriate story and deciding how to introduce it to your students. In selecting the story, you must be sure that it will be enjoyable for second grade students and that it reflects the structure employed in most stories, Consequently, you may select a book such as Mercer Mayer's picture and words book called *There Is a Nightmare in My Closet*. Second graders love it and it follows the familiar story structure of setting, character, problem, a series of events relating to the problem, and a resolution of the problem. In introducing the story, you decide to read it once for enjoyment and then to read it again during the discussion to point out the story parts.

To expedite identification of the story parts, step 2, you decide to show your students the pictures most closely associated with a particular part of the story, decide on key statements you must make to ensure a smooth discussion, and decide on any support materials (chalkboard illustrations, handouts, etc.) that might help achieve the goals. Once the story parts are identified, you prepare students for writing by modeling how the same story parts guide an author who is writing a story like Mayer's.

For step 3 of the lesson, you invite your students to use the same story parts to create a story like Mayer's. To ensure that the task does not become overwhelming and therefore frustrating, you give each student a booklet. On each page, you have written a component of story structure to guide the students (the first page is for *setting*, the second for *character*, the third for *problem*, etc.). Further, you elicit a story idea from each student before they begin writing, thereby ensuring that no one is left without a story to write.

At the conclusion of the lesson, you assess its success by determining which students attained the performance specified in the objective. Those students who wrote their own story using the story structure have achieved the conceptual understanding that reading involves predicting and that there is a strong relationship between reading and writing.

You might have a follow-up lesson that emphasizes the interrelated nature of reading and writing by having your students read the books they have written to younger children. Your first decision regarding this lesson involves choosing indirect instruction. Since the goal of having students better understand the interrelated nature of reading and writing involves developing a concept about reading and writing, indirect instruction seems appropriate. You state the objective in the following way: "Given a self-authored story, the student will read the story to younger children." The three-part lesson format for indirect instruction would consist of the following: students read their own stories; you discuss with them how to introduce their stories to younger children; and students introduce and read their own stories to younger children. You can then have students evaluate how the reading went and how well they read their story to the younger children.

LESSON PLANNING USING DIRECT INSTRUCTION

When using direct instruction to achieve process and content goals, you assume a much more overt instructional role. You define the task for students through verbal mediation; that is, you directly and explicitly explain to your students how to use a reading strategy or how to extract content from the text. Hence, the lesson planning format for direct instruction for process goals focuses on using a strategy to make sense out of text; the lesson planning format for direct

With direct instruction, teachers carefully explain what students must do to accomplish a task.

instruction for content goals focuses on the information the student is to extract from the text.

Planning Direct Instruction for Process Goals

There are eight steps for planning direct instruction of process goals. They are described in the modified direct reading lesson presented in Chapters 4 and 13 and outlined in Figure 13.2.

When you teach a process goal, you want students to consciously use their knowledge. To develop such metacognitive awareness of story structures, for instance, use the MDRL and state the objective something like this: "Given an appropriate basal text, the student will state how story structure was used to make predictions about meaning in each of five different stories." In short, you want your students to state how they used story structure to predict meaning in five different basal text stories so you can determine if they are metacognitively aware.

Once you state the objective, begin planning the lesson using the MDRL. The first step is to select a basal text story in which story structures can be applied. Introduce the story by giving your students background information that activates their prior knowledge about the topic of the story, that develops new vocabulary associated with that topic, that gets them thinking about the author's purposes for writing the story (whether it is to inform, to entertain, to provide a moral lesson, or whatever), and that establishes what will be applied while reading the story. In this case, it is conscious use of story structures to predict meaning.

In the next section of the lesson, tell your students explicitly what they will be learning, where in the basal text selection they will apply it, and what they must attend to in order to learn it. This introductory step requires that you do a task analysis. A **task analysis** is just what the name implies: it is an analysis of the task being taught. Its purpose is to arm you with specific information about what to tell your students about how to perform the process goal (i.e., using story structures to predict meaning).

A task analysis has three parts, as can be seen in Figure 14.3. The features and sequence identified in the task analysis become the mental process (or thinking) you want students to consciously apply when using knowledge to make sense of text. Using our current example, the goal is the conscious use of story structure to make predictions about what will happen in a story; the language principle is the common story format; the features are the elements of the story structure; and the sequence might be identifying the story part, noting the information contained there and using that information along with general information about the topic to predict what will happen next.

Once you have introduced knowledge of story structures, you should model its use. This is a crucial step since it is during modeling that you actually show students how good readers consciously apply structural knowledge to make pre-

---

FIGURE 14.3 Task Analysis

Goal
What is the goal I am after? What do I want my students to be able to do?

Critical features
What do readers pay particular attention to as they do this?

Sequence
What sequence do readers follow in thinking through the task and achieving the goal?

Result: A mental process, consisting of features and sequence, which students can use as a starting point when trying to do what you are trying to teach them to do.

---

dictions. While you might use visual aids and other devices at this stage, the best way to model is by explaining your own thinking processes. When teaching story structures, for instance, select a sample story and start by saying, "When reading this story, I first look at setting, characters, and problem. I see that it is about...." In short, you make explicit the mental process identified in the task analysis by showing your students exactly how you use it. In so doing, you ensure that your students have a model to follow as they attempt to use the knowledge. They are not left to figure it out for themselves. This is referred to as **mental modeling.**

In the next step, you mediate students' acquisition of the learning objective by providing guided practice. Mediation includes much assistance at first, with a gradual lessening of this assistance as students begin to catch on. For instance, you will initially provide students with many statements to direct their use of the knowledge or strategy, as well as cues and highlighting (such as underlining or pointing to particular elements) to assist them in thinking through the process. Gradually, you withdraw the cues and statements until your students are thinking with no assistance.

In teaching story structure, for instance, you will give students sample stories and ask them to use story structures to predict meaning and to explain how they do so. Initially, you may point to each of the three major story parts and make prompting statements regarding the next step in making predictions. As students do their thinking out loud, you listen for knowledge of story structures and provide assistance whenever they exhibit confusion regarding its use. Gradually, you provide less and less assistance as your students begin using the mental process without assistance.

Once students demonstrate an understanding of how the knowledge is used, guide them in applying it to the basal story that was introduced at the beginning. In a story structure lesson, for instance, you will not only talk to students about the content of the story they are reading, but will also tell them that the story follows the same three-step format they just learned about and that they should use the thinking process they just practiced to make predictions about content while reading the story. Then you have students read the story with these two purposes in mind.

In the case of story structures, you may wish to combine the reading and the discussion by having the story read in sections corresponding to the major story parts and, as students finish each section, discuss with them their predictions about what will happen next. In any case, monitor their application of what was taught, and then close the lesson by having them summarize both the story content and the way story structures were used to predict that content.

Once your students have successfully applied the process goal to a basal story, you must still transfer the learning to other settings. For instance, remind students to use the knowledge of story structures when doing uninterrupted silent sustained reading and when reading textbooks. You can also use other activities in the literate environment to accomplish transfer. A particularly useful technique is to have your students write their own stories using a story structure. This not only reinforces the knowledge taught, but also strengthens their understanding of the reading-composing relationship.

As can be seen, teaching story structures by direct instruction is significantly different from teaching story structures in a more indirect way. The planning format used for direct instruction of process goals is different, requiring careful task analysis, explicit teacher explanation, and careful teacher mediation and guidance throughout. Figure 14.4 illustrates the steps for deciding the progression of the instructional sequence for process goals.

Planning Direct Instruction for Content Goals

The lesson format for direct instruction of content goals is the directed reading lesson, not the modified directed reading lesson, because when teaching content goals, you are less concerned with whether students understand how they get meaning. Instead, you simply want to make sure students understand the message.

FIGURE 14.4　Decisions to Make in Planning Direct Instruction of Process Goals

1. Assess to determine whether students need to learn the knowledge or strategy.
2. Decide whether to use direct or indirect techniques.
3. State the learning as a specific instructional objective.
4. Do a task analysis of what you want the student to be able to do.
5. Select a text in which the knowledge or strategy can be used.
6. Select examples to be used for your own modeling and for student practice.
7. Decide on the substance of what you will say and on the sequence of the lesson, following the eight-step format for direct instruction of process goals (MDRL).
8. Assess your instruction and decide whether it was effective.

To illustrate, let's go back to the process lesson on story structures described above. A content lesson involving the same story focuses on the story, not on how to use story structure to predict meaning. You might ask questions about the story in a sequence paralleling the story structure. However, your objective is that your students learn the content, not story structure.

Content lessons are also different from process lessons in the kind of direct instruction provided. In a process lesson, you make visible the thinking processes used to make sense out of text. In the story structure illustration, for instance, the lesson focused on how thinking about story structure can affect comprehension. In a content lesson, however, you focus on the topic, the author's purposes, and the information to be gleaned from the text. The intention is that your students will demonstrate understanding of information in the story or selection.

Although the lesson-plan format for content and process lessons is similar in this first step, subsequent steps differ greatly. In an MDRL for process goals, you carefully explain how the targeted reading strategy works and how it is to be applied to the story. In a DRL for content goals, however, you move directly to the story, carefully stating the purposes for reading the selection (the value of the information contained in the text) and providing whatever study aids (guides, notes, summaries) students might need. The differences continue as your students read and discuss the text. In an MDRL, the discussion deals with how the reading strategy was used to make sense out of the selection, whereas in a DRL the discussion deals with the pertinent information in the text. Similarly, the lesson closure differs. In a content lesson, only the content is summarized; in a MDRL, both the content and the strategy used to understand the content are summarized. Figure 14.5 illustrates the decisions to make in planning direct instruction for content goals.

To summarize, direct instruction for content differs greatly from direct instruction for process despite similarities in the lesson-plan format. To be effective, you must first decide if you are developing an understanding of content or an understanding of process. Only when this decision is made should you proceed with planning and conducting the lesson.

FIGURE 14.5   Decisions to Make in Planning Direct Instruction of Content Goals

1. Decide whether the selection is worth reading.
2. State an objective for the content knowledge you want students to learn.
3. Analyze what the students need to know about the words, topic, purpose, and text structure in order to get the content knowledge.
4. Decide how you will aid students in using the words, topic, purpose, and text structure to get the content knowledge.
5. Decide the sequence of the lesson and what you will say in the lesson.
6. Decide how you will evaluate whether the lesson has been a success.

Analyzing Planning Decisions

Like all good instruction, direct instruction requires careful planning, whether the goal is process or content. You must have a clear concept of the intended goal and must have the techniques and examples to be used firmly in mind. This does not mean that direct instruction involves no spontaneity on your part; on the contrary, unanticipated student responses frequently require you to spontaneously modify your lesson plans. Such interactive decision making is only effective if you carefully make the preceding planning decisions. The better prepared you are, the more likely it is that you will be able to spontaneously create good responses to unanticipated happenings.

To illustrate the planning decisions in direct instruction of process, assume once again that you are teaching a second grade class. You note that prefixes is one of the skills suggested by the basal text being used by one of your groups and students in that group cannot figure out the pronunciation of an unrecognized prefixed word. Since your assessment indicates a need for instruction, you make your first decision: You decide to teach prefixes.

Second, you decide which of the three major goals you are after and what kind of instruction to use. Since you want your students to use prefixes to repair blockages to meaning caused by unrecognized words, you are teaching a process goal. Since strategies are better taught by direct than by indirect instruction, you decide to use direct instruction.

Third, you decide to state the goal as an instructional objective. In this case, you state your objective as follows: "Given a text containing unrecognized words having a known root prefixed by *dis-* or *un-*, the student figures out how to say the unrecognized word and explains the thinking used to figure out the word in each of the five samples of real text."

The fourth decision is to do a task analysis of how readers think through the process of figuring out the pronunciation of unknown words having prefixes. You know the goal is to consciously apply a strategy to pronounce unrecognized prefixed words; the language principle is that new words can be built by adding prefixes and suffixes; a sequence to follow in identifying a prefixed word could be identify the root, identify the prefix, separate the two, pronounce each separately, pronounce them as one word, and see if the word makes sense in the sentence.

The fifth decision is to select a text that will give your students a real opportunity to apply the strategy. Usually, basal text stories are used, although you must ensure that the basal selection does indeed contain prefixed words that your students might not recognize so there is really an opportunity to apply the strategy. If there is no text situation and you teach it in isolation, students may never learn to apply it to text.

Sixth, collect examples that can be used when explaining the strategy. There must be examples you can use for modeling and examples students can use to try out the strategy. Not only must there be enough examples, they must all be ones which reflect the critical features of the strategy.

Seventh, decide what to say during the course of the lesson. Since direct instruction is heavily dependent upon your ability to explain things, it is necessary that you plan what to say. This does not mean that you must write out everything you will say ahead of time. It *does* mean, however, that you think carefully about what needs to be said, make notes about the sequence of your explanation, decide on key statements, on what to display on the chalkboard, on what material (if any) students should have in hand during the explanation, and so on. It is helpful to use the MDRL format to guide your thinking in this regard. Example 14.1 illustrates what a carefully stated lesson in prefixes looks like when it follows this format and shows how a teacher might talk through each step.

Finally, assess the effect of your instruction and decide whether you were successful or not. Did your students learn to use prefixes? Do they exhibit the behavior specified in your objective? In this regard, it is sometimes useful to interview students following instruction. If, after your lesson is over, students can answer the questions "What were you learning to do? When would you use it in real reading? How do you do it?" you have probably been instructionally successful.

The decision patterns are similar when teaching a content goal. However, rather than starting with a skill contained in the basal, you start with a selection that needs to be read. Your first decision is whether this selection is worth reading. You then decide why it is worth reading, and develop an objective describing what student behavior will be when the targeted content has been learned. Instead of doing a task analysis as you would with a process goal, you analyze what knowledge sources (words, topic, purpose, and text structure) the student might use to get meaning from the text. On the basis of this analysis, you decide what learning aids to provide your students to ensure that they get the targeted content. Such aids might take the form of an explanation or could be paper-and-pencil aids such as study guides that focus students on the right section of the text or on certain relationships being developed by the writer. In any case, decide how you will talk to students during the lesson. Finally, as with the process lesson, decide how to evaluate the success or failure of the lesson.

To summarize, direct instruction is *not* a matter of planning an instructional script and then reading it to students. It is a carefully developed, well-structured, and explicit effort to achieve particular curricular goals with the particular group of students you are teaching at the moment. Careful planning is essential for two reasons. First, teaching students how to make sense from text is a complex and difficult task. If you do not think carefully about it, the instruction can become jumbled and confusing. Second, all instruction demands that you be able to respond spontaneously during instruction to your students' unanticipated responses while still maintaining an instructional focus on the intended goal. Such focused spontaneity is not possible unless careful planning has been done beforehand. Consequently, good planning is crucial to effective direct instruction.

EXAMPLE   14.1   Sample Lesson for Direct Instruction of Process Goals: Teaching Prefixes as a Strategy for Pronouncing Unrecognized Words

1. Introducing the basal text lesson

"Today we are going to read a story about a monkey that lived in the zoo. How many of you have been to the zoo? What do you see at the zoo? We are going to read about the monkeys that lived in the zoo and the special problem a monkey named Clyde had with his brothers and sisters. Now in this story there are some hard words that you have never had before. Here's one right here [*shows students*]. Here's another [*shows students*]. I'm going to teach you a strategy for figuring out these words and others like them so that, when you come to them in the story, you will be able to figure them out yourselves and go right on finding out about what happens to the monkey."

2. Introducing the strategy

"Sometimes when you are reading you run into a word you don't recognize, like the words I just showed you which are in the story we'll read today. Because you don't recognize it, you can't understand the story. So we need to stop and figure out the word. Today I'm going to show you how to figure out unrecognized words that have prefixes on them. At the end of the lesson, you will have a strategy for pronouncing in your basal text story or in other books you read those unrecognized words that begin with the prefix *dis-* or *un-*. This strategy will help you figure out the pronunciation of prefixed words so you can continue getting the author's meaning despite these hard words. In order to do this, you need to look for the root word, then look for the *dis-* or *un-*. Then you separate the two, pronounce each one separately, then say the prefix and the root together."

3. Mental Modeling

"I'll explain how I figure out words like these. You'll do this in a moment, so pay attention to the way I figure these words out. Let's say that I'm reading along in my basal story and I run into the word *unhappy*. If I've never seen this word before, I say to myself, 'Oh, oh. I need to figure this word out if I'm going to continue getting the author's meaning.' So I stop, look at the word and think about what strategy I can use to make sense out of this word. I see that it is a prefixed word, so I think about a prefix strategy. I find the root [*circles it*]. I separate the root from the prefix [*draws a line between them*]. Then I pronounce the prefix—*un-*. Then I pronounce the root—*happy*. Then I say the two parts together—*unhappy*. Then I put the word back into the sentence in the story to make sure it makes sense. Now let's review what I did. You tell me the steps I followed, and I'll list them up here on the board. Susie, what did I do first? Yes, first I...[*writes on board*]... then I...[*writes on board*]..., [etc.]."

4. Mediating students' initial attempts to apply the strategy using directives and cues

"Can you use my strategy to figure out unrecognized words? Let's try one and I'll help you. Let's assume that you are reading your story and you come to this unknown word [*writes* dislike *on the board, circling the prefix and root and drawing a line between them*]. Let's see if you can use the strategy I used to figure out this word. You have two things to help you: the steps in the strategy listed on the board here [*points*] and the circles and lines in the word you're trying to figure out here [*points*]. Mary, show me how you use the strategy to figure out this word." [*Mary responds by starting with the recognition of a break in meaning getting caused by an unknown word and by going through the steps of the strategy aloud, ultimately identifying the word as* dislike *and checking to see if it makes sense in the sentence.*]

• **Interaction with questions and faded cues**

"Okay. That was good because you thought about how to figure out words that begin with the prefix *dis-* or *un-*. Now let's see if you can do the same thing when I give you less help. I'm going to erase from the board the steps of my strategy, and you see if you can use a strategy of your own that is like mine. And when I put our word [*writes* unkind *on the board*], I'll just circle the prefix and root but leave off the dividing line [*circles prefix and root*]. Now, Sam, what would you do first to figure out this word? Can you show me how you'd figure out the word?" [*Sam responds by just pronouncing the word, says* unkind.] "You said the word correctly Sam, but I don't know whether you were doing the thinking correctly. What did you do first? Talk out loud so I can hear how you figured that word out." [*Sam responds, stating the steps he used.*] "That's good, Sam. You stated the steps you used to figure out the word correctly. This strategy doesn't work all the time, because some of our words look like words with prefixes but really aren't." [*Illustrates the word* under.] "See if this word can be pronounced using our prefix strategy." [*Leads students through the process showing them where the strategy doesn't work and why.*]

• **Interaction with fewer cues**

[*Continues to elicit responses from the students, but gradually phases out the amount of assistance until the students are doing all the thinking without help and are figuring out the prefixed words independently. Provides other nonexamples, such as* unless, *having students state whether the strategy works and why.*]

• **Interaction with supportive feedback and no cues**

"Okay, Now before I give you practice in doing this alone, let's make sure we all know how to figure out words like these." [*Has students tell how they figure out prefixed words when no cues are provided. Also provides nonexamples for contrast.*]

5. Setting purposes for reading the basal selection

"Now we are going to read the story about the monkey named Clyde. We talked about the fact that Clyde had a problem with his brothers and sisters and we want to find out what that problem was and whether you have had similar problems in your house. There are some hard words in this story, which you haven't seen before. When you come to these words, say to yourself, 'Oh, oh. I'm going to have to figure this word out.' Then see if your prefix strategy will work, and, if the hard word does have a prefix, use what we learned about figuring out prefixed words to figure out the word in the story."

6. Silent or oral reading

[*Students read the story. The reading may be oral in primary grades but will almost always be silent reading in the middle and upper grades.*]

7. Discussion

[*Leads a discussion in which questions are posed about both the content and the application of the prefix strategy while reading the story. The intent is to assess whether students understood the content and the application of the prefix strategy.*]

8. Lesson closure

[*Closes the lesson by having students summarize what happened in the story and how the prefix strategy was used to help understand the story. May also do some kind of culminating activity, enriching activity, or broadened language experience activity at this stage as a means for bringing closure to the lesson. The closure should also include a statement such as the following.*] "All right. Now that you have successfully used the prefix strategy to figure out hard words in the basal text story, we have to be sure to use it in other things you read. What other things do you read where you could use this strategy? What if you ran into an unknown word when reading in your USSR book? Could you use this strategy in that situation? Can you tell how you would use the prefix strategy in reading a newspaper?"

PLANNING FOR THE SUBTLETIES OF INSTRUCTION

The foregoing suggestions for planning lessons are important and practical. However, good lesson planning is not simply a matter of following a format. Instruction requires subtle distinctions and decisions, some of which are described below.

Lesson Length

Many people think of lessons as confined to a definite length of time, usually a single class period. However, lessons are seldom started and finished in one day. What is planned for either direct or indirect instruction often extends over several class periods, even if everything goes perfectly.

In reality, however, things seldom go perfectly. No matter how well you plan, something always needs improving. Consequently, a lesson plan initiated one day will often need to be modified overnight and presented again in order to clarify points of confusion. Often the second day of instruction will begin with a review of the first day and, depending on the review, will either remain at the first phase of the lesson or move on to the next phase. Lesson plans are not permanent documents. They are constantly being tinkered with, modified, adjusted, and improved to meet the needs of your students. This tinkering requires careful attention and subtle decision making.

Introducing the Lesson

Direct instruction requires that students be told what the lesson is about at the outset. However, when the targeted goal is the use of a strategy, three factors complicate the seemingly simple task of introducing the lesson.

First, there is the difficulty of translating skills into strategies. It is easier to introduce a lesson on main idea by saying, "Today, we are going to learn *about* main ideas" rather than saying, "Today, we are going to learn *how to figure out* the main idea the author is trying to convey." The distinction is subtle, but crucial. If your students are to learn how to be strategic readers, you must emphasize strategic thinking, not knowledge about the skill.

Second, although it is easier to think in terms of separate and isolated lessons, in actuality lessons cannot be isolated from one another. Instead, each lesson is a minor variation of earlier ones. All share certain characteristics: the goal of sense making, active student thinking, student use of text and prior knowledge to predict, and student confirmation or rejection of predictions based on whether the result makes sense in context. Consequently, you make better progress when you emphasize common themes instead of teaching isolated lessons. Again, the difference is subtle, but critical.

Third, being a good reader means understanding where and when to use the strategies that have been learned; application is crucial. Hence, you should specify when a strategy is to be used in real reading. Rather than saying that a strategy "will make you a better reader," it is better to start with a passage from real text, illustrate how one might lose the gist of such a passage, and state that "this strategy will help you fix situations like this when they happen to you." Again the distinction is subtle, but essential.

Showing Students How

All lesson plan formats include a section in which you explain and demonstrate what is being learned. Your explanations must reflect three subtle distinctions.

First, keep the desired goal firmly in mind. For instance, if the object is to teach a strategy, you must not get sidetracked into emphasizing the story's content. Explanations must focus on the process of understanding the strategy, not on the content itself. This is a subtle distinction because process can never be totally separated from content, so we often end up emphasizing story content. Note what happens in the following lesson where a main-idea strategy is being taught, but student responses indicate that they do not understand how to figure out the main idea. The teacher uses a paragraph about bears hibernating in the winter to reexplain.

T: Let's talk about animals that hibernate. You know what hibernate means, right? What does *hibernate* mean?

S: [*inaudible*]

T: Okay, animals that sleep through the winter, right? Now, what are some animals that might hibernate?

S: A bear.

T: Okay, a bear.

S: Rabbit.

T: Rabbit.

S: Fox.

T: I'm not sure about all the animals. Squirrels, okay. But don't you see squirrels out in the winter?

S: Yeah.

S: Yeah.

T: Then are they hibernating?

S: No.

S: Yeah.

T: Maybe they do. I don't know. Maybe that is something that I should check out, too.

At this point, the teacher realizes that she is not teaching students a strategy for figuring out main idea, but is focusing on story content about animals that hibernate. She tries to shift to a process focus—that is, to the strategy for figuring out main idea. She generates the following nonexample:

T: Okay, let's say we were talking about those animals that hibernate and I said, "Oh, many, many animals sleep through the winter. Some of the animals are bears. Bears hibernate in caves." And I talk about bears, but then all of a sudden I say, "Fish swim in the sea."

S: How do fish hibernate in that cold water?

T: I didn't say they hibernate. I said "Fish swim in the sea." "Birds fly south." Is that about animals that hibernate?

S: No.

S: Yeah.

T: No. So, would this be included in my paragraph?

S: No.

T: No. So, what is a main idea? A main idea is a group of sentences that do what?

S: [*in chorus*]:
Hibernate.

Despite this teacher's best efforts, instruction failed because she slipped into discussing the content of the story when she should have continued to emphasize how to figure out the main idea. Maintaining a focus on the intended goal is the crucial component of effective instruction.

A second subtlety in lesson explanation involves showing students how to do something. Because reading is an invisible mental process, it cannot be demonstrated like a swimming instructor demonstrates a new stroke. Instead, you must make visible the thinking that led to the answer. To do this, say aloud the mental steps you perform when using the strategy (or that you have analyzed to be the steps a novice would need to use). Such thinking out loud models the thinking you want students to do. Hence, it is helpful to say, "When *I* use this strategy, I think first about the important words. For instance, in this paragraph, I read along and identify these words as important. Then I. . . ." In so doing, your students can initially "do as the teacher does" when employing the strategy. Such modeling is an essential part of explanation. Without it, your students may not know how to begin the task.

A third subtlety in making effective explanations requires that you not be too prescriptive. No one knows precisely how humans process information. The best that you can do is analyze your own thinking, show your students what you do, and encourage them to adapt your model to their style and needs. Allowing for student adaptation is the key. Your model must be descriptive, not prescriptive. Say, "Here is a way I think about this problem. Now I want to see if you can use my demonstration to help you solve similar problems." Don't say, "Here is *the* way to do this; you must employ it as I do."

Mediating Student Acquisition

A major part of a process lesson is the interactive phase, sometimes called **guided practice.** It is here that you attempt to move your students gradually to the point where they can use strategies independently. As in the other sections of the lesson, subtle verbal distinctions are crucial.

Explanation implies that a teacher does all the talking. However, when you do that, learning does not occur. There must be a gradual transition from teacher modeling to student control, and you must carefully judge how quickly or slowly to effect this transfer. Moving too quickly leaves students unclear about what to do; moving too slowly is boring. In order to control this transfer process, probe for how students get their answers, emphasizing mental processing rather than answer accuracy. For instance, when you direct a student to the main idea of a paragraph, it is better to ask, "How do you know what the main idea is?" than to ask "What is the main idea?" If your students show understanding of how to use the strategy, the lesson can progress; if they do not, more explanation is needed.

If student responses indicate a misunderstanding of the strategy, you must spontaneously generate a reexplanation. Such reexplanation is difficult because it requires instant decision making. In the following illustration taken from a lesson on main ideas, the teacher reads a paragraph to the group, then proceeds as follows.

T: Now, of these three titles, which one would be the best main idea? Mary?

S: A trip downtown.

T: Okay, John, what do you think?

S: The new shirt.

T: Bib, what was your choice?

S: The new shirt.

T: Joan, what about you?

S: A trip downtown.

At this point, it is clear that her students have not understood the teacher's explanation. The situation calls for an elaboration or reexplanation of how one figures out the gist of a paragraph. Instead, the teacher says:

T: I think the girls decided on a trip downtown and the boys like the new shirt. Mainly, what was the story about?

S: A trip downtown.

S: Getting a new shirt.

T: Getting a new shirt, wasn't it?

The teacher *does* try to elaborate by referring to what the story was mainly about. However, she is not explicit. Compare it to the following spontaneous reexplanation.

T: We seem to have some confusion. The main idea is the author's major message in the paragraph. Look at the paragraph here on the chalkboard. What words did we say were important in this paragraph? Sam, can you read them?

S: Store, shirt, buy, long-sleeved, downtown mall.

T: Good. Now, the topic of all these words—that ties them together—is what? Mary?

S: They're all about a new shirt.

T: Good. The new shirt is what it's about. That's the topic. Now I've got to think about what the author's major message is regarding the new shirt. So I think to myself, "What does the author want me to understand about the new shirt? What is his main message to me?" To do that, I think of how these words and sentences can be combined into a message. When I think about them together, it's more than just a new shirt. Let's combine them together like this [*writes on the board*]. What message ties all these words together? John?

S: It's about how to buy a new shirt.

T: Right. There are many words in paragraphs, but we have to decide what the main message is—what idea ties it all together. How did you know what ties this paragraph together, John?

S: I looked for words that would tell me what the topic was and then thought about what the author wants me to understand about the topic—about the shirt.

This spontaneously generated reexplanation is more helpful than the first sample because it's more explicit. This difference, though subtle, is crucial.

It is not unusual to use various kinds of highlighting to focus student attention on salient features of the strategy. For instance, you may use the chalkboard and underline key words, draw arrows from one meaning relationship to another, circle particular structures, or write out steps to help students learn to use the strategy. However, you must ensure that your students learn the intended goal, not the cues and prompts (such as your underlining or the steps in the procedure). You can be very explicit about salient features, steps, and sequences but, in the process, unintentionally make reading into a mechanical activity of rote memory rather than a strategic, sense-making activity.

Practice

All lesson plan formats all for practice, and all practice calls for repetition of a task to make it habitual. Here, again, the subtleties are crucial. An important consideration in the practice part of the lesson is in choosing the proper form of practice. Most teachers use workbooks or ditto sheets. However, these tend to emphasize artificial reading tasks. Since your object is to get students to use strategies in reading real text, we recommend that practice occur in guided reading of real text—for example, the basal text selection, the social studies text, library books, or some other real reading material. Then the learning can be practiced in contexts similar to where it will ultimately be used.

Another important decision involves the nature of the activities assigned students. In traditional basal instruction, students are asked to read and answer questions and are then assigned grades based on the number of correct answers. When teaching reading strategies, however, you are more interested in the thinking processes students go through to get the answer than in the answer itself. Good practice activities, therefore, call for repetitive use of the *thinking* involved. The goal is thoughtful, not automatized, application.

A third decision regarding practice involves the student behaviors you choose to reward. Since you want to develop a strategic approach to text, you should praise students for "knowing how they know." There is a fine distinction between being praised for thinking strategically and being praised for getting the right answer. The most effective instruction praises the former.

Transfer to Real Reading

Application is the most neglected part of all lessons. When teaching for strategic reading, application requires more than an opening statement about a strategy's usefulness or a general reminder of the possibility of applying it to a basal story. Application must include a genuine reading situation where, once a meaning breakdown occurs, students can be guided through their storehouse of strategies, select the appropriate one, fix the difficulty, and continue processing text. The subtlety here involves knowing how to help students recognize when a strategy is called for, how to access the proper one, how to use it in a real situation, and how to determine whether the strategy worked or not. This part of a teacher's explanation is perhaps more crucial than any other.

To summarize, using lesson plan formats helps guide the planning of indirect and direct instruction. These provide a structure that aids your decision making as you plan. However, good instruction also involves fine distinctions that you must anticipate. If you follow the lesson plan formats as a rote procedure, your instruction will be boring and ineffective. If, however, you use the lesson formats as a guide and think about the subtleties of the task, your students, and the intended application to read text, your instruction will be more successful, more interesting, and more relevant.

SUMMARY

The essence of instruction is its intentionality. That is, instruction is designed to develop specific objectives through direct instruction, indirect instruction, or a combination thereof. To achieve intentionality, you must state objectives for both long-term units that build cohesive networks of understandings and for individual lessons that develop specific goals. The objective should not only state what the student should be able to do and how well, it should also state the situation and conditions under which it is to be done. If your instruction is to be mainly indirect, decisions revolve around the three steps of indirect lessons; if your instruction is to be mainly direct, decisions revolve around the eight steps of the modified directed reading lesson when teaching a process goal and around the directed reading lesson when teaching a content goal. For either kind of instruction, you must do a task analysis to decide where to direct your students' attention. However, instruction is a fluid, complex enterprise. You must be prepared with lesson formats, but also must be prepared to make spontaneous subtle distinctions and adjustments as you teach.

SUGGESTED ADDITIONAL READING

ALLINGTON, R. L., & STRANGE, M.   (1977). The problem with reading games. *Reading Teacher, 31*(3), 272–274.

ATWELL, A. A., & RHODES, L. K.   (1984). Strategy lessons as alternatives to skill lessons in reading. *Journal of Reading, 27*(8), 700–705.

BEED, P., HAWKINS, E., & ROLLER, C.   (1991). Moving learners toward independence: The power of scaffolded instruction. *Reading Teacher, 44*(9), 648–655.

COGNITION AND TECHNOLOGY GROUP AT VANDERBILT.   (1990). Anchored instruction and its relationship to situated cognition. *Educational Researcher, 19*(6), 2–9.

DAVEY, B.   (1983). Think aloud: Modeling the cognitive processes of reading comprehension. *Journal of Reading, 27*, 44–47.

DUFFY, G., & ROEHLER, L.   (1987). Improving reading instruction through the use of responsive elaboration. *Reading Teacher, 40*, 514–521.

DUFFY, G., & ROEHLER, L.   (1987). Teaching reading skills as strategies. *Reading Teacher, 40*, 414–418.

DUFFY, G., ROEHLER, L., & HERRMANN, B. A.   (1988). Modeling mental processes helps poor readers become strategic readers. *Reading Teacher, 41*(8), 762–767.

GAMBRELL, L. B.   (1980). Think-time: Implications for reading instruction. *Reading Teacher, 34*(2), 143–146.

GUTHRIE, J. T.   (1982). Teacher effectiveness: The quest for refinement. *Reading Teacher, 35*(5), 636–638.

GUZZETTI, B. J., & MARZANO, R. J.   (1984). Correlates the effective reading instruction. *Reading Teacher, 37*(8), 754–758.

ISAACS, M. L.   (1979). The many facets of language arts: Helps and handbooks for lesson planning. *Language Arts, 56*(5), 577–580.

JOHNS, J. L.   (1982). Does our language of instruction confuse beginning teachers? *Reading Psychology, 3*(1), 37–41.

KITAGAWA, M. M.   (1982). Improving discussions or how to get the students to ask the questions. *Reading Teacher, 36*(1), 42–45.

RILEY, J. D.   (1979). Teachers' responses are as important as the questions they ask. *Reading Journal, 32*(5), 534–537.

SADOW, M. W.   (1982). The use of story grammar in the design of questions. *Reading Teacher, 35*(5), 518–522.

SHAKE, M. C., & ALLINGTON, R. L.   (1985). Where do teachers' questions come from? *Reading Teacher, 38*(4), 432–438.

SPIEGEL, D.   (1990). Materials for integrating science and social studies with the language arts. *Reading Teacher, 44*(2), 162–163.

STAAB, C.   (1990). Teacher mediation in one whole literacy classroom. *Reading Teacher, 43*(3), 548–552.

STIEGLITZ, E., & OEHLKERS, W.   (1989). Improving teacher discourse in a reading lesson. *Reading Teacher, 42*(6), 374–379.

STRICKLAND, D., & MORROW, L.   (1990) Integrating the emergent literacy curriculum with themes. *Reading Teacher, 43*(3), 604–605.

THE RESEARCH BASE

ANDERSON, R., WILKENSON, I., & MASON, J.   (1991). A microanalysis of the small-group, guided reading lesson: Effects of an emphasis on global story meaning. *Reading Research Quarterly, 26*(4), 417–441.

COMMEYRAS, M.   (1990). Analyzing a critical-thinking reading lesson. *Teaching and Teacher Education, 6*(3), 201–214.

DUFFY, G., ROEHLER, L., SIVAN, E.   (1987). Effects of explaining the reasoning associated with using reading strategies. *Reading Research Quarterly, 22*(3), 347–368.

PEARSON, P. D.   (1985). Changing the face of reading comprehension instruction. *Reading Teacher, 38*(8), 724–738.

ROEHLER, L., & DUFFY, G.   (1991). Teachers' instructional actions. In R. Barr, M. Kamil, P. Mosenthal, & P. D. Pearson (Eds.), *Handbook of reading research, volume II.* New York: Longman.

WEBER, R., & SHAKE, M.   (1988). Teachers' rejoinders to students' responses in reading lessons. *Journal of Reading Behavior, 20*(4), 285–299.

ACTIVITIES FOR REFLECTING, OBSERVING, AND TEACHING

Reflecting on Planning and Teaching Units

PURPOSE: Learning to plan and teach units and lessons takes much thought and analysis. This activity is designed to help you make some of the distinctions which are crucial to good planning and teaching.

DIRECTIONS: Answer each of the questions posed below.

1. To say that objectives are important is almost a platitude. It is easy to answer a question about why objectives are important with jargon and high sounding phrases. But objectives are important because they are practical. Give one hypothetical example of when a lesson or unit objective would be practical.

2. There is a big difference between following a unit as provided in the teacher's guide of a basal textbook and developing a unit with your students. It is obviously easier to follow directions someone else has already thought out. The obvious advantage of developing your own unit with your students is that units planned with your students will be genuinely interesting to them, will capitalize on their particular current concerns, and will be tailored to their background. Describe below one hypothetical scenario regarding how you might get your students interested in a particular unit that you and they plan together.

3. We have talked in earlier chapters about the fact that instruction can be thought of as a continuum moving from totally indirect to totally direct. Describe briefly below a unit you might teach at your grade level, and then describe lessons within that unit which would represent the various degrees of indirect and direct instruction represented.
   Your unit:

   A very, very indirect lesson might be:

A somewhat indirect lesson might be:

A somewhat direct lesson might be:

A very direct lesson might be:

4. Four crucial aspects of a direct instruction lesson are introducing the lesson, showing students how, mediating students' understanding, and transferring what they learned to real reading. Select a strategy you might teach at your grade level. Then describe what you would do for each of the four parts:

Introducing the lesson:

Showing students how:

Mediating students' understanding:

Transferring to real reading:

Watching Others Plan and Teach Units and Lessons

PURPOSE: Because your understanding of unit and lesson instruction will be enhanced if, after watching other teachers teach units and lessons, you see what the students themselves were thinking and then analyze the results, this activity is designed to help you get students perceptions on units and lessons.

DIRECTIONS: Arrange to observe a teacher teaching several consecutive lessons in a unit. Following each lesson, interview five students selected at random. Ask each student the following three questions:

What was your teacher teaching you today?

When will you use what you are learning?

Explain to me how to do what you were learning to do today.

Following the interviews, analyze students' responses. Did the students understand the purpose of the lessons in the same way the teacher did? If there were differences, what do you think caused the differences? What could the teacher have done to alter the quality of the students' understandings?

Doing It Yourself

PURPOSE: At some point in time, you will have to prepare and teach units and lessons yourself. This activity is designed to help you do so.

DIRECTIONS: Arrange to teach a class of elementary or middle school children. Plan a unit for that group of students, following a sequence like the following.

Think about the topics that interest your students. How could you transform students' interests into a problem to be solved? Write down such a problem.

Does this problem call for the genuine use of reading and writing in solving the problem? Write down how reading and writing can be used to solve the problem.

Can the problem be organized into a project? What would the project be?

Will the project culminate in some sort of activity at the end of the unit? State what the culminating activity might be.

What content goals will you be able to accomplish in this unit (i.e., what expository and/or narrative text will students be asked to comprehend and what is the content they should understand from these texts)? List the subject matter understandings to be developed and the texts you will use (these are your content goals for the unit).

What attitude goals will you be able to develop in this unit (i.e., what feelings and concepts can you develop)? List these (they are your attitude goals for the unit).

What skills will your students need to learn in order to read the texts you want them to read during the unit? What strategies will you want your students to apply to the texts they will be reading during the unit? List these (they are your process objectives for the unit).

Now list a series of lessons you will teach. Start with how you will introduce the unit to the students and list the lessons you will teach to develop your content, attitude, and process goals. Conclude by describing the culminating activity.

How to Manage Reading Instruction

15

GETTING READY

More than any other single thing, the scarcity of time makes classroom teaching difficult. There are many things to do and not enough time in which to do them. Consequently, time is your most important instructional resource.

To get the most from the time you have, you must manage it well. Expert teachers manage reading instruction in three ways: they allocate time to reading, they assure effective activity flow, and they ensure sustained student engagement in tasks. This chapter develops each of these three management techniques.

The hard truth of teaching is that you can do all the organizational steps specified in previous chapters—create a literate environment, assess students' abilities, adapt the basal, and plan good lessons—and still be ineffective if you cannot get your students on task and keep them there. Consequently, management is crucial to getting organized for instruction.

FOCUS QUESTIONS

- What can you do to ensure that enough time is allocated to reading?

- What techniques can you employ to achieve smooth activity flow?

- What can be done to make sure that students remain engaged in tasks?

ALLOCATING TIME TO READING

In most classrooms, reading period occurs first thing each morning and lasts for an hour or an hour and a half. Typically, all this **allocated time** is taken up by basal text instruction. Usually a teacher meets with three or four reading groups during this time, teaching one group while the other groups do seatwork.

To develop all three goals of reading, however, you must think more broadly about how to allocate time for reading. Because reading permeates all aspects of the school day, you can integrate reading instruction into other school activities; that is, reading goals can be achieved during times other than the hour or hour and a half planned for reading. In the area of attitudes, for instance, you can develop conceptual understandings about the communication function of reading in conjunction with any subject matter; you can develop concepts about the reciprocal nature of reading and writing during a writing period; and you can develop positive responses to reading at any point in the school day when you are sharing stories and poems. Similarly, you can teach certain process goals about how the reading system works from a social studies or science textbook as well as from a basal reader. Finally, you can develop content goals anytime a text is used. In short, reading goals can be developed all day long.

Likewise, you can integrate other school content into reading time. Students can read science materials as seatwork during the reading period, read stories and poems during reading group time, and share quality books in collaborative student groups as seatwork while you work with another reading group. You can arrange for direct and indirect instruction to occur simultaneously. For instance, while you directly instruct one reading group, other reading groups can be engaged in indirect instructional activities.

Reading goals can be achieved while sharing stories.

Accomplishing such integration, however, requires careful year-long planning. You must identify when certain goals will be developed, and you must consciously allocate instructional time for reading beyond the usual hour or hour and a half. For instance, you must examine the year-long language arts or social studies curriculum and decide when objectives in those areas can be integrated with reading goals. Integrating reading with other content areas does not occur by accident; you must consciously plan instructional time to make the integration happen. By doing so, you create more instructional time for reading.

Another way to create more reading time is to look for **nook-and-cranny time** in the school day. All school days have "dead spots" of 5 to 10 minutes duration. It may be a transition time from one activity to another, a short period of time between two special teachers, or any other time that is too short to start a formal lesson. These nooks and crannies of time are gold mines for you if you are looking for extra reading time. For instance, these are good times for sharing and other activities designed to develop concepts and positive feelings. Similarly, these short periods of time are useful for direct instruction about how certain words convey emotional connotations, how to make predictions about what meaning is being communicated, or how to get content meaning from various kinds of texts.

PLANNING FOR EFFECTIVE CLASSROOM ACTIVITY FLOW

Successfully engaging students on tasks demands a smooth flow of classroom activity. Smooth **activity flow** depends on the physical arrangement of your room, the patterns you use, and your behaviors in managing academic content.

Physical Arrangement

If you plan to use both large- and small-group instruction and have an average size room, then space becomes a problem. Many teachers find that the traditional rows of seats take up too much space, and they use seating clusters instead. Other teachers use a large rug in the middle of the room for whole-group instruction and have students sit at independent learning centers around the edges for beginning and closing exercises. There are many ways to physically arrange a classroom. The only limitations are the dimensions of the room and your creativity. Some teachers are very elaborate and use portable screens, old furniture, large floor pillows, and hanging screens as part of the physical setting. Some simply move the existing furniture. Others organize the room into a noisy half (interaction areas, physical activity areas, and small-group instruction areas) and a quiet half (listening centers, reading centers, and study areas). Whatever the arrangement, when teaching small groups you should place yourself where you can see the entire room. This allows you to monitor students who are not in the group and to help students in the small group remain attentive. Figure 15.1 shows two ways to create space by organizing classroom desks. Organizing

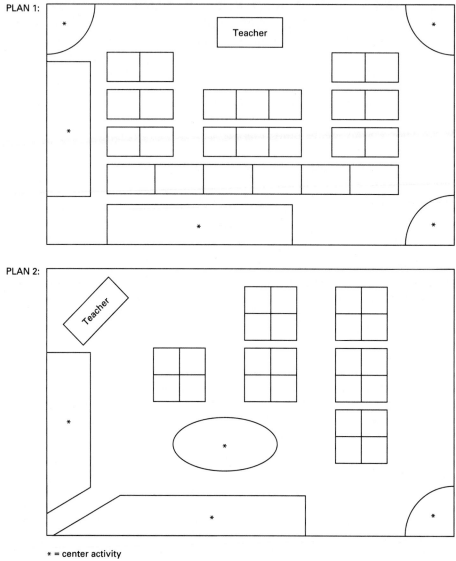

* = center activity

FIGURE 15.1 Creating Space by Organizing Classroom Desks

student desks into rows, as in Plan 1, uses up too much floor space; space for learning centers and other activities is created by eliminating rows, as in Plan 2.

Patterns

When teachers work with a reading group, students not in the group must work independently. If students are to work independently, you must firmly establish patterns or routines on which both you and the students agree. For instance, if you want your students to complete a workbook page or a practice game independently during the reading period, you should provide them with a pattern of steps to follow. It is vital that students understand these patterns and use them frequently enough to acquire habits that operate without your direct supervision. You must develop patterns for independent activities, safety-valve activities, procedures, and interaction between teacher and students.

Independent Activities   Students who are not in the participating reading group will require **independent activities.** While you teach a small group, the other students work by themselves on activities such as reading for pleasure, applying and practicing skills, reading basal stories, completing science or social studies assignments, creative writing, or practicing oral and written language skills. They can complete these independent activities as individual seatwork or at centers located in various spots within the room.

Assume that you want to develop a classroom library and reading center for your students' independent activity when they are not in a small group. You need to make decisions about where to put these, what types of books to include, what types of furniture to use, and what patterns will govern its use. You might bring in shelves that are easily accessible to your students, a piece of carpeting or rug to mark the reading center, several beanbag chairs, and several large pillows for comfortable reading. You could file books on shelves alphabetically or by interest areas (mystery books, horse stories, stories of today's world, and so forth). The patterns you develop for using the reading center may include considerations such as: Where can your students read in the room? How are books to be returned? How long can a student stay in the center? Can your students return to their seats whenever they wish? Are there follow-up activities? Can your students choose whether to work in the center or at other places? You need to decide on these patterns and then have students practice them until they become routine. Giving attention to such detail may seem mundane, but it is crucial to the success of independent activities.

Safety Valves   Once you create independent activities for your students to pursue while you are teaching small groups, you must be prepared for them to finish their assignments at varying times. Some will get done before you finish with a reading group, and if you have not anticipated this, disruptions may result. Consequently, you should plan safety valves that your students can fall back on when they finish their independent work early.

Safety valves usually take the form of learning centers or activities in which your students can participate at any time. They are different from independent activities because they do not change daily, they are not always associated with ongoing academic work in the classroom, and students think they are fun. Appropriate safety valves include recreational reading, writing in journals, vocabulary games, phonics games, chess or backgammon, art centers, or anything else that appeals to both you and your students. The important thing is that they can be completed with little assistance from you. You will, of course, need to establish with students the patterns to follow in using safety valves.

Procedural Patterns **Procedural patterns** include routines on how to start, change, keep track of progress, and stop. You should carefully establish each of these patterns.

You use **how-to-start patterns** to get initial information, such as directions and opening procedures, to your students. One way to handle this is to provide students with mailboxes, each containing directions for the period and other needed information. You can duplicate these directions on ditto sheets to minimize preparation time. The direction sheets tell your students what to do first, second, and so on. Using such a technique saves time and gets students engaged more quickly. For nonreaders, how-to-start procedures can make use of color. A manila folder that has been folded to form a pocket can hold needed materials color coded to correspond to different centers. Numbered clothespins could also be used. The intent is to keep your students well informed about procedures so they get on task as quickly as possible. Students can go to their mailboxes, pick up their directions and needed materials, return to their designated places, look at their directions, and begin. Transition time is minimized and instructional time is increased.

After how-to-start patterns are developed, **how-to-change patterns** are required. The options here are as varied as your preferences. Activities can be changed on a signal from you or when students have completed an activity. If you want students to change activities independently, one of your problems will be unfinished activities. For some activities, such as reading or ditto sheets, interruption poses little problem. However, an independent activity involving complicated steps (art projects, science experiments, and so forth) may create a problem. You can circumvent this by offering independent activities that can be interrupted during the reading period only. However you decide to change activities, your students need to know the patterns for change and to be able to implement them independently.

Once the reading period has started and is running smoothly, you need a way to keep track of students' activities. There are many ways to keep records efficiently. A good record-keeping device should not be bulky or cumbersome. It should require little time or effort to record your students' progress, and it should provide an immediate picture of where each student is in relation to desired reading goals. It should also assist in the development of reading groups. Further, it should allow you and your students to see progress. The things to remember are that it should be manageable in size and easy to use, while providing a good visual image of your students' progress relative to your goals.

A record-keeping device we have used with success consists of graph paper and a looseleaf notebook (see Figure 15.2). Arrange your students' names down the side of the paper and make divisions across the top for each of the three major goals. Within each square in each curricular category, list the objective for that

	Attitudes			Process					Content	
	Reading as communication	Reading as a tool	Positive response to reading	Language conventions	Linguistic units	Strategies: initiating predictions	Strategies: during reading	Strategies: post-reading	Functional text	Recreational text
Mary										
John										
Sue										
Frank										
Allen										

FIGURE 15.2 Sample Record-Keeping Device

outcome. As objectives are assessed, taught, retaught, practiced, or applied, note it in the squares for that objective. Keep the notebook handy to record events or behaviors as they occur, and inform students of the patterns for keeping track of progress.

Contracts are also useful for keeping track of reading progress. You and your students develop a contract, which may vary in length of time for completion (several days, a week, etc.). The completed contract is an individual record of what each student intends to complete, and it can be placed in each student's folder.

Whatever techniques you use, students should keep as many of their own records as possible. This eases your time problem and gives students a continued awareness of their own progress.

Finally, it is also important to establish patterns for putting away materials, storing incomplete activities, and handing in completed activities at the end of the reading period. This requires that you teach all your students where various materials belong and what kinds of filing systems and storage arrangements are used. You need to develop such **how-to-stop patterns** before fully implementing a reading program.

Interaction Patterns   **Interaction patterns** include procedures for socialization among students and between you and your students. Socialization is an important factor in any elementary school classroom and it occurs with or without your forethought. In order to make socialization work, you need to develop patterns for it.

There is no single way to manage interaction in the classroom. Major guidelines are that you establish some sort of patterns and that you adjust these patterns for particular students and situations. One way to regulate interaction is to divide the classroom into a noisy half and a quiet half. All verbal communications occur in the noisy half, leaving the quiet half relatively noise free. Some teachers, because of personal preference or special circumstances, confine social interaction to a designated center where their students go to talk, or to a communication center, such as a listening center or a drama center, where interaction has a set purpose.

Regardless of the interaction patterns you establish, there will never be enough for some students. Establishing times for written interaction can help alleviate this difficulty. For instance, each person in the room may have a mailbox where messages can be left, thereby allowing all members of the class to interact via letters or notes. The patterns specify when mail can be left and when you and your students can pick up and read mail.

After you have developed interaction patterns for independent activities, you must develop interaction patterns for small-group instruction. Efficient reading instruction depends upon a smoothly operating group. You should identify a section of the room as the small-group learning area where students know to come quickly and with any needed materials. You also should have your materials ready and be prepared to instruct. Finally, just as you need a way to get independent activities started, you need a way to start small-group instruction. The use of some sort of signal is often helpful.

Many teachers find that the use of a buffer helps minimize interruptions during small-group instruction. A **buffer** is another adult or a student who handles unanticipated situations while you are teaching a group. Ideally, the buffer would be a trained paraprofessional or teacher's aide, but it could also be a volunteer parent. The buffer could also be a high school student who has been released from school to help with such duties. Another source is students from higher grades in the same school. Finally, the buffer can be a student assistant from your own classroom. Responsibilities include handling minor problems such as unexpected interruptions and directions for assignments, supervision of practice activities, participation in learning games, listening to students read aloud, completing assessment activities, correcting papers, and generally providing any kind of nonprofessional classroom assistance.

To summarize, when establishing patterns, it is important that you be clear and consistent about expected behaviors. This requires careful planning. It is also important to remember that your students have a much more difficult time unlearning a pattern and then learning a new one than learning one initially. Once you set a pattern, it becomes a permanent part of a classroom routine. Make sure that the patterns you start are the ones you want. It will be necessary to give students much directed assistance early in the school year (including models, walking students through the patterns, talking over modifications, and dress rehearsals), but this assistance will diminish as they get used to the patterns. Once patterns are established, you can begin instruction with confidence that your students will be engaged on task.

MANAGING THE ACADEMIC CONTENT OF READING

Before instruction starts, you must make certain decisions about managing the reading content. The following six decision areas are particularly important:

1. Your lessons should focus on academic content.

2. You need to be aware of your students' personal concerns.

3. You need to accurately assess skill levels and provide learning tasks of appropriate difficulty.

4. You need to know how to focus attention.

5. You need to know how to provide appropriate challenges.

6. You need to help your students be responsible and cooperative.

First, you should keep the instructional focus on targeted academic content during a lesson. If it is a process lesson, keep the focus on the process; if it is a story being read for enjoyment, keep the focus on the content of the story; if it is a lesson on developing a concept of reading, keep the focus on that concept. This means that you must resist students who try to steer you into discussions of other topics. If you want students to learn what the lesson is designed to teach, you must keep the focus on that content.

Second, you need to be sensitive to your students' personal concerns. The focus may be on academic content, but students' personal concerns need to be woven into lessons. For instance, when a lesson is on tornadoes, and students live in an area where tornadoes occur, you should be aware of their related worries.

Third, you need to determine your students' instructional level (see Chapter 12) and create learning tasks that challenge them intellectually. You must know which curriculum goal you are working on and where your students are with regard to that goal. For instance, if the goal is to develop an understanding that reading involves making predictions and confirming or modifying those predictions, and your students have never worked on this goal, assume that they are at an initial learning phase. If they have worked on this goal in previous years, estimate whether they are still in the initial learning phase or in a subsequent one and if they need more presentation, just practice, or guided application. In any case, the more precise you can be in assessing needs, the easier it will be to match instructional activities to student developmental levels and thereby ensure a high degree of task engagement.

Fourth, you must know to focus your students. Knowing what your students attend to depends on knowing what their personal concerns are. To focus their attention, you must have the targeted goal clearly established in your mind. If the goal is a memory task, focus the students' attention on the salient features; if the goal is a procedural task, focus students' attention on the procedural steps, and so on. Once you know what the goal requires, you need to focus students on that.

Fifth, you need to provide appropriate challenge for your students. If they can do a task without assistance, there is no challenge. If they cannot do the task even with appropriate assistance, then the challenge is too great. Providing the appropriate challenge means selecting a learning task with which your students need some assistance but which is not so hard that it is frustrating.

Finally, you need to cultivate student responsibility and cooperation. The ultimate goal of schooling is to have all students responsible for their own behaviors and actions. Classrooms characterized by responsible behavior naturally create an optimum environment for learning. Similarly, each member of a group is affected by the other members. Cooperative behaviors allow a group to make decisions and move ahead. Anything you do to promote group decisions and cooperative behavior helps create optimum conditions for achievement.

ENSURING SUSTAINED STUDENT ENGAGEMENT

Allocating time to the three major curricular outcomes is fairly easy; keeping students on task is harder. Younger students will become engaged just because you want them to, but older students rarely do so. In both cases, it is difficult to keep students engaged once instruction has started. The following discussion of teacher behaviors that encourage continued **student engagement** is divided into those behaviors that apply to all or most teaching situations and those that relate to specific problems.

General Teacher Action

Six general teacher behaviors help maintain student engagement on task. First, you should make students accountable for all work, whether it is completed independently or in groups. Once work has been assigned, it should be completed. If they are not held accountable for completing their work, students find other things to do. This means that you must correct and provide feedback for all academic work assigned in the classroom. Attention to student accountability helps ensure engaged time on task.

Second, you should ensure all students are not only attentive but actively involved during instruction. It is not enough to have their eyes on you. In order to keep their attention, you must actively involve them in thinking, observing, doing, listening, speaking, reading, or writing. The hardest activities to sustain are thinking, listening, and reading. After students have thought for a moment or two, or listened or read for a short time, allow them to speak or write. Continued active involvement requires opportunities to both receive information (listen, observe, or read) and express information (speak, act, or write). Younger children can sustain only short periods of receiving and giving information, while older children can sustain their involvement for longer periods of time.

Third, seatwork should include both activities you have assigned and student-choice activities. Seatwork can be completed either individually, in pairs, or in small groups. The activities assigned can vary from the practice of newly learned skills, to applying activities, to reading and writing, to informal assessment activities. In any case, variety is important.

Students should be held accountable for all assigned work.

Fourth, you should adjust the pace of instruction to the needs of your students. For both high-aptitude and low-aptitude students the pace should be brisk enough to keep their attention, but not so brisk that they become frustrated and stop attending. You can expedite pacing by breaking instruction into small steps that students can easily understand. Clarifying the purpose or the usefulness of a lesson also encourages a brisk pace because your students understand why they are doing a task.

Fifth, you should ensure high success rates for your students. Generally, success rates should be above 80 percent. All students, but particularly low-aptitude students, must have high success rates in order to maintain a high level of perseverance. Students persevere and remain on task when success is high; as the failure rate increases, they get discouraged and their engagement diminishes rapidly.

Finally, you should give your students frequent opportunities to respond. Students need to speak, write, or do in order for learning to occur. Frequent response opportunities encourage their learning because it is through these responses that you determine their understanding and provide the positive feedback that solidifies learning.

To summarize, you can increase your students' engagement on tasks by holding them accountable, involving them, providing a variety of seatwork, ensuring brisk pacing, ensuring success, and having frequent responses.

Specific Teacher Action

You will use many of these general teacher behaviors whenever you teach. However, some teacher behaviors relate only to specific problems of student engagement.

Helping Students Become Engaged   To help students become engaged, you must get their attention. You can do this by using verbal statements, written statements, or some type of an attention-getting device such as an object or a figure drawn on the board. Once your students are attentive, you can establish procedures for the activity. It may be necessary to have students remain in their seats, to form a large circle on the rug, or to complete the activity in small groups at learning centers. Whatever procedures apply, students need to know them early in the activity.

You can also promote student engagement by providing thorough, lucid directions for the task they are to complete. Most elementary students can keep only a limited number of things in their minds at one time. This means that you can give only three or four directions at a time; otherwise, some of your students will be unable to complete the work without help. Therefore, it is sometimes necessary to provide directions for the first half of a task and then for the second half, or to provide written directions to supplement oral directions. Remember, however, that written directions are more easily followed when they reflect a pattern of behavior that is familiar. By providing directions within the limits of the students' memory capacity and according to established classroom patterns, you help promote student engagement.

How teachers distribute materials can also effect engagement. If you pass out materials before you provide directions, the chances are good that some of your students will pay more attention to the materials than to you. Many problems can be avoided by giving directions first, then distributing materials.

After everyone knows what is to happen and what their role is, students need a signal to begin the activity. Although you can simply tell them to begin, an established signal helps ensure that all students will begin at the same time.

Once started, you can enhance engagement by ensuring that students' personal needs have been considered. For instance, are the activities pleasant ones from the students' point of view? Do they understand your rationale for the lesson and concern for their work? Is there variety in the activities, and are there opportunities for their students to express themselves about the lesson content? Are student concerns heard and clarified? Are you reinforcing appropriate student behavior? By attending to personal needs such as these, you help ensure sustained engagement on tasks.

Question asking also helps your students become engaged because it allows them to demonstrate their understanding of the lesson and to be attentive during it. For instance, if you are teaching a content goal, you should ask questions to activate knowledge about the topic of the story; if you are teaching a process goal, you should ask questions to activate knowledge about the target strategy. Questions serve a dual role by helping students become engaged and preparing them to focus on the lesson content.

In summary, initial student engagement is enhanced if you get their attention, give thorough, lucid directions before distributing materials, signal when to begin, consider their personal needs, and ask questions to focus their attention on the lesson.

Helping Students Sustain Engagement Just as there are things you can do to help students become engaged, there are others that help students maintain that engagement. This requires sensing a pending break in the activity flow and doing something to prevent its occurrence. A teacher who lacks this sensitivity allows a break to occur and then has to restore the activity flow. Obviously, when a teacher can prevent such breaks, students will learn more because they will be engaged longer.

There are a number of teacher behaviors that help maintain activity flow. One relates to the steps within the lesson. You should break lessons into small steps to keep the cognitive demands within the capabilities of your students. The size of the steps varies with the age and aptitude of your students and must be adjusted to their needs.

Another teacher behavior is to look for signals that a group is not working well together and to deal with the potential problems quickly, before activity flow is disrupted. Often a student's body posture signals that off-task behavior is about to occur. Similarly, students' eyes or the type of noise coming from a group signals a need for your assistance. When you are alert and can assess a group's problem before a disruption occurs, you can solve problems without a break in activity flow.

You can also prevent breaks in activity flow by letting students know what to do with completed work. If everything has to pass through your hands, valuable instructional time will be lost. If your students have to ask you what to do with their work, activity flow is broken. Established patterns for turning in work and recording the results aid in sustaining activity flow.

Your use of humor and affection can also help sustain engagement because it releases the tension associated with concentration, fear, and insecurity. Students who are working hard benefit from a moment of humor, as do students who want to work hard but do not quite understand the task and those who experience a high degree of anxiety during a lesson. Make sure that your humor is funny to all students, however. Sarcasm can make a situation worse, as can laughter directed at a particular student. Similarly, you must use affection wisely. All students need to know that they are important, but artificial affection is quickly spotted and is usually counterproductive. Honest affection makes everyone feel good and aids in developing feelings of belonging.

You can also help sustain student engagement by monitoring involvement in lessons. Everyone, but especially low-aptitude readers, needs to be checked and to receive appropriate feedback. Regardless of the focus of the lesson, the only way to determine students' understanding is to monitor their responses. This monitoring helps sustain engagement on task. While monitoring, you can move near potentially disruptive students and use nonverbal signals— a lifted eyebrow or a finger on their lips—as a way to head off disruptions. Redirection away from inappropriate behavior and toward the expected behavior, reinforcement of appropriate behavior, removal of potential distractions, and assisting students who are showing signs of frustration are other ways of combating disruptions.

Your interactions with students also help sustain engagement. When you stop to talk with students, you should talk about the activity at hand. If a group of students are completing a task about favorite books, you should talk about that assignment. If you are taken off task by discussing something else, that too creates a break in engagement, a situation that is often hard to repair.

Your sensitivity to students' constraints also helps sustain engagement. This includes sensitivity to intellectual limits, where the content demands more than your students can deliver; to emotional limits, where the content is so unrelated that your students have no interest in learning; to concentration limits, where no matter how exciting the lesson is your students have been attending for too long. Teachers who are sensitive to the constraints of their students' learning abilities can use that knowledge to stop lessons before a break in the activity flow occurs.

Sustained engagement is also aided by planned, brief breaks. Few people can concentrate on a task for long periods without an opportunity for the brain to rest. Therefore, breaks are necessary if your students are to sustain attention to the lesson. Long breaks, however, allow students to become involved in something entirely new, so short breaks are better. They allow for rest while minimizing chances that attention will wander.

In summary, it is important to remember that students will vary in their ability to remain engaged. A room that is uncomfortable will shorten the time of engagement, as will an exciting upcoming event or hunger. High motivation and interest will lengthen it. The trick is to use what is known to be successful in sustaining high engagement rates while also being sensitive to your students' needs.

STEPS IN CREATING A MANAGEMENT SYSTEM

This chapter focuses on how to enhance student engagement during lessons. However, the organization and management of a reading program requires the melding of many little pieces. It is a difficult task, but the following guide offers structured assistance. You can adapt this guide in developing your own personalized management system.

Before the opening of school and the assignment of your students

1. Using the three goals of reading instruction as a guide, develop curriculum goals for the year.

2. Within each curriculum goal, collect and categorize activities for assessment, instruction, practice, and application.

3. Develop a teacher resource file for oral reading, independent reading, interest grabbers, independent activities, safety valves, guided application (basals, other commercial activities), room arrangements, and others.

4. Collect and categorize children's books and other printed material by interest and general reading levels to be used for independent reading, grabbing interest, and guiding application.

5. Develop student activity card files for learning centers, independent activities, safety valves, and interest grabbers.

6. Collect and develop informal and formal assessment tools, including graded oral-reading paragraphs, games, and interest inventories.

7. Develop a general pattern for reinforcement that can be adjusted after you know your students.

8. Develop patterns for how-to-start procedures.

9. Develop patterns for how-to-change procedures.

10. Develop procedures for keeping track of students.

11. Develop patterns for the optional activities (independent activities and safety valve activities).

12. Develop patterns for how-to-stop procedures.

13. Develop patterns that allow for interaction among teacher and students.

14. Develop the general role of the buffer and the steps in training the buffer.

15. Develop your philosophy about approaches (basals, language experience, and personalized reading) to reading instruction and how the three outcomes can be integrated into your philosophy. What balance will you strike in developing these three outcomes?

Before the opening of school, after you have been assigned to a classroom

1. Continue to develop curriculum goals and activities for the three outcomes of reading instruction. Collect source books, activity cards, assessment tools, materials for instruction and application, and lists of recreational books. Develop procedures for the various patterns for the buffer, and refine your philosophy of reading instruction.

2. Develop a floor plan for the physical arrangement of your classroom.

3. Make an inventory of the materials and facilities you have for the coming school year.

After the school year begins

1. Implement instruction for developing attitude outcomes.

2. Implement patterns for procedures and interactions.

3. Implement independent activities and safety valves.

4. Implement the role of the buffer.

5. Evaluate progress so far, including patterns and procedures.

6. Determine the reading preferences of each student.

7. Initiate plans for students to begin developing their own lifelong reading habits.

8. Administer the informal and formal assessment devices for year-long needs.

9. Implement instruction for developing process and content outcomes.

10. Evaluate the progress of your reading program to date.

Continued growth and evaluation

1. Continue to develop materials, ideas, sources, a library, patterns, and a teaching style.

2. Be alert for ways you can vary safety-valve activities as the year progresses, and be alert for new ideas and materials. Try not to alter established safety-valve patterns.

3. Continue to evaluate the ongoing reading program. Are your expectations reasonable? Are patterns developing as expected? Are positive attitudes and an understanding of reading being established? Are content outcomes being achieved? Are you implementing and maintaining the reading program as successfully as you want?

SUMMARY

Management—making the most of the time you have—is a crucial component of effective reading instruction. There are many specific techniques to use to increase time for reading by looking beyond the allocated reading period. By establishing routine patterns for enhancing activity flow in the classroom and by employing procedures to ensure that your students' attention to tasks is sustained, you can achieve maximum student-engagement time.

SUGGESTED ADDITIONAL READING

BURNS, M. (1981). Groups of four: Solving the management problems. *Learning, 10,* 46–51.

CASTEEL, C. P. (1984). Computer skill banks for classroom and clinic. *Reading Teacher, 38*(3), 294–297.

CHERNOW, F. B., & CHERNOW, C. (1981). *Classroom discipline and control: 101 practical techniques.* West Nyack, NY: Parker.

EMMER, E., EVERTSON, C., & ANDERSON, L. (1980). Effective management at the beginning of the school year. *Elementary School Journal, 80,* 219–231.

KLEIN, M. L. (1979). Designing a talk environment for the classroom. *Language Arts, 56*(6), 647–656.

LASLEY, T. (1989). A teacher development model for classroom management. *Phi Delta Kappan, 71*(1), 36–38.

NEVI, C. N. (1983). Cross-age tutoring: Why does it help the tutors? *Reading Teacher, 36*(9), 892–898.

REUTZEL, D. R., & COOTER, R. (1991). Organizing for effective instruction: The reading workshop. *Reading Teacher, 44*(8), 548–554.

WELCH, F. C., & HALFACRE, J. D. (1978). Ten better ways to classroom management. *Teacher, 96,* 85–86.

WOOD, K. D. (1983). A variation on an old theme: 4-way oral reading. *Reading Teacher, 37*(1), 38–41.

THE RESEARCH BASE

ANDERSON, L., EVERTSON, C., & BROPHY, J. (1979). An experimental study of effective teaching in first grade reading groups. *Elementary School Journal, 79*(4), 183–223.

ANDERSON, L., EVERTSON, C., & EMMER, E. (1980). Dimensions in classroom management derived from recent research. *Journal of Curriculum Studies, 12,* 343–346.

BROPHY, J. (1983). Classroom organization and management. *Elementary School Journal, 83,* 265–286.

DOYLE, W. (1986). Classroom organization and management. In M. Wittrock (Ed.), *Handbook of research on teaching* (3rd ed.) (pp. 392–431). New York: Macmillan.

EVERTSON, C. & WEADE, R. (1989). Classroom management and teaching style: Instructional stability and variability in two junior high English classrooms. *Elementary School Journal, 89*(3), 379–393.

KARWEIT, H. (1988). Quality and quantity of learning time in pre-primary programs. *Elementary School Journal, 89*(2), 120–133.

KOUNIN, J. (1970). *Discipline and group management in classrooms.* New York: Holt, Rinehart & Winston.

TAYLOR, B., FRYE, B., & GAETZ, T. (1990). Reducing the number of reading skill activities in the elementary classroom. *Journal of Reading Behavior, 22*(2), 167–179.

TAYLOR, B., FRYE, B., & MARUYAMA, G. (1990). Time spent reading and reading growth. *American Educational Research Journal, 27*(20), 351–362.

ACTIVITIES FOR REFLECTING, OBSERVING, AND TEACHING

Reflecting on How to Manage Reading Instruction

PURPOSE: Teachers who are good managers make classroom management look easy and natural. However, in reality, good classroom managers have a characteristic which has been come to be known as "with-it-ness." That is, good classroom managers are good at managing instruction because they are "with-it" in the sense that they know what they are about and think carefully about how to manage smoothly and efficiently. This activity is designed to help you become more conscious of what you need to be thinking about in order to be a "with-it" manager.

DIRECTIONS: Think about the grade level you intend to teach. Keeping that level in mind, answer each of the questions below.

1. What ways can you think of to help squeeze out more time for reading and writing from an already overcrowded school day at the grade level you wish to teach?

2. Thinking of the grade level you want to teach, what techniques do you think would be most effective in promoting smooth activity flow?

3. No matter what grade level you teach, there is a lot of content to be covered in reading and writing. That is, there are lots of attitudes, processes, and subject-matter content you have to be thinking about. Given the grade level you hope to teach, what do you plan to do to manage all that academic content?

4. Thinking again of the grade level you want to teach, how do you plan to keep students engaged on tasks once you have them started? What techniques will be particularly effective at your grade level?

Watching Others Manage Reading Instruction

PURPOSE: You can learn a lot about how to be a good classroom manager by watching a teacher who knows how to manage instruction. This activity is designed to help you structure such an observation.

DIRECTIONS: Arrange to observe a teacher teaching at a grade level you are interested in teaching. As you watch the teacher, note particularly the following:

1. How much of the time are students actively engaged in learning tasks? What does the teacher do to ensure that this happens?

2. How does the teacher's arrangement of the room promote efficient management?

3. How does the teacher use independent activities to ensure smooth management?

4. What patterns and routines do you notice the teacher using? Are there standard ways to start? To interact? To stop?

5. How are interruptions from the students handled? How are interruptions for other sources handled?

Trying It Yourself

PURPOSE: It is very difficult to develop a classroom management system for yourself until you have your own classroom. As a student teacher or visitor to another teacher's classroom, the best you can do is work within the management system the teacher has already established. However, it would help you establish your own management system if you understood the process teachers go through in establishing such systems. This activity is designed to help you develop such an understanding.

DIRECTIONS: Arrange to interview a teacher you have been observing or working with. Using the "Steps in Creating A Management System" provided in the last part of this chapter as a guide for asking questions, interview the teacher about what he or she did to establish an effective management system before school started, early in the school year, and as the year progressed. Also ask questions about how the teacher evaluates his or her management system, when decisions are made to change the system, and how those changes are made.

Part 4

Conducting Instruction at Various Grade Levels

Earlier sections of this book provided information designed to help you construct general understandings about the reading curriculum and how to organize for instruction. However, since reading instruction differs in specific ways depending on the grade level being taught, this general information must be augmented. The four chapters in this section offer specific guidelines about how to conduct reading instruction when you teach preschool or kindergarten (Chapter 16), primary grades (Chapter 17), middle grades (Chapter 18), or upper grades (Chapter 19).

16 | Teaching Preschool and Kindergarten Reading: Emergent Literacy Stage

GETTING READY

To teach a preschool or kindergarten class, you must adapt what you have learned in earlier chapters to students who, for the most part, do not yet know how to read. This chapter helps you do this. It describes language instruction for the emergent literacy stage and provides a general background, the major curricular emphases, and instructional activities to help you develop the intended curricular goals.

FOCUS QUESTIONS

- What special problems are associated with teaching reading to prereaders?
- How are attitude goals developed in preschool and kindergarten?
- How are process goals taught in preschool and kindergarten?
- How are content goals developed in preschool and kindergarten?
- How are reading and writing integrated at the emergent literacy stage?
- What does a typical preschool and kindergarten instructional day look like?

OVERVIEW OF PRESCHOOL AND KINDERGARTEN READING

There has been much debate in recent years about how and whether to teach reading in preschools and kindergartens. On one side of the debate are those who argue that emphasis should be limited to socialization in which children are taught the personal and social responsibilities associated with going to school. Here, the major instructional activity looks much like play, and the expectation is that children will learn reading goals incidentally while engaging in socialization activities. On the other side of the debate are those who argue that preschool children can and want to learn to read, and, therefore, schooling at this level should emphasize formal, systematic reading instruction.

Although the debate still rages in some quarters, most educators have settled on a middle-ground position. In this position both socialization and reading are included, but reading instruction receives less formal emphasis. "Less formal" does not mean there is an absence of direct instruction; in fact, both direct and indirect instruction are found in good preschool and kindergarten programs. It does mean there is less emphasis on the trappings of formal education: Basal text reading groups are seldom found in kindergartens or preschools; similarly, the use of workbooks, although more prevalent than basal texts, is generally frowned upon. Instead, teachers provide students many opportunities to expand background experiences, to communicate about these experiences, to use listening and speaking, to perceive reading and writing as exciting and useful activities, and to understand the graphic nature of written language.

At the emergent literacy stage, teachers provide many opportunities for speaking and listening.

The emergent literacy stage is actually a broad introduction to language. It seldom looks like the formal "book learning" associated with the basal-text reading instruction found in first grade and above, but teachers do structure a learning environment that broadly emphasizes communication. Because most children at this level cannot yet read, communication is mostly oral and the emphasis is on speaking and listening. Content goals focus almost entirely on listening to the teacher and other adults read texts for functional and recreational purposes; process goals stress how comprehension works in listening situations; and positive attitudes toward reading are often created when students listen to a teacher read good children's literature. The major encounter with written text at the emergent literacy stage is through language experience stories, and reading skills focus on students' awareness of print and the graphic nature of reading. Table 16.1 summarizes the instructional emphasis at the emergent literacy stage.

TABLE 16.1   Instructional Emphasis at the Emergent Literacy Stage

OUTCOME	INSTRUCTIONAL EMPHASIS	MAJOR INSTRUCTIONAL ACTIVITY
Attitude goals		
Concepts about reading	Reading is talk written down What you are reading was written by someone Reading is for enjoyment Reading is for getting information	Indirect instruction using language experience and USSR activities
Positive responses to reading	Reading is exciting Reading is satisfying Reading results in knowledge	Indirect instruction using language experience and USSR activities
Process goals		
Routing skills Vocabulary	Discuss experiences that employ new words Emphasize concrete words	Direct instruction of word meanings
Word recognition	Develop print awareness related to recognizing words instantly Develop letter and word awareness	Direct instruction of letters and words Direct instruction in how to use knowledge sources of listening and comprehension
Metacognitive strategies		
Initiating strategies	Active background knowledge of content using picture and title Use story structure and author purpose to make predictions	Direct instruction of strategies in listening situations Direct instruction of how to use story structure to make predictions when listening to recreational text

DEVELOPING ATTITUDE GOALS

Since many children first encounter reading and writing in preschool and kindergarten, their attitudes are often determined by what happens to them there. At this level, then, the most important goal is to create experiences that will develop accurate concepts and build positive feelings about reading and writing.

Two concepts—the message-sending nature of reading and the potential rewards of reading—are fundamental to reading success, and you should strongly emphasize them at the preschool and kindergarten levels. First, develop the understanding that language is a communication system, with both reading and writing as parts of the system, because it is crucial for students to understand that what they read is a message from someone else; it is like an oral message

TABLE 16.1 continued

OUTCOME	INSTRUCTIONAL EMPHASIS	MAJOR INSTRUCTIONAL ACTIVITY
During-reading strategies		
Monitoring strategies	Monitor accuracy of predictions Monitor fluent sense making	Direct instruction of monitoring skills in listening situations

Fix-it strategies	Recognize disruption in sense making while listening
	Access strategies to solve the problem
	  Word recognition
	  Vocabulary
	  Author's meaning
	  Beyond the author's meaning
	Determine which strategy is needed
	Implement the strategy
	Verify repair of sense making
		Direct instruction of fix-it strategies for listening comprehension

Post-reading strategies		
Organizing strategies	Recall what is important through story structure (beginning, middle, end)	Direct instruction of recalling story structure in listening comprehension
Evaluating strategies	Judge real or make believe	Direct instruction in listening comprehension
Content goals		
Recreational	Get meaning from story narratives that the teacher reads orally	Directed listening activity
Functional	Get meaning from simple expository text that the teacher reads orally	Directed listening activity

except that it has been written down. Second, show students that reading has an important role to play in their lives, that constructing meaning from text can be both functional (provides information and helps solve problems) and recreational (brings enjoyment and enriches lives).

You should also place heavy emphasis on developing positive feelings about reading. Your students should be involved in activities that help them see that reading is exciting, is satisfying, and results in new knowledge. Conversely, if their initial encounters with text are boring, frustrating, or of little personal use, students will develop negative feelings. The importance of creating positive responses cannot be overemphasized.

Creating a Literate Environment

A strong literate environment is crucial to the success of preschool and kindergarten programs. Meaningful activities and communication should play an integral role. The intent, as it always is with the literate environment, is to create an atmosphere that encourages students to engage in representative literacy activities.

Make sure the physical environment in your classroom includes tangible evidence of the importance of communication. Emphasize listening, reading picture books, writing, and language-experience stories. Maintain a room arrangement that promotes communication, and have displays in the room that celebrate the products of individual and collaborative communication efforts. Your classroom's physical environment should clearly show that participants engage in important and exciting activities that require them to communicate.

Much of the physical environment of a classroom is a reflection of the intellectual environment you create. If you plan and promote exciting class projects, students will be engaged in meaningful activities. If you set the expectation that students will work collaboratively on these projects, real communication will result. Similarly, a good social-emotional environment in the classroom promotes student collaboration and sharing, thereby maximizing opportunities for communication and developing targeted concepts and responses about language.

Hence, it is through a literate environment that you create the atmosphere, activities, and interactions that preschoolers and kindergartners associate with literacy.

The Major Instructional Approach

At the emergent literacy stage, the major instructional approach is language experience. By engaging students in collaborative writing based on common experiences, you highlight several reading concepts: the communication function of written language; the writer-reader relationship; and the relationship among listening, speaking, reading, and writing. In addition, creating real text about meaningful experiences is exciting and satisfying for preschoolers and kindergartners and does much to build positive feelings.

Preschool and kindergarten teachers spend much time developing language experience stories with students. Since these stories are based on real experiences, it is important to organize common experiences that are worth writing about. For instance, you might plan field trips to places of interest in the community, have students share their most exciting experiences with each other, and plan special classroom events such as guest presenters, parties, and plays. Children's literature that is read aloud in the classroom can also be an effective source of language experience stories since it can be the genesis for student-written stories.

Once you have selected an experience, you can use it as an occasion for message sending and receiving. For instance, before visitors to the classroom arrive, you and your students can write invitations, write signs directing the guests to their seats, create posters depicting classroom activities, and write stories for display. Once the activity is over, students may write thank-you notes, keep journals, create summaries, generate a report to parents, or write a newspaper that chronicles the events and experiences. You can represent in collaboratively developed language the experience of writing any kind of text associated with the real world. Through participation in these activities students develop the concepts and responses that are the foundation for continued growth in reading. The lesson shown in Example 16.1 shows how to incorporate language experience activities into the emergent literacy stage.

EXAMPLE   16.1   How to Develop Positive Attitudes

Background	You want to develop the concept that reading is talk that has been written down. You decide to do so by involving students in a language experience activity.
Activity 1	Arrange a field trip to the fire station, city hall, or some other community agency. Prepare students for what they are to learn on the trip.
Discussion	In the classroom after the trip, have a conversation about what was learned. Direct students to the need to thank the people who provided the information. Point out that you could speak your thanks if you saw them, but since you probably will not see them, you can send a note.
Activity 2	Work with students to write a thank-you note on chart paper. As the note is composed, point out that what they say can be written down, and that what is written down can be read by the receivers of the thank-you note.

ACTIVITIES TO DEVELOP ATTITUDE GOALS

Here are some useful preschool and kindergarten activities to supplement development of positive attitudes toward reading.

1. Have students write short letters to classmates that are mailed and then delivered by a child who plays the role of a postman. The children can then read the letters they have received. Emphasize the concept that reading and writing are communication tools.

2. Using the special kinds of animal or adventure stories that children are interested in, encourage them to collect or print words essential for reading and enjoying their particular interests. List these words in a special book to develop positive responses toward reading.

3. Show pictures of some of the same things your students draw, such as a dog or an airplane. Say, "These pictures tell a story. Do you know what this picture is?" Call on a child as you point to the picture. After the correct response is elicited, ask another child, "What is this picture?" When all the picture details have been discussed, ask more general questions, such as "What do you think they are doing? Have you ever seen an airplane land? Where did you see it? Was anyone you know in it?" These questions help students develop the concept that pictures and words convey information.

4. Use the covers of children's books for a game. Have students sit in a circle, then hold up a cover and have the students guess what the story is about if it is new, or tell about it if it is familiar. Call on several children to get a variety of stories and ideas. Picture postcards, magazine pictures, and travel pictures may all be used if old covers are not available. The concept that reading is both enjoyable and informational is developed while also developing predicting skills.

5. Have students write or dictate their own stories, which you type in primary type. They may then read their stories and exchange them with other students. These stories may be bound into books. This helps students develop positive attitudes toward reading.

6. Have students read simple poetry. They should read it over until it becomes easy for them, developing the idea that language is fun.

7. Feltboard characters provide an excellent vehicle for storytelling. Using a feltboard and teacher- or student-made characters from books, have students talk about the books they have read. This develops positive attitudes about reading.

8. Puppets are as much fun to make as they are to operate. A large packing box or a table turned on its side can serve as the stage. Kindergartners enjoy making small drawings of characters introduced in picture books or

storytelling sessions and then pasting them on pencils or sticks to use as puppets. The concept of what reading is, as well as positive attitudes toward reading, is developed.

9. Have students write their own concept books (what is round, what is heavy, what is loud, and so on); this will develop positive attitudes toward reading.

TEACHING PROCESS GOALS

Process goals help students understand routine skills that are applied automatically and metacognitive strategies that are consciously applied. Since most preschool and kindergarten students are unable to read text independently, the process goals taught at this level are preparatory in nature.

Routine Skills

In preschool and kindergarten, you teach students routine skills associated with language conventions and linguistic units in two ways. First, you use language experience activities to teach abut the conventions of print in our language. When constructing language experience stories, point out the top-to-bottom and left-to-right sequencing of language, that spoken words can be represented by written words, that they can tell where a word ends because there is a space, that a spoken sentence can be represented as a printed sentence, and that there are certain conventions (capital letters and periods, for instance) that signal when a sentence begins and ends. Help students learn that words are made up of letters and teach them these letters. At first, preschoolers and kindergartners can see no sense in how letters are formed and have difficulty visually discriminating such letters as *u* and *n, w* and *m,* and *d* and *b.* It is important that you show them how the system of discrimination among letters works. A sample of how to teach such language conventions in preschool and kindergarten is provided in Example 16.2.

Second, you need to increase vocabulary. All students need a large store of word meanings they understand in oral language. Most children come to school with an oral vocabulary of approximately 4,000 words, but they need many more to be successful. In preschool and kindergarten, you need to provide many opportunities for students to hear about, experiment with, and interact with words. **Concept books** are one good way to do this. Students can brainstorm things that are round, square, soft, hard, and so on, and then you can introduce other words that fit into that category. Drawings and pictures of new words that fit the category can be put into books. Whenever you introduce new words, it is important that you be as concrete as possible.

Teachers often overestimate children's capacities for understanding the words they use in oral language. They assume that because students say the

EXAMPLE 16.2   How to Teach Visual Discrimination

Background	Your students continually confuse the letters *b* and *d*. You decide to teach them how to visually examine the letters.
Lesson Sequence	
Introduction	Point to examples of the letters they are confusing in the story you have been reading to them. Indicated that being able to read the story themselves requires their being able to tell the letters apart and that you are going to show them how to do that.
Modeling	Explain the way you visually examine print to tell letters apart. In the case of *b* and *d*, visual examination emphasizes left-to-right orientation, with the "stick" of the letter being encountered first in *b* and the "ball" of the letter being encountered first in *d*.
Interaction with students	Give students several opportunities to distinguish *b*s from *d*s in text. Give them considerable help in the early stages as they talk out loud about how they are visually examining the letters, and gradually reduce this assistance as they demonstrate a consistent pattern in their visual examination.
Closure	Return to the text you have been reading to them. Point out the letters again, and have them use their strategy to visually examine the letters and to distinguish between them.
Desired Outcome	Given printed text, students will use the conventional ways of visually examining text to distinguish letters.

words, they share the adult meaning for it. For instance, a group of kindergartners were discussing an upcoming parents' night. All of them entered the conversation about how to best prepare for the event. Yet, when it came time to write invitations to their parents, the children did not understand that parents were their mothers and fathers. They used the word *parents*, but they did not share the adults' meaning.

Function words, such as *not, same,* and *or,* are particularly crucial since preschoolers and kindergartners need these words to operate successfully in school. When teaching the meanings of these words, it is important to do so within the students' physical world by using language modeling. Modeling use of function words such as *not, same,* and *or* during instruction might be as follows: "Who is sitting down? Who is *not* sitting down? Is the rabbit the *same* as the table? Is the desk the same as the floor *or* is it different?" A sample of how to teach vocabulary in preschool and kindergarten is provided in Example 16.3.

Metacognitive Strategies

At this level, three categories of metacognitive strategies are taught, mostly in listening situations: initiating strategies, during-reading strategies, and post-

EXAMPLE   16.3   How to Teach Vocabulary

Background	Your students understand that many words can be grouped as round, but they seem to be confusing round with square. You decide to teach them distinctions between round and square.
Lesson Sequence	
Introduction	Explain that you are going to show them how to decide whether a picture fits with something round or square by highlighting corners and no corners.
Modeling	Use concepts books for *round* and *square*. Go through the books naming each entry and modeling how you use corners to determine if it is round or square.
Interaction with students	Give students many opportunities to decide if a picture should be placed with one concept or the other. Have them verbalize how they made their decision. Gradually reduce assistance as they demonstrate their understanding.
Closure	Return to the concept books and have students draw new pages. When they have completed their drawings, have them explain to each other or to you why the drawings fit in one concept book or the other.
Desired Outcome	Given spoken words that stand for something round or square, students will categorize words according to which fits each grouping.

reading strategies. Each is discussed below. Study strategies are not used at this stage.

Initiating Strategies   The initiating strategies include activating prior knowledge of topic, story structure, and author's purpose. At the preschool and kindergarten level, messages are presented orally, not in print. Activating prior knowledge depends on the topic of the reading selection and what students already know about it. Begin by providing statements and asking students questions about their prior experiences with the topic. For instance, in preparing for a lesson on mail deliverers as community helpers, you would provide statements and ask questions like: "We have people who deliver mail. Do you know how mail is brought to your houses? Have you ever seen or talked to the people who bring the mail? Let's see what all of us know about mail carriers."

To activate prior knowledge, you might begin by reading text to your students and showing them how understanding the words, topic, purpose, and text structure helps to figure out meaning. For instance, you might read a story about a mailman and then talk about (1) how the words in the story provide clues to the topic, (2) how recognizing the topic (or what is talked about) triggers thinking about that topic and predictions based on what they already know, (3) how the purpose (having fun or getting information) makes them listen for certain things, and (4) how their general knowledge of stories helps them predict what will happen next in this story. Although it is a listening situation, the process of getting the meaning is very similar to that used when reading. Consequently, when students get to formal reading, they will already be familiar with this strategy. Example 16.4 illustrates how to structure such a lesson in preschool and kindergarten.

During-Reading Strategies   The during-reading strategies are monitoring and fix-it strategies. Since preschoolers and kindergartners do not actually read when first learning how to monitor text or when learning their first fix-it strategies, they use listening situations and simulated situations involving language-experience stories.

At the emergent literacy stage, monitoring involves simply listening to a story to see if it makes sense. When reading a story to your students, stop periodically, have students recall what has just happened, and ask them if that makes

---

EXAMPLE 16.4   How to Use a Listening Situation to Teach an Initiating Strategy for Getting Meaning

Background	As part of getting your students ready to read, you want them to be aware of how to get meaning—how to make predictions about meaning based on our knowledge of the words, topic, purpose, and type of text. You use a listening activity to develop the goal of activating prior knowledge.
Lesson Sequence	
Introduction	After reading a story to students, discuss what happened in the story. Ask them how they know what the story means. Tell them you are going to show them how readers and listeners get meaning from stories.
Modeling	Read sections of the story orally and explain what you think of as you hear the first group of words, how hearing those words causes you to predict a topic, how your knowledge of the topic causes you to expect certain things, how your understanding of the author's purpose and the normal pattern of stories gives you clues to where the story is going, and how these predictions continue to be refined as you hear more of the story.
Interaction with students	Using other story samples, have students do as you did. At first, give them much assistance as they try to talk out loud about their thinking while processing text. Gradually diminish this assistance until the students can make predictions about meaning without assistance.
Closure	Read another story having the students explain what happened and how they know what the story meant.
Desired Outcome	Given oral text, students can explain how they use knowledge of the words, topic, purpose, and type of text to make predictions about meaning.

sense. In this way you provide many opportunities for students to realize that reading and listening are sense-making processes. Eventually you want students to tell you when the story does not make sense. When this occurs, text monitoring has begun.

At the emergent literacy stage, the most emphasized fix-it strategy relates to vocabulary—what to do when students encounter a word unknown in meaning. You do this by using listening situations to teach students how to use oral context to predict a word that is unknown or left out. For instance, play games with them in which they have to complete sentences such as, "When I went to the store, my mother told me to buy a pair of _____." Or have students predict words that will fill certain slots in sentences such as, "The _____ went to the fair." In this case, a defensible noun would have to be used, whereas in "I saw a horse in _____ barn," a defensible article or adjective would have to be used; and so on. By engaging students in such exercises you help them learn that language is a sense-making activity, and they develop a solid foundation for using context to figure out unknown words. The thinking process used by readers is similar to that used by listeners, so listening instruction becomes a preparation for reading. Example 16.5 shows how to teach oral context.

EXAMPLE 16.5   How to Teach Oral Context Clues for Getting Meaning

Background	As part of your effort to get students ready to read, you want them to know how to use context to predict what unknown words mean, but you must teach this strategy in an oral situation.
Lesson Sequence	
Introduction	Selection a story to read to the students. Pick a word the students are not likely to know an present it to them. Tell them you are going to teach them how to figure out such words as they listen to the story.
Modeling	Read aloud a section of the story that contains the word. Explain how you used the other words in the sentence and your own background knowledge to figure out the unknown word.
Interaction with students	Present to students other difficult words embedded in context. Have them talk out loud demonstrating how they used the other words and their experience to predict the meaning of the unknown word. Give them much help initially, but gradually diminish this help as you go along.
Closure	Read the story aloud. Afterward, discuss the story content with them. Have conversations about how they used their strategy to figure out word meaning while they were listening.
Desired Outcome	Given a listening situation, students will use context to figure out the meaning of unknown words.

Another strategy emphasized at the emergent literacy stage relates to word attack or word analysis (or decoding), particularly as it relates to phonics. In order to use phonics to figure out unknown words encountered in print, students must know letters, must be able to distinguish one letter sound from another, and must be able to associate the correct letter sound with the correct letter in print. Some preparatory work for using phonics occurs in the preschool years and much of it occurs in kindergarten. Most teachers introduce phonics by creating simulated situations in the language-experience stories that have been written with students. For instance, while reading a language experience story, you might say to a student, "Let's pretend that you didn't know this word. When you came to it, you would have to stop and try to figure it out. How could you use what you know about the sounds of letters to figure out this word?"

These situations must be simulated because most children in the process of creating the story will learn the words in a language experience story as sight words, meaning that they no longer have to figure them out. The simulation, however, will help prepare them for figuring out unknown words when they encounter them in their reading at the initial mastery stage. Having children com-

---

EXAMPLE 16.6   How to Teach Letter Sounds

Background	As part of your effort to get students ready to read, you want them to know letter sounds. Then if they encounter a word they do not recognize in print, they can use initial consonant sounds together with context to predict the unknown word.
Lesson Sequence	
Introduction	Using a story you have read orally, point out the words and show students how the words begin with letters they know by name. Say that if they know the sound letters make, they can begin to say the words on the page and that you are going to teach them those letter sounds.
Modeling	For each letter in turn, demonstrate how you point at the letter and simultaneously say its sound.
Interaction with students	Have students do what you did (point to each letter in turn and say the sound). At first provide much assistance by pointing to the letter and saying the sound with the students. Gradually reduce such help as the students begin associating the sound with the letter.
Closure	Return to the story. Point out the words that begin with the letter sounds. Have students use those sounds and the context of the sentence (which you can read orally) to predict what the word is.
Desired Outcome	Given a word unrecognized in print, students will use the initial letter sound and the sentence context to predict what a word is.

bine this sounding technique with the context strategy just discussed provides an even stronger preparation for reading since the two strategies in combination are a powerful and efficient way to figure out words unknown in print. Example 16.6 provides an illustration of how to prepare students for phonics.

Post-Reading Strategies   The post-reading strategies are organizing and evaluating content. The organizing content strategy taught at the preschool and kindergarten level is recalling what is important through use of simple story structures (beginning, middle, and end). This means that you signal where the beginning, middle, and end sections are in stories and have conversations about each section with students in terms of what happened. At the initial mastery stage it is not important to be concerned with what constitutes the sections of the story; it is more important that students understand that stories have beginning, middle, and ending sections and that important information is found in each section. A more refined level for organizing content occurs at later stages. Example 16.7 illustrates how to structure a lesson on organizing oral content in preschool and kindergarten.

EXAMPLE   16.7   How to Teach Organizing Content

Background	Your students try to remember everything, or they remember only the last things they heard about in stories. You decide to teach them how to organize story information by remembering what happened in the beginning, middle, and end sections of a story.
Lesson Sequence	
Introduction	Read a story orally. Note for the students where each section is started and completed as you read.
Modeling	Explain that it is helpful when organizing story information to remember it in terms of the beginning of the story, the middle of the story, and the end of the story. Read each section and demonstrate how you remember the important information in that particular section. Then demonstrate how to organize important information based on where it is in the story.
Interaction with students	Give students several opportunities to remember information by organizing it in terms of the story structures of beginning, middle, and end. Start with single sections and gradually move to entire stories. As students demonstrate their understanding and use of this strategy, gradually reduce your assistance.
Closure	End the lesson series with another story. Point out the beginning, middle, and ending sections and have students use their strategy to organize information for remembering.
Desired Outcome	Given oral stories, students will organize story information by remembering the content found in the beginning, middle and end of stories.

The major emphasis in evaluating content at this stage is judging stories to be real or make-believe. This strategy is developed in terms of your students' background experiences. It is not important that every story be judged real or make-believe; it is important that preschoolers and kindergartners understand that some stories present information in ways that could really happen and other stories do not. Your students judge stories to be real or make-believe based on what their background experiences tell them could or could not really happen. Example 16.8 illustrates how to structure a lesson on evaluating content taken from oral stories.

ACTIVITIES TO DEVELOP PROCESS GOALS

In preschool and kindergarten, many of the activities to develop process goals are created by the teacher and focus on language conventions and linguistic units associated with word recognition and vocabulary. Certain commercial materials may be used (such as word games, work sheets, and so on), but the bulk of the activities grow naturally out of the communication activities being pursued in

---

EXAMPLE 16.8 How to Teach Evaluating Content

Background	Your students do not understand how to judge stories as real or make-believe. You decide to teach them how to judge whether a story is real or make-believe when it is read to them.
Lesson Sequence	
Introduction	Read a story that could happen based on students' backgrounds. Note and discuss those events that could really happen. Repeat the process using a story with events that couldn't really happen.
Modeling	During conversations, explain and demonstrate how to decide if events are real or make-believe. Continue to model by demonstrating how background experience signals whether a story is real or make-believe. Repeat the process using a make-believe story.
Interaction with students	Give students several opportunities to judge whether a story is real or make-believe. Start with real stories, move to make-believe stories, and then intermix both types. Gradually diminish your assistance as students demonstrate they can judge stories as either real or make-believe based on their background experiences.
Closure	End the lesson series with stories that are either real or make-believe. Have students judge whether stories are real or make-believe.
Desired Outcomes	Given orally read stories, students will judge story content as real or make-believe based on their background experiences.

the literate environment. Here are some activities you can use to supplement your teaching of process goals in preschool and kindergarten. Be cautioned that these are practice activities to be used after students understand how the various process goals are to be used in real reading.

1. Cut an oak tag into cards of handy size, such as 3" by 5", and have students paste on them pictures cut from old books, magazines, and newspapers. Under each picture print the word or phrase that tells about the picture and print the same word on the reverse side of the card. This helps students associate printed symbols with pictures (language convention).

2. Use an activity like bingo. Give each player a card marked off into 12 square blocks. In each block a sight word has been printed. On a small pack of cards, each the size of a block, words have been printed. Show the cards one at a time. The student whose card has the displayed word raises her or his hand, pronounces the word, points to it, is given the small card, and places it over the appropriate word. The first student to cover a line of words in any direction is the winner. This helps students learn to recognize words at sight (linguistic units).

3. Have all the words your students learn put into their vocabulary book, *My Word Book*. Students may illustrate this book or cut pictures from other sources and paste them under each word. This helps students build meaning vocabulary (linguistic units).

4. Labeling is a worthwhile device only if it is made meaningful. Label toys students bring to class; label shelves in the classroom closet to indicate places for various supplies. Label children's hooks in the wardrobe and encourage children to learn the names of their classmates. Use complete sentences when labeling—for example, "This is a Tonka truck." This helps students learn to recognize words at sight (linguistic units).

5. Write jumbled sentences on cards or on the board and have your students reassemble the sentences. This helps students search for meaning

    that makes sense and left-to-right directionality (language conventions). Examples:

    > baby down slid
    > a puppy black and white spots had

6. Place phrase cards along the blackboard ledge. Read one of these phrases and ask a student to go to the board and pick out the phrase that was read. Then have the student read the phrase to the class. This helps students recognize words at sight (linguistic units).

7. Give students several phrase cards based on a story they have read. Write on the board a question that can be answered by one of the phrase cards. Ask all students who think they have a phrase that answers the question

correctly to raise their hands. Ask students to first read the question from the board and then the answer from their card. Write the answer on the board and then write another question to be answered as before. Example: *Charlotte's Web,* by E. B. White, provides phrases such as *Charlotte and Wilbur, at the fair, in the barn,* and so forth. A question could be "Wilbur and Charlotte lived _____?" or "Charlotte said good-bye to Wilbur _____?" This helps students develop recall for what is read.

8. Place a large box filled with small objects or pictures before your students. Arrange printed word cards corresponding to the objects or pictures along the blackboard ledge. Have students close their eyes and draw an object or picture, for which they must then find the corresponding word. This helps students recognize words at sight (linguistic units).

9. Number a large cardboard clock face from 1 to 12 and fit the clock with a large moveable hand. Print and number twelve words or phrases either on the blackboard or on a large sheet of paper. Call on a student to spin the hand, see the number at which it stops, then read the corresponding printed word or phrase. This helps students recognize words at sight (linguistic units).

10. Prepare cards with black and white drawings of objects that have a characteristic color. Print directions under the objects such as, "This is a ball. Its color is blue." Because the picture is black and white, you will know your students can read the colors.

11. Show a picture to a group and have students discuss either the main idea, the figures in the foreground or background, or the colors. Occasionally ask specific questions, such as, "What is the little boy holding in his hand? Where do you think he is going?" Some students may be able to make up a short story of two or three sentences about the picture, while the others listen for the sequence of ideas. This helps students develop comprehension.

12. Have students learn sequencing of common activities by dividing a large sheet of oak tag into four or six squares and putting a picture showing one part of an action sequence into each square. Put the same pictures on small cards cut the same size as the squares on the large card. Ask students to take the small pictures and assemble them in a sequence that tells the same story as that on the large sheet. This helps students develop understanding of sequencing (language conventions).

13. Have students learn letter memory of upper and lower case letters (linguistic units) by giving them sheets prepared with short rows of letters. Tell students to circle either the capital or the small letters.

		AAaa	aaaA	AAAa	aaaA	
		BBBB	BBBB	bbbb		
CCC	Ccc	ccC	CCc	ccc	cCC	CCC
	DdD	DDd	ddd	DDD (etc.)		

14. Have students fish for sight words. Fold word cards and pin the open ends together with a large straight pin. (Take care to use steel pins, or hairpins, because a magnet will not pick up ordinary pins.) Place the cards in a container. Have students use a piece of string attached to a small magnet to pull out one of the "fish." If they can read the word on the card, they may keep it; otherwise it must be thrown back. Keep records of the number of words correctly read each day. This helps students learn words at sight (linguistic units).

15. Place pictures of objects that rhyme on the blackboard: pictures of a *pie* and *sky*, a *hand* and *sand*, and so on. Point to the first picture and ask what it is. "Yes, it is a *pie*. Who can find another picture that rhymes with *pie*?" This helps students develop auditory discrimination (linguistic units).

16. Say, "We are going to play a new guessing game today. This little boy is Bill." Point to a picture or to a child whose name is Bill. "He lives on a high _____. Who can tell me where Bill lives? It is a word that sounds like *Bill*. Yes, it is a *hill*. Bill likes to sit on the window _____. Yes, *sill*. Who can give me another word that sounds like *Bill* and *sill*?" This helps students develop auditory discrimination (linguistic units).

17. Perform or have a student perform a short series of acts, such as tapping on the desk, lifting a book, and then picking up a piece of chalk. Ask students to replicate the acts performed to develop auditory memory and sequencing (language conventions).

18. Have students practice letter recognition by playing the game "Concentration". Use six different letters at one time with each letter on two separate cards. Place the 12 cards randomly on the table, letter side down. Students find the pairs and keep each pair they find. This develops memory for letters (linguistic units).

19. Have students use concentration to recognize sight words. Follow the same procedure as in Activity 7. This develops memory for words (linguistic units).

20. Use recorded sound patterns in which each pattern is repeated. Direct students to listen to a sound pattern, stop the recorder, repeat the pattern, start the recorder, and check their accuracy. This develops auditory discrimination (linguistic units).

21. Play the airport game with students using a game board, a toy airplane, and someone to give the oral sound patterns to each child in turn. If the child reproduces a sound correctly, he or she moves the airplane one space down the runway. As each plane reaches the end it may be flown briefly. The same technique can be used in reverse to return the airplanes to the hangar. This develops auditory discrimination (linguistic units).

22. Play a game in which students pair off and then take turns clapping two sound patterns to each other. This develops auditory discrimination (lin-

guistic units). The partner must respond to each pair of sound patterns by identifying them as the same or different. Determine the winner either by recording the number each child gets right or by adapting the game to a game board such as the one described in Activity 10.

23. Play the game monkey hear, monkey do, using pairs of players and a game board. Have one child clap or say a sound pattern and tell the partner to mimic it. If the partner is correct, he or she moves forward one space on the game board. Auditory discrimination is developed (linguistic units).

24. Play a dot-to-dot game, using any connect-the-dots picture. Pair students and have one say letter-sound patterns. Tell the other to mimic it and, if correct, to connect as many dots in the picture as there are letter-sound units in the pattern. This develops memory for letter sounds (linguistic units).

25. Play a remembering game in which one student says a word, the next student repeats it and adds another word, the third student repeats the first two words and adds a third, and so on. Continue until one student cannot remember the sequence. The object is to develop memory for words (linguistic units).

26. During story time or reading time, purposely distort some word in the story by leaving off its first sound. Stop and say, "Oh, I didn't say that word correctly! What should I have said?" Do this during any daily oral activity. This develops predicting skills.

27. Have students bring to class pictures cut from magazines, with each picture or series of pictures showing something that has the same sound at the beginning, end, or middle. This develops readiness for phonics (linguistic units).

28. Bring in a group of magazine pictures, and direct students to tell what each picture shows and to sort the pictures according to the common beginning, middle, or ending sounds. For instance, all the pictures that begin with the same sound heard at the beginning of *kite* go in one pile, all the pictures that begin with the same sounds heard at the beginning of *top* go in another pile. This helps students learn phonics (linguistic units).

29. Spread a group of pictures on the floor. Have students point to a picture that has the same sound heard at the beginning, end, or middle of the word you say. This helps students discriminate among sounds (linguistic units).

30. Play games with students that follow this pattern: "I'm thinking of something on your desk that begins with the same sound heard at the beginning of the word *pig*. What am I thinking of?" You may also adapt this activity to middle and ending sounds. This helps students use phonics in combination with predicting (linguistic units).

31. Divide a shallow box into four squares. Place a key picture in each of the top two squares. Provide students with a group of pictures, and tell them to sort the pictures and place them in the square beneath the picture that has the same sound at the beginning, middle, or end. This helps students learn to categorize while also developing phonics (linguistic units).

32. Make a shutter device out of tagboard in which the opening of the shutter can be controlled. Insert a card that has the letter to be learned at the left, followed by a picture of an object beginning with this sound. Open the shutter to reveal first the letter and then the picture. Have students form the letter sound with their mouths and blend that sound into the picture name as it is exposed. This helps develop phonics as a word-analysis strategy (linguistic units).

33. Give each student a group of pictures, some of which begin with the letter to be worked on and some of which do not. Hold up a letter card and direct students to hold up any picture they have that begins or ends with the sound of that letter. This helps develop phonics (linguistic units).

34. Give students a group of letter cards. Have each student take turns saying the letter name and a word beginning with the letter, as in, "I have a letter. *Money* begins with the letter *m*."

DEVELOPING CONTENT GOALS

As previously mentioned, much preschool and kindergarten language activity is oral, and this is especially true of content goals. Because your students cannot read yet, you teach listening comprehension of functional and recreational text. Consequently, what becomes a reading activity at the higher grades is often a listening activity at the emergent literacy stage.

Many students receive their first formal introduction to recreational and functional text at the preschool and kindergarten level. Students should begin to understand the content of simple narrative text and simple expository text that you read to them. In both cases the selections should be simple in structure because this is typically your students' first formal encounter with text. Listening comprehension is emphasized because students have not progressed to the point where they can read independently.

Directed Listening Activity

Since your students listen rather than read at the preschool and kindergarten levels, you will often use the directed listening activity (DLA). This is similar to the standard directed reading lesson (DRL) used with many basal texts (see Chapters 4 and 13). The difference, of course, is that the DRL is used with written text, whereas the DLA is used with listening activities.

A directed listening activity helps kindergartners focus on text content.

The DLA works like this. Before you read to your students, introduce the topic to activate their background knowledge and develop the meaning of unknown words. With this background established, specify what your students are listening for (set the purpose). Then begin reading, stopping periodically to remind students what they are listening for. After the reading, hold a conversation in which everyone shares what they learned, focusing primarily on the purposes that were set at the beginning. Finally, close the lesson by having students summarize what was learned and by engaging them in an activity that applies (or enriches) this learning.

The DLA can be used to guide your students' listening of either recreational or functional text. For instance, if you are reading students a story, you can activate schemata about the setting and the problem encountered in the story, cite the purposes for listening, and hold a conversation after the story to share what was learned about the established purposes. If you are reading a functional text, you can activate schemata related to that topic, establish the purposes, and hold a conversation about those purposes. In both cases student listening is guided and, as a result, there is a greater chance that the content will be understood. An illustration of how to use the DLA is provided in Example 16.9.

Preschoolers and kindergartners create both functional and recreational text as part of their language-experience activities. For instance, language-experience activities that result in written invitations, lists of activities the class

EXAMPLE 16.9   How to Use a Directed Listening Activity for Content Goals

Background	You are reading a story to your students. You want to be sure they understand what happens to the main character and why it happens. To ensure they get this content, you guide their listening using a directed listening activity.
Lesson Sequence	
Introduction	Tell students what you are going to read to them. Discuss the setting and the circumstances surrounding the story and elicit student prior knowledge. Identify any words they may not have heard before and explain their meanings.
Set purposes	Specify the particular things you want students to listen for.
Oral reading	Read the story and be sure students are listening for the right information.
Discussion	Discuss what they found out about the purposes set at the beginning.
Closure	Have students summarize what was learned and/or have them use what was learned in a subsequent activity.
Desired Outcome	Given a text that is read orally, students will be able to discuss the story in terms of the specific purposes set.

pursued, or a recipe are all examples of functional text. Similarly, language-experience activities that result in stories or poems are recreational text. However, it is seldom necessary for teachers to guide students' understandings of these texts. Because students create them, they understand them. They have strong backgrounds for the words used, the topic, the purpose, and the text structure. As a result they comprehend the content without guidance.

ACTIVITIES TO DEVELOP CONTENT GOALS

Almost any occasion when you read functional or recreational text to children can be used to develop content goals. Here are some activities to supplement your teaching of content goals in preschool and kindergarten.

1. Have a news corner for announcements or for news pertaining to students themselves, such as "We are going to the market tomorrow." This leads to an understanding of uses of functional information.

2. Place interesting pictures with an explanatory word or two about them in very simple language on the bulletin board. You may also use colorful book jackets from children's books, which develop the understanding that reading is recreational.

3. Use bulletin boards to show all the enjoyable elements of books such as adventure, excitement, and laughter.

4. Use concept books that have been written by the students as functional texts for other students. Concepts can include the following: What is round? What is soft? What is exciting?

5. Use puppets to act out information that has been read to students.

INTEGRATING READING AND WRITING

One of the advantages of the language-experience approach is the way it dramatizes the integration of reading and writing. In fact, when students are creating language-experience charts and stories to read, they are engaged in writing. You can use these occasions for language experience to develop positive feelings about writing as an activity. While actually producing the written text associated with language experience, you can demonstrate process goals such as how writers use the conventions of language to signal meaning to readers, how authors monitor the text they are producing, and how they use certain techniques to focus, reorganize, and clarify their meaning. Regarding content goals in writing, you can use language experiences to model how decisions are made in the planning stage about whether the writing is to be functional or recreational and what meaning is to be conveyed.

As important as language experience is, however, it is not the only time that preschool and kindergarten students engage in writing activities. Very young children enjoy what they call writing, even though we might call it doodling. They will sometimes draw a picture of something and put a lot of squiggles on the page, which they describe as "a story I have written." This preliterate writing is an important part of learning to write. You can use these activities to build important concepts about writing, what people use it for, and how it works, as well as to build positive feelings toward writing.

Writing is an integral and important part of the preschool and kindergarten experience. It is evident both in the language-experience activities and in the pretend writing that students engage in at this age. Both kinds of writing activities are important to reading because they provide additional experience with written language that, in turn, strengthens students' desire and ability to use written text.

There are many ways to integrate the various language modes in preschool and kindergarten. One of the most effective is to teach units that carry over several days and develop a variety of objectives, as described in Chapter 14. Two examples follow. The first example, found in Figure 16.1, is an illustration of a unit on friendship. The second example, Figure 16.2, is a more detailed illustration of a unit on the postal system. Both might be taught at the preschool or kindergarten level.

ADDITIONAL INTEGRATED READING AND WRITING ACTIVITIES

Here are some additional activities to supplement your integration of reading and writing in preschool and kindergarten.

1. Provide pictures from magazines and have students write titles to them. Put pictures and titles on display for all to read.

2. Read a *Weekly Reader* to students and do the writing activities suggested there. This is usually completed as a group activity.

3. Have students write and illustrate a group story. Place the words and pictures on a roll and show them as a television program. Have students read the words as they appear on the "screen."

4. Have students create class stories after field trips. Place the stories in a travel folder and refer to them for future trips or for review.

5. Have students create concept books such as: what is trying, what is big, what is old, and so on. Each student creates a page with a sentence and an illustration.

6. Have students create a collage with a theme such as happy, sad, excited. Once the collage is created, have the class create a poem such as "Happiness is _____," "Sadness is _____," and so on. Display the collage and poem for reading and enjoyment.

7. Begin an alphabet book for each student, with a page for each letter. Add appropriate pictures of illustrations to each page throughout the school year.

8. Read *The House that Jack Built*. Discuss the book's repetitive pattern. Discuss other content. Write a group story using the repetitive pattern.

9. Using a story such as *Jack and the Beanstalk*, read the story to the point where Jack wakes up the golden harp. Insert into the story the harp saying, "You are as noisy as _____." Discuss with your students what things are *noisy*. Have each student create an ending to the sentence. Read the revised story with each student's insertion.

CHARACTERISTICS OF AN INSTRUCTIONAL DAY

Of all the levels of elementary school, preschool, and kindergarten have the most distinctive characteristics for three reasons.

First, almost all public preschool and kindergarten are half-day rather than full-day sessions. Consequently, the total daily allocated time for instruction is typically between 2½ and 3 hours. This characteristic has several consequences. For you, it usually means two completely different classes in a day, one in the

---

FIGURE 16.1 Emergent literacy.

Theme: Developing and keeping friends

Objectives:
1. Provide opportunities to explore that friendships are and why they are important
2. Foster understandings about how friendships are developed and maintained
3. Expand knowledge of picture books that contain information about friendships
4. Use picture books as a stimulus for reading, writing, and conversations
5. Develop understandings about picture books through the use of patterned books
6. Develop expertise in predicting and verifying predictions during pre-reading activities
7. Provide opportunities for the student to move through the literacy cycle using reading, writing, and conversations
8. Compose individual and class books on friendship
9. Develop conceptual understandings about authoring and the interrelationships of reading, writing, and conversations
10. Develop reflection as a post-reading strategy
11. Develop understandings about point of view
12. Encourage the knowledge that reading, writing, and listening lead to understanding

Summary:

The students moved through the literacy cycle while developing their understanding about gaining and keeping friends. A series of picture books on friendships were used. The students read, listened, talked, acted out, and wrote stories in order to develop conceptual understandings about authoring, the interrelationships of reading, writing, and conversations, and the strategies of predicting, verifying predictions, and point of view. The unit began with sharing the book *Sherwood Walks Home* by James Flora. Through conversations and creative drama, the students created a classroom book patterned after *Sherwood Walks Home*. Additional books, *Corduroy* and *Pocket for Corduroy* by Don Freeman, *Amos and Boris* by Steig, *May I Bring a Friend* by the D'Auliers, and the *Toad and Frog* books by Lobel, continued development of understandings as the students moved through the literacy cycle. In addition, students read poems as Toad did in "Garden," a chapter in *Toad and Frog Are Friends*, and did creative drama activities for all the stories. The unit culminated with a classroom collection of books about friendship, including *Helpful Hints for Being Friends* and *My Favorite Stuffed Animal Friend*.

> The friendship unit was developed by Laura R. Roehler and Cheryl Latham at Spartan Village Elementary Professional Development School, East Lansing, MI.

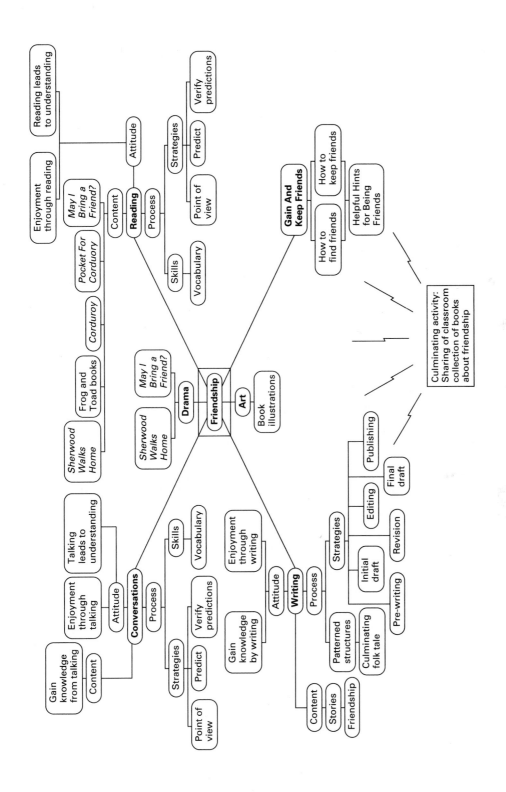

Reading leads to understanding

Enjoyment through reading

Attitude

May I Bring a Friend?

Content

Reading

Pocket For Corduroy

Process

Corduroy

Strategies

Predict

Verify predictions

Point of view

Frog and Toad books

Skills

Vocabulary

Sherwood Walks Home

May I Bring a Friend?

Drama

Sherwood Walks Home

Friendship

Art

Book illustrations

Gain And Keep Friends

How to find friends

How to keep friends

Helpful Hints for Being Friends

Culminating activity: Sharing of classroom collection of books about friendship

Talking leads to understanding

Enjoyment through talking

Attitude

Gain knowledge from talking

Content

Conversations

Process

Skills

Vocabulary

Strategies

Predict

Verify predictions

Point of view

Enjoyment through writing

Gain knowledge by writing

Attitude

Writing

Process

Strategies

Publishing

Editing

Final draft

Revision

Initial draft

Pre-writing

Patterned structures

Culminating folk tale

Content

Stories

Friendship

FIGURE 16.2   Sample Teaching Unit: Using the Postal System

LEVEL
Preschool and kindergarten, emergent literacy stage

OBJECTIVES
Content Objective: Given a trip to the Post Office and various listening activities and experiences with mail transportation, students will describe how to communicate using the mail.
Attitude Objective: Given opportunities to communicate by mail, students will state the reader-writer relationship in a postal communication and will eagerly engage in letter writing.
Process Objective: Given letter writing experiences, students will use a friendly letter structure in both composing and interpreting letters.

CULMINATING ACTIVITY
Use the mail system to invite parents to visit the classroom to have tea or coffee.

DAY 1
Warm-up activity: Bring a letter to class from a parent or several parents telling about something they like about the class. Have a conversation about how exciting it is to get mail. Read the letter to the class.
Focusing activity: Discuss the letter and lead a conversation to the point where the students decide they want to invite their parents to a tea or coffee.
Reading-writing activity: Construct a group letter telling where and when the parents should come. Read the letter together.
Assessment: During the letter-writing process, assess students' knowledge about the form of a friendly letter. Directly teach the form to those students who need it.

DAY 2
Reading-writing activity: Print the letter to parents neatly, using letter form.
Assessment: Assess students' ability to print letters and words found in letters. Directly teach penmanship skills to those students who need it.

DAY 3
Warm-up activity: Using an overhead or an opaque projector, present a model envelope like the one that will be used to send the letter to parents.
Focusing activity: Directly teach how to address an envelope.
Reading-writing activity: Students practice on sample paper (same size as an envelope) how to address an envelope to their parents.
Assessment: Assess students' ability to address an envelope. Note whether students know their address.

DAY 4

Focusing activity: Have a conversation about the purpose and structure of the postal system.

Reading-writing activity: Address the envelopes. Take the letters to the mailbox and mail them.

DAY 5

Reading-writing activity: Draw the steps the students' letters will go through in the process of being delivered. Have them predict when the letters will arrive. Have them verify the arrival.

Note: A trip to the post office would be appropriate at this time.

DAY 6

Warm-up activity: Brainstorm with students about all the interesting things they've been doing in class.

Focusing activity: From the brainstorming list, select activities to show parents during the coffee or tea.

Reading-writing activity: Decide how to show parents work, songs, plays, and so on.

DAY 7

Focusing activity: With the students' help, decide what refreshments will be served at the coffee or tea.

Reading-writing activity: The results of the conversation can lead to reading recipes to make whatever is served, measuring the ingredients to be used, and cooperatively serving refreshments.

DAY 8

Culminating activity: The coffee or tea with parents.

Assessment: Assess the success of the coffee or tea. Did the parents enjoy it? Did the students successfully show the parents what they have learned? Did the letters arrive at their homes? Were the reading and writing uses successful? Was information conveyed?

---

morning and one in the afternoon. This poses a real problem since much language instruction should be individually tailored to students' needs, but when you have 50 to 60 students each day, it is hard to keep track of their individual needs. In terms of planning for individual development, more preparation time is required for the preschool and kindergarten teacher than for teachers at the higher levels.

A second distinguishing characteristic of instruction in preschool and kindergarten is the dominance of playlike activities. Because children at this age cannot read and are not yet socialized into the behaviors associated with traditional schooling, you cannot give them traditional seatwork tasks that require independence and good work habits. Instead, find a variety of shorter activities, most of which are fun, such as story sharing, games, and creative drama.

The third distinguishing characteristic of preschool and kindergarten is the absence of designated periods for reading, mathematics, and social studies. Although these subjects are taught at this level, the allocated instructional time is divided by activities (manipulative objects, animals, children's literature, and so on), with each activity often calling for the integrated use of reading, mathematics, and social studies. This allows teachers to focus on activities that relate to students' real experiences. It also offers the option of brisk pacing, a crucial aspect of teaching at this level since preschool and kindergarten children have relatively short attention spans and must have a variety of activities in a relatively short period of time.

The instructional day in preschool and kindergarten is unlike that found at any other grade level. Students do not sit at desks, they do not have reading groups in the traditional sense, they seldom use basal readers, the activities often look like play time, and many different kinds of activities are squeezed into a relatively brief half-day period. Even though the school day looks quite different, teachers at these levels are teaching to the same three goals as teachers at the higher levels and are striving to lead students to the same ultimate outcome.

SUMMARY

Reading instruction at the preschool and kindergarten level provides the foundation for literacy. A special problem at this level centers on whether to have formal reading instruction or to focus on socialization. A balance of these two forms is recommended to ensure a broad introduction to literacy. Attitude goals are developed through the literate environment where students are engaged in important and exciting tasks involving sharing, cooperation, and collaboration. Process and content goals are also taught within the literate environment, primarily with language-experience activities, during which students learn about conventions of print, vocabulary and word-recognition strategies, and about stories and simple texts. The reading-writing connection is also stressed. The typical instructional day looks different than at other elementary grades: Subjects are not differentiated, the instructional tasks are more playlike, and oral language and listening are emphasized.

SUGGESTED ADDITIONAL READING

ALLEN, R. V., & ALLEN, C. (1976). *Language experience activities.* Boston: Houghton Mifflin.

ANSELMO, S. (1978). Improving home and preschool influences on early language development. *Reading Teacher, 32*(2), 139–143.

BAILEY, M. H., ET AL. (1982). Preparation of kindergarten teachers for reading instruction. *Reading Teacher, 36*(3), 307–311.

BLANCHARD, J., & LOGAN, J. (1988). Letter-naming knowledge in kindergartners: What's happening? *Reading Psychology, 9*(3), iii–xi.

BURRIS, N. A., & LENTZ, K. A. (1983). Caption books in the classroom. *Reading Teacher, 36*(9), 872–875.

CAZDEN, C. (1985). Research currents: What is sharing time for? *Language Arts, 62,* 182–188.

CLAY, M. (1991). Introducing a new storybook to young readers. *Reading Teacher, 45*(4), 264–273.

COATE, S., & CASTLE, M. (1989). Integrating LEA and invented spelling in kindergarten. *Reading Teacher, 42*(7), 516–519.

COMBS, M. (1984). Developing concepts about print with patterned sentence stories. *Reading Teacher, 38*(2), 178–181.

CROWELL, D., KAWAKAMI, A., & WONG, J. (1986). Emerging literacy: Reading-writing experiences in a kindergarten classroom. *Reading Teacher, 40,* 144–151.

DEGLER, L. S. (1979). Putting words into wordless books. *Reading Teacher, 32*(4), 399–402.

ELLERMEYER, D. (1988). Kindergarten reading programs to grow on. *Reading Teacher, 41,* 402–405.

ELLIS, D. W., & PRESTON, F. W. (1984). Enhancing beginning reading using wordless picture books in a cross-age tutoring program. *Reading Teacher, 37*(8), 692–698.

GAMBY, G. (1983). Talking books and taped books: Materials for instruction. *Reading Teacher, 36*(4), 366–369.

GOODALL, M. (1984). Can four year olds "read" words in the environment? *Reading Teacher, 37*(6), 478–482.

KAISEN, J. (1987). SSR/Booktime: Kindergarten and first grade sustained silent reading. *Reading Teacher, 30,* 532–537.

LARRICK, N. (1976). Wordless picture books and the teaching of reading. *Reading Teacher, 29*(8), 743–746.

LASS, B. (1982). Portrait of my son as an early reader: *Reading Teacher, 36*(1), 20–28.

MARTINEZ, M., & TEALE, W. (1987). The ins and outs of kindergarten writing program. *Reading Teacher, 40,* 444–451.

MCGEE, L. & RICHGELS, D. (1989). "K is Kristen's": Learning the alphabet from a child's perspective. *Reading Teacher, 43*(3), 216–225.

MCGEE, L., & RICHGELS, D. (1990). *Literacy's beginnings: Supporting young readers and writers.* Boston: Alyn & Bacon.

PONTECORVO, C., & ZUCCHERNIAGLIO, C. (1989). From oral to written language: Preschool children dictating stories. *Journal of Reading Behavior, 21*(2), 109–126.

ROBINSON, S. (1987). Kindergarten in America: Five major trends. *Phi Delta Kappan, 68*(7), 529–530.

SIPPOLA, A. (1985). What to teach for reading readiness: A research review and materials inventories. *Reading Teacher, 39,* 162–167.

STRICKLAND, D., & MORROW, L. (1990). Sharing big books. *Reading Teacher, 43*(4), 342–343.

STRICKLAND, D., & MORROW, L., (1989). Oral language development: Children as storytellers. *Reading Teacher, 43*(3), 260–261.

STRICKLAND, D., & MORROW, L. (1989). Interactive experiences with storybook reading. *Reading Teacher, 42*(4), 322–323.

TEALE, W. H., & SULZBY, E. (Eds).). (1986). *Emergent literacy: Writing and reading.* Norwood, NJ: Ablex.

TRACHTENBURG, P., & FERRUGGIA, A. (1989). Big books from little voices: Teaching high risk beginning readers. *Reading Teacher, 42*(4), 284–289.

VALENCIA, S., & SULZBY, E. (1991). Assessment of emergent literacy. *Reading Teacher, 44*(7), 498–500.

WEEKS, T. E. (1979). Early reading acquisition as language development. *Language Arts, 56*(5), 515–521.

WISEMAN, D. L. (1984). Helping children take early steps toward reading and writing. *Reading Teacher, 37*(4), 340–344.

THE RESEARCH BASE

BRUNER, J. (1979). From communication to language: A psychological perspective. In V. Lee (Ed.), *Language development.* New York: Wiley.

CALKINS, L. (1980). Children learn the writer's craft. *Language Arts, 57,* 2.

MASON, J. (1984). Early reading from a developmental perspective. In P. D. Pearson (Ed.), *Handbook of reading research* (pp. 505–544). New York: Longman.

MORROW, L., O'CONNOR, E., & SMITH, J. (1990). Effects of a story reading program on the literacy development of at-risk kindergarten children. *Journal of Reading Behavior, 22*(3), 255–275.

RESNICK, L., & WEAVER, P. (1979). *Theory and practice of early reading.* Hillsdale, NJ: Erlbaum.

REUTZEL, D. R., ODA, L., & MOORE, B. (1989). Developing print awareness: The effect of three instructional approaches on kindergartners' print awareness, reading readiness, and word reading. *Journal of Reading Behavior, 21*(3), 197–217.

SULZBY, E., & TEALE, W. (1991). Emergent literacy. In R. Barr, M. Kamil, P. Mosenthal, & P. D. Pearson (Eds.), *Handbook of reading research, volume II* (pp. 727–758). New York: Longman.

WEIR, B. (1989). A research base for kindergarten literacy programs. *Reading Teacher, 42*(7), 456–460.

ACTIVITIES FOR REFLECTING, OBSERVING, AND TEACHING

Reflecting on Teaching Preschool and Kindergarten Reading

PURPOSE: Good instruction puts students in situations where they are engaged in genuinely literate activity for a purpose which makes sense to them. The postal unit provided as a sample in this chapter is one such example. Your success as a preschool or kindergarten teacher will depend in large part upon your ability to create similar units and to teach necessary reading and writing processes within such authentic activity. This activity is designed to give you experience doing so.

DIRECTIONS: Using both the sample unit provided in this chapter and the suggestions provided in Chapter 14, create a unit which will involve preschoolers and/or kindergartners in authentic literate activity in pursuit of a genuine goal. Include specific content, attitude, and process objectives, and a day-by-day schedule of activity.

Watching Others Teach Preschool and Kindergarten

PURPOSE: The more you watch others teach preschool and kindergarten, the more extensive your experience background will be. Such experiences will hold you in good stead in doing your own teaching. Consequently, this activity helps you structure such observations.

DIRECTIONS: Arrange to observe a preschool or kindergarten teacher for a period of several consecutive days. During these observations, specifically note the following:

- the instructional emphasis (relative to Table 16.1)
- the literate environment
- the use of language experience
- how attitudes are developed
- what routine skills are taught and how they are taught (look particularly for lessons on visual discrimination and vocabulary)
- what strategies are taught and how they are taught (look particularly for initiating strategies, oral context clues, letter sounds, organizing content, and evaluating content)
- what content is taught and how it is developed
- whether activity is organized into units and, if so, the nature and characteristics of the unit

Trying It Yourself

PURPOSE: The more opportunities you have to teach preschool and kindergarten yourself, the better off you will be when you get to your own classroom.

DIRECTIONS: When you are observing in a preschool and/or kindergarten classroom, accept all invitations to teach and look for opportunities to volunteer to teach. On those occasions when you can teach, use the suggestions in this chapter to help you decide what to do and how to do it.

Teaching Primary Grade Reading: Initial Mastery Stage

17

GETTING READY

First and second grade are important to literacy development because it is here that most students first receive formal reading instruction. If they are well taught in first and second grade, reading success often follows; if they are poorly taught in these grades, a cycle of failure is initiated that sometimes persists for a lifetime. This chapter focuses on teaching reading at the initial mastery stage. It provides a background for primary grade reading instruction, describes the major curricular emphases, and provides specific instructional activities to help you develop the intended curricular goals.

FOCUS QUESTIONS

- What special problems are associated with teaching primary grade reading?

- How are attitude goals developed in the primary grades?

- How are process goals taught in the primary grades?

- How are content goals developed in the primary grades?

- How are reading and writing integrated at the initial mastery stage?

- What does a typical primary grade instructional day look like?

OVERVIEW OF PRIMARY GRADE READING

Teaching grades 1 and 2 places special demands on teachers. Both the students and the curriculum are unique. The students are unique because they are newcomers to formal reading instruction. They may have engaged in emergent literacy activity of the kind described in Chapter 16 while in kindergarten, but few have actually read a book on their own. It is not until first grade that students become conscious of learning reading skills or strategies, and it is then that students often form lasting impressions about what reading is. Primary grade students are at a particularly sensitive stage in their academic careers. Primary grade teachers, like kindergarten teachers, must make special efforts to provide experiences that develop positive attitudes and accurate conceptions of reading. The development of such attitude goals is a major effort in grades 1 and 2.

TABLE 17.1 Instructional Emphasis at the Initial Mastery Stage

OUTCOME	INSTRUCTIONAL EMPHASIS	MAJOR INSTRUCTIONAL ACTIVITY
Attitude goals		
Concepts about reading	Reading is a message written by an author Reading is for enjoyment Reading is for information	Indirect instructional using language experience and USSR activities
Positive responses to reading	Reading is exciting Reading is satisfying Reading results in knowledge Reading satisfies curiosity	Indirect instruction using language experience and USSR activities
Process goals		
Routing skills Vocabulary	Building vocabulary through discussion of vicarious and direct experiences Emphasize concrete words	Direct instruction of words
Word recognition	Identify words at sight Recognize words easily confused Fluent recognition of sight words in connected texts	Direct instruction of words
Metacognitive strategies		
Initiating strategies	Active background knowledge of content using predicting Activate prior knowledge of how the reading system works using story structures, expository structures, and author's purpose	Direct instruction of initiating strategies
During-reading strategies		
Monitoring strategies	Monitor for unknown words, for unknown words, for fluent sense making and accuracy of predictions	Direct instruction of monitoring strategies

There is a second curricular focus in first and second grade: It is decoding—figuring out what the printed squiggles on the page say. This is because, although reading is a matter of getting meaning, the first task readers face is graphic—interpreting the letters and words on the page. Therefore, primary grade reading instruction emphasizes letters, their sounds, techniques for recognizing printed words instantly, and strategies for figuring out unrecognized words. Comprehension instruction is not neglected, however. It continues to be taught in the listening mode until students can decode words.

The tension that exists between the need to develop attitude goals and the need to develop decoding ability is a particularly difficult aspect of primary grade reading instruction. The experiences you provide your students result in concepts and feelings that stay with them for a lifetime, so you must emphasize the sense

TABLE 17.1 (continued)

OUTCOME	INSTRUCTIONAL EMPHASIS	MAJOR INSTRUCTIONAL ACTIVITY

Fix-it strategies	Recognize disruption in sense making while reading or listening
	Access strategies to solve the problem
	  Word recognition
	  Vocabulary
	  Author's meaning
	  Beyond the author's meaning
	Determine which strategy is needed
	Implement the strategy
	Verify repair of sense making
		Direct instruction of fix-it strategies for comprehension

Post-reading strategies		
Organizing strategies	Recall what is important by story and text structure Classify words and phrases Determine main idea of expository text	Direct instruction of organizing strategies
Evaluating strategies	Distinguish between reality and fantasy	Direct instruction in making judgments
Content goals		
Recreational	Get meaning from story narrative texts Get meaning from various literature genres Use listening comprehension in recreational text	Directed reading lessons using basal text selections
Functional	Get meaning from simple expository texts Use listening comprehension in functional text	Directed reading lessons using basal text selections

making, meaning getting, and communication aspects of reading. At the same time, you must emphasize decoding—the letters, the sounds of letters, individual words, and other linguistic units and language conventions that govern how print represents oral language. This conflict often means that first and second grade teachers overemphasize decoding and neglect attitudes. Most basal textbooks have a relatively heavy emphasis on word recognition, which reinforces this inclination.

Your unique challenge when teaching primary grade reading is to create positive and accurate experiences with real reading and language, while simultaneously providing a solid foundation in how to decode. The first and second grade reading curriculum reflects this conflict, as seen in Table 17.1, which illustrates the instructional emphasis at this level.

DEVELOPING ATTITUDE GOALS

Attitude development is crucial at the initial mastery stage of developmental reading growth. Positive attitudes result from positive experiences that help students build accurate concepts of what reading is and positive feelings about reading activities. Specifically, we want first and second graders to develop the concepts that reading is a message from an author to a reader, an enjoyable pastime, and useful for getting information as well as feeling excited, satisfied, and fulfilled about reading.

Creating a Literate Environment

In the primary grades, your intent is to establish a literate atmosphere that emphasizes comprehension while it simultaneously supports a curricular emphasis on letters and words.

In the physical environment include special centers to display recreational books, lounging areas for relaxed reading, displays of children's writings and language-experience stories, collections of class-written books, clusters of messages, and objects that have been labeled and tagged. Because labeling should feature words in context rather than words in isolation, a chair would not be labeled "chair" but "This is a chair."

Organize the intellectual environment by planning for many genuine reading and writing opportunities. You and your students can engage in language-experience activities to construct, send, and receive messages. You want to establish the expectation that you and your students will engage in meaningful reading, that you will model this reading by leading your students in language-experience activities, and that your students will be given choices of both topic and activity.

Organize the social-emotional environment by emphasizing working together. This, in turn, encourages communication and interaction with oral language, which supports literacy development.

In creating a literate environment in grades 1 and 2, then, you make a deliberate effort to have students conceptualize reading as a meaning-getting activity that is an integral part of language, and to instill feelings about reading that will motivate them. You highlight the prominent role of language in the physical environment, you stimulate engagement in real language through the intellectual environment, and you encourage genuine language interactions through the social-emotional environment. In addition, you emphasize the graphic code because you display printed words everywhere and frequently refer to its relationship with oral language.

Instructional Approaches

In the primary grades, you will make heavy use of the language-experience approach to develop attitude goals. Look for opportunities to create text to illustrate to your students that reading is a message from an author to a reader. Similarly, create language experiences to illustrate that reading is enjoyable and can convey information. Such activities also get your students excited about reading.

Make use of literature-based reading activities to develop positive feelings about reading. Usually, these activities take the form of uninterrupted sustained

Building positive attitudes about reading and writing is critical at the initial mastery stage.

EXAMPLE 17.1 How to Develop Positive Attitudes

Background	You want to develop the concept that reading and writing are related aspects of language communication. You decide to do so by involving students in a language experience activity.
Activity 1	Arrange to take the class on a field trip to a farmer's apple orchard where students are shown how apples are grown, harvested, and marketed.
Discussion	In the classroom after the trip, organize students into collaborative groups, have them conduct conversations on what they saw and learned in the trip, have each group develop a thank-you note to the farmer, and then work with the whole group to combine the ideas into a single thank-you note.
Activity 2	Have students read a recipe for making applesauce, and then engage them in actually making applesauce from the apples picked at the orchard.

silent reading or some other kind of free reading activity. Even though first and second graders are just beginning to learn to read, you can nevertheless involve them in reading books of their choice. Such books may include picture books with words, wordless books, and student-authored language-experience books. By organizing such personalized reading activities for your students, you help them develop the concepts that authors write to convey messages to readers and that reading can be done for enjoyment and for information. Similarly, such self-selected reading helps your students feel excited and satisfied about what they are reading.

Lessons associated with language experience and literature-based reading are organized in the three-step format for indirect instruction described in Chapter 14 (activity-discussion-activity) and make use of collaborative groups as described in Chapter 12. For instance, assume that you want your students to feel knowledgeable as a result of reading (positive response) and to understand that reading involves receiving a message from a writer (concept of reading). After you decide to develop these goals through indirect instruction using a language experience activity, you might plan and conduct a lesson like the one shown in Example 17.1. Such indirect instruction helps first and second grade students feel knowledgeable as a result of reading (they know how to make applesauce) and helps them understand that reading involves a writer who has a message to send (they were the writers with a message of thanks to send to the apple farmer).

ACTIVITIES TO DEVELOP GOALS

Here are some useful first and second grade activities to supplement development of positive attitudes toward reading.

1. Develop a continuing contact with the expressive writing of skilled authors so students have the opportunity to develop appreciation of literature.

2. Place interesting pictures with a word or two about them in very simple language on the bulletin board. Colorful book jackets from children's literature are also good bulletin board material. Such bulletin boards help develop positive attitudes.

3. Have students read or recite favorite poems to help develop positive attitudes toward reading and language and to stimulate further reading of poetry by the group.

4. Hold informal conferences with students to stimulate continued reading, using both student-authored books and library books. This helps set expectations that reading is enjoyable.

5. Plan a field trip to the public library to develop positive attitudes about the lively world of books.

6. Develop a class book in which each student has one page to review his or her favorite book. Each page should include a brief statement of what it is about, why it is a favorite, and the title and author. Encourage students to include an illustration of the best part.

7. Pair students and let each pair read to each other from books they choose. A buddy system is a good way to encourage students to use library books.

8. Have each student write or dictate a story that is typed in primary type. Have students read their stories and exchange them with other children. Bind these stories into books and place the book in the classroom or school library. This helps develop positive feelings about reading.

9. Have students read and dramatize conversation, and then write the conversation for them to read. This develops the concept that reading is talk written down.

10. Trace or draw cutouts of favorite characters from illustrations. Use these drawings to provide a constantly changing population of book friends in displays.

11. Draw life-sized figures of favorite characters on mural paper and display them in the classroom or hall. First and second graders like to draw the animals they have read about including Paddington, Curious George, and other well-known book characters, and it helps them develop positive attitudes toward reading.

12. Make a class list of favorite books in chart form to offer students an opportunity to express their interests and preferences. Revise the list periodically as the children's tastes and interests develop.

13. Create a library corner. Responsibility for management can be a buffer's role. Include fairy tales, poetry, picture books, and concept books in the selections.

14. Introduce new books to the class. Tell what is special about each new book to help students develop an interest in them.

15. Model reading and writing often for your students. If students never see adults read or write, they are not likely to value reading and writing. What you do is just as important as what you say. Let students see you writing notes to friends, business letters, and expressive stories and poems to share. During nook-and-cranny time, read aloud what you have written and ask students to comment on your writing. Let students be a part of your revision process for all types of writing.

16. Encourage students to write for free samples and information. Many books and magazines include sections that list companies and addresses. This develops the concept that reading is a useful tool.

17. Be alert to occasions when students can be involved in writing and reading activities such as adding notes at the end of letters to parents, making and sending holiday and birthday cards, writing notes to friends, and drafting school notes for parental signature. When such occasions are used in these ways, students are encouraged to build accurate concepts about what literate persons do when they know how to read and write.

TEACHING PROCESS GOALS

Two process goals are emphasized in the primary grades: routine vocabulary and decoding skills and metacognitive strategies for figuring out unknown words.

Routine Skills

In the primary grades you will spend much time teaching your students about words and the role words play in reading. Your first emphasis should be on vocabulary—developing meanings for words. You do this in two ways: teach specific word meanings and teach about words. In the former, determine what words your students do not know by asking them to use specific words in sentences. If students cannot, provide either direct or vicarious background experiences as a conceptual base, then develop the distinguishing characteristics of the concept, using examples and nonexamples and, finally, ask students again to use the word correctly in a sentence. Example 17.2 illustrates how to teach word meaning.

When you teach *about* words in the primary grades, focus mainly on the fact that words can have multiple meanings. For instance, the word *strike* can be associated with unions, clocks, baseball, bowling, fishing, and matches. The correct meaning in a particular sentence depends upon the context of the message

EXAMPLE 17.2 How to Teach Vocabulary

Background   To increase your students' vocabulary, you decide to introduce the new words in conjunction with a text about trains being read in class. You decide which words need to be taught by asking students to use a word in a sentence. If the word is used correctly, students have a concept for the word; if it is used incorrectly or not at all, students do not have a concept for the word.

Lesson Sequence

Introduction   State what word meaning is to be learned (diesel locomotive) and why it is important to have a meaning for the word at this time (in preparation for reading a selection on trains).

Background experience   Discuss students' real experiences or provide a vicarious experience for diesel locomotive as a basis for identifying the concept's distinguishing characteristics.

Developing characteristics   Illustrate the conceptual characteristics of the word using a chart such as the following:

What is it?
(part of a train)

What are
some nonexamples
(a steam locomotive)
(a caboose)
(a diesel truck)

↑
←**diesel locomotive** →
↓

What is it like?
(it pulls the train)
(powered by diesel fuel)
(big)

What are some examples?
(the one we saw at the train station)
(the one in this picture)

Engage students in a conversation about the distinguishing characteristics of *diesel locomotives*.

Closure   Have students use the word in a sentence. Then assign guided reading in which the new word appears.

Desired Outcome   When students encounter the word in real text, they will have an accurate mental picture of the word and will be able to use this knowledge to construct the author's message.

in which it is embedded. In a sentence about bowling, *strike* means one thing; in a sentence about unions, it means another. You want your primary grade students to know that words have multiple meanings and that the "correct" meaning is determined by the context of the message.

It is also important to teach first and second graders to be automatic in identifying words in print. When a reader instantly identifies words, the reading is smooth and uninterrupted. To achieve fluency, most words should be sight words. That is, they must be firmly embedded in the reader's memory, and when they appear in the text, they must be identified immediately and without conscious effort. Efforts to build your students' sight-word vocabulary begin with the print-awareness tasks (letter naming, visual discrimination, and visual memory) described in Chapter 16. Once students can discriminate among letters and words and remember their visual form, you can teach individual sight words. Normally, you teach first the most utilitarian words, such as *a, the, in, are, is,* and other high frequency words because they are essential for students to read real text. The list provided in Figure 7.1 shows examples of high-utility words.

Also among the first sight words to teach are those which are less utilitarian but which appear in the particular text to be read. For instance, if the text is about going to school, teach sight words such as *school, teacher, desk,* and *chalkboard.* As students recognize more and more words, begin teaching easily confused sight words. It is not uncommon for primary grade students to confuse words that look alike. They may say *was* for *saw, where* for *there, them* for *then.* Such miscues are not disastrous when reading for meaning since the reader will detect the dissonance, look back, and make a correction. However, repeated miscues of this kind disrupt fluency and should be corrected. Some students confuse *was* and *saw* because they examine the words from right to left instead of from left to right; some confuse *where* and *there* because they fail to discriminate the initial letter; and some confuse words such as *after* and *father* because of hasty and partial visual examination. As students progress through the grades, they learn more and more sight words. You decide what words to teach your students by examining the next selection your students will read and by determining which of the words used in a particular selection need to be taught. Examples 17.3 and 17.4 show how to teach sight words.

Metacognitive Strategies

Three categories of metacognitive strategies receive emphasis at the initial mastery stage: initiating strategies, during-reading strategies, and post-reading strategies.

Initiating Strategies   The initiating strategies are activating prior knowledge for topic, text structure, and author's purpose.

Activating prior topic knowledge at the primary level involves helping students bring to a conscious level what they know about a topic. This can be accomplished with concrete objects, representations of objects such as illustrations or pictures, and teacher-student conversations. For instance, if the topic is how to care for pets, rabbits in particular, there are three ways to activate background knowledge. First, you can have a live rabbit to activate what students know and generally provoke conversation. Second, you can use films, filmstrips,

EXAMPLE 17.3   How to Teach Sight Words

Background	You want your students to recognize words by sight. To decide which words need to be taught as sight words, note which frequently appearing words are not instantly recognized or anticipate which words in the text to be read are not known as sight words. Be sure students have concepts for *letter, word, first, last, top, bottom, left, right, alphabet, sight word,* and *instantly* if you intend to use these words when teaching sight words.
Lesson Sequence	
Introduction	Show students a text they are going to read and tell them what words they are going to learn to recognize instantly, so that they can read the story fluently. Tell them they must understand both the visual form (what it looks like) and the "name" of each word. Show students where they will encounter the words in the text they will read.
Modeling	Print the words in phrases on cards. Present the cards one at a time. Point to the phrase, say it, and use it in a sentence.
Interaction with students	Have students do what you did (point to the phrase, say it, and use it in a sentence). Write a sentence containing the word on the back of the card, underlining the sight word. Then have student read the sentence containing the word, read the underlined sight word, write the sight word, and say it. Repeat this procedure (with variations) until students instantly recognize the word.
Closure	Have students demonstrate which sight words they have learned by flashing them the words and having them name them. Also have students state why it is important to know these words at sight and when these words will be used in the story to be read. Then guide the reading of the story that contains these new words.
Desired Outcome	When reading text, students will instantly recognize the words in print and will be able to state why it is important to instantly recognize such words.

or pictures, which are not as stimulating, so you will have to provide more statements and questions. Third, you can simply talk about rabbits; here you provide statements and questions as the way to activate prior knowledge. Conversation alone does not stimulate students as much as concrete objects or their representations, but it can be effective if you provide information and ask questions that are tied to your students' background experiences about rabbits and pet care. Statements broaden students' range of background activation while questions narrow it, so use statements interspersed with questions. Rather than simply asking your students what they know about how to take care of rabbits, combine statements and questions as follows: "People have kept animals as pets throughout history. Rabbits are sometimes kept as pets. Think about what you know

EXAMPLE 17.4 How to Teach Easily Confused Sight Words

Background	Your students confuse *was* and *saw* when reading. You want them to examine the word carefully for its distinctive visual, or graphic, characteristics. Be sure students have concepts for *letter, word, first, last, top, bottom, left, right, alphabet, sight word,* and *instantly* if you intend to use these words in your teaching.
Lesson Sequence	
Introduction	State which two words are to be learned, why they are being taught together, your evidence that the student is indeed confusing the words, and why it is important to fluent reading that they not be confused. In the case of *was* and *saw,* students must be sure to visually examine the word from left to right.
Modeling	Present the two words simultaneously on separate cards. Point to each word, say its name, and use it in a sentence. Then show how *was* and *saw* do not look alike when you read them from left to right. Model moving across the page from left to right, encountering the first letter, visually examining the word from first letter to last letter, and saying the word.
Interaction with students	Have students do what you did (move across the page from left to right, visually examine the word from first letter to last letter, and say the word). Present the word repeatedly in various phrases and sentences, and have students visually examine the word and say its name until the two words are no longer confused.
Closure	Have students state which words they have learned, what they have learned about visually examining words which will prevent similar miscues in the future, and when they will use what they have learned in real text. Then guide reading that contains these easily confused words.
Desired Outcome	When reading text, students will instantly recognize look alike words that were previously confused and will be able to state how to visually examine such words to avoid confusion.

about rabbits as pets. Do you have a pet rabbit? Do you know someone who has a rabbit as a pet? Let's see what we know about rabbits as pets."

Not only is it necessary to activate what students know about the topic, it is also necessary to activate what they know about purpose and text to predict initial meaning. From the very beginning, give students real text to read and teach them directly that reading involves making predictions about the meaning of text. Show them how knowledge about an author's purpose helps us predict the message, and how the text structure itself can be used to predict an author's message. For instance, during nook-and-cranny time or when guiding students' reading of stories, you may discuss how to decide whether an author's purpose is one of entertaining or informing and to use this knowledge to help predict the meaning; and teach them to use their knowledge of story structure to predict what will happen next. Your aim is to make your students aware of how they use their knowledge of purpose and text to construct meaning so they can be in control of the meaning-getting process. Example 17.5 illustrates how to structure such a lesson.

During-Reading Strategies   The during-reading strategies include monitoring and fix-it strategies related to decoding. Primary age students have had experiences with monitoring strategies and fix-it strategies in oral situations in kindergarten (see Chapter 16). As they learn to decode words, they move these strategies into printed texts.

Monitoring is crucial for early reading. Even though instructional emphasis is on development of word recognition, your students need to understand that reading is accomplished only when the text makes sense. This is difficult for many students to understand because so much instructional time is spent on decoding. You can help students with this problem by continuing to emphasize

---

EXAMPLE   17.5   How to Use Text Structures to Predict Meaning

Background	You have recently read two books to the class about hermit crabs, one written as a narrative text that gives a hermit crab human characteristics and another written as expository text that provides factual information about hermit crabs. You decide to use nook-and- cranny time to help students understand how different text structures can be used to make predictions.
Lesson Sequence	
Introduction	Initiate a discussion about the two books with a purpose-setting statement such as, "Let's see how these two books are organized differently and how that helps us predict meaning.
Modeling	Show how the narrative follows a story structure and that you can predict what will happen next if you know the parts of a story. Show how the expository text structure helps you predict meaning and how you used, these knowledge sources to predict the author's message.
Interaction with Students	Using other narrative and expository texts, have students follow your model and describe how they used text structure to construct meaning.
Closure	Summarize the discussion by having students state what they have learned about how to use text structure to construct meaning.
Desired Outcome	When reading text students should be able to predict the author's message and explain how they used text structures to help make their predictions.

monitoring during orally presented stories and by teaching them how to monitor when using printed materials. You want your students to understand that text that does not make sense is a problem to be solved. They monitor to see if it does make sense—to see if there is a problem.

Because of the emphasis in primary grades on words, fix-it strategies focus on what to do when you come to a word that you do not recognize at sight. This category of fix-it strategy is sometimes called word attack or word analysis because when you do not instantly know a word, you must attack it or analyze it to figure it out. There are three major ways for figuring out unrecognized words.

First, teach students to use context to predict an unrecognized word. For instance, if students do not recognize the printed word *engine* in the sentence, "The airplane's engine stopped and it crash-landed in a field," they can use their knowledge of airplane crashes to predict that the unknown word is either *engine* or *propeller*. This strategy is the most efficient way to solve word recognition problems because it is fast and it emphasizes meaning getting. For instance, even if a student predicts *propeller* in the example above, the essential meaning of the message remains intact. Consequently, teach your first and second grade students to turn first to the strategy of contextual prediction when they encounter words they do not know. Even before formal reading begins, teach your students to supply endings for oral sentences such as, "I went to the store and bought a pound of _____" or "I went to the store and bought a pair of _____." Later, require more difficult predictions, such as filling in the blanks in an exercise like the following:

The elephant went around the circus _____, performing his tricks and entertaining the _____. He did not seem very happy. _____ master was whipping him and he _____ slowly through one trick after another.

Examples of the various kinds of context are provided in Chapter 7.

Your instruction in context emphasizes monitoring meaning getting so readers know when they encounter an unrecognized word and so they first use context to identify the word. Later, when they have also learned to use phonics and structural analysis to figure out unknown words, teach your students to combine these methods with context clues. In the airplane example, if you teach first and second grade students to use context in combination with phonics they would not predict that the unknown word is *propeller* because, although it makes sense in the sentence, propeller does not begin with the letter *e*. Consequently, the reader searches for a word that both makes sense and fits the phonic and structural constraints of the unknown word (see Example 17.6).

Second, teach students to figure out unrecognized words using structural analysis. This involves teaching them to examine an unknown word for structural meaning units and root words which, when broken apart, make it easier to figure out what the word is. For instance, when readers encounter the unknown word *unneeded*, they can separate the root word *need* from the prefix *un* and from the

EXAMPLE 17.6   How to Teach Context Clues as a Strategy for Figuring Out Unrecognized Words

Background	When students encounter an unrecognized word in print, you want them to first use context as a means for figuring out the word. You decide to teach them the language principle that words in any text are related through meaning and through syntactical relationships. Be sure students have concepts for *predict, indentified words, unidentified words, context,* and *relationships* if you intend to use these words when teaching context.
Lesson Sequence	
Introduction	State what kind of reading problem you are trying to fix, the specific kind of context strategy to be used, why context is a preferred strategy, and the situation in which it will be used. Stress the need to look at the particular syntactic and meaning relationships between the unknown word and the known words around it. Show students where the strategy will be used in text to be read.
Modeling	Present an example in which you encounter an unknown word when reading. Explain how you encountered the problem while reading, how you decided to use context to fix it, how you examined the context for the particular syntactic or meaning relationship you are teaching, how that relationship gave you clues to what the unidentified word was, how you tested the predicted word to see if it made sense, and how, if it did fit the context, you then continued reading for meaning.
Interaction with students	Give students similar examples of text containing unknown words and have them explain as you did. At first, provide directives in the form of verbal and visual cues to aid students, but gradually phase these out in successive attempts as students become more successful. Be prepared to explain again and remodel if students are confused about how to use the strategy.
Closure	Have students state what they have learned, when it will be used and the mental process one goes through when using it. Then assign guided reading in which the context strategy can be used in real text.
Desired Outcome	Given real text and a blockage in getting the meaning caused by a word unknown in print, students will use a context strategy (or a context strategy combined with other kinds of cues) to figure out the unknown words, remove the blockage, and continue with meaning getting.

inflectional ending *ed* and pronounce each part in turn. This strategy is more efficient than phonics because it focuses on meaning units rather than on sound units and because it is faster than phonics (there are normally fewer meaning units in a word than sound units). However, for it to be useable, the unknown word must contain structural units. In teaching structural analysis, you progress from the most common structural units to the less common ones. Consequently, instruction begins with analyzing compound words, then common inflectional endings (such as -s, -ed, and -ing), contractions, common prefixes and suffixes, less common prefixes and suffixes, and Greek and Latin roots. A list of common structural units is provided in Figure 7.3.

Teach your students to examine unknown words for recognizable structural units, to break the units apart, to pronounce the units in turn, and to check the results with the sentence context to see if the word makes sense. To use this strategy, readers must be aware of the various kinds of structural units so they can recognize them and they must not confuse structural analysis with syllabication (which is analysis by sound unit or phonics, not analysis by meaning unit). Also, your students must not confuse structural analysis with "looking for the little word in the big word," which does not always work (sometimes it does, as when one looks at the *at* in the unknown word *chat*, and sometimes it does not, as when one looks for the *at* in the unknown word *father* or the unknown word *plate*). Structural analysis is illustrated in Example 17.7.

Third, teach your primary grade students phonics. Teach them the sound of each of the letters (or letter combinations) and how to blend those sounds together to pronounce an unknown word. In the word *umbrella*, for instance, teach students to divide the word into parts (um-brel-la) and to pronounce each part by saying the letter sounds individually and then blending them together. Students will say the short *u* and the consonant *m* to get *um*; the consonant blend *br*; the short *e* and the consonant sound for *l* to get *brel*; and the consonant sound for *l* and the schwa sound to pronounce the unaccented final syllable *la*. Then they say the three parts one after another, blend them together, and identify the unknown word (assuming that the reader's pronunciation is accurate enough and that *umbrella* is a word they have heard or used before).

You can see that phonic analysis often requires more time and effort on the reader's part than either context or structural analysis. Consequently, phonics is the least efficient of the strategies for attacking unknown words. Also, it is sometimes inaccurate since, unless you know virtually all there is to know about phonics, you may produce an approximation of the unknown word rather than an exact reproduction of the actual pronunciation. Finally, phonics is difficult to teach because there are so many letter sounds, letter-sound combinations, generalizations, and exceptions to be learned. Despite these disadvantages, however, phonics is an important word-attack strategy because almost all words can be pronounced (or pronounced almost the way they are supposed to be said) by using phonics. When a sentence does not provide enough context clues to make an accurate prediction about a word, and the word does not contain meaning units for structural analysis, readers can turn to phonics in the expectation that a reasonable facsimile of the word's pronunciation will result. For this reason, it is important to spend considerable time teaching primary grade students to use phonics to attack and sound out unknown words.

Begin instruction in the prereading stage with emphasis on auditory discrimination of sounds and letter-sound associations (see Chapter 16). Teach your students the various sound elements, beginning with single consonant letter

EXAMPLE 17.7   How to Teach Structural Analysis as a Strategy for Figuring Out Unrecognized Words

Background   When students encounter a word unknown in print which has a root and affixes, you want them to use such structural elements as an aid in identifying the word. You decide to teach the principle that the meaning of many English words are changed by adding prefixes, suffixes, and inflectional endings. By separating these affixes from the root, an unrecognized word sometimes becomes recognizable. Be sure students have concepts for *prefix, suffix, inflectional endings, roots,* and *structural analysis* if you intend to use them when teaching structural analysis.

Lesson Sequence

Introduction   State what kind of reading problem you are trying to fix and the specific kind of structural analysis to be used to fix it. Describe when this strategy would be used, and state that students must attend to the affix in question and separate it from the root. Show students where the strategy will be used in text to be read.

Modeling   Present an example in which you encounter an unknown word when reading. Explain how you decided to use structural analysis to fix this blockage, examined the unknown word for the affix in question, separated the affix in question, separated the affix from the root, pronounced the two separate parts, pronounced them together, tested the newly pronounced word to see if it made sense, and continued reading if it did make sense.

Interaction with students   Give students similar examples of text containing unknown words that have structural units. Have them explain their mental processing in figuring out the word. Assist them at the early stages with verbal and visual directives but gradually diminish these as students demonstrate success. Reexplain and remodel as dictated by the quality of student response.

Closure   Have students state what they learned, when they will use it, and how to do it. Assign guided reading containing unknown words to which structural analysis can be applied and have students use the strategy in this real reading situation.

Desired Outcome   Given real text and a blockage in getting the meaning caused by an unknown word composed of structural units, students will use structural analysis (in combination with context) to figure out the unknown word, remove the blockage, and continue with meaning getting.

sounds, consonant blends and digraphs, letter substitution in common phonogram patterns (such as substituting initial consonants in *mat, bat, fat,* and *sat*), short vowel sounds, long vowel sounds, vowel combinations, vowel generalizations, and syllabication. As students progress through the grades, more and more of these phonic units are presented. Place your emphasis on examining words for specific phonic elements (to determine, for instance, whether the unknown word *chow* should be attacked as c-h-o-w or as ch-ow), breaking the word apart by these units, applying the appropriate sounds to the units, pronouncing the separate sounds, blending them together, and checking to see if the resulting pronunciation makes sense in the context of the sentence. See Example 17.8 for an illustration of how to teach phonics as a strategy in the primary grades.

EXAMPLE 17.8 How to Teach Phonics as a Strategy for Figuring Out Unrecognized Words

Background	When an unrecognized word cannot be figured out using context or structural analysis, you want students to use phonics. You decide to teach the language principle that alphabetic letters and phonogram units have assigned sounds that can be blended together to approximate the sound of the unknown word. Be sure students have concepts for *letters, words, sounds, first, last, middle, same, different, blending, phonogram,* and *phonics* if you intend to use these words when teaching phonics.
Lesson Sequence	
Introduction	State what kind of reading problem you are trying to fix, the specific phonic element to be used, and when it will be used. Tell students to look at the visual form of the phonic element and its associated sound. Show students where this strategy will be used in text to be read.
Modeling	Present an example in which you encounter an unknown word while reading. Explain about how you decided to use phonics to fix the blockage, how you examined the word to find the phonic elements you knew how to use, how you supplied the appropriate sound and blended it with other letter sounds, how you tested the approximation that resulted to see if it made sense, and how you then continued reading if it did.
Interaction with students	Give students similar examples of text containing unknown words made up from the phonic element being taught. Have them explain the mental processing they used to figure out the word. Assist them at the early stages with verbal and visual cues, but diminish these gradually until they are doing the task independently. Be prepared to reexplain and remodel if student responses indicate confusion.
Closure	Have students state what they have learned, when they would use it, and how to do it. Assign guided reading containing unknown words to which phonics can be applied and have students use the strategy.
Desired Outcome	Given real text and a blockage to getting the meaning caused by an unknown word composed of known phonic elements, students will figure out the word using phonics (in combination with context) and continue with meaning getting.

To be good readers, students must first understand the relationship between sight words and word analysis. Most words in any given text must be recognized at sight. In fact, the rule of thumb used by most teachers is that unless 95 percent of the words are sight words, a text is too difficult. Only the 5 percent that are not instantly recognized should require word attack using context clues, structural analysis, and phonics. Students must monitor their own word identification as they read. They must determine if they recognize a word visually, if they require word-attack skills, and if so, how to select the appropriate strategy. Strategy use must be preceded by self-monitoring. Good reading ultimately demands that readers use these strategies in combination—they use visual characteristics, contextual meaning, structural units, and phonics because using them together is more efficient than using them separately.

EXAMPLE 17.9   How to Teach Organizing Content

Background	Your students have been organizing content for listening situations. You decide to teach them how to organize information from stories and texts that are read by remembering what happened in the beginning, middle, and end sections.
Lesson Sequence *Introduction*	Have students read a story or text. Direct them to read the beginning section and stop, the middle section and stop, and the ending section and stop. You signal each section.
Modeling	Explain that it is helpful when organizing information that has been read to remember it in terms of the beginning, middle, and end sections. Explain that the usefulness of organizing content by beginning, middle, and end sections helps the memory process and makes it easier to remember it at a future date. Be specific about the future use of the strategy. All students read each section, and you demonstrate how you remember information in a particular situation. Then demonstrate how to organize information based on where it is in the story or text.
Interaction with students	Give students several opportunities to remember story or text content through use of the beginning, middle, and end sections. Start with single sections and gradually move to entire selections including both narrative and expository texts. As students demonstrate their understanding and use of the strategy, gradually reduce your assistance.
Closure	End the lesson series with another selection. Point out the beginning, middle, and end sections, and have students read the selection and use their organizing strategy to remember information.
Desired Outcome	Given narrative and expository texts that are read by students, students will remember information by organizing into beginning, middle, and end sections.

Word recognition, then, involves a four-step procedure. First, the reader examines the word visually and tries to identify it as a sight word. If that does not work, the reader turns to context and tries to predict the unknown word by reference to meaning cues. Then, the unknown word is examined for structural units and, if they are present, these are used in combination with context to figure out the word. Finally, the word can be sounded out and the pronunciation confirmed by reference to the sentence context (if it makes sense, it is probably the right word). As you introduce each of these four procedures, teach your students to use them in combination.

Post-Reading Strategies   The post-reading strategies are organizing and evaluating content. During the initial-mastery stage, these strategies are emphasized more than they were at the readiness stage.

Organizing content is a strategy that becomes increasingly important as first and second graders learn how to recognize words. For organizing content, the major strategy taught at this level is recalling what is important through use of simple story structures and text structures. This means that students need to recognize where the beginning, middle, and end sections are in stories and texts, and then each section as a way to organize content. You need to teach your students how to do this. Example 17.9 illustrates how to structure a lesson on organizing content of narrative texts or stories.

In the initial-mastery stage, students continue to evaluate the content of narrative and expository texts as real or make-believe, but it is taught when students are reading, not listening, as was the case in kindergarten. You want your students to judge whether or not information they read could really happen. It is not important that every story students read be classified real or make-believe. Students judge stories and texts based on what their background experiences tell them could really happen or could not happen. Example 17.10 illustrates how to structure a lesson on evaluating content after reading narrative or expository text.

Role of the Basal

Basal textbooks emphasize many process goals and, therefore, frequently are the basis for process instruction in primary grades. However, you should be cautious about basing your process instruction on the basal in grades 1 and 2.

First, what the basals recommend is not necessarily what needs to be taught. For instance, only a few current basal texts recommend much instruction in using prior knowledge, purpose, and text structure in combination with construct meaning. Similarly, not all basals have carefully structured programs of word meaning and sight-word vocabulary; others do not make a distinction between instant word recognition and word analysis; still others teach word-analysis techniques as skills to be memorized rather than as strategies to be consciously applied; and still others put a priority emphasis on phonics (rather than context) as a word-attack technique.

EXAMPLE 17.10 How to Teach Evaluating Content

Background	Your students may already know how to judge stories they listen to. You decide to teach them how to judge stories or texts as real or make-believe when they read them.
Lesson Sequence	
Introduction	Have students read a narrative or expository text that is real. Then have them read a make-believe selection. Note and discuss the events that make each selection real or make-believe.
Modeling	During discussion, explain and demonstrate how to decide if events are real or make-believe by using background experiences.
Interaction with students	Give students several opportunities to judge whether a selection is real or make-believe after it has been read. Gradually diminish assistance as students demonstrate they can judge selections as real or make-believe based on their background experiences.
Closure	End the lesson series with narrative and expository texts that are either real or make-believe. Have students judge whether the selections they read where real or make believe and then support their decisions.
Desired Outcome	Given stories that students have read, students will judge selection content as real or make-believe based on their background experiences.

Second, your intention in teaching process goals is that your students will *apply* process knowledge when reading real text. Most basal texts, however, make only minimal attempts to transfer skills from the instructional context of the workbook to the application context of real books and stories. In fact, many basals do not even recommend that skills taught in a particular lesson be applied in the reading of that lesson.

Consequently, you should modify basal text prescriptions to ensure that what needs to be taught is indeed taught and that what is taught is actually applied by students to real text. The recommendations made in Chapter 13 should be used to guide your decision making when making these modifications.

ACTIVITIES TO DEVELOP PROCESS GOALS

Here are some activities you can use to supplement your teaching of process goals in first and second grade. The activities at this level tend to focus on words, because this is a process emphasis in primary grades. Be cautioned, however, that understandings about words are best developed within a literate environment and that these activities should not be used in isolation from real reading situations.

1. Hold up familiar objects to elicit descriptive words such as *round, heavy, square,* and so forth. As the object is shown, ask questions such as: "What is this? What shape is it?" You may also use pictures. This helps develop oral vocabularies, which are essential for reading success.

2. When students begin to read, they need to recognize certain words for directions. This includes such concepts as *same, different; smaller, larger; big, bigger, biggest; up, down; circle, underline; left, right.* Games are good for this purpose. For example, to develop correct ideas for *left* and *right*, have students play the game "Simon says, turn left, turn right." Or have them dramatize or give directions as they say the nursery rhyme "Jack and Jill."

   Activities 3 through 12 can be used to help students develop sight words.

3. Make up racing games in which students progress in the race by pronouncing at sight the words to be learned. For instance, construct an auto-racing course and divide the track into equal-sized squares. Give each student a toy racing car. Using a pack of cards upon which are printed the words you want the class to learn, flash one word to each student in turn. Students who pronounce a word instantly move their racing car one square closer to the finish line. Students who are unable to pronounce the word do not move their car. The first student to get his or her car to the finish line wins.

4. Help students construct self-help references for the words they find difficult. For instance, each student can be provided with a 3" by 5" file box and a supply of file cards. Have students write difficult words on a file card, and glue a picture or other aid to the card to help remember the word. Tell students to refer to the file frequently to study the words and to remind themselves when they are unable to identify words in reading.

5. Place the words to be learned at sight on the chalkboard. Send one student into the hall, and have another go to the board and point to one of the words. Tell the rest of the class to pronounce the word to be sure that all the students know it. Then bring the first student back into the room and tell him or her to guess the target word. Have the student point to one word and say, "Is it _____?" The student continues this way until the word is identified.

6. Construct ladder games in which a paper ladder leads to a place where a reward of some kind is waiting. For instance, the ladder can lead to the upper branches of a paper apple tree that has many paper apples on it. Each rung of the ladder has a sight word attached to it. Tell students to instantly pronounce the word on each rung of the ladder to reach the top. The reward is knowing all those words. Other rewards can be used, such as a real apple or a check on a progress chart.

7. A multitude of games for building sight words can be based on the idea of a trip. This trip may be a reconstruction of the adventures of some famous

story character (such as Peter Rabbit), it may be a trip that the students are actually going on, or it may be a trip that is completely imaginary (such as a trip to the moon, a trip to a distant city, and so on). In any case, construct a game board and draw the path to be followed in reaching the destination as well as the hazards to be overcome along the way. Each student progresses on the trip by correctly pronouncing the words that are flashed. The first student to complete the trip wins the game.

8. Play a fishing game in which students are given a pole constructed of a stick and a string with a magnet tied to the end. Place paper fish with sight words printed on them in a box or in some other object that will serve as a pond. Attach a paper clip to each fish. Have students drop their line into the pond until the magnet attracts the paper clip on a fish. They pull the fish out and get to keep it if they can correctly pronounce the word printed on its side. Each student tries to increase the number of fish caught each time the game is played.

9. Make nine packs of ten cards each. The nine packs represent the nine holes of a golf course, and the words printed on the cards are the words to be learned at sight. Shuffle the cards and tell the player to put the pack for the first hole face down on the desk. Have the student turn each card over in turn, pronounce it, and go on. Every time a word is incorrectly pronounced, put a mark on the score card. The number the student gets wrong on the first hole (first pack of cards) is his or her score for that hole. Have the student continue in this manner through the nine packs of word cards, trying to get as low a score as possible. Encourage students to keep a record of their scores so they can note their progress in mastering the course. Construct new courses offering new challenges as new words need to be learned.

10. Put some sight words on cards, placing a numerical value from 1 (low) to 3 (high) in the upper right-hand corner of each card in accordance with its degree of difficulty in being remembered. For instance, *dinosaur* is a fairly easy word for learners to identify and would only be given a value of 1, but *the* is very difficult for young students to recognize and would be given a value of 3. Students take turns drawing the cards, reading the words, and noting their scores. If they pronounce the word correctly, their score is the numerical value noted on the corner of the card. Each student tries to increase the number of points each time the game is played.

11. Play a treasure hunt game in which some packets of ten or more word cards are hidden around the classroom. Give each student the first packet and direct students to read each word. Have students go through the words as quickly as possible and try to get to the last card that tells them where the next packet is hidden. They go to that packet and repeat the process. The final packet directs them to a spot where each student will receive a reward for having completed the game.

12. Play a variation of the television game "Concentration". Place the words to be learned on cards and put them face down on the table. Tell students to try to remember where there are two cards exactly alike and to pick up matching pairs. As students turn over each card, they must pronounce the word on the card. If they succeed in picking up a card that matches the first word, they get another turn. All students try to increase the number of pairs each time the game is played.

13. Help students write headlines to develop an understanding of how reading works. Popular first and second grade books may lead to such headlines as "Dinosaur Missing from Museum," "Fish Saves Family," or "Sharing Is Fun." This helps students learn to focus on main ideas.

14. Read three or four lines of a story not known to your students, and have them create an ending. Later have students compare their version with the original. This activity helps students learn to predict.

15. Play a game in which you (or a student) start off with a word, such as *Wilbur.* Ask the next student to add a new word. Continue the game with each student adding a word until a complete story sentence about the initial word is given. This game shows how the reading-writing system works.

16. Line up a series of objects for students to see. Tell them to look carefully and to remember the objects from left to right. While their eyes are closed, you (or a student) shift the order of one or two objects, then ask some of the other students to recreate the original order.

17. Present the following to students orally or in written form:

    Sugar is sweet, but pickles are _____?
    A jet is fast, but a bicycle is _____?
    The clouds are above, the dirt is _____?

    This type of procedure helps students with comparisons and relationships. For example:

    Bread is made by a baker; boats are made by a _____?
    A dog runs on its legs, but a car moves on its _____?
    In the morning the sun rises; at night the sun _____?

18. Once students develop a sight-word vocabulary, you can use those words to create written sentences and ask students to provide the missing word. If students cannot yet read independently, you can do the same thing as in a listening activity by putting the sentences on tape or having them spoken by another student, an aide, or you. This helps develop skill in using context clues.

19. Read a paragraph to students and state that you will stop reading every once in a while and hold up a letter card. Direct them to keep the paragraph in mind, to look at the letter on the card, to think of the sound associated with that letter, and to say a word that both begins with that letter sound and fits the sense of the paragraph. This helps develop using context and phonics in combination.

20. Play games that require students to use both context and sound-symbol connections. For instance, direct them to listen to a sentence such as, "I went to the store and bought a mouse, a _____, a _____, and a _____." Hold up a letter card to indicate the beginning letter of each word required to fill the missing spaces. Students expand the sentence by adding words that begin with the letter sounds you show.

21. Group students in pairs. Give each pair a supply of letter cards. Let each take a turn in making up a sentence in which one word is left out. One student must hold up the beginning letter of the missing word at the appropriate spot in the sentence, while the other uses the sense of the sentence and the sound-symbol connection of the letter card to guess what word goes in the space. After correctly identifying the missing word, that student must make up a sentence. This helps students use context clues and phonics in combination.

22. Give students riddles in which the context supplies only a minimum outline of the missing word. For instance, you could provide the sentence, "The swimmer dived into the _____." Elicit student responses and encourage a variety of answers, such as water, pool, lake, river, and so on. Then place a letter card (such as the letter w) at the left of the blank space and say, "What word must now go in the blank space?"

23. Use context activities to develop structural analysis. Provide students with sentences in which one word is missing and give them a choice of a root word or a root plus its structural ending to fill the space. For instance, a sample sentence might be, "The two (boy, boys) went to the store." Students choose the correct word to fill the blank, pronounce it, and tell why that word is the correct one. This helps students learn to use context clues and structural analysis in combination. Caution: The successful use of this technique presupposes that students already know orally the correct form of the word. Certain dialects will not contain many of these inflected and derived forms of words. Teach these as oral responses prior to the activity.

24. It is sometimes helpful to reverse the decoding process. That is, ask students to create words with prefixes and suffixes, or to compound words. Print the known words and word parts on separate cards, scramble them up, and have students choose a card. Then have the student choose another word card that goes with that word, making it either a prefixed word,

a suffixed word, or a compound word. Be sure to have students pronounce each word they have created.

25. To help develop structural-analysis skills, make a chart or a work sheet in which root words or parts of compounds are listed down the left side and suffixes or the second part of the compound are listed down the right side. Attach strings to the words on the left-hand column and direct students to connect the string with the suffix or other part of the compound listed at the right to make a new word.

26. Make up crossword puzzles in which only compound and/or prefixed and suffixed words can be used as answers.

27. Play a card game in which each player is dealt cards with root words written on them. Place the rest of the deck, with prefixes and suffixes on the cards, in the center of the table. Have students take turns drawing cards from the deck to try to match the drawn card with one of the root words to form a new word. If they can do so, they lay the two cards down together and pronounce the new word. If students draw a card they cannot use, it is put back on the bottom of the pile. The first player to get rid of all his or her cards is the winner.

28. Plan activities in which students must complete a series of sentences using the same root word in each. For instance, you might provide them with the root word *play* and tell them to use it with suffixes to complete the following sentences (see caution in Activity 2).

> He is a baseball _____.
> She is _____ in the game.
> Yesterday he _____ football.
> When she _____ she is happy.

29. Make a shutter device out of tagboard so that you can control the opening of the shutter. Insert a card that has the letter to be learned on the left and a picture of an object with the beginning sound of that letter on the right. Open the shutter to reveal first the letter and then the picture. Have students form the letter sound with their mouths and blend that sound into the picture name as it is exposed. This helps develop phonic skills.

30. Use the same device as described in Activity 29, but this time insert a picture first, then the letter, then the picture again. Have students say the picture name, then its beginning letter sound, and then blend that sound into the picture name as it is exposed the second time.

31. Use flash cards containing the letters to be learned. Flash a letter to students and direct them to respond with a word that begins (or ends) with that letter sound. This helps students develop phonic skills.

32. To help your students connect letters and sounds, display pictures of common objects (dogs, money, and so on) with the letter the object begins with printed at the left. Encourage students to use these pictures when trying to remember the sound of a particular letter.

33. Make a box and label it with a large printed form of the letter you are teaching. Place in the box pictures and objects whose names begin (or end) with the letter to be practiced. Direct students to reach into the box, draw out a picture or object, name it, and tell what letter it begins with. Make sure students look at the letter on the box while saying the object's name.

34. For students who need to review a number of letters and their sounds, modify Activity 33 by putting several letters on the outside of the box and placing objects that begin with all these letters in the box. The students then draw an object, name it, and point to the letter on the box that begins the object's name.

35. Give each student a group of pictures, some of which begin with the letter to be worked on and some of which do not. Hold up a letter card and direct students to hold up any picture they have that begins (or ends) with the sound associated with that letter. This helps develop phonic skills.

36. Using a flannelboard or a pocket chart, place a letter card to the left and a row of three pictures to the right. Two of the pictures should begin with the sound associated with the letter and one should not. To help develop phonic skills, direct students to select the beginning sound of the two pictures that begin the same.

37. Make a bulletin board or a large chart showing the letters to be learned in one part and in the other, next to each one and under a flap, a picture whose name begins with the sound associated with that letter. When students cannot remember the sound of *m*, for instance, they can go to the bulletin board, look under the flap next to *m* and say, "Oh, the sound of *m* is what we hear at the beginning of *money*" (or whatever the picture is under the flap).

38. Make a tagboard chart with the letters to be learned listed down one side and pictures beginning (or ending) with the sounds of these letters listed down the other. Attach pieces of string to the letters, and have students who need help with phonics connect the string from each letter to an object that begins with its sound.

39. Provide students with a number of letters. Play a game in which you say, "I see a letter whose sound we hear at the beginning of the word *money*. What letter do I see?" Tell students to hold up the proper letter card, look at it, and say, "*Money* begins with the letter *m*."

40. Make a set of picture cards for each letter sound. Teach students to play a card game in which several cards are dealt to each player. Tell students to pair picture cards beginning with the same letter sound. Have each player take turns asking their partner "Do you have a picture card beginning with the letter *m*?" If a student has such a card, he or she gives the picture card to the student requesting it and then has the opportunity to draw a card from the student's hand in return. Tell students to keep track of the number of pairs they possess.

41. Give students a group of letter cards. Tell each student to take turns saying, "I have a letter. *Money* starts with the sound of my letter. What letter do I have?" The student who responds correctly is the next one to select a letter.

42. To help review phonics, play a dramatization game with students in which you hold up a letter card and ask them to act out something that begins with the sound of that letter. Tell those who are not acting to guess what begins with the letter sound being dramatized.

43. To develop student use of context clues and ending sounds, use activities in which you provide the student with a key word and a sentence in which one word is missing. Direct them to supply a word to fill the blank. This word must rhyme with the key word. For instance, give the key word *cat* and the sentence, "Hit the ball with the _____." Students must supply and pronounce the word *bat*.

44. Play games in which you start with a common spelling pattern (phonogram) written on the board. To help develop phonic skills, students change either the initial or final letter, substitute another, and pronounce the new word. The next student must change it again and pronounce the new word. The pattern of words might look something like this:

> *cat* is changed to *bat*
> *bat* is changed to *bag*
> *bag* is changed to *bad*
> *bad* is changed to *had*
> *had* is changed to *has*

45. Have one student write on the chalkboard a word illustrating a common phonogram pattern. He or she must then pronounce the word and make up a sentence using that word. Tell the next student to go to the chalkboard, change either the initial or final consonant in the word, pronounce the new word, and use it in a new sentence. At first, you may want to accept any sentence students produce. As they become more skillful, however, modify the activity to have them produce successive sentences that are related to each other and that tell a story so that students are using phonics and

context clues in combination. For instance, the sentences might proceed in this manner:

> The *cat* is in the house.
> He is sleeping near the *bat*.
> A man put the cat in a *bag*.
> He must be a *bad* man.

46. Make word cards using words incorporating common phonogram patterns you have been working on. Include also a number of cards that have the word *changeover* written on them (meaning that the phonogram pattern may be changed). Deal each student five cards. Tell one student to start by laying down any word card and naming it. The next student must lay down and name a card in his or her hand that has the same phonogram. If the student cannot play because he or she does not have such a word, he or she must draw from the deck until finding a word that fits or drawing three cards. When the *changeover* card is drawn, the student can play that and name any word with a different phonogram pattern. The first person out of cards wins the game.

47. Play a variation of crazy eights by making a deck of 40 cards that have printed on them words containing the phonogram patterns you have been working on. Make six cards with the numeral 8 on them. Give each student four cards, and place the rest of the cards in the center of the table. Tell the first student to lay down a card that contains the same word element or an 8 card. If students have neither a word card that fits nor an 8 card, they must draw a card from the deck. The first person out of cards is the winner.

DEVELOPING CONTENT GOALS

Ultimately, the ability to read is measured by noting how much of the content of particular texts is understood by the reader. Teaching to these goals begins in the primary grades and builds from the listening comprehension activities initiated in preschool and kindergarten (see Chapter 16).

Both recreational and functional texts are used at the primary level. Recreational texts are usually short stories with a simple story structure. Typically, they include a character, a setting, a problem the character must solve, a brief series of incidents relating to the character's problem, and a resolution of the problem. Many stories of this type appear in primary grade basal textbooks. However, primary grade recreational reading is not limited to basal-text stories. Trade books (picture books and easy-to-read stories) and magazines (*Jack and Jill, Humpty-Dumpty*) are also read recreationally.

The predominant functional texts in grades 1 and 2 are simple expository articles conveying factual information. These are usually brief and straightforward, following a format of introduction-body-conclusion. Many times such functional text will be presented as a story; that is, expository text about animals may convey factual information by personifying an animal and telling a story about it. Some functional text of this kind is found in basal textbooks, and examples are also found in current-events magazines and newspapers designed for use by primary grade students (such as *Weekly Reader* and *Scholastic Magazine*).

EXAMPLE 17.11 How to Use a Directed Reading Lesson for Content Goals

Background	You want your students to read the next selection in the basal textbook, and you want to make sure they comprehend the content. You guide the reading using the steps of the directed reading lesson. At the primary grade level, the selection to be read will almost always to be narrative text.
Lesson Sequence	
Introduction	Introduce the story in a manner designed to activate the students' prior knowledge about the topic or problem encountered. Extend students' schema for the topic or problem by teaching the meaning of new words that appear in the story, using a technique similar to that described in Example 16.2. When appropriate, also activate student knowledge about text structure and how this knowledge is used to predict meaning.
Purpose-setting	There are many ways to comprehend a story. You may wish students to focus on certain casual relationships, on how story problems are reflected in real life, or on broad themes. To ensure that students are focusing on the type and level of comprehension you intend, state the purposes for reading the selection and point out the author's purpose for writing the selection. Then tell how these two purposes are compatible.
Reading	Have students read the selection. At the early primary level this reading will often be oral, since students may not yet know how to read silently. Also you may ask students to have conversations about the story in sections as it is being used.
Discussion	Follow a question-answer format for the discussion. Base questions on the purposes stated at the outset and guide the conversation to ensure that students comprehend the story in the intended way.
Closure	Have students review what was learned from the selection particularly in terms of the purposes set earlier. Usually you will also plan some type to follow-up activity that will extend and enrich the content knowledge. Frequently such follow-up activities involve writing or otherwise emphasize how reading and writing are integrated.
Desired Outcome	Students will be able to state what current knowledge has been gained from reading the selection.

In first and second grade, you want students to comprehend the content of both kinds of text. Plan your instruction to guide students to acquisition of content.

Directed Reading Lesson

As noted in Chapter 16, instruction in comprehending the content of recreational and functional text begins in preschool and kindergarten when virtually all comprehension is listening comprehension. The major technique to guide listening comprehension is the directed listening activity. In grades 1 and 2, you will continue to develop listening comprehension using directed listening activities.

After your students develop a sight-word vocabulary and an accurate concept of reading, however, you can begin to guide students' reading of recreational and functional text using the directed reading lesson. The DRL can be used with either recreational or functional text. In either case, you clearly communicate the purpose of the reading before beginning. If you involve students in this step, you will guarantee more student involvement in the reading (and, hence, more comprehension) while also establishing the importance of having clear purposes for reading. Example 17.11 illustrates how to use a directed reading lesson with a basal-text selection.

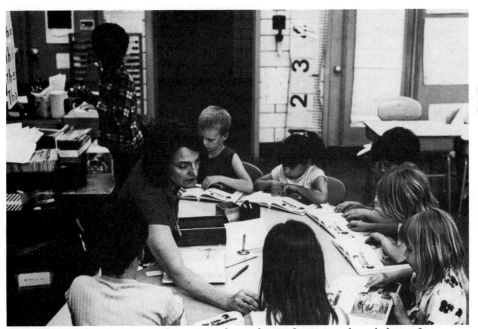

Teachers must decide whether they are teaching a lesson for content knowledge or for process goals.

Role of the Basal

It is important to make connections between process goals and content goals. Process goals should not be taught in isolation; in fact, the lesson format for teaching process goals (the MDRL) begins with discussion of the selection to be read for content. Consequently, there are times when both process and content are taught together, with the intention of helping students apply process knowledge while reading for content information.

Part of your responsibility is to decide whether you are teaching a particular lesson only for content knowledge or whether you are trying to help your students consciously use process knowledge. If the lesson is to ensure comprehension of content, you can use the directed reading lesson as described in Example 17.11; if the lesson is for applying process knowledge to content, use an MDRL.

Both forms of the DRL are typically used with basal textbooks. That is, you can use basal-text selections to teach content goals alone or to teach how process knowledge is applied to content. In either case, however, you must override the basal-text prescriptions, make a decision about why you want to use the selection, and then plan the lesson to achieve that objective. By making such decisions, you maintain cognitive control of instruction.

ACTIVITIES TO DEVELOP CONTENT GOALS

Here are some activities you can use to supplement your teaching of content goals in first and second grade. The suggestions are not extensive because instructional activities for content goals depend on your choice of text. Thus your task is not to collect activities, but to use different kinds of text.

1. Have students find an action picture in a newspaper or magazine. Have them discuss how the picture helps develop the information in the text.

2. Have students cut out questions in the weekly reader newspaper. Tell them to exchange questions and then provide answers. Have students compare answers given by the newspaper to their own.

3. Have students choose an advertisement that intrigues them. Have them conduct conversations about what might have happened before the ad was placed, then have them discuss the uses of advertisements.

4. Have students read aloud particularly the "most interesting" or "most exciting" parts of a story. This helps them develop and comprehend the meaning of recreational text.

5. Have students sell some toys they no longer want. Have them examine some ads for toys and then write an ad that will help sell the toys. This will illustrate the functional use of newspapers.

6. Discuss a news article. Divide the class into groups of four or five and have each one recount the article. Have them rewrite the article as if they had been an eyewitness. Members of the group then share their stories with one another.

INTEGRATING READING AND WRITING

The language-experience approach provides endless opportunities for you to integrate reading, writing, and oral language. Such integrated activities help primary grade students develop positive attitudes about both reading and writing. During an integrated unit where students first read and then write their own books, an understanding of the reading and writing systems can be directly taught and used while they are involved in activities leading to content goals (such as finding out how the local government works). When integrated activities are used, time is not only used efficiently, but also is used effectively since integrated instruction more closely represents the writing and reading in everyday life. Following are examples of two integrated language units. The first one, found in Figure 17.1, is an illustration of a unit on bats. The second one, Figure 17.2, is a more detailed unit on saving the whales.

ADDITIONAL INTEGRATED READING AND WRITING ACTIVITIES

Here are some additional activities to supplement your integration of reading and writing in grades 1 and 2.

1. Provide pictures from magazines and other sources. Have students discuss what led up to the events in the pictures. Have students write a story about an event. Put their stories in books to be added to the classroom or school library.

2. Have students write riddles and place them in riddle books to be read during free time or nook-and-cranny time.

3. Have students share a story and retell it in a rebus. Example:

    Three little _____s build _____s.

4. Write comparison books with a variety of comparisons. Examples:

    As big as a _____, as little as a _____.
    As warm as _____; as cold as _____.
    As light as _____; as heavy as _____.

    Books for each set of comparisons can be added to the classroom or school library.

FIGURE 17.1 Initial mastery.

Theme: Understanding the community life of bats

Objectives:
1. Provide opportunities to explore the lives of bats
2. Develop understandings about the various types of bats and why they have special characteristics
3. Develop understandings about echo location
4. Increase conceptual understandings about the relationships of reading, writing, and conversations while authoring books
5. Introduce literature that develops factual knowledge about bats
6. Use literature and conversation as a stimulus for reading and writing
7. Develop expertise in reasoning through generating and answering questions
8. Provide opportunities for students to work through the literacy cycle from guided reading and writing to publishing
9. Develop positive attitudes about reading, writing, and conversations

Summary:

The instruction revolved around the literacy cycle where students progressed through the reading of books on bats interspersed with instructional conversations about the content triggered by student-generated and teacher-generated questions. Students talked aloud about their reasoning during conversations. This type of activity was followed by brainstorming, in which the students generated lists and cognitive maps about what they had learned. The lists and maps became the basis for stories and books. A class book about vampires was created, refined, published, and presented to the school librarian. The unit started with invitations and questions, followed by questions generated during reading and conversations. In order to activate background knowledge, students were asked to generate what they knew about bats and what they wanted to know. Early in the unit, the students were taught what questioning during reading is, when to use it, how to do it, and how this type of questioning fit into the unit on bats. Over 10 instructional lessons, the students and teacher shared knowledge about bats and had instructional conversations about that knowledge while generating questions and seeking answers to those questions. At the beginning of each lesson, the teacher reviewed questions that had not been yet answered, asked for any additional ones, presented a new book, read from it while talking out loud how the text made sense, and asked for comments and questions. The teacher always brought in a book to be shared during the lesson and additional books for independent reading. Gradually, the students also brought in books they had found, and all of them were used during the lessons and independent reading. Classroom books about vampires and other bats were created, revised, and published. The classroom book about vampires was presented to the school librarian as part of the permanent collection.

> The bat unit was developed and taught by Laura Roehler and Cheryl Latham at Spartan Village Elementary Professional Development School, East Lansing, MI.

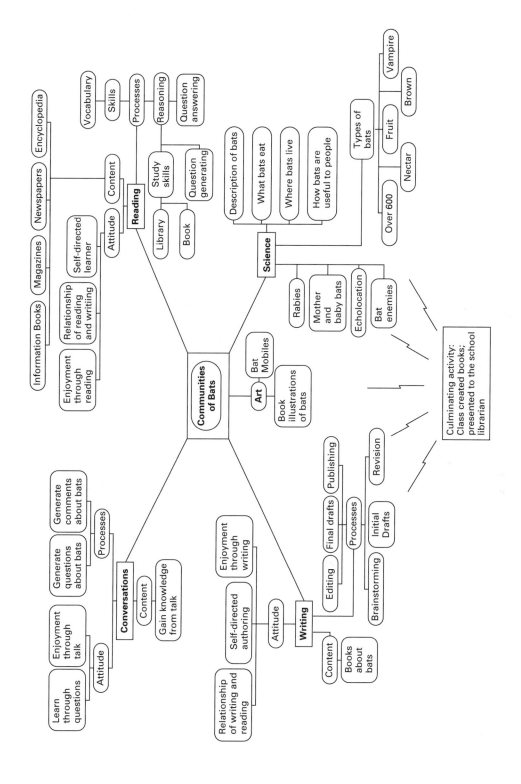

FIGURE 17.2   Sample Teaching Unit: Saving the Whales

LEVEL:
First and second grade, initial mastery stage

OBJECTIVES:
Content Objectives: Given multiple experiences in reading about, viewing, and discussing whales and the environmental issues involving whales, students will state the reasons why they feel they must save the whales, supporting their position by reference to scientific knowledge about whales.

Attitude Objectives: Given experiences with the environmental issues involving whales, students will state that reading and writing gives them a feeling of power because it allows them to take action on issues of importance to them.

Process Objectives: Given reading and writing to be completed as part of a "Save the Whales" project, students will instantly recognize in print and spell certain high-utility words and will use context to figure out the words they do not know. Given the need to write a letter to the President, students will use a business-letter format as the structure for communicating their message.

CULMINATING ACTIVITY
At the conclusion of the unit, students will compose and mail letters to the President of the United States, protesting current environmental policy and recommending specific changes.

DAY 1
Warm-up activity: Use prior student interest to introduce the issue of the whales and related environmental issues to the whole group. Lead students to consider what they might do about this issue. Surface a suggestion that letters could be written to the President.

Focusing activity: Get the students to list what we would have to learn if we were going to write letters to the President regarding the problem with whales.

Reading-writing activity: Have conversations about the kinds of reading that could be done in order to learn needed facts.

Assessment: While students are generating a list of what needs to be learned, assess what common words they know at sight and their ability to use context.

DAY 2
Warm-up activity: Bring in many books, magazines, and other texts regarding whales. Discuss these sources of information with students.

Focusing activity: Identify common words associated with reading about whales. Note the need to learn those as sight words and proceed to teach them.

Reading-writing activity: Have students work in collaborative groups to read selected whale material, using new sight words.

Assessment: Continue assessing students' sight-word vocabulary.

DAY 3

Reading-writing activity: Students continue reading various whale texts in collaborative groups. They begin listing content which will need to be included in the letter to the President.

Focusing activity: As new words are encountered during reading, note how context can be used to figure the words out.

Assessment: Note students who need particular help with using context clues.

DAY 4

Reading-writing activity: Students continue gathering information on whales. Teacher coordinates listing of important scientific content in discussion with students in their groups.

Focusing activity: As needed, individual and/or small groups of students are provided extra help learning needed sight words and/or learning to use context.

Assessment: During small-group instruction, assessment relative to sight-word acquisition and context clues continues.

DAY 5

Focusing activity: Teacher meets with whole group and collects from each group the content information they have gathered on whales.

Reading-writing activity: Teacher helps students organize this material, and discusses with them how the information should be used in the letter to the President.

Assessment: During the discussion, determine students' background relative to business letters and the structure used.

DAY 6

Focusing activity: Teacher develops students' understanding of the form and structure of business letters.

Reading-writing activity: Working in a whole group, students begin to frame out the content of the letter to the President.

Assessment: Teacher notes how many of the sight words learned in the unit are now accurately spelled.

DAY 7

Reading-writing activity: Students work in their collaborative groups, with each group composing a letter.

Assessment: The teacher works in small groups with students having trouble spelling the sight words learned in the unit.

DAY 8
Reading-writing activity: Students continue to work in small groups on their letters. The teacher helps each group revise and edit.

DAY 9
Culminating activity: Students share the letters written in each of the collaborative groups. Letters are addressed and mailed. Discussion focuses on what kinds of responses to expect.

5. Have students discuss a sport they are knowledgeable about, such as soccer, tennis, or swimming. As a group, have students write one line about how it feels to play, then one line about how it feels to watch.

6. Have students think like a vendor at a baseball or football game. Discuss how vendors might sell their products, then have students write a chant about selling them. During nook-and-cranny time, have students read their chants.

7. Have students select their favorite story and rewrite it in playscript. Ask other students to read the new stories, with each person taking a character role.

8. Have students select their favorite food and create the recipe for its preparation. Place all recipes in a book, duplicate it, and send each parent a copy to be read and enjoyed.

9. Have students create recipes for a "good kid" cookie. Discuss all the important ingredients by starting with the statement, "A good kid is _____." Have students write individually or in groups their recipes for a "good kid" cookie.

CHARACTERISTICS OF AN INSTRUCTIONAL DAY

First and second grade reading instruction has a number of unique characteristics. One of the most obvious is the heavy allocation of time. In most primary grades, there are two designated times for reading instruction, one in the morning and another in the afternoon. This allocation of extra instructional time for reading is another example of how crucial reading is at this level.

Another distinguishing characteristic is the way in which time is used. Time tends to be allocated in large blocks: It is more typical to find reading being conducted for $1\frac{1}{2}$ hours than for the 50 minutes we normally associate with instructional "periods." Moreover, most first and second grade teachers do integrate reading with the other language arts. Hence, reading periods normally include listening comprehension, writing, language experience activities, oral sharing of ideas and experiences, creative drama, and teacher reading, as well as the typical basal-text activities normally associated with reading instruction.

This difference in time usage reflects the curricular emphasis in the primary grades. Because attitude goals are so important at the primary grade level, you plan many diverse activities to develop language concepts and positive responses. This diversity is also a reflection of the shift from listening comprehension to reading comprehension, which accompanies the move from the readiness stage to the initial mastery stage.

Another distinctive characteristic is the self-contained instructional day in which one teacher is responsible for teaching virtually all subjects. Primary teachers usually place more emphasis on the classroom library than on the school library, do much more of their own art and music instruction, and integrate such activities into on-going reading instruction.

First and second grade often have a highly integrated curriculum that includes many diverse activities with little evidence of different subjects being taught. Within this framework, reading is heavily emphasized. However, the emphasis is not just on skills—it is also on developing conceptual understanding about language and positive responses. Consequently, instruction in first and second grade is dominated by language, in that all modes of communication (listening, speaking, and writing, as well as reading) are in evidence.

SUMMARY

While comprehension is always a priority in reading, teachers in grades 1 and 2 place a relatively heavy emphasis on attitude and decoding. A particularly difficult aspect of teaching in the primary grades is the need to develop well-rounded conceptions of reading while also emphasizing word-level skills and strategies. To achieve this balance, teachers place heavy emphasis on creating a literate environment and on using language experiences to develop attitude goals; they also use directed reading lessons and modified directed reading lessons with a basal textbook to develop content and process goals. Typically, primary grade reading instruction integrates reading instruction with general language activities and includes two allocated instructional times, one in the morning and one in the afternoon.

SUGGESTED ADDITIONAL READING

BRIDGE, C. (1979). Predictable materials for beginning readers. *Language Arts, 56*(5), 503–507.

BRIDGE, C. A., WINOGRAD, P. N., & HALEY, D. (1983). Using predictable materials vs. preprimers to teach beginning sight words. *Reading Teacher, 36*(9), 884–891.

CARR, K. S. (1983). The importance of inference skills in the primary grades. *Reading Teacher, 36*(6), 518–522.

CLARK, A. (1989). Helping primary children write about reality. *Reading Teacher, 42*(6), 414–416.

CUDD, E., & ROBERTS, L. (1987). Using story frames to develop reading comprehension in a 1st grade classroom. *Reading Teacher, 40,* 656–663.

CUDD, E., & ROBERTS, L. (1989). Using writing to enhance content area learning in the primary grades. *Reading Teacher, 42*(6), 392–404.

CUNNINGHAM, P., HALL, D. & DEFEE, M. (1991). Non-ability-grouped multi-level instruction: A year in a first-grade classroom. *Reading Teacher, 44*(8), 566–571.

DOWHOWER, S. (1989). Repeated reading: Research into practice. *Reading Teacher, 42*(7), 502–507.

DYSON, A. H. (1982). Reading, writing and language: Young children solving the written language puzzle. *Language Arts, 59*(8), 829–839.

EEDS, M. (1985). Bookwords: Using a beginning word list of high frequency words from children's literature K-3. *Reading Teacher, 36*(2), 176–184.

FOWLER, G. L. (1982). Developing comprehension skills in primary students through the use of story frames. *Reading Teacher, 36*(2), 176–184.

FRIEDMAN S. (1985). If you don't know how to write, you try: Techniques that work in first grade. *Reading Teacher, 38*(6), 516–521.

FRIEDMAN, S. (1986). How well can first graders write? *Reading Teacher, 40,* 162–167.

GIPE, J. P. (1980). Use of relevant context helps kids learn new word meanings. *Reading Teacher, 33*(4), 398–402.

HEALD-TAYLOR, B. G. (1984). Scribble in first grade writing. *Reading Teacher, 38*(1), 4–8.

HEALD-TAYLOR, B. G. (1987). How to use predictable books for K-12 language arts instruction. *Reading Teacher, 40,* 656–663.

HICKEY, M. G. (1989). Developing critical reading readiness in primary grades. *Reading Teacher, 43*(3), 192–193.

KLEIN, A. (1989). Meaningful reading and writing in a first grade classroom. *Elementary School Journal, 90*(2), 186–192.

MANNING, M., MANNING, G., & HUGHES, J. (1987). Journals in 1st grade: What children write. *Reading Teacher, 41,* 311–315.

MILLER, R. (1982). Reading instruction and primary school education. *Reading Teacher, 35*(8), 890–894.

PILS, L. (1991). Soon anote you tout me: Evaluation in a first-grade whole language classroom. *Reading Teacher, 45*(1), 46–50.

RASINSKI, T. (1988). The role of interest, purpose and choice in early literacy. *Reading Teacher, 41,* 396–401.

REUTZEL, D. R. & FAWSON, P. (1989). Using a literature webbing strategy lesson with predictable books. *Reading Teacher, 43*(3), 208–215.

SPACHE, E. B. (1982). *Reading activities for child involvement* (3rd ed.). Boston: Allyn & Bacon.

SPIEGEL, D. L. (1978). Meaning-seeking strategies for the beginning reader. *Reading Teacher, 31,* 772–776.

STAUFFER, R. G., & CRAMER, R. (1968). *Teaching critical reading at the primary level.* Newark, DE: International Reading Association.

THE RESEARCH BASE

BARR, R. (1984). Beginning reading instruction: From debate to reformation. In P. D. Pearson (Ed.), *Handbook of reading research* (pp. 545–608). New York: Longman.

CALFEE, R., & DRUM, P. (1986). Research on teaching reading. In M. Wittrock (Ed.), *Handbook of research on teaching* (pp. 804–849). New York: MacMillan.

CLAY, M. (1972). *Reading: The patterning of complex behavior.* Auckland, New Zealand: Heinemann.

HIEBERT, E. (1988). The role of literacy experiences in early childhood programs. *Elementary School Journals, 89*(2), 163–171.

JUEL, C. (1991). Beginning reading. In R. Barr, M. Kamil, P. Mosenthal, & P. D. Pearson, (Eds.), *Handbook of reading research, volume II* (pp.759–788). New York: Longman.

WORDEN, P., & BOETTCHER, W. (1990). Young children's acquisition of alphabet knowledge. *Journal of Reading Behavior, 22*(3), 277–292.

ACTIVITIES FOR REFLECTING, OBSERVING, AND TEACHING

Reflecting on Teaching First and Second Grade

PURPOSE: As has been noted in previous chapters, it is important to situate students' instruction in genuinely literate activity. The "Save the Whales" unit provided as a sample in this chapter is one example. You will be a good teacher to the extent that you, too, can create such units. This activity is designed to help you do so.

DIRECTIONS: Using both the sample unit provided in this chapter and the suggestions provided in Chapter 14, create a unit which will involve first and second graders in authentic literate activity in the pursuit of a genuine goal. Include specific content, attitude, and process objectives, and a day-to-day schedule of activity.

Watching Others Teach First and Second Grade

PURPOSE: The more you watch others teach first and second grade, the more experienced you will become and the better you will get at teaching yourself. Consequently, this activity helps you structure an observation experience for yourself.

DIRECTIONS: Arrange to observe a first or second grade for a period of several consecutive days. During these observations, specifically note the following:

- the instructional emphasis (relative to Table 17.1)
- the literate environment
- the use of language experience, literature-based instruction, and other approaches to develop attitude goals
- what routine skills are taught and how they are taught (look particularly for vocabulary, sight words, and easily confused sight words)
- what strategies are taught and how they are taught (look particularly for using text structures to predict meaning, context clues, structural analysis, phonics, organization of content, and evaluation of content)
- what content is taught and how it is taught
- whether activity is organized into units and, if so, the nature and characteristics of the unit.

Trying It Yourself

PURPOSE: The more you teach first and second graders yourself, the better you will get.

DIRECTIONS: When you are observing in a first or second grade classroom, look for opportunities to do some teaching yourself. When you have such opportunities, use the suggestions in this chapter to guide you.

Teaching Middle Grade Reading: Expanded Fundamentals Stage

18

GETTING READY

If things go well in grades 1 and 2, young readers come to grades 3 and 4 with accurate conceptions and positive feelings about reading, an understanding of how to handle words, and an understanding of how to use topic, purpose, and type of text to predict an author's message. Grades 3 and 4 expand these fundamentals. This chapter describes how third and fourth grade teachers teach reading. It describes the characteristics, curricular emphases, and instructional techniques needed to teach reading in the middle grades.

FOCUS QUESTIONS

- What particular characteristics are associated with teaching middle grade reading?

- How are attitude goals developed in the middle grades?

- How are process goals taught in the middle grades?

- How are content goals developed in the middle grades?

- How are reading and writing integrated in the middle grades?

- What does a typical middle grade instructional day look like?

OVERVIEW OF MIDDLE GRADE READING

The middle grades represent the bridging years between learning the fundamentals of reading (the initial mastery stage) and applying these fundamentals in a variety of specialized content areas (the application stage). Hence, third and fourth grade reading instruction expands on fundamentals taught in grades 1 and 2 in preparation for the greater reading demands in the upper grades.

Because of the middle grades' bridging function, the reading curriculum is unique. Emphasis on attitude goals shifts from helping students build accurate concepts and positive feelings about reading to helping them build accurate concepts and positive feelings about themselves as readers; emphasis on process goals shifts from print to comprehension; and emphasis on content goals shifts from simple narrative stories and simple expository text to a variety of literature and expository texts.

As the curriculum shifts, instructional emphasis also shifts. For instance, group language-experience activities, which are relied on heavily in the primary grades, give way to individual language-experience activities and more collaborative grouping; direct instruction shifts to metacognitive comprehension strategies and fluency; and teachers guide reading using techniques that are more complex than the standard directed reading lesson. The relative emphasis in curriculum and in instructional activities in the middle grades is shown in Table 18.1.

The bridging function of grades 3 and 4 provides a special challenge for teachers. Because different students progress at different rates, virtually every child in grades 3 and 4 is at a different point in crossing the bridge from beginning reading to upper grade reading. Some are still trying to make sense out of the print, while others are eagerly demanding more challenging texts. This diversity is a major instructional challenge in teaching third and fourth grade.

DEVELOPING ATTITUDE GOALS

Developing positive attitudes is always a major outcome of reading instruction because, without good attitudes, students are unlikely to become literate people. The heavy attitude emphasis in the primary grades continues at the middle grade level. There is continued development of concepts about the communicative nature of reading and its recreational and functional purposes. There is also continued emphasis on making reading exciting and satisfying. But the greatest emphasis at the middle grade level is on helping students perceive themselves as readers with a lifelong habit of reading.

Creating a Literate Environment

The literate environment in grades 3 and 4 must encourage students to become involved in real reading. You can do this by designing the physical environment of your middle grade classrooms so that it looks like a place where literate people live and work. Make sure you have a room library consisting of a large selection of children's books (about three or four books per student, representing a variety of genres and topics). Be sure the library is prominently located, attractively decorated, and comfortable looking (some teachers use throw pillows and beanbag chairs to entice students to settle down with a book) to create the image

TABLE 18.1   Instructional Emphasis at the Expanded Fundamentals Stage

OUTCOME	INSTRUCTIONAL EMPHASIS	MAJOR INSTRUCTIONAL ACTIVITY
Attitude goals		
Concepts about reading	Reading is communication between writer and reader Reading is predicting meaning Reading is sense making Reading is a tool	Indirect instruction using projects, language experience, USSR activities, and writing
Positive responses to reading	Reading is exciting Reading is satisfying Reading results in knowledge Reading satisfies curiosity Reading is a source of power	Indirect instruction involving projects, language experience, USSR activities, and writing
Process goals		
Routing skills Vocabulary	Building vocabulary through direct study of words associated with content being studied Emphasis shifts from concrete words to multiple meaning words, homonyms, synonyms, antonyms, and other special categories of words	Direct instruction of words
Word recognition	Recognize a wide variety of words instantly and fluently	Direct instruction of words using basal text recommendations
Metacognitive strategies		
Initiating strategies	Active prior knowledge of content using predicting Activate prior knowledge about how different types of text and author's purpose help make initial predictions about meaning	Direct instruction of initiating strategies

that reading is a natural part of life in your classroom. You can reinforce this by arranging other aspects of your physical environment, for instance, by including a variety of projects that require written directions and student writing. Your physical environment will thus communicate that your classroom is an exciting place where literate people read books of their choice.

Also create an intellectual environment to stimulate many reading and writing activities. Set up the room library, encourage various projects and written communications, establish collaborative groups to exchange ideas, and gener-

TABLE 18.1 (continued)

OUTCOME	INSTRUCTIONAL EMPHASIS	MAJOR INSTRUCTIONAL ACTIVITY
During-reading strategies		
Monitoring strategies	Monitor for unknown words, for unrecognized words, for fluent sense making, and for accuracy of predictions	Direct instruction of monitoring strategies
Fix-it strategies	Recognize disruption in sense making Access strategies to solve the problem Word recognition Vocabulary Author's meaning Beyond the author's meaning Determine which strategy is needed Implement the strategy Verify repair of sense making	Direct instruction of fix-it strategies for comprehension
Post-reading strategies		
Organizing strategies	Recall what is important by recognizing different types of text structure (stories, articles, poems, letters), classifying sentences, and determining main idea	Direct instruction of organizing strategies
Evaluating strategies	Judge content of message by author's word usage • denotative and connotative words Judge content of message by completeness of content development	Direct instruction of evaluating strategies

ally establish the expectation that your students will participate in language in real ways. These expectations are an intellectual stimulation that promotes development of goals. Similarly, arrange the social-emotional environment to help students perceive themselves as readers and develop the habit of reading. Create an environment where students work together, usually in collaborative groups. Because reading and writing are a natural part of such cooperative learning situations, it is easier for your students to develop the desired concepts and responses.

Instructional Approaches

Basal textbooks play a relatively minor role in developing attitude goals in the middle grades. Rather, you should use language experience and personalized reading activities to promote attitude goals.

TABLE 18.1   (continued)

OUTCOME	INSTRUCTIONAL EMPHASIS	MAJOR INSTRUCTIONAL ACTIVITY
Study strategies		
Locational strategies	Use book strategy of table of contents and glossary to locate information Use library strategy of card catalog to locate books by title or author Use reference source strategy of dictionary to find word meanings Use graphics strategy of simple bar and line graphs to gain meaning	Direct instruction of study strategies
Study habits	Follow written directives involving three or more parts	Direct instruction of study habit strategies
Rate strategies	Develop a slow pace for careful reading and a fast pace for skimming	Direct instruction of rate strategies
Organizing strategies	Use semantic maps to organize content	
Remembering strategies	Use summarizing to remember content	
Content goals		
Recreational	Getting meaning from various types of narrative text Understanding various literary devices used by authors	Directed reading lessons
Functional	Getting meaning from expository texts found in content area textbooks	Guided reading of context area texts

Literature-based reading plays a particularly heavy role in the middle grades. Uninterrupted sustained silent reading (USSR) is an integral part of every instructional day. In addition, look for other ways to involve students in free reading. You can place a heavy emphasis on sharing books, and use collaborative groups to plan and organize puppet shows, skits, creative drama, simulated newscasts, and other non-book reporting activities. These kinds of activities help your students see themselves as readers and promote the reading habit.

Language experience also plays a role in the middle grades. In contrast to the primary level, however, much of the language experience at this level is individual rather than group work. Have your students use their reading experiences as the basis for writing an imaginary story or use a field trip as the basis for writing a poem, for instance. You, of course, create the opportunities for such writing and encourage your students to make use of the experiences that are present. However, instead of a jointly produced language experience story, such as those typically found in the primary grades, have individuals do the writing.

EXAMPLE 18.1   How to Develop Positive Attitudes

Background   You want to develop the feeling that reading makes one feel empowered. You establish a situation in which students are unable to do what they want to do because they lack information.

Activity 1   As part of the literate environment, establish an activity that the students very much want to pursue, such as setting up an aquarium. Although you know they do not have enough information to complete the task, allow them to work on it. When frustration occurs because they lack the necessary information, initiate a discussion.

Discussion   Discussion the problem with the students and identify the lack of information as the source of the frustration. Help them locate the needed information in reference books. Point out that reading provided them with the power to complete a task that had previously frustrated them.

Activity 2   Have students return to the original activity and complete it.

These efforts are not necessarily unstructured. Indeed, you can use the three-step format for indirect instruction (see Chapter 13) to give these activities some structure. For instance, this format might be used to plan and conduct a lesson like the one shown in Example 18.1. Such instruction is designed to help students derive a sense of empowerment from reading while also building the concept that reading is a useful tool.

ACTIVITIES TO DEVELOP ATTITUDE GOALS

Here are some activities you can use to supplement development of positive attitudes in the third and fourth grade.

1. Have students act as evaluators for first and second grade books to help middle graders develop a positive attitude toward reading. Ask students to present their evaluations to first and second graders.

2. Present radio shows using a tape recorder. By writing, reading, and speaking favorite stories, students develop the concept of the integrative nature of language.

3. Use quiz shows, patterned after "What's My Line?" or "Jeopardy" or "Wheel of Fortune" or "I've Got a Secret," to help middle grade students become acquainted with book characters. This type of activity helps develop the concept that reading is life captured in print.

4. Use newspaper and magazines articles about children's books, authors, or illustrators to stimulate development of a positive attitude toward reading. Have students bring these articles to class for discussion.

5. Use collaborative group reporting of children's literature to provide an opportunity for comparisons and contrasts of similar books. Use books about animals, family life, periods of history, etc., as the basis for these discussions. Such discussions stimulate student interest in books.

6. Use feltboard characters to provide an opportunity for storytelling and development of positive attitudes. Ask students to develop and present their favorite stories to younger children.

7. Put questions in envelope pockets on the bulletin board to help students develop a positive attitude toward reading. Label an envelope "Who Am I?" and put in clues about popular characters. Label another "Where did it happen?" and include clues about events in various books. Tell students to add their own questions about books they have read.

8. Have students make bookmarks illustrated with "the part I liked best" or "my favorite character." They make lasting momentoes of enjoyable reading experiences and help to develop positive attitudes toward reading.

9. Have students make a video of a book by illustrating and connecting scenes from the book. The series of scenes, rolled on a wooden rod, may be passed through a frame cut from a box. You can also use an opaque projector. Such activities help students develop positive feelings about reading.

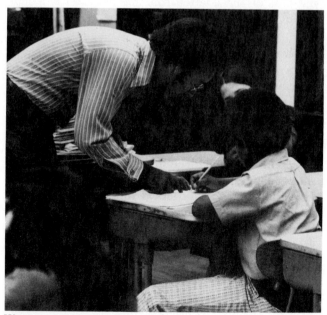

Written communication is emphasized at the expanded fundamentals stage.

10. Use student-developed book jackets, illustrations, or advertising posters to illustrate a book that has been read. These make excellent bulletin board displays and develop positive attitudes toward reading.

11. Have students illustrate maps to show a character's travels or the area encompassed by a story. These offer a good way of sharing a book. Historical fiction books are especially effective.

12. Have students conduct interviews on selected topics with an adult or students from upper classes. Use them in activities where positive attitudes toward reading are being developed.

13. Have students prepare and make appeals before another class on behalf of school or community drives that can be related to selected reading topics.

14. Have students correspond with hospitalized children and adults. Have them share interesting information about reading topics and favorite books. This helps develop the concept of the interrelatedness of language as well as positive feelings about reading.

15. Have students take characters from books such as *Charlotte's Web* or *Pippi Longstocking* and rewrite the story in a setting suitable to the present. This activity promotes the concept of integrated language usage.

16. Have students write and then display a letter from one character in a book to another. Suggest they tell about something that might have happened had they both lived at the same time and place. Such activities help students learn to appreciate reading.

17. Have students create a magazine for the classroom by compiling voluntary artwork and writing projects completed during reading. Publish the magazine for classroom distribution to help students learn to value reading and its communicative function.

18. Hold a book fair. This opportunity to share a wide variety of books is an ideal device for getting middle grade children involved in book reviewing. Have students assume responsibility for reviewing important books before the fair, and ask representatives to travel to other classes to review the books before the exhibit. Students then use the reviews as guides for locating at the fair books that may be of particular interest to them.

19. Have students take responsibility for reviewing Caldecott Award winners for the primary grades. Have them present these reviews orally.

20. Keep a library corner, complete with bulletin board display. Such access to books helps develop positive attitudes toward reading. Relate themes for the displays to popular authors (Cleary, Wilder), genres of books (realistic fiction, mysteries, informational), or topics (animal, sports).

21. New books in the classroom library deserve recognition. A few well-chosen words about selected books will help build student interest and will keep the books circulating.

TEACHING PROCESS GOALS

Because the middle grades are bridging years, process goals are emphasized. There is a continued emphasis on the routine skills of knowing word meanings and sight words, and on the metacognitive strategies of knowing how to use prior knowledge and strategies to remove word-level blockages when getting meaning from text. In addition, however, middle grade reading emphasizes fluency and fix-it strategies to repair breaks in comprehension. Also, study skills are introduced in the middle grades. In short, middle grade teachers must continue the development of primary grade goals, begin placing special emphasis on metacognitive comprehension strategies, and introduce new strategies for study that will be emphasized in the upper grades.

Routine Skills

In the middle grades, there is less emphasis on the routine skill of sight words. Students progressing at a normal rate should have a large store of sight words, which should increase as they practice and use words that appear frequently in their texts. You do not need to focus on the learning of sight words, but sight word development does continue.

Do continue to emphasize vocabulary development, however. Within vocabulary instruction you continue to build meaning for many words, helping students understand the characteristics, properties, and examples for these words and how various words fit together into categories. You should continue to emphasize words that are useable: Ask yourself whether your students will need the words five years from now. If the answer is yes, teach the meanings of those words in instructional situations that actively involve students. Also continue vocabulary development through use of context clues for multiple-meaning words, structural analysis, and understanding and using synonyms, antonyms, and homonyms, so that students become independent in figuring out word meaning.

In addition, emphasize fluency in the middle grades; that is, how smoothly and accurately students interpret meaning of text. If your students read a text with no hesitations or miscues and use intonation patterns consistent with the text's meaning, they are reading fluently. If, on the other hand, they read in a slow, choppy manner with many errors and poor intonation patterns, they are not fluent.

Fluency is a concern in both oral and silent reading. However, it is emphasized instructionally in oral reading situations because the easiest way to observe fluency is to listen to your students read out loud. You can then observe exactly where in the text the fluency began to break down and you can generate hypotheses regarding both causes and appropriate corrective instruction. However, you can also assess fluency during silent reading by timing students. If, for instance, your third and fourth grade students take much longer to silently read a particular text than you do, you can assume that their fluency is not good.

Poor fluency is often associated with poor sight-word recognition because, when students instantly recognize all the words in a selection, they tend to read it fluently. Similarly, fluency is associated with general language competence because it is reasonable to assume that students who have limited oral-language backgrounds, who have limited exposure to oral reading, or who have recently learned English as a second language would find it difficult to be fluent.

When such problems are the cause of fluency difficulties, the remedy is straightforward. If unfamiliar words cause readers to hesitate, teach the needed words as sight words before assigning text reading. If inadequate general language competence is the problem, establish a strong oral language program that includes frequent listening to oral reading and frequent participation in other forms of oral language.

Many times, however, students are not fluent, even though there is no difficulty with sight words or with general language ability. Such students need direct instruction on how to be fluent. Begin such fluency instruction with the concept that authors expect their text to have a certain sound when read—that it should sound the way it would be said. In order to "say" the text properly, one must know what it means. Therefore, to be fluent a reader must understand the author's message; if it does not sound right, it probably is not the message intended by the author. Monitoring of the meaning, then, is the first instructional emphasis in helping nonfluent readers become fluent.

You can aid monitoring for fluency by encouraging students to think about intonation patterns when reading. For instance, encourage them to read as the author would say it. Then show them how to draw lines under clusters of words that could be "said together," and how to change boundaries of such word clusters until the text sounds right. Similarly, help students improve their fluency by teaching them to attend to the typographic cues embedded in the text, particularly the punctuation cues. These cues are direct aids to intonation and, hence, to fluency.

Another frequently used technique is **repeated readings.** To use this technique, have students first read a text for understanding. Then direct them to read it aloud again and again until it sounds the way they would say it. This technique works because it sets the expectation that reading should sound like real language and because it challenges students to strive for natural sounding reading until it becomes almost second nature to them.

Fluency is a major process goal at the middle grades. It is closely tied to comprehension since appropriate voice intonation depends on understanding the meaning of the text. An example of how to teach fluency is illustrated in Example 18.2.

EXAMPLE 18.2   How to Develop Fluency

Background	Some of your students read in a choppy, hesitant manner despite knowning the words at sight and having strong language backgrounds. You want to help them develop fluency.
Lesson Sequence	
Introduction	Set a purpose for orally reading a particular text; for instance, plan to have students read a book to a group of first graders. Explain that they must read fluently so the first graders will enjoy their reading. Give examples of fluent reading and nonfluent reading.
Modeling	Explain how the meaning of a passage signals what the intonation should be. For instance say, "This is a dangerous situation. The story character must be scared. I need to read it like I'm scared." Then read it that way.
Interaction with students	Give students sample pieces of text and ask them to do the same kind of thinking that you did. At first, help them by pointing out what is happening and how that helps us say it. Gradually diminish the amount of help until students are independently making decisions about how to say the text passage.
Closure	Have students apply what they have learned about fluency to the text they are to read to the first graders. Guide their practice of the oral reading, and then have them read to the first grade.
Desired Outcome	When reading a text, students will monitor the meaning of the text and use this meaning to decide how to say the words in the text.

Metacognitive Strategies

At the expanded fundamentals stage, metacognitive strategies expand into four categories. In the initiating reading category are strategies for activating prior knowledge for topic, text, and purpose. During-reading strategies emphasize monitoring and fix-it strategies for getting the author's meaning. Post-reading strategies emphasize organizing and evaluating knowledge. The fourth category—study strategies—includes locational strategies, rate strategies, organizing strategies, remembering strategies, and study habits.

Initiating Strategies   In the middle grades, initiating strategies include activating knowledge of topic, text structures, and purposes of both the author and the reader.

Activating background knowledge for topic involves helping your students bring to a conscious level what they know about a topic. The best way to accomplish this continues to be using concrete objects such as animals or people, or representations of objects such as films, pictures, and drawings, as described in Chapter 17. Whether concrete objects or representations are used, it is important also to use teacher statements to activate student prior knowledge and to ask questions as the way to initiate talk. For instance, in a lesson on developing friendship, you might activate your students' prior knowledge as follows: "Having friends is an important part of third graders' lives. We need to know how to make friends. Think about the times you have made friends. Remember what you did that seemed to help. Let's see what we can remember. Who wants to be first?"

It is also important to continue developing strategies about using prior knowledge to make predictions. During the expanded fundamentals stage, continue to give students real text to read and show them how knowledge about topic, purpose, and type of text all combine to help readers predict the meaning being conveyed. Since this is introduced in the primary grades, in the middle grades it often takes the form of a reminder. Nevertheless, you must be conscious of the need to keep meaning getting in the forefront and to continuously illustrate for your students how various knowledge sources can be used to predict what an author is conveying.

During-Reading Strategies This category contains strategies to monitor reading and to fix meaning blockages. Although students were introduced to monitoring their reading in primary grades and have probably developed a beginning understanding of it, the middle grades especially emphasize monitoring. Students learn to monitor for words unrecognized in print, for words unknown in meaning, for what the author means, and for meaning beyond the author's intention. That is, readers check themselves to make sure they know what each word says, they know what each word means, they know what the author means, and they can make critical judgments and conclusions that go beyond the author's meaning.

To enhance monitoring, teach students to see if the text is making sense—to determine whether the anticipated meaning is what actually emerges while reading. In the course of such monitoring, readers occasionally become aware of something that does not make sense or that is unanticipated. At these times, most readers first look to see if there are words they did not say correctly; then they look to see if they have the appropriate meaning for each word; then they look to see if they understand the author's meaning; and finally they check to see if the judgments they are making about the author's meaning are appropriate in light of what the author is saying.

If the problem is a word they did not say correctly or an incorrect word meaning, then the word recognition and vocabulary strategies developed in Chapter 7 and emphasized in the primary grades (see Chapter 17) are accessed and applied. However, if the problem is the author's meaning or judgments that go beyond the author's meaning, comprehension strategies are accessed and applied. Example 18.3 illustrates one way to teach monitoring for the author's meaning.

EXAMPLE 18.3   How to Teach Students to Monitor Predictions

Background	You want your students to monitor their sense making when reading and to look back to generate new predictions when meaning getting breaks down.
Lesson Sequence	
Introduction	Using a basal text selection the students are to read, locate an ambiguous passage that might generate an erroneous prediction. State that you are going to show them how to check meaning and to generate new predictions until a sensible one is found.
Modeling	As you read, explain your thinking to students. Model your continuous monitoring of the meaning in light of your initial prediction, you puzzlement when the prediction no longer fits the subsequent text, your looking back for clues, your examination of these clues to produce new predictions (such as words have multiple meanings or reversals in the usual word order), your generation of a new prediction, and your testing of this prediction in the text.
Interaction with students	Give students examples of ambiguous text so they can do as you did. Have them explain their thinking so you can evaluate it. Gradually reduce the help you provide until students are generating new predictions without assistance.
Closure	Return to the basal text selection. Set the purpose for reading the selection, including the reminder to use the strategy for generating new predictions if they encounter situations where their initial prediction is not confirmed.
Desired Outcome	When reading text, students will monitor their meaning getting, will look back when sense making breaks down, and will use clues to generate new predictions.

When the problem is the author's meaning, it is helpful to look back at the typographic cues (punctuation, italics, bold print, etc.), or for key words or word elements (prefixes, suffices, etc.), or for certain context clues. These cues are all visible in the sense that they are right there on the page. By looking for visible cues, a reader may note that the author's meaning can be determined by attending to a previously ignored comma, a misread prefix or suffix, the sequence of key words, or a missed relational word such as *finally, since,* or *but.* Example 18.4 illustrates one way to teach students to use such visible cues to determine an author's meaning.

Similarly, you can help your students understand an author's meaning that is not explicitly stated. Readers search for clues and infer what has been implied but not stated. They look inside themselves for knowledge they already have that can be combined with clues to make inferences. For instance, readers can often determine the gist of a written message by classifying, that is, by grouping together similar words or ideas and using them to infer the meaning. Readers use

EXAMPLE   18.4   How to Teach Students to Use Visible Cues for Comprehension

Background	You want your students to know how to look for meaning through visible cues embedded in the text. For instance, when they lose track of the story sequence, they do not know that you can look for key words used by the author.
Lesson Sequence	
Introduction	Find a basal text selection in which the author uses visible cues to sequence, such as *first, next, then,* and *finally.* Tell students you will teach them a look-back strategy to use if they lose track of the story sequence.
Modeling	Show students how, after losing track of story sequence, you look back for key words. Explain what you think about as you encounter the problem, as you search for cues, and as you find the cues.
Interaction with students	Provide a series of similar textual examples for students and have them do as you did (determine story sequence by using key words). Provide help at first, but gradually phase out assistance as students' explanations provide evidence they understand how to use the strategy.
Closure	Have students read the basal text selection. Have them use the key word strategy if they lose track of the sequence.
Desired Outcome	Given a real text containing sequential events signaled by key words, students will be able to use key words as a strategy for determining story sequence.

their own prior experience with similar situations to predict an author's implied meaning. And readers make inferences about relationships in text (chronological, causal, compare-contrast, etc.). By thinking of a similar situation from their own experience and determining the similarities between it and the text situation, they combine the text clues with their related prior knowledge and infer the author's meaning. Example 18.5 illustrates one way to teach students to use prior knowledge to determine meaning implied by the author.

Strategies for making judgments that go beyond the author's meaning require critical thinking. These strategies are described in Chapter 19.

Post-Reading Strategies   Organizing and evaluating content are both post-reading strategies taught in the middle grades. Organizing content is important because this is where students restructure text information and store it in long-term memory for future use. This helps counter rote memory and simplifies the process of understanding and remembering through conscious grouping and storing. The major strategy to teach your students is based on purposes for reading. If the purpose is to find answers to predictions, then the information to remember is organized by the predictions; if the purpose is to remember sensory details,

EXAMPLE 18.5   How to Teach Inferencing

Background	You want your students to use invisible knowledge from their prior knowledge of the topic to make inferences.
Lesson Sequence	
Introduction	Use a basal text selection that poses questions requiring students to draw inferences. Note the need to answer such questions at the outset, and state that you are going to show them how to answer these kinds of questions.
Modeling	Use a basal selection, explain the thinking in making inferences. Show how you attend to the clues in the text while also thinking of similar situations for your prior knowledge. Talk about how you relate the text clues to your own prior experience and uses it as a basis for drawing inferences about what the author is implying.
Interaction with students	Using similar text passages, have students follow your model in drawing inferences. Provide much help initially, but gradually reduce this assistance. Be sure you have students talk out loud to determine whether they are using a viable strategy.
Closure	Have students read the basal text selection, using their strategy to answer questions, using their strategy to answer questions that require drawing inferences.
Desired Outcome	Given a real text to read, students will use their prior knowledge and text cues to answer questions that require drawing inferences about meaning authors imply but do not explicitly state.

then the information could be remembered by organizing information by senses. Teach your students to organize around whatever the purpose is. Example 18.6 illustrates how to structure a lesson on organizing content according to purpose.

The second post-reading strategy is evaluating content. A specific strategy taught in the middle grades is judging content by author's word choice. Teach your students to consider the purpose of written materials and the text structure used, and then to judge if the words used are appropriate. Your students should not consider all words that carry meaning, but select words that seem to be important. Such words might be repeated often or might have extensive definitions, descriptions, or explanations within the text. Example 18.7 illustrates how to structure a lesson on evaluating content by author's word choice.

Study strategies is a new set of metacognitive strategies emphasized for the first time in grades 3 and 4. Up to now, students have focused on learning how to read. During the middle grades, the emphasis moves gradually to reading to learn. Accordingly, middle grade students are introduced to study strategies. However, the greatest instructional emphasis on study strategies occurs in the upper grades. Consequently, they are discussed in detail in Chapter 19.

EXAMPLE 18.6 How to Teach Organizing Content

Background	Your students have been orgainizing content of narrative and expository texts by the beginning, middle, and end sections. You decide to teach them how to organize information from books by focusing on purpose.
Lesson Sequence	
Introduction	Have students read a book selection after the purpose is set. The purposes is to compare and contrast two positions. Proceed with the lesson using small segments of text.
Modeling	Explain that when organizing text information it is helpful to remember it in terms of purpose. Explain how this strategy is useful when we need to remember information that is read. Describe generally how students will use the strategy in the future. Demonstrate specifically how you remember text information about the two positions discussed in the particular text being modeled.
Interaction with students	Give students opportunities to organize text information according to different purposes. Start with simple purposes and gradually move to more complex ones. As students demonstrate their understanding and use of the strategy, gradually reduce your assistance.
Closure	End the series of lessons with another text. Have students read the selection and use their strategy of organizing text information by purpose as a way to remember.
Desired Outcome	Given selections that are read, students will remember text information by organizing it according to purposes set.

Role of the Basal

Most process strategies are taught in conjunction with basal textbooks. However, teachers must use considerable caution in following basal prescriptions for two reasons. First, most basal texts do not present comprehension strategies as they are presented in this book. The reason is that most basals reflect only research that has long been accepted by the public to whom publishers must sell the books. Since the strategies presented here reflect current research findings, they are not always found in basal texts. What is often found instead is reference to the more traditional "skills" of comprehension, such as main idea, cause-effect relationships, looking for details, and so on. Consequently, you must modify the prescriptions of the basal text and recast them as strategies (see Chapter 13).

Second, as has been previously mentioned, most basal textbooks tend to isolate process goals, teaching them in association with workbook and ditto sheets. Seldom are the "skills" of comprehension applied to real text. Consequently, you must make the necessary modifications so that strategies are taught in real contexts.

EXAMPLE 18.7 How to Teach Evaluating Content through Word Choice

Background	Your students already know how to judge the selections they read as real or make-believe. You decide to teach them how to evaluate content by analyzing word choice.
Lesson Sequence	
Introduction	Establish what the author's purpose was for writing the selection (to inform, to entertain, to persuade, etc.). Have students note words that seem important.
Modeling	During discussion of the selection, explain and demonstrate word choice using words you think are important. Demonstrate whether you think the author used an appropriate word and explain why. Explain that this strategy is particularly useful when reading persuasive writings, such as advertisements or editorials. Be specific about when students will use the strategy.
Interaction with students	Give students many opportunities to judge whether author's word choice is appropriate according to the purpose gradually diminish your assistance as the students demonstrate they can judge author's word choice.
Closure	End the lesson series with another selection. Have students judge the author's word choice and then have them support their decisions.
Desired Outcome	Given selections that have been read students will state how the author's word choice was designed to influence the meaning obtained from the text.

In sum, while you will teach most comprehension strategies in direct instruction situations employing basal textbooks, you must be prepared to modify basal text prescriptions regarding comprehension, both in terms of *what* strategies to teach and in terms of *how* to teach them.

ACTIVITIES TO DEVELOP PROCESS GOALS

Here are some instructional activities you can use to supplement your teaching of process goals in third and fourth grade. Be cautioned that these activities are best used within a literate environment and that they should not be used in isolation from real reading situations.

1. Draw a runway with a hangar at the end of it. Divide the runway into sections on which are printed new words. Pair students and give each an object representing an airplane. Have the game begin with both planes in the hangar. Tell the first player to spin and move the number of spaces that the spinner signals if he or she can use each word correctly in a sentence. Have the players take turns until one plane reaches the end of the runway. Such activities help students build vocabulary.

2. Have students select an article from a newspaper and list all the pronouns in it. Then have them write the nouns the pronouns refer to beside each pronoun. This helps students use pronouns to determine an author's meaning.

3. Use exercises in which students replace words with synonyms. Encourage students to supply another word that means about the same thing. Group discussion can judge the appropriateness of the synonyms. This helps students use different words in determining author meaning.

4. Teach word opposites. One way to discriminate a concept is by knowing not only what it is but what it is not. Activities with word opposites help students develop vocabulary.

5. Encourage students to associate words with mental pictures of that concept. Let them draw or describe their mental pictures to help create meaning for words.

6. Have students note on 3″ by 5″ cards the word meanings they have learned and the key characteristics and/or synonyms they have created. In this way you not only build meaning vocabulary, but also a synonym source for use in writing assignments.

7. Have students work in pairs with concrete objects. Tell one student to manipulate the objects and make a sentence. Tell the other student to change the word order in the sentence. Then have the first student put the sentence back in correct order. This helps students become sensitive to how syntactic order influences meaning.

8. Use exercises in which you present a string of words orally. Tell students to create sentences using those words. Determine appropriateness by correct positioning of the words to communicate a meaning.

9. Use the "telegram" technique. Direct students to read a paragraph and decide what words could be omitted without losing the meaning. Explain that they are going to send the paragraph as a telegram and will have to pay for each word. What is left will be the main idea and essential supporting details. This helps students learn to summarize.

10. Make "stand-up" paragraphs. They can be fun, and they can teach skills for comprehending both the main idea and details. Select a student to stand in front of the class and think up a key topic sentence. (This might have to be supplied at first). Tell other members of the class to think up details that elaborate on the topic sentence. As each adds an important detail, have the child stand behind the student who made the topic sentence. The paragraph becomes a row of students starting at the front of the room. When all the "sentences" have taken their places, have them repeat their sentences one after the other and then construct the paragraph. Don't be afraid to have sentences rearranged or even omitted if they do not belong.

11. Have students find five words with prefixes or suffixes in a newspaper or magazine, and then have them write new sentences using each one of them. This helps students focus on how meaning can be changed through structural analysis.

12. Have students combine simple, known words to create either real compound words or invented compounds, then discuss the new concept created when two simple words are made into one compound word. This helps students focus on meaning.

13. Put words on the chalkboard that signal certain meaning relationships (such as cause-effect) and have students think up sentences using these words. This helps students understand the role certain words play in signaling meaning.

14. Say words or show objects to students and ask them to tell how they are alike in meaning or which one does not belong. This helps students learn to look for common meaning and to classify.

15. Have one student call out a category (such as *groceries*) and another student supply as many things that would go in that category as possible. This helps build classification skills.

16. Select a well-written informational paragraph. Put the paragraph's individual phrases on the chalkboard, and direct students to examine each phrase and use their classifying skills to write the overall theme.
Example:

> Brush teeth regularly
> Bath frequently
> Eat well-balanced meals
> Get enough rest
> Get regular exercise

> Main idea: good health habits.

17. Have one student create a sentence and another change one word or phrase to indicate a change in meaning.

18. Provide unpunctuated sentences for students. Have them punctuate each sentence several times, each time communicating a different meaning by using different punctuation. Then have students read each sentence, using the correct intonation according to the punctuation supplied and describing how the meaning changed.

19. Before directing students to read a selection, set a purpose by asking them how many things they can learn while reading. Direct students to keep a tally while reading, with each mark standing for something learned. This helps focus students on meaning getting.

20. Before reading a selection from a textbook or reader, put the following purpose-setting formula on the board: Who? Where? When? How many? What happens? Ask students to use this formula as a guide in their reading. Such a guide invariably will result in increased comprehension and helps students learn the importance of setting purposes for their reading.

21. Have students find five examples of connotative words. Tell them to group words according to where they found them (newspaper editorial, news article, magazine article, and so forth). Discuss the relationship between the words and their source, and how the words influence the reader's interpretation of the author's meaning.

22. Have students choose two sports writers, then analyze and discuss the structure each writer uses in writing stories about sporting events. Let students try to develop their own sports articles based on such structures.

23. Begin a sentence with a function word. Have students complete the sentence using words appropriate to the relationship signaled by the function word. Example:

The book is on _____.
Because Tommy was late _____.

DEVELOPING CONTENT GOALS

In the middle grades, students begin reading various types of text, and content goals become more complex. In terms of recreational text, third and fourth grade students will not only read increasingly complex stories but also will read biographies, autobiographies, plays, poems, diaries, cartoons, and riddles, as well as folk literature, fantasy, realistic fiction, and humorous stories.

Functional text also becomes more complex. In addition to simple expository articles typical of primary grade reading, third and fourth grade students encounter content area textbooks, that is, textbooks dealing with academic fields. Middle grade students are expected to comprehend this more complex material.

Techniques that Promote Comprehension

The directed reading-thinking activity (DRTA) can be used to help students achieve content goals in the middle grades. It has the advantage of helping students develop the habit of making predictions. An example of how to teach using the directed reading-thinking activity with recreational text is provided in Example 18.8.

The DRTA can also be used with functional text. You follow the same format, but instead of making predictions about what is going to happen in the story or to the main character, focus predictions on expository information. For instance, in a text about the pyramids of Egypt, your students would examine the text,

EXAMPLE 18.8   An Example of How to Use a Directed Reading-Thinking Activity to Ensure Comprehension of Recreational Text

Background	You want your students to read the next selection in the basal text, and your major objective is that they comprehend the content of the story. You decide to use a directed reading-thinking activity.
Lesson Sequence	
Introduction	Provide a story introduction designed to activate students' background knowledge about the topic, the purpose, and the text structure. Teach new vocabulary as needed.
Purpose-setting	Direct students to survey the selection, examining illustration, headings, and other clues to story content. Have them use these clues to make predictions about what they are going to encounter in the story. List their predictions on the board, then direct them to read the story to see if their predictions were accurate.
Reading	Have students read the selection for the story content and check their predictions.
Discussion	Discuss the story content and the accuracy of students predictions.
Closure	Review the content of the selection. You may wish to follow up the story with an enriching activity that calls for using the knowledge gained from the story.
Desired Outcome	Students will be able to state what has happened in the story selection.

note the clues in the form of titles, headings, subheadings, photographs, and so on, and then make predictions regarding what they are going to learn about pyramids.

Another guidance technique that you will find particularly useful when teaching content goals with functional text is **survey, question, read, recite, and review (SQ3R)**, a five-step process designed to recall text information. It works like this. First, you direct your students to survey the material to be read, noting titles, headings, subheadings, pictures, and other clues to text content. Next, have them list questions they should be able to answer after reading the text. They can get the questions from you or from the end of the chapter, but it is best to have students formulate their own questions by turning what they surveyed into questions. For instance, a text on the pyramids of Egypt might include a subheading such as "The Pyramids: An Engineering Marvel" which you teach students to turn into a question such as, "Why are the pyramids an engineering marvel?" Once questions are listed, have your students read text to answer the questions. When they finish reading, have them look at the questions again and answer them. Finally, if they cannot answer one or more questions, tell them to go back into the text, review it, and then try again.

SQ3R is a very systematic technique and works well for many of the same reasons as the directed reading-thinking activity. It involves readers in establishing purposes for reading; it allows them to get a feel for the text through an initial survey; it encourages confirming or disconfirming predictions embodied in the questions; and it promotes the habit of checking to make sure that predictions have indeed been confirmed. An example of how to use SQ3R is provided in Example 18.9.

The middle grades, then, strongly emphasize content goals. There is particular emphasis on more complex forms of recreational and functional text. These are bridging experiences from the relatively simple content goals at the primary level to the increasingly more complex and diversified reading demanded in the upper grades.

Role of the Basal

Basal textbooks are often an excellent place to teach and apply techniques such as DRTA and SQ3R. Middle grade basals typically include a variety of recreational and functional text. If your major goal is for students to comprehend these samples of text, then you should use DRTA and SQ3R with these selections.

The important thing to remember about using basal texts, however, is that they serve two purposes: they contain samples of recreational and functional text that you can use for teaching content goals or for applying process goals. Consequently, you must consciously decide whether you are using a particular selection primarily as an application of a process goal or as a selection to be comprehended because of its inherent content value. Both are important, but

---

EXAMPLE   18.9   How to Use SQ3R to Ensure Comprehension of Functional Text

Background	Your students are reading a selection from a science textbook on photosynthesis. To help them understand this difficult scientific content, you decide to guide their reading with SQ3R.
Lesson Sequence	
Survey	Activate students' experience with leaves and trees, and elicit their conceptions of how trees get food. Have students look over the chapter to determine what the text is about.
Question	Have students examine the headings subheadings, illustrations, and end-of-chapter discussion points. Have them pose a question for each. These questions become the purpose setters for reading the chapter.
Read	Have students read the chapter to determine the answers to their questions.
Recite	Discuss their answers for each of the questions.
Reread	For questions that have not been answered, direct students to the appropriate place in the text and have them try to answer it again.
Desired Outcome	Students will remember and recall the important information in the text.

you must know when you are teaching for one goal and when you are teaching for another.

ACTIVITIES TO DEVELOP CONTENT GOALS

Unlike attitude and process goals, for which you can specify a variety of activities, the activities for content goals are limited because specific activities depend on the text you use. Consequently, you must decide on the particulars of the activity once you have selected the text. Here are some activities you can use to supplement your teaching of content goals in third and fourth grade.

1. Have students sell a book to the class as a novel way of presenting an oral report. Tell the reader-salesman to convince the rest of the class that the book is the best book of its kind.

2. Use a book tree to develop both functional and recreational reading. As a book is read, label a leaf on the tree with the title and author, and place it on the functional or the recreational side. The goal is to keep the tree balanced in terms of number of leaves.

3. Use pantomime to share the content of a story that has proved especially popular with the class. One or more students can put on the pantomime while the rest of the class tries to guess who or what the performers represent and/or the type of content represented.

4. Use puppets, which are as much fun to make as they are to operate, as an excellent way of sharing content. Make puppets using clay or paper-mâché for the heads and simple cloth squares for the bodies.

5. Construct mobiles in the form of major characters from a story. You can also use settings or illustrations of the major content as a display.

6. Make dioramas and shadow boxes to illustrate content from a book. Again, either recreational or functional books can be the basis. Have students indicate their purpose for reading the book.

7. Have students make a miniature stage setting with pipe-cleaner figures to describe part of the information learned from a book. Have them display the stage setting and figures and give a two-minute talk explaining the content they represent and why they were selected.

8. Have students write using the patterns employed in favorite books. Mercer Mayer's books can lead to original stories, Rudyard Kipling's *Just So Stories* can be used to generate fanciful explanation, the poems on color in O'Neil's *Hailstones and Halibut Bones* can stimulate poems about sounds, smells, and so on.

9. Have students turn to the food advertisements in a newspaper and pick four items they would want for dinner. Write down how much each of these items will cost and the total food costs for preparing dinner.

FIGURE 18.1 Sample unit on pioneers.

Theme: Overcoming challenges through the pioneer spirit

Objectives:
1. Provide opportunities to explore the lives of settlers, focusing on how they overcame challenges in order to survive
2. Foster understandings and critically analyze the relationships between Western settlers and Native Americans
3. Develop knowledge of historical fiction that addresses the theme of survival and the pioneer spirit
4. Explore the many challenges of female settlers
5. Develop understandings of tall tales and discover reoccurring patterns and motifs
6. Develop predicting as a pre-reading strategy
7. Provide opportunities for students to move through the literacy cycle using reading, writing, and conversations
8. Introduce students to explanation papers as an example of expository text structures
9. Develop and present research projects at the culminating campfire festival
10. Extend understandings of sense-making as a during-reading and during-writing strategy
11. Encourage reflection as a post-reading and post-writing strategy
12. Enhance understandings of reading, writing, and conversations as ways of communicating and as useful tools
13. Develop understanding of the relationships among reading, writing, and conversation
14. Develop planning and organizing as a pre-writing strategy

Summary:

The students began the unit by forming cooperative groups and researching an area of interest about settlers. Each group researches its topic, composed the information, and created a mural to teach other class members. This learning and teaching aid the conceptual framework for the culminating activity. For two weeks, the students developed understandings about settlers and Native Americans by listening to the *Bread and Butter Indian*, discussing it, and writing about it in their literature logs. The following three weeks, students listened to tall tales, had conversations about the common elements, created tall tales, and published the tales in a class book. This was followed by the oral reading of several historical fiction stories about the settlers and the composing of explanation papers by students. The eight-week unit culminated with a campfire festival for which students choose an area about settler life and presented their published research. In social studies, students learned about history, map skills, and communities through the movement of the settlers. Science was developed through explorations of the settlers' dependency on animals and their inventions which helped improve their lives. In art, students created a life-sized log cabin, murals, toys, and quilt squares for a classroom quilt.

> The survival unit was developed and taught by Danise J. Cantlon and Pam G. Seales at Elliott Elementary Professional Development School, Holt, MI.

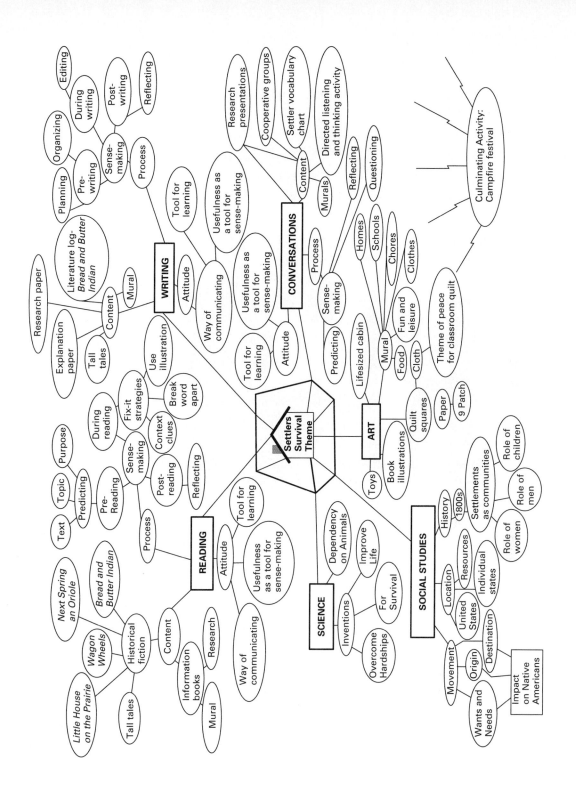

WRITING

Content
- Research paper
- Explanation paper
- Tall tales
- Mural
- Literature log–*Bread and Butter Indian*

Tool for learning

Attitude
- Usefulness as a tool for sense-making
- Way of communicating

Process
- Sense-making
  - Pre-writing
    - Planning
    - Organizing
  - During writing
  - Post-writing
    - Reflecting
    - Editing

CONVERSATIONS

Content
- Research presentations
- Cooperative groups
- Settler vocabulary chart
- Directed listening and thinking activity
- Murals

Process
- Sense-making
  - Predicting
  - Reflecting
  - Questioning

Tool for learning

Attitude
- Usefulness as a tool for sense-making

Mural
- Homes
- Schools
- Chores
- Clothes
- Fun and leisure
- Food
- Cloth
- Lifesized cabin

Theme of peace for classroom quilt

Culminating Activity: Campfire festival

ART

Quilt squares
- Paper
- 9 Patch

Book illustrations

Toys

READING

Sense-making
- Pre-Reading
  - Predicting
    - Topic
    - Text
    - Purpose
- During reading
  - Fix-it strategies
    - Context clues
    - Break word apart
  - Use illustration
- Post-reading
  - Reflecting

Process

Tool for learning

Attitude
- Usefulness as a tool for sense-making
- Way of communicating

Content
- Historical fiction
  - *Next Spring an Oriole*
  - *Bread and Butter Indian*
  - *Wagon Wheels*
  - *Little House on the Prairie*
- Tall tales
- Information books
- Research
- Mural

SCIENCE

- Dependency on Animals
- Improve Life
- Inventions
  - For Survival
  - Overcome Hardships

SOCIAL STUDIES

History
- 1800s
- Settlements as communities
  - Role of women
  - Role of men
  - Role of children

Location
- Resources
- United States
  - Individual states

Movement
- Origin
- Destination
- Wants and Needs
- Impact on Native Americans

Settlers Survival Theme

427

Third and fourth graders are expected to do more individual creative writing.

10. Using advertisements, have students find at least seven things they drink. Have them note their favorites and the cost for a week's supply.

11. The class or school newspaper should have a good feature section devoted to children's books. The sections can classify books as recreational or functional and highlight their novel aspects. Have a different theme for each issue, such as Pioneers, Life in Other Lands, Science Fiction, Magic and Fantasy, Biography, Natural Science, etc. The class or classes responsible for this section ought to concentrate on novel ways of stimulating interest in the books presented.

12. Use original posters, illustrations, or book jackets to illustrate the contents of a book. These become excellent displays and can be used also to develop positive attitudes to reading.

13. Illustrate maps to show a character's travels or the area encompassed by a story as a novel way to show the content of a book. This helps students decide whether to read the book for entertainment or information.

14. Draw murals to depict either functional or recreational content, and include sample book titles associated with the content.

15. Have the class publish booklets about various subjects (science, ecology, World War II). Tell contributors to do research and then write their portion of the booklet.

16. Have students present a "You are There" show where they enact the content of a book they have read.

17. Have students present a talk show and interview the central characters of a book they have read.

INTEGRATING READING AND WRITING

There are many opportunities to integrate subject matter and the various language modes when teaching the middle grades. The following units are examples. The first one, shown in Figure 18.1, is an illustration of a unit on pioneers. The second one, Figure 18.2, is an illustration of a unit on mummies.

FIGURE 18.2   Sample Teaching Unit: Egyptian Mummies

LEVEL:
Third and fourth grade, expanded fundamentals stage

OBJECTIVES
Content Objective: Given the opportunity to visit a museum exhibit on Egyptian mummies, students will in preparation for the visit state historical and cultural conditions of ancient Egypt which contributed to the death rituals of the time and obtain specific additional information from the museum curator during the visit.
Attitude Objective: Given opportunities to investigate death rituals of ancient Egypt, students demonstrate positive feelings about satisfying curiosity through literacy activity.
Process Objective: Given the task of gathering information about Egyptian mummies, students will use knowledge of various kinds of text structures to predict where needed information will be found.
   Given the task of gathering information about Egyptian mummies, students will use locational strategies associated with book parts and card catalogs to find the information they need.

CULMINATING ACTIVITY
Students will visit the mummy exhibit at the museum, ask the additional questions generated in the course of their study, satisfy their curiosity about death

rituals, and make comparisons between the death rituals of ancient Egypt and those of our own culture.

DAY 1

Warm-up activity: Comment on the fact that a mummy exhibit will be available at the local museum. Get students talking about their prior knowledge about mummies, and the questions they have about mummies. Introduce the possibility of visiting the museum as a way to answer some of their questions.

    Assessment: Assess group knowledge about mummies and students' ability to generate and state questions.

    Focusing activity: Read aloud and show pictures from an appropriate book on Egyptian mummies. Tell students to listen and observe so they will be able to answer questions (information gathering) that have been generated in the warm-up activity, and perhaps generate additional questions.

    Reading-writing activity: Have students develop questions that can be answered from the text. Tell them to list questions that should have been asked. After the conversation, classify questions into answered and unanswered categories. Have students generate sources for answering the unanswered questions (library, museum, guest speaker, etc.).

    Assessment: Assess students' knowledge about mummies, ability to develop and state questions, and knowledge of where to go for information. Teach these skills to students who could not develop questions or locate information.

DAYS 2 & 3

Warm-up activity: Using the questions generated in the prior lesson, have students play the game, pick and seek. Place each question on a card and have enough cards with duplicate questions so that each student will have at least one question to sort. Tell students to decide where to look for the answer to the question on their cards. Have a student stationed at each location (library, *Mummies Made in Egypt*, museum, speaker, etc.) to verify the choice. By the end of the activity all questions are classified for further research.

    Focusing activity: Have library researchers go the library to gather information about the art, artifacts, pyramids, rituals, and so on, of the ancient Egyptians and the process of mummifying and burying their Pharaohs, as well as the discovery of such famous tombs as that of Tutenkhamen.

    Reading-writing activity: Have students share the information found in the library with one or more students acting as recorders during the conversation. Have the recorders write a report of the conversation that will be shared and verified by their classmates.

    Assessment: Assess students' knowledge about ancient Egypt, some students' abilities to record and report an oral discussion, and all students' abilities to participate in oral conversations. If a skill lesson for locating information was taught previously, it could be checked during the focusing activity.

DAY 4

Warm-up activity: Have students read the written record of the previous day's conversation and alter or approve it. Give each student an approved copy of the written record.

Focusing activity: Have students revise and update the questions generated for the guest speaker. New questions can also be generated at this time.

Reading-writing activity: Have groups of four or five students interview another student who is role playing a guest speaker knowledgeable about ancient Egypt. Tell students to check their own knowledge of ancient Egypt and the validity and form of their questions. Have students give their questions to the guest speaker.

Assessment: With the students, assess their knowledge of ancient Egypt, the ability to record and report oral conversations, and the skill of interviewing. (If a skill lesson had been taught earlier on questions, it could be evaluated during the focusing activity. All needed skills should be taught.)

DAY 5

Warm-up activity: Have students brainstorm all the words they can think of that relate to ancient Egypt. Then tell them to classify words according to the questions prepared for the guest speaker. Have them put words that cannot be classified under a question in a separate group.

Focusing activity: Give each student the responsibility of asking one question. Then have the speaker present knowledge of ancient Egypt.

Reading-writing activity: After the oral presentation, have students ask their questions individually. Encourage additional questions. Have students write an answer to their question. Duplicate questions and answers, and give them to each member of the class.

Assessment: Evaluate knowledge of Egypt (brainstorming or written answers to questions), ability to classify, skill in careful listening, skill in interviewing.

DAY 6

Warm-up activity: Have students list the sources of information (book presented in class, library, speaker, etc.), and how they can use each source to locate knowledge about Egyptian burials.

Focusing activity: Have students sort and discuss their questions and answers about burials in ancient Egypt.

Reading-writing activity: Have students select parts to play in re-enacting the burial of an Egyptian king and the later discovery of his tomb. Some students may be artists who create jewelry, others may be embalmers, others discoverers, etc. Then have them enact the ritual, using the information they have gathered. After the tomb in the pyramid is secured, have the contemporary discoverers find the tomb and carefully dismantle it, telling of the artifacts they find.

Assessment: Assess students' ability to classify, recall information about Egyptian burials, and dramatize Egyptian burials.

DAYS 7 & 8

Warm-up activity: Have students create their own time line with 12 inches of string and five cards. Have each student select five important events in his or her life and put one event on each card. Hieroglyphics may be used, but the pictures should tell a story to people who might find them many years later. Tape each card on the line in sequential order so that each student has a time line (informing). Have students read each other's time lines.

Focusing activity: Discuss how the kings of Egypt, like the students themselves, had five important events in their lives. Discuss how those events could be illustrated with hieroglyphics. Lead the conversation to Egyptian burials of the kings where personal artifacts as represented in the time lines might be buried with them.

Reading-writing activity: Have students list the personal artifacts they would choose to have buried with them if they were kings of Egypt. Share these lists with other classmates. Compare the similarities and differences among the items selected, as well as their implied values. Do not allow students to criticize each other's selections. Have students orally compare and contrast the artifacts and picture they would have in their tomb with the artifacts found in the tomb of King Tut.

Assessment: Assess students' ability to sequence events and enumerate similarities and differences of items selected for burial with King Tut's burial.

DAY 9

Warm-up activity: Brainstorm items that have been discussed so far in the unit and that people would consider important. List items by people.

Focusing activity: Tell students that in a way the Egyptian tombs are like time capsules. Identify a local time capsule (i.e., cornerstone of a school, church, or courthouse) that has been opened recently, or a famous time capsule such as the one on top of the John Hancock Building in Chicago. Ask: "How do the items included in these time capsules reflect their society? What items would you put in a time capsule to reflect your society for those who open it in 100 years?"

Assessment: Assess classification skills, justified choice skills, and abilities to recall, inform, and imagine.

Culminating activity: Visit the museum and pose the unanswered questions about mummies to the curator. Follow the visit with a conversation of the similarities and differences between rituals in the ancient Egyptian culture and rituals in our culture.

ADDITIONAL INTEGRATED READING AND WRITING ACTIVITIES

Here are some additional activities to supplement your integration of reading and writing in grades 3 and 4.

1. Provide pictures of action. Have students discuss what might have happened earlier to cause this action. Have students write a story of the events

that led to the action. Have students read the stories to each other or to younger students for enjoyment.

2.   Have students write riddles and place them in riddle books to be read during free time.

3.   Have students share a book about a spaceship. Ask: "If you could turn your chair into a spaceship, what would you do?" Have students write their answers.

4.   Have students read a well-known story (fairy tale, tall tale, etc.). Then have them discuss how the story would change if it were told from another point of view, for example, Hansel and Gretel from the witch's view, Paul Bunyan from the Blue Ox's view, *It's Like This Cat* from the cat's view. Have students write a new version of the story from a different view.

5.   Have students discuss what new inventions might occur in the future. Have them illustrate their invention and write a paragraph to explain its use. Place a compiled book in the classroom library. Examples: automatic surfboard, robot hairdresser, a plane-boat-helicopter, an automatic comb, a pencil that knows all the answers.

6.   Have students discuss nicknames such as Slim, Bones, and Speedy. Have them select a nickname and write a paragraph on how that person got the name. File paragraphs in the writing center to be used in future stories.

7.   Have students read a humorous story such as those about Pippi Longstocking or Amelia Bedelia. Have them select one incident and create a cartoon strip for it. Share the cartoon strips with another class.

9.   Have students create a What If book. Include topics such as: What if there were no cards? What if you were the teacher? What if you were asked to travel on the space shuttle? What if you were invited to the White House to receive a bravery award? What if you were asked to show the Queen of England around your school? Have the students create either a book for the class or their own book. Share books with other classes or schools.

9.   Have students create a Liar's Club with a "biggest whopper" award. Tell students to write about topics such as heroic deeds, family, travel, funniest event, strangest event, etc. Publish all whoppers in the classroom newspaper. Publish the winners in the school newspaper.

10.   Have students think like a football player, getting ready to begin a play. Have them write what the player would say to a player on the other team. Have students write what the player's response would be. Keep dialogues for future stories.

CHARACTERISTICS OF AN INSTRUCTIONAL DAY

Because the middle grades are bridging years between the primary and the upper grades, the instructional day takes on some characteristics associated with both. For instance, in many schools third and fourth grade retain the self-contained classroom arrangement typically found in first and second grade. That is, your students remain with you all day, rather than having different teachers for different subjects as is typically the case in the upper grades. At the same time, however, the middle grades do make a sharper distinction between subjects taught in school than the primary grades do. While the school day at the primary grade level is primarily devoted to language (especially reading), reading is but one of several subjects taught in the middle grades. For instance, most middle grades have a reading period, another period for language arts other than reading (usually emphasizing writing, but including elements of listening and speaking), another for mathematics, another for social studies, and another for science, with "special" subjects (such as art, music, and physical education) taught once in a while (often by specialists in these areas). Hence, the school day in third and fourth grade is often a combination of the self-contained classroom unit found in the typical primary grade and the subject-by-subject arrangement found in the typical upper grade.

Time allocation in the middle grades is different from that found in the primary grades: Reading is only taught once a day in most third and fourth grades. Also, it is often harder to integrate the various language arts in the middle grades because of the shift in emphasis to specific subjects. There is a tendency to teach only reading during reading period, only social studies during social studies period, and so on. This is regrettable, of course, since all these "subjects" offer opportunities for genuine communication using all the language modes. The best third and fourth grade teachers do strive to integrate subject matter that promotes genuine language uses. In their classes you will find students reading for content goals during social studies, being reminded of how to apply certain fix-it strategies during science, reviewing reading content while doing mathematical story problems, being shown how certain reading strategies can be converted into writing strategies, and so on.

Also typical of the middle grades are attempts to involve students in individual reading and writing efforts. Because students in first and second grade are just beginning to read, many of their activities are group oriented and result in group products. The language-experience story is one example. In the middle grades, however, the emphasis shifts to individual efforts and individual products. Third and fourth graders are expected to do much more independent silent reading and individual writing. This does not mean that there is no place for groups in the middle grades. Indeed, many of the individual projects designed to develop attitude goals are preceded by collaborative groups in which students help one another before working alone. Similarly, process and content goals are often initiated in the basal text reading groups and then move to individual work.

The middle grades retain many of the characteristics of the primary grades while also adapting some of the characteristics students will encounter when they get to fifth, sixth, seventh, and eighth grades. Although reading usually becomes a separate subject that gets taught in a certain time slot, teachers strive to integrate it into the other subjects, thereby requiring students to be involved in real language activities.

SUMMARY

The middle grades are a bridge from learning how to read in the primary grades and using reading to learn in the upper grades. During these years, the instructional emphasis is on comprehension. Third and fourth grade teachers typically rely on directed reading lessons and modified directed reading lessons to develop content and process goals, although every effort is made to also develop attitude goals through the literate environment and to integrate reading instruction with instruction in other content areas. Generally reading instruction at this level occurs during a single time allocation designated as the reading period.

SUGGESTED ADDITIONAL READING

ALLINGTON, R. L. (1983). Fluency: The neglected reading goal. *Reading Teacher, 36*(6), 556–561.

ALVERMANN, D. (1991). The discussion web: A graphic aid for learning across the curriculum. *Reading Teacher, 45*(2), 92–99.

ALVERMANN, D., DILLON, D., & O'BRIEN, D. (1987). *Using discussion to promote reading comprehension.* Newark, DE: International Reading Association.

ARNOLD, R. D., & WILCOX, E. (1982). Comparing types of comprehension questions found in fourth grade readers. *Reading Psychology, 3*(1), 43–49.

BABBS, P. J. (1984). Monitoring cards help improve comprehension. *Reading Teacher, 38*(2), 200–204.

BAKER, D. T. (1982). What happened when? Activities for teaching sequence skills. *Reading Teacher, 36*(2), 216–218.

BECK, I. L., & MCKEOWN, M. G. (1983). Learning word well—A program to enhance vocabulary and comprehension. *Reading Teacher, 36*(7), 622–625.

BERGQUIST, L. (1984). Rapid silent reading: Techniques for improving rate in intermediate grades. *Reading Teacher, 38*(1), 50–53.

BLACHOWICZ, C., & LEE, J. (1991). Vocabulary development in the whole literacy classroom. *Reading Teacher, 45*(3), 188–195.

BRAUGHT, L. (1992). Student operated paperback bookshops: A program to encourage middle grade literacy. *Reading Teacher, 45*(6), 438–450.

CHAPMAN, J. (1979). Confirming children's use of cohesive ties in text: Pronouns. *Reading Teacher, 33*(3), 317–322.

COHEN, R. (1983). Self-generated questions as an aid to reading comprehension. *Reading Teacher, 36*(8), 770–775.

CROWHURST, M. (1979). Developing syntactic skill: Doing what comes naturally. *Language Arts, 56*(5), 522–525.

FARRAR, M. T. (1984). Why do we ask comprehension questions? A new conception of comprehension instruction. *Reading Teacher, 37*(6), 452–456.

FRICK, H. (1986). The value of sharing stories orally with middle grade students. *Journal of Reading, 29*, 300–303.

HOFFMAN, J. V. (1979). Developing flexibility through reflex action. *Reading Teacher, 33*(3), 323–329.

IRWIN, J. (1991). *Teaching reading comprehension processes* (2nd ed.) Englewood Cliffs, NJ: Prentice Hall.

KIMMEL, S., & MACGINITIE, W. (1985). Helping students revise hypotheses while reading. *Reading Teacher, 38*(8), 768–771.

KLEIN, M. L. (1988). *Teaching reading comprehension and vocabulary: A guide for teachers.* Englewood Cliffs, NJ: Prentice Hall.

KOSKINEN, P., & BLUM, I. (1986). Paired repeated reading: A classroom strategy for developing fluent reading. *Reading Teacher, 30*, 70–77.

MARTINEZ, M., & ROSER, N. (1985). Read it again: The value of repeated readings during story time. *Reading Teacher, 38*(8), 782–786.

MCGEA, L., & RICHGELS, D. (1985). Teaching expository text structure to elementary students. *Reading Teacher, 38*(8), 739–749.

MCINTOSH, M. (1985). What do practitioners need to know about current inference research? *Reading Teacher, 38*(8), 755–761.

MCKEOWN, M. G. (1979). Developing language awareness or why *leg* was once a dirty word. *Language Arts, 56*(2), 175–180.

MOLDOFSKY, P. B. (1983). Teaching students to determine the central story problem: A practical application of schema theory. *Reading Teacher, 36*(8), 740–745.

REUTZEL, D. R. (1985). Story maps improve comprehension. *Reading Teacher, 38*(4), 400–404.

REUTZEL, D. R., & FAWSON, P. (1990). Traveling tales: Connecting parents and children through writing. *Reading Teacher, 44*(3), 222–227.

SMITH, M., & BEAN, T. W. (1983). Four strategies that develop children's story comprehension and writing. *Reading Teacher, 37*(3), 295–301.

STAUFFER, R. G., & HARREL, M. M. (1975). Individualized reading-thinking activities. *Reading Teacher, 28*(8), 765–769.

TAYLOR, B. M. (1982). A summarizing strategy to improve middle grade students' reading and writing skills. *Reading Teacher, 36*(2), 202–205.

TAYLOR, B., & FRYE, F. (1988). Pretesting: Minimize time spent on skill work for intermediate readers. *Reading Teacher, 42*(2), 100–104.

WONG, J. A., & HU-PEI AU, K. (1985). The concept-text-application approach: Helping elementary students comprehend expository text. *Reading Teacher, 38*(7), 612–618.

WOOD, K. D., & ROBINSON, N. (1983). Vocabulary, language and prediction: A prereading strategy. *Reading Teacher, 36*(4), 392–395.

THE RESEARCH BASE

GARNER, R. (1982). Resolving comprehension failure through text lookbacks: Direct training and practice effects among good and poor comprehenders in grades six and seven. *Reading Psychology, 3*(3), 221–231.

GORDON, C. J., & BRAUN, C. (1983). Using story schema as an aid to reading and writing. *Reading Teacher, 37*(2), 116–121.

MASON, J. M.   (1983). An examination of reading instruction in third and fourth grades. *Reading Teacher, 36*(9), 906–913.

SAMUELS, S. J.   (1979). The method of repeated readings. *Reading Teacher, 32*(4), 403–408.

SAMUELS, J., SCHERMER, N., & REINKING, D.   (1992). Reading fluency: Techniques for making decoding automatic. In J. Samuels & A. Farstrup (Eds.) *What research has to say about reading instruction* (2nd ed). (pp. 124–144). Newark, DE: International Reading Association.

SCHWARTZ, R., & RAPHAEL, T.   (1985). Concept of definition: A key to improving students' vocabulary. *Reading Teacher, 39*(2), 198–205.

ACTIVITIES FOR REFLECTING, OBSERVING, AND TEACHING

Reflecting on Teaching Middle-Grade Reading

PURPOSE: As students get older, it is more and more important that instruction be situated in authentic activity which is important to the students. The unit on Egyptian mummies provided as a sample in this chapter is an example of such activity. This activity is designed to help you develop your own ability to generate such authentic learning experiences.

DIRECTIONS: Using both the sample unit provided in this chapter and the suggestions provided in Chapter 14, create a unit which will involve third and fourth graders in authentic literate activity in pursuit of a genuine goal. Include specific content, attitude, and process objectives, and a day-by-day schedule of activity.

Watching Others Teach Third and Fourth Graders

PURPOSE: You become better and better at teaching yourself as you gain more and more experiences with what it means to teach third and fourth grade. That is why it is so helpful to observe other teachers who are teaching third and fourth grade. This activity helps you structure such an activity.

DIRECTIONS: Arrange to observe a third or fourth grade for several consecutive days. During these observations, specifically note the following:

- the instructional emphasis (relative to Table 18.1)
- the literate environment
- the use of literature-based reading and language experience, especially in developing attitude goals
- what routine skills are taught and how they are taught (look particularly for vocabulary and fluency)
- what strategies are taught and how they are taught (look particularly for lessons on monitoring, using visible cues to comprehension, inferencing, organizing content, and word choice).
- what content is taught and how it is developed
- whether activity is organized into units and, if so, the nature and characteristics of the unit

Trying It Yourself

PURPOSE: The more you teach yourself, the better teacher you become. Consequently, this activity suggests ways to get more teaching opportunities.

DIRECTIONS: When you are observing in a third or fourth grade, look for opportunities to relieve the teacher or to fill in for the teacher. When these occasions arise, use the suggestions in this chapter to help you determine what to teach and how to teach it.

Teaching Upper Grade Reading: Application Stage

19

GETTING READY

The upper grades are significant because it is here that students move from elementary to middle school or junior high school and take a major step toward eventual adulthood. Students are moving further from learning how to read to using their reading abilities to learn in other content areas. This stage of reading growth is called the application stage—students apply what they know about reading to the learning of content subjects. This chapter describes the difficulties of teaching reading at this level and makes suggestions to help you overcome them.

FOCUS QUESTIONS

- What are the unique difficulties of teaching reading in the upper grades?
- How are attitude goals developed in the upper grades?
- How are process goals taught in the upper grades?
- How are content goals developed in the upper grades?
- How are reading and writing integrated in the upper grades?
- What does a typical upper grade instructional day look like?

OVERVIEW OF UPPER GRADE READING

The shift from middle grade reading to upper grade reading is almost as dramatic as the shift from kindergarten to the primary grades for four reasons.

First, the move to fifth, sixth, seventh, and eighth grade often means a physical move from one school building to another. Typically, American students attend an elementary school for grades 1 through 4 or 5 and then move to a middle school or a junior high school in grade 5 or 6. This change to a new, unfamiliar physical environment is dramatic for children, making it a significant time in their lives.

Second, the shift heralds important organizational changes in the way schooling is conducted. In elementary school, students typically have one homeroom teacher for most of the school day and receive almost all instruction from that person. In grades 5 through 8, however, the homeroom teacher is the person to whom students report at the beginning of the day, but they may receive instruction from as many as five or six other teachers over the course of the day. Hence, the organization of the school shifts from self-contained classrooms in which one teacher provides most of the instruction to a departmentalized setting in which specialists teach one subject to five different groups of students each day.

Third, the upper grades represent a dramatic psychological change for students. While the environment in the first four or five grades is consistent and stable, the environment in the upper grades is more diverse and requires much more flexibility. The upper grades are intentionally designed as a bridge from the lower grades to high school, and, as such, are designed as a bridge from the lower grades to high school, and, as such, are designed to ease students into high school behaviors. Nevertheless, the change is still a dramatic one for many students.

Finally, the upper grades have traditionally taken a different approach to curriculum and instruction, especially as it relates to reading. In fifth, sixth, seventh, and eighth grade, reading is not a formal part of the curriculum, and typically there is no specialized reading teacher as there is for the subject areas. The assumption is that reading has been mastered from preschool to fourth grade and does not need to be emphasized thereafter. Recently, however, there has been a growing awareness of the need to continue reading instruction into the upper grades and to have subject matter teachers show students how to read the specialized materials associated with their content area. The basal text, however, is not as prevalent as it is in the earlier grades because reading is not normally taught as a separate subject.

All these characteristics make teaching reading in the upper grades a unique and challenging endeavor. The building is different, the school organization is different, the students themselves are at a unique psychological stage, and the context in which reading is taught is different. The result has often been that upper grade teachers feel a pressure unlike that felt by teachers at any other level. They are in a unique position between elementary school and high school, charged with bridging the gap from learning how to read to applying reading knowledge to the learning of specialized subject matter. The task is not an easy one.

Despite these differences, however, the overall instructional goal in reading remains essentially unchanged in the upper grades—to develop students who control their meaning getting as they read functional and recreational text. However, the context for reading instruction becomes the various content areas and their specialized texts. There is also a growing emphasis on critical reading (teaching students to make judgments about what is read), study skills (guiding the efficient handling of more complex reading materials), and content goals (providing guidance in reading difficult text).

These curricular emphases are reflected in the instruction found in the upper grades. The curricular and instructional emphasis in the upper grades is shown in Table 19.1.

DEVELOPING ATTITUDE GOALS

Because reading in the upper grades is so closely associated with reading in the content areas, attitude goals often receive less attention than they should. Teachers emphasize learning content, and they often assume that students' elementary years provided them with all they need to know about reading and with a positive attitude toward reading. Such is not the case. The development of concepts and responses that make for positive attitudes toward reading is still important in the upper grades.

One of the major tasks of an upper grade teacher is to maintain the earlier emphasis on positive attitudes. You do this by providing your students with reading experiences that reinforce both the conceptual understanding of reading and the positive responses developed in previous years. You should reinforce reading as a communication process, that it is a functional tool, and that it is a medium for enrichment and enjoyment. You ensure that reading is enjoyable so positive feelings develop.

Creating a Literate Environment

Because of academic departmentalization in grades 5 through 8, students encounter many classroom environments on any given day. Departmentalization makes it difficult for teachers to physically arrange their classrooms to stimulate literate activities when they switch rooms every period. They cannot establish a preferred physical arrangement because each classroom is the homeroom of a colleague.

Despite this limitation, you can create a literate environment by relying on intellectual and social-emotional characteristics more heavily. You can create a literate environment intellectually by involving students in meaningful reading and writing tasks and by setting the expectation that they will pursue those tasks in literate ways. To organize the social-emotional environment, you can involve students in collaborative groupings that encourage intellectual diversity and cooperation in pursuing assigned language tasks. Some teachers counter the changing physical environment by creating posters that can be carried from classroom to classroom. Others put physical decorations in cartons and take them from room to room as they move.

Because upper grade teachers often specialize in a particular content area, the literate environment is frequently associated with that content. For instance, an eighth grade social studies teacher teaching a unit on the Civil War may involve students in examining real documents from that era and in drawing

TABLE 19.1 Strategies for Taking Tests

OUTCOME	INSTRUCTIONAL EMPHASIS	MAJOR INSTRUCTIONAL ACTIVITY
Attitude goals		
Concepts about reading	Authors have purposes for writing text; readers have purposes for reading text Reading can clarify knowledge, feelings, and attitudes Reading can expand knowledge, feelings, and attitudes Reading is a valuable tool that meets needs	Indirect instruction using projects, language experience, USSR activities, and writing
Positive responses to reading	Reading is exciting Reading is satisfying Reading results in knowledge Reading is curiosity Reading is a source of power	Indirect instruction involving projects, language experience, USSR activities, and writing
Process goals		
Routine skills		
Vocabulary	Build vocabulary through direct study of words encountered in content-area subjects Emphasize abstract words	Direct instruction of vocabulary
Word recognition	Recognize a wide variety of words instantly and fluently	Direction instruction of word recognition
Metacognitive strategies		
Initiating strategies	Activate background knowledge of content using predicting Activate background knowledge about different types of text structures, author's purpose, and reader's purpose	Direct instruction of initiating strategies
During-reading strategies		
Monitoring strategies	Maintenance Monitor for unknown words, for unrecognized words, for author's meaning, and for meaning beyond what the author says	Direct instruction of monitoring strategies

Fix-it strategies	Recognize disruption in sense making
	Access strategies to repair sense making
	    Word recognition
	    Vocabulary
	    Author's meaning
	    Beyond the author's meaning
	Employ strategies
	Verify repair of sense making
		Direct instruction of fix-it strategies of comprehension

TABLE 19.1 (continued)

OUTCOME	INSTRUCTIONAL EMPHASIS	MAJOR INSTRUCTIONAL ACTIVITY
Post-reading strategies		
Organizing strategies	Recall what is important by using knowledge of the different types of text structure, classifying paragraphs, and determining main idea Draw conclusions Summarize content	Direct instruction of organizing strategies
Evaluating strategies	Judge content of text in reference to prior experience Judge author's structuring of text in reference to content	Direct instruction of evaluating strategies
Study strategies		
Locational strategies	Use book strategies of table of contents, glossary, and index to locate information Use library strategies of card catalogs and the Dewey Decimal System to locate information Use reference source strategies of dictionaries, encyclopedias, atlases, thesaurus, etc., to locate information Use graphics strategies of using graphs, charts, tables, etc., to locate information	Direct instruction of study strategies
Study habits	Organize time Develop test-taking strategies	Direct instruction of study habit strategies
Rate strategies	Develop scanning pace, skimming pace, and slow pace	Direct instruction of rate strategies
Organizing strategies	Develop note taking Develop outlining	Direct instruction of organizing strategies
Remembering strategies	Maintain semantic map useage Use SQ3R and variations	
Content goals		
Recreational	Get meaning from various literature genres Get meaning from various froms of narrative text	Guided reading
Functional	Get meaning from text containing heavy conceptual loads	Guided reading
	Get meaning from expository texts found in content area textbooks	Guided reading
	Use QARs to get meaning from expository text	Guided reading

conclusions about how people in various parts of the country felt about the morality of the war. Although such reading tasks are closely associated with the content being studied, they nevertheless help students conceptualize reading accurately and feel positive about it. They are, in short, literate activities.

Instructional Approach

Upper grade teachers expedite attitude development by planning units of instruction that are characterized by a unifying project or culminating activity within a content area. Such projects can easily be done within the departmentalized organization typically found in the upper grades. Students in an English class studying various forms of free verse poetry may study them in preparation for creating a book of poetry. Students in a social studies class may study state government in preparation for holding a mock legislative sessions in their school. The unifying theme provides a meaningful and interesting context in which to learn and promotes attitude development.

For the unit approach to help attitude development, you must choose projects that are motivating to students and necessitate learning some targeted content. Here are some sample project ideas you can use in fifth through eighth grade science, social studies, and mathematics classes as a culminating activity for an integrated unit of instruction.

Science and Social Studies Projects

1. After a current events unit where issues related to city, state, or country have been discussed, have students list five changes they would make. Have students read each other's lists and create a class list.

2. After a science unit on health needs, tell students to select what they feel was the most important point, then to put this point in a poster. Place posters in prominent spots in the school.

3. After a unit on budgets, provide students with a budget, a family, and the local newspaper advertisements from grocery stores. Have students buy food for a week's time.

4. During election year have students conduct a mock election of those running for office.

5. After a science unit on ecology, have students select an important point and create an editorial to be placed in the class or school newspaper.

6. End a science unit on weather with daily written forecasts that include maps. Record and graph the accuracy of the forecasts.

Mathematics Projects

1. After a travel unit, have students plan an itinerary for a motor trip in the United States. Given mileage, meal, and hotel costs, have students develop the costs for the trip.

2. After a unit on mapping, have students measure and map the school, the neighborhood, or their route from home to school.

3. After a unit on measurement, have students measure and record the weights of unknown rocks. Using the sizes and the weights, have students predict in writing the types of rocks they have.

Within units, use indirect instruction to develop particular concepts about reading and particular responses to reading. For instance, an English unit on newspapers may have as its culminating activity the publication of a student newspaper. During this unit, you may wish to develop the concept that newspaper editorials represent an attempt to persuade readers to the paper's view on some issue. To do this, you may plan a trip to the local newspaper and a visit with the editorial writer. Your instruction would follow the three-step format for indirect instruction. An illustrative example is shown in Example 19.1.

ACTIVITIES TO DEVELOP ATTITUDE GOALS

Here are some activities you can use to supplement development of positive attitudes toward reading in fifth through eighth grade.

1. Have students sell a book to the class as a novel way of presenting an oral report and developing positive attitudes. Tell reader-salesmen to convince the rest of the class that the book they read is the best book of its kind.

EXAMPLE 19.1 How to Develop Positive Attitudes

Background	As part of a unit on newspapers, you want your students to learn that newspaper editorials are written by people trying to influence the reader to share the same viewpoint as the publisher of the paper. You can develop this concept indirectly.
Activity 1	Arrange to take students on a field trip to the local newspaper office. Schedule an interview with the editorial writer, and prepare students to ask questions about how the topics are chosen, why certain positions are taken and what the writer's techniques are in composing the editorials.
Discussion	In the classroom after the trip, have conversations about what students found out about the editorial writer and the purpose of editorials.
Activity 2	Organize students into collaborative groups to analyze recent editorials written by the writer they interviewed and to draw conclusions about the persuasive nature of editorials. Then have students produce their own newspaper and include editorials. Establish an editorial policy to determine the positions to be taken by the newspaper, and assign someone the task of writing editorials that will convince others to share the views of students.

Upper grade teachers must maintain the earlier emphasis on positive attitudes toward reading.

2. Use index cards with brief summaries and reactions to books read independently. These can be a valuable asset to the class if other students are allowed to use them to get ideas for future reading.

3. Illustrate maps to show a character's travels or the area encompassed by a story. These offer a novel way of sharing all kinds of books ranging from historical fiction to realistic fiction.

4. Suggest that the school newspaper include a feature section devoted to children's books. The section might have a different theme for each issue, such as Science Fiction, Magic and Fantasy, Biography, Natural Science, etc. The class responsible for writing this section concentrates on novel ways of stimulating interest in the books presented.

5. Have students broadcast a book review, as if they were radio or television critics. Tape record the review, and have others listen and state whether or not they would like to read the book and why. This helps develop students' interest in reading.

6. Have students write a script and produce a radio or television program about a favorite book. Have them present it to another group of students.

7. Have students develop and present commentaries about favorite books for a silent movie, a filmstrip, or a slide show. Have them use their own photographs or slides, if possible.

8. Have students write an imaginary letter from one story character to another. Have them tell about something that might have happened had they both lived at the same time and place. This helps students develop interest in reading about others in books.

9. Have students create "tall tales" like those they read. Have them write, illustrate, and share at least two of the tales they create. This activity helps develop interest in and appreciation for reading.

10. Have students identify comic strips that reflect contemporary social values, and have them discuss how comic strips relate to concepts of reading such as communicating messages, providing enjoyment, and so on.

11. Authors are important. Your students, especially by the upper grades, should begin to be aware of prominent authors. This awareness can lead to discussion of various authors and comparisons of their works, which strengthens students' concepts of reading and the author-writer relationship.

12. Have students discuss value-laden problems that appear in advice columns to develop the concept that language communicates shared values.

13. Have students write a letter to the editor that is constructively critical of the editorial position of the newspaper on some given issue. This develops the concept that language allows us to communicate.

14. When reading a story aloud to your students, have them keep a journal of the story as if they were a character in it, or simply have them record their reactions to the story. Periodically share the journals. This helps develop students' interest in recreational reading.

15. Have students draw a series of comic strips, basing them on a short story, fairy tale, or myth. This helps students develop interest in various forms of literature.

TEACHING PROCESS GOALS

One of the major tasks for teachers in grades 5 through 8 is to continue developing the process goals introduced in earlier grades. You will continue developing some routine skills, and you will continue to develop students' understanding of how to use various knowledge sources to make predictions, to monitor comprehension, and to apply fix-it strategies when text no longer makes sense. In addition, you will extend post-reading strategy instruction into the area of critical reading and heavily emphasize study strategies.

Routine Skills

Although you no longer place instructional emphasis on teaching sight words, students' sight word knowledge continues to grow independently. This occurs primarily because students read widely, and as they read they are exposed to words repeatedly; those words gradually become sight words. To expedite this process, you need to provide many opportunities for your students to read a wide range of texts.

Instruction in vocabulary development continues, for few relationships have been so clearly documented as the relationship between word meanings and reading performance. The more words your students know, the better they read. Continue developing word meanings and providing opportunities for students to use their new words in reading and writing.

Metacognitive Strategies

All four metacognitive strategies are emphasized in the upper grades: initiating strategies, during-reading strategies, post-reading strategies, and study strategies.

Initiating Strategies   You will continue to emphasize how to activate background knowledge of the topic and how to predict in the upper grades. For instance, you might help students activate prior knowledge of the topic in preparation for a story on mummies by saying, "Today we have a video clip on mummies. I know many of you think of horror movies when I say mummies, and that's valid—there are often mummies in horror movies. However, today we're going to read about the process of mummifying people. Start thinking about what you know about mummifying people as we watch the video clip. Take notes on what you didn't know. Later, we will learn more from our reading selection." The important element is to start students thinking about the process of mummifying people.

During-Reading Strategies   During-reading strategies are grouped into two categories: monitoring and fix-it strategies for word recognition, vocabulary, and getting the author's meaning. The strategies in these categories are introduced and taught at earlier grade levels. They are maintained and reviewed in the upper grades, particularly in the reading of content materials in academic subjects such as English, social studies, science, and mathematics.

Post-Reading Strategies   Organizing and evaluating content are both post-reading strategies taught in the upper grades. Organizing content is important because this is where students restructure information found in texts and store it in long-term memory for future use. This strategy helps counter rote memory and starts the process of understanding and remembering through conscious grouping and storing. Teachers at this level continue to maintain the organizing strategies of classifying paragraphs, determining main ideas, and drawing conclusions developed in earlier grades.

Beyond these things, though, you should develop your students' critical reading. Critical reading involves making judgments about what is read based on the knowledge that something is not necessarily true just because it appears in print and that writers sometimes compose text to persuade readers to do or believe something. Critical reading is taught throughout the grades, usually as a post-reading comprehension strategy, but it is emphasized more in the upper grades. Teachers want their students not only to make judgments, but to be enthusiastic about what they agree with, to get angry at writers they disagree with, to feel justified about modifying positions with which they disagree, and so on. Hence, in the upper grades they not only help students make post-reading judgments as in earlier grades, but also develop new concepts and responsible responses associated with critical reading.

For instance, you might focus on connotative language, that is, language that triggers emotional responses. Its opposite is denotative language, which refers to the use of neutral terms that tend to be objective in nature. To illustrate, saying that a person is slim is a use of denotative language; saying that the person is skinny is a use of connotative language. Calling a person proud has a positive connotation; calling a person arrogant has a negative connotation. Through skillful use of denotative and connotative language, writers subtly influence a reader's feelings about a person, topic, or issue. Consequently, plan instruction that familiarizes students with connotative language techniques and shows them how to make their own decisions about issues despite an author's choice of words. Example 19.2 illustrates how to do this.

A second way in which authors influence readers is through using a set of techniques known as propaganda devices. These techniques, which are listed in Figure 19.1, are used to influence readers in much the same way as connotative language. You should make sure upper grade students are aware of these techniques as they read.

When teaching critical reading, try to make your students aware that writers can use the language system to influence their feelings and opinions, and that good readers can recognize these techniques and avoid being unwittingly influenced. Consequently, teach your upper grade students the propaganda techniques writers use and how to make independent judgments about a writer's objectivity in presenting information.

Study Strategies   Teachers in upper grades emphasize study strategies to handle students' unique study demands. The first category focuses on study habits. For study habits you teach your students to use their free time efficiently. Help them estimate available study time, prioritize study assignments, and make a time budget that distributes available time according to priorities.

A second category focuses on reading rate. Students who are falling behind everyone else may need to make more efficient use of their study time. Since the study load is typically light in elementary school and students are not routinely expected to spend their free time studying until they get to the upper grades, it is not unusual that this kind of problem arises. Upper grade students can learn to control the problem by using a variety of reading rates and by organizing their free time.

Using a variety of reading rates is not the same as speed reading. In fact, speed reading has no real place in the elementary reading curriculum because it is highly specialized and of limited use. Adjusting the rate of reading, however,

EXAMPLE 19.2 How to Develop Understandings about How Word Choice Influences Meaning

Background	You want students to reflect after reading on how authors choose words that influence readers' feelings about the topic at hand.
Lesson Sequence	
Introduction	Show examples of text in which authors have used emotion-laden, biased, stereotyped, or mood words to influence readers. Discuss the need to understand such words so that readers will not be unknowningly manipulated.
Modeling	Read sample pairs of sentences such as the following: He *quickly* put away his books. He *frantically* put away his books. Explain how the italicized word is objective and neutral in the first sentence and is emotion-laden and suggestive in the second sentence (it causes readers to associate haste and panic with the student). Discuss how you came to agree or disagree with the author's word choice, and how you decided for yourself about the issue at hand.
Interaction with students	Present a series of similar sentences such as: The *new* tool was on the table. The *new-fangled* tool was on the table. Have students do as you did, talking out loud about whether the italicized words are objective or are designed to trigger emotional responses and influence opinion.
Closure	Return to the examples you used in the introduction and have students use their understanding to determine whether the authors are trying to influence their thinking.
Desired Outcome	When reading real text, students will recognize when authors are using connotative language to influence them and will make objective post-reading decisions about the topic rather than being influenced by the author's choice of words.

FIGURE 19.1 Propaganda Devices

Glittering generalities General statements, the exact meanings of which are not clear.

Bandwagon Statements that encourage one to follow the crowd.

Authority endorsement Statements in which an authority recommends use, i.e., company president, etc.

Hero endorsement Statements in which a hero or heroine recommends use, i.e., sports star, movie star, etc.

Plain folk Statements that identify a product or position with the average person.

Name-calling Statements that assoicate a product or position with something that is disliked or undesirable.

Wealthy endorsement Statements that associate a product or position with an exclusive, well-to-do group.

---

is something all students can learn to do, and it is applicable to many content area reading situations. It involves teaching your students to read at a normal pace if the materials are easy and are being read for recreational purposes, at a slow pace if the materials are difficult and are being read for factual information, at a rapid, skimming rate when looking for a key word or key idea, and at a very rapid scanning pace when previewing material. By adjusting the reading rate to the purpose for reading and to the difficulty of the material, students can make much better use of their study time. To teach reading rates, you must explain to students that there are various rates, show them how to move their eyes more quickly across the page, and show them how to move at different rates depending on what they are trying to find out. Most important, you must provide practice in reading material at different rates. Example 19.3 is an example of how to organize a lesson on reading rate.

A third category of study strategies is locational skills, taught to help students locate information. For instance, students may need to find information in a particular type of book, graphic material, or other reference information storage device typically found in libraries and other public agencies. When this occurs, they need to stop and think, "What do I know about finding information in this situation?" Locational skills are taught to answer that question.

EXAMPLE 19.3   How to Teach Students to Read and Study Efficiently

Background	In a class on various forms of written communication, you have asked students to read several different kinds of text in preparation for the next lesson. The kinds of text include encyclopedia articles, newspaper articles, fiction books, magazine articles, and speeches written by politicians. You want to help them study efficiently.
Lesson Sequence	
Introduction	In the reading assignment, make sure that each student gets at least two different types of text to read. Emphasize the need for reading both while also using study time efficiently.
Modeling	Demonstrate how to tie reading speed to the purpose for reading and to the difficulty of the material. Explain how to make this decision and how to think about reading rate as you read the text.
Interaction with students	Have students examine their tests and explain how they decide how fast to read and how they monitor their reading.
Closure	Have students use various reading rates when reading the various forms of written communication.
Desired Outcome	When students have assignments to read they will examine the difficulty of the text and the purpose of the assignment and then select an appropriate reading rate.

Upper grade students need to learn a variety of locational skills in order to locate information efficiently. You should provide instruction in these strategies following the format for direct instruction. Example 19.4 illustrates how to teach one such skill.

The fourth category of study strategies is organizing. Organizing strategies help students put information into order; they include note taking and outlining. To illustrate, Example 19.5 provides a sample summarizing lesson.

The final category of study strategies is remembering. Remembering strategies help students recall information and include systematic reading techniques such as SQ3R. Direct instruction can be used to teach these strategies.

Role of the Basal

Because reading is seldom taught during a separate period as it is in the earlier grades, reading in upper grades is integrated into the content areas and, sometimes, is associated with literature studies conducted in English class. As such, the prevalent textbook is not a basal reading text, but rather a text for the content: a social studies text, a science text, a literature text.

Consequently, basal reading textbooks are found less frequently in the upper grades. Instead, when you teach reading strategies such as critical reading

---

EXAMPLE 19.4 How to Teach Locational Skills

Background	Your students are completing a social studies unit on regions of the United States. Each student has volunteered to make an oral report on one particular region and what it is famous for. You help them understand how to get all the information they need from the social studies textbook.
Lesson Sequence	
Introduction	Discuss the task of locating in the textbook the information about specific regions of the country. Suggest that a quick way to answer the question "How am I going to find the information I need?" is to use the index.
Modeling	Model for students the mental steps you go through in using the index to find specific information about a topic. Explain what you are thinking at each step so they can do what you did.
Interaction with students	Give students tasks similar to the ones they will pursue in their reports on regions of the country. Have them demonstrate how they would do as you did to locate the information in the textbook.
Closure	Have students use the index to locate the information each needs to make the required oral report on regions of the country.
Desired Outcome	When faced with the need to locate specific information in a textbook, students will successfully use the index.

EXAMPLE   19.5   How to Teach Students to Organize Information Using Summarization

Background	In a class on the lives of famous American presidents, students have been assigned to read short biographies of selected presidents. You want them to organize the essential points by summarizing them.
Lesson Sequence	
Introduction	When students have finished reading the biographies, set the purpose for summarizing by emphasizing the need to organize information into manageable chunks.
Modeling	Show students how you summarize the main events and themes in the life of persons they read about by puttings all the details into categories and then labeling the categories.
Interaction with students	Have students demonstrate the same mental steps in summarizing what they have read. Have them explain their reasoning so you have a window into their thinking and can provide appropriate assistance if they get off track.
Closure	Use students' summaries as the next step in the unit on American presidents.
Desired Outcome	When students are trying to organize content information, they will summarize it using a strategy that calls for categorizing.

---

or study strategies, have students apply what they learn in a content area text rather than in a selection from a basal textbook. However, decision making is much the same. Use a modified directed reading lesson (MDRL) as you would in the lower grades, but apply it to a textbook instead of to a basal selection.

ACTIVITIES TO DEVELOP PROCESS GOALS

Here are some activities you can use to supplement your teaching of process goals, particularly critical reading and study skills, in fifth through eighth grade. Be cautioned that these activities should be used in conjunction with a literate environment and that they should not be used in isolation from real reading situations.

1. Have students compile a reading notebook containing excerpts from their reading that are unusually expressive. Have them use expressive language in their own writing as a way to increase their sensitivity to how word choice can influence meaning.

2. Have students compare the language of an editorial column with that of a news article on the same topic to increase understanding of the need to be critical when reading.

3. Have students find an article that arouses emotional response. Have them rewrite it in their own style as a straight newspaper article. This will help them understand how text can be used to influence readers.

4. Have students compare the quality of advertised goods by noting what is omitted from various ads. Note the use of propaganda devices.

5. Have students identify examples of technical vocabulary used in various types of articles (e.g., foreign policy, sports, business news) and the way this influences meaning getting.

6. Have students write an article persuading people to their point of view by using biased words and propaganda devices.

7. To help students with reading rate, give students an entire page from a newspaper. Have them find, as quickly as possible, an article about some subject you have discussed in a story. Time them. To increase their ability to quickly spot articles in which they are interested, have them select a subject and then list as many key words as possible for that subject to help them identify articles on it.

8. At the upper grade levels it is useful to study homonyms or pairs of words that sound and look alike but have different meanings. Present students with a list of words that are frequently confused. Develop the meanings and have students use the words in sentences. Give such words as: *alleys, allies; aloud, allowed; bare, bear; board, bored; borough, burrow; bough, bow; bridal, bridle; cell, sell; break, brake; course, coarse; desert, dessert; except, accept; lose, loose; lesson, lessen; peace, piece; cue, queue; quiet, quite; receipt, recipe; rein, rain; sensible, sensitive; site, sight; tide, tied.*

9. To develop sensitivity to word choice in conveying meaning, have students list words found in their reading which they think may some day disappear from our language. Examples: *pullover, skillet.* They may also list new words or phrases that have come into common use. Example: *yuppie.*

10. Have students locate and organize information from three or four authorities on a given subject, and then list the various facts each advances to support his or her opinion. This combines the use of study strategies and critical reading.

11. Have students evaluate the reliability of articles by judging the source (e.g., the president said, the White House announced, an informed spokesman said, all Washington believes, etc.). Rank the reliability of the sources.

12. Have students pick an editorial and list all the persuasive language used. Have them write their own editorial for some subject covered on the editorial page.

13. Have students pick an editorial and list the following: The nature of the problem, facts supporting and contradicting the writer's position, and opinions supporting and contradicting the writer's position.

14. To help develop students' abilities to locate information using an index, give students a list of questions in each of which one word is underlined. This is a key word. Have them draw two lines under another word in each question that would also be a key word to look for in an index. For example:

> What percentage of the industry in <u>Kentucky</u> is devoted to <u>coal</u> mining?

> What is the value of the annual <u>orange</u> crop in the state of <u>Florida</u>?

> Do the seasons affect the formation of <u>icebergs</u> in the <u>North Atlantic</u> Ocean?

15. Have students predict the response of a governmental official or agency to a current news event. Discuss why critical reading is important when reading such responses.

16. To develop students' use of a table of contents, have them open a book. Ask questions that may be answered from the table of contents, such as, "Is there a chapter in this book about mammals? On what page is the chapter? How many pages are there in the chapter?"

Much upper grade reading is done in content area textbooks.

DEVELOPING CONTENT GOALS

Content goals are especially emphasized in the upper grades because the curriculum at this level focuses on content-area subjects such as social studies, English, and science. Indeed, the purpose of reading in these subjects is to understand and be able to answer questions about such content.

Since much of upper grade reading instruction occurs in subject area classrooms, it is often referred to as content-area reading, from instruction provided by subject-matter teachers to help students understand the content of textbooks being read in those areas. Content-area reading, like content goals, can be divided into two major categories: recreational and functional. Recreational reading occurs mostly in English classes where students read and study literature, whereas functional reading occurs mostly in subjects such as social studies and science where students read textbooks loaded with factual information. In both types of classes, use various guided reading techniques such as DRL or DRTA to ensure that students comprehend their texts.

There are special problems associated with developing content goals in upper grade reading. For instance, when teaching literature in the upper grades, good authors use special literary devices, such as foreshadowing, flashbacks, symbolism, and allegory, and they employ special language forms, such as idioms,

---

EXAMPLE 19.6 How to Teach Students to Interpret Literary Devices to Comprehend Content of Recreational Text

Background	The book *The Island of the Blue Dolphins* by Scott O'Dell contains many idioms that must be understood in order to understand the story. You decide to teach your students how to interpret idioms.
Lesson Sequence	
Introduction	After introducing the novel, point out in the text several examples of idioms (such as "night had fallen"). Tell students that the author uses several idioms in his story and that you are going to show them how to interpret idioms.
Modeling	Give several examples of idioms and model how you use your background experience and the context of the passage to interpret them figuratively rather than literally. Explain your thinking so that students have an opportunity to use your model when they try a similar passage.
Interaction with students	Provide several more examples of text containing idioms. Have students do as you did in figuring out what the idioms mean.
Closure	As students read sections of *The Island of the Blue Dolphins,* point out the idioms and have them interpret their meaning in the context of the passage.
Desired Outcome	Given an example of literature in which an author uses idioms, students will be able to interpret the author's meaning in that passage.

---

similes, metaphors, and onomatopoeia. These literary devices are best taught while reading literature. Example 19.6 illustrates what such a lesson might look like.

Similarly, when using functional texts, you can apply techniques such as a DRL. However, the increased complexity of reading material in upper grades often means that additional guidance is needed. For instance, you can guide functional reading by teaching a technique called question-answer relationships, also known as QARs. Since much upper grade reading is guided by questions asked by authors and teachers, the QAR technique helps students decide where answers to various types of questions might be found. For instance, teach your students that answers can be found in a sentence on the page (right there) or in several sentences or paragraphs (think and search) or in your own prior knowledge (on your own). Hence, when faced with the task of answering questions in functional texts, students think about the question, its relationship to what is said in the text, and where to go to find the answer. A sample lesson on teaching the QAR technique to upper grade students is contained in Example 19.7.

EXAMPLE   19.7   How to Teach Students to Use QARs to Comprehend the Context of Functional Text

Background	In a science class on systems of the body, students have been directed to read a chapter in their science text and answer the questions found at the end of the chapter. You want your students to use question-answer relationships (QARs) as an aid for finding the correct answer.
Lesson Sequence	
Introduction	After the purposes of the science unit have been set, explain to students that they will more easily find the answers to the questions if they use a technique called QARs.
Modeling	Demonstrate how you identify whether the answer to a question requires one of three strategies: right there (because the answer is found right on the page), think and search (because the answer requires information from more than one sentence or paragraph), or on my own (because the answer is not in the selection, but instead is found in the reader's own prior knowledge). Explain how you thought about the question, the information in the text, and where to find the answer.
Interaction with students	Give students samples of text and related questions. Have them explain how they looked through the information provided in the text and then decided how to answer the question. Gradually increase the complexity of the text material as students become more proficient at answering questions.
Closure	Have students apply their understanding of QARs in answering the questions at the end of the science chapter on systems of the body.
Desired Outcome	When required to answer questions about textual material, students will first analyze the question in terms of where the answer is to be obtained.

You can also guide students' reading of functional text by giving them study guides. Study guides are precisely what the name implies: guides to the study of the material in the text. It is helpful for you to prepare your own study guides, gearing them to a particular chapter or text. For instance, if a science chapter on classifying animals is organized in a particularly complex way, provide a study guide that directs students to particularly relevant sections of the text. If a social studies text requires literal thinking at one point, requires thinking about implied relationships at another, and requires generalizations beyond the text at another, write a study guide that cues students to the kind of thinking required in each section. If you want your students to pay particular attention to certain charts and illustrations or certain sections of the text, write a study guide directing them to those particular materials. Study guides can take many forms: lists of questions; matching tasks; simple directions for what to do first, second, and third; complex charts that students must complete as they read. Whatever their form, their purpose is to help students comprehend functional text.

A third technique for guiding students' reading of functional text is using structured overviews, which are particularly useful for text that introduces many new words. (Figures 2.1 and 2.2 are a type of structured overview.) Structured overviews usually consist of a schematic diagram of the important words in the text and show how these words are related to each other. Such overviews enable students to preview and relate the major ideas that will be covered in their reading and thereby create expectations that are helpful in comprehending the text. Example 19.8 illustrates how to use structured overviews.

There are many modifications of QARs, study guides, and structured overviews that you can develop and use when teaching content subjects using functional text. All these modifications have one thing in common, however—they are all attempts by you to direct your students' comprehension of targeted content.

ACTIVITIES TO DEVELOP CONTENT GOALS

Here are some activities you can use to develop content goals in fifth through eighth grade.

1. Have students follow published weather reports for your location for an extended period and then try to account for them by applying meteorological theories found in relevant functional text. Have them try forecasting the weather.

2. Have students use functional text to identify examples of social and technological changes by comparing historical accounts of some event or activity with its contemporary counterpart. Some examples of issues that have persisted in American history include:

Isolationism vs. foreign involvement

How wealth is distributed

EXAMPLE 19.8   How to Use Structured Overviews to Ensure Comprehension of Functional Text

Background	You want your students to read the appropriate chapter in the social studies textbook on the branches of the federal government and how the system of checks and balances works. You are concerned about the heavy conceptual load and decide to use a structured overview.
Lesson Sequence	
Introduction	Select the words in the chapter that represent the key concepts about how the branches of the federal government work, and arrange them into a network of concepts that shows the relationship of one concept to another and the relationship of these concepts to previously learned ideas. Encourage students to add related ideas from their own prior knowledge.
Modeling	While showing the structured overview, talk about the concepts, their relationships to each other, and how these concepts are the framework for the chapter to be read.
Interaction with students	As students begin reading sections of the chapter and encounter the various concepts in the structured overview, have them discuss how one concept is tied to another, how new information is added to old information, and how their prior knowledge is expanded.
Closure	After the chapter has been read, modify the structured overview to reflect the new ideas that emerged during discussion. Display this modified overview and discuss it as a means for summarizing the chapter.
Desired Outcome	Given a content area text on a given topic, students will understand the relationships among various key concepts.

Race relations

Civil liberties

Industrialization vs. conservation

The balance of power between state and federal governments

3. Have students choose an item of current interest or concern and read a variety of functional and recreational text on it.

4. Have students collect folklore such as rope-jumping rhymes, mottoes, counting out rhymes, legends, myths, or folk songs related to the area as a way to develop understanding of various forms of recreational text.

FIGURE 19.2 Sample teaching unit on whales.

Theme: Developing understandings about whales as mammals who live in water

Objectives:
1.   Provide opportunities to explore the world of whales
2.   Expand knowledge about informational books about whales
3.   Use informational books as a stimulus for reading, writing, and conversations
4.   Provide opportunities for researching, developing, and presenting papers to class members
5.   Develop understandings about the roles and responsibilities of presenters and active listeners during report presentations
6.   Develop conceptual understandings about communication and the relationships among reading, writing, and conversations
7.   Develop inquiry as an ongoing reading and listening strategy
8.   Develop the understandings of the structure of report writing
9.   Develop vocabulary about whales
10.   Provide opportunities for the students to work through the literacy cycle from guided reading and writing to publishing

Summary:

After expressing interest in whales, the students generated lists of the concepts they knew about whales and then generated questions about what they wanted to know about whales. This knowledge and set of questions led to the generation of new knowledge about whales as the students moved through the literacy cycle. As information was shared during lessons, the students noted new information, commented on what they had learned, and generated questions about whales. The new information was periodically placed in a cognitive structure, providing a visual map of the accumulating knowledge about whales while conceptual understandings that reading, writing, and conversations are ways of communicating information and that the language modes are interrelated were developed. The strategies of question generating and answer seeking, semantic maps and composing, and the skills of vocabulary development and report structures were developed and used as needed throughout the unit. The unit culminated in a research seminar where the students interactively discussed their research on whales.

> The whales unit was developed by Laura Roehler and Meredith McClellan at Spartan Village Elementary Professional Development School, East Lansing, MI.

---

5.   To develop understanding of how to use functional text such as road maps, have students plan an automobile trip they would like to take. Use road maps to determine exact routes.

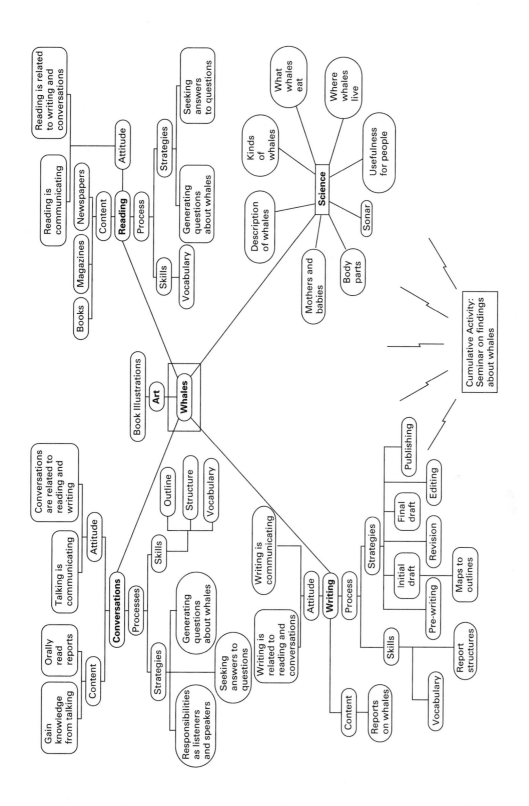

461

6. Have students use various forms of functional text to create travel brochures.

7. Analogous stories written in the manner of old favorites offer a challenge to older students and help them learn to use various forms of recreational text. Edward Lear's nonsense limericks can lead to original limericks and Rudyard Kipling's *Just So Stories* to other reports on how something happened.

8. Hold panel discussions of various kinds of recreational text. Even though no two members of the panel may have read the same book, students can discuss stories in terms of problems faced by main characters. They can compare stories with one another and react in terms of the kind of solution presented in each story: Did the solution involve magic, accident, or effort on the part of the particular character who is being discussed? Would the students have handled the problem in a different way if they had been there? Why or why not? How is each solution different from (or the same as) solutions mentioned by other members of the panel?

9. As a way to broaden understanding of functional text, select a topic and search for original manuscripts, old page proofs, first editions of books, book jackets, taped interviews with authors and other interesting persons in the community, or any other documentation related to the topic. Have students write history from original sources.

10. Have students keep diaries about memorable historical experiences as if they had lived through the period being read about. Add the diaries to the functional text resources available for studying the topic.

INTEGRATED READING AND WRITING

Upper grade English, social studies, mathematics, and science teachers should involve students in writing activities associated with their content area. Most of the reading and writing that occurs in fifth through eighth grade is embedded in topical units from content areas. Social studies teachers may have units on the Civil War, on the development of laws, or on the relationship between geography and economics; science teachers may have units on simple machines, electricity, or on photosynthesis. Although these units primarily focus on content goals associated with social studies and science, they also include reading and writing outcomes. This is because teachers intentionally structure their content-area units to include reading and writing. Following are two examples of such units. The first example, found in Figure 19.2, is an example of a unit on whales. The second one, in Figure 19.3, is more detailed and is taught as a social studies unit. It includes both reading and writing.

FIGURE 19.3   Sample Teaching Unit: Resolution of Conflicts

LEVEL
Fifth through eighth grade, application stage

OBJECTIVES
Content Objective: Given the opportunity to read literature in which conflicts are encountered, students catalog ways conflict is dealt with.
Attitude Objective: Given opportunity to read about conflict in human encounters, students will state how reading can clarify and help them understand their own feelings and emotions.
Process Objectives: Given literature containing incidents which can be viewed from various points of view, students construct meaning from one perspective and then for the other.

Given a series of conflicts caused by differing points of view, students will employ techniques of persuasive writing to write a position paper on the degree to which differing points of view are at the root of most conflicts.

Given a series of literary experiences dealing with conflicts, students will draw conclusions about how they can apply what they have learned to their own lives.

CULMINATING ACTIVITY
Based on the results of their reading, students apply what they have learned from their reading by using it to resolve the conflicts in their own lives which they identified at the outset of the unit.

DAY 1:
Warm-up activity: Engage students in conversation about the conflicts they have experienced and are currently experiencing in their lives. Have students discuss their feelings about these conflicts. Establish the fact that frustration often accompanies such conflicts, especially when we do not know how to resolve them. Suggest that some of that frustration might be diminished if we could read about others who have had similar conflicts.
Reading-writing activity: Introduce a book that focuses on conflict and resolutions such as *My Brother Sam Is Dead* by James Lincoln Collier and Christopher Collier (New York: Fourwinder Press, 1974).
Focusing Activity: Have students categorize their various conflicts and list them. Establish that the reading will be pursued in order to find examples of how others have resolved conflicts similar to these.

DAY 2
Reading-writing activity: Students read the book. Teacher conducts conversations about various incidents with individual students, helping them identify the relationship between conflicts in the book and their own conflicts which they had identified the day before.

DAY 3

Warm-up discussion activity: Have students discuss their feelings about the book, especially those that relate to the characters.

Reading-writing activity: Have students categorize the feelings that were expressed and group those feelings according to various character's (father, Tim) points of view. Have students conclude with written statements of the varying points of view.

Assessment: Teach the students who cannot determine points of view.

DAY 4

Discussion activity: Sam's brother, Tim, was often asked to state publicly which side he was on. Using this as a springboard, tell the class to generate other areas of conflict with which they are familiar (weekend privileges, propositions to be voted on, school rules, etc.). For each topic provided, create an affirmative statement and a negative statement. Assign students to collaborative groups, one group taking the affirmative position, the other the negative position.

Collaborative group activity: Have students collaborate to develop their positions using examples and elaborations to support them.

DAYS 5 & 6

Discussion activity: Have students discuss how Tim had to defend his point of view. Using the examples generated, instruct students in persuasive writing.

Discussion activity: Have students discuss how Tim had to defend his point of view. Using the examples generated, instruct students in persuasive writing.

Strategy instruction: Instruct students in components of persuasive writing, i.e., persuasive writing contains a statement indicating the importance of the audience, examples, and elaborations that support the positions, and an appeal for the audience to act on the position.

Writing-reading activity: Have students collaborate to write a position paper using the components of persuasive writing.

DAY 7

Discussion activity: Have students review the varying points of view and how that led to intrapersonal conflicts within the characters.

Reading-writing activity: Have students list the conflicts in the story *My Brother Sam Is Dead* and support each stated conflict with examples.

DAYS 8 & 9

Discussion activity: The story *My Brother Sam Is Dead* contains three types of conflict: intrapersonal conflicts within individuals who were torn between different points of view; personal conflicts among family members who believed differently; and national conflicts among those who wanted linkage with England and those who wanted to separate. Have students discuss these conflicts in terms of how people try to persuade others to their view.

These include appeals to authority (credibility or power of the source), motivational appeals (needs, fears, etc. of the receiver), and substantive appeals (relations between phenomenon such as cause and effect, analogy, and deductive or inductive reasoning). For instance, on page 6 of the book, Sam's father said, "In my house I will decide what constitutes treason." His argument depends on his perceived authority. Center discussion around questions such as, When can conflict be handled by talk? How many of the conflicts in the book could have been resolved by talk? What parallel examples of national, intrapersonal, or interpersonal conflict can be identified? Which of these can be resolved through talk?

Focusing activity: Teach a strategy lesson on how to draw conclusions. Use as motivation for the lesson the fact that they will be drawing conclusions the next day—that, specifically, they will be concluding how the conflicts they read about relate to their own conflicts. At the conclusion of the lesson, assign students to use their strategy in preparation for the culminating activity.

Culminating Activity: Have a conversation with the students about the various conflicts encountered in the reading they did. Identify those conflicts that relate to their own as identified on the first day of the unit. Have them use their strategy for drawing conclusions to conclude how the conflicts in the stories they read can be useful in resolving their own conflicts. For each of their own conflicts which apply, determine a way in which the conflict could be resolved, using what was learned in their reading.

ADDITIONAL INTEGRATED READING AND WRITING ACTIVITIES

Here are some additional activities you can use to supplement your integration of reading and writing.

1. Provide pictures in which an emotion is clearly illustrated (exaltation, anger, happiness, etc.). Have students discuss what events led to the emotion and then write a story that climaxes with this emotion. Have stories read in collaborative groups to judge if the story line is appropriate and to provide feedback about the best sections.

2. Have students write "think-pinks" (two one-syllable words that rhyme, such as *sad lad*) and provide definitions (What is an unhappy boy?). They make books with the questions on one page and the answers on the next page. "Thinky-pinkies (two-syllable words) can also be written. (What is an angry devil? A steamin' demon.) "Thinkity-pinkities" can also be written (What is an exact car accident? A precision collision.)

3. Have students read a mystery story, such as the one about Encyclopedia Brown (*Encyclopedia Brown and the Case of the Dead Eagles,*), by Donald J. Sobal), either individually or in groups. Discuss different endings

that could have occurred. Have students answer "what-if" questions. Have students write their new ending for the story.

4. Have students read a number of ghost stories (*The Haunted Trailer*, by Robert Arthur, *Ghost Story*, by Genevieve Gray, *Hix House*, by Betty Levine). Have them discuss what makes ghost stories scary and then write ghost stories using the results of the discussion.

5. Have students discuss sayings such as the following: Sometimes you get more by giving; It's better to give than to receive; The grass is always greener on the other side of the fence; You only get what you take for yourself. Have students select a saying and write a short critical essay about it. Then have other students read and critique the essay.

6. After sharing a book together, have students write a letter from one of the book's characters to another, describing what happened after the story ended. Example: Using the character Kit in *Witch of Blackberry Pond* (by Elizabeth Speare), a student might write to a cousin about what happened after the witch trial.

7. Have students create lists of things to do before they finish school. Compile the lists in a book and note when each item is completed. Add to the list when convenient.

8. Have students create poems and compile concrete poem books made up of poetry formatted to visually reflect the subject of the poem. Example:

m

erry

christma

shappynewy

earmerrychristma

shappynewyearmerryc

hris

tmas

happ

ynew

year

9. Have students place themselves in the role of a famous sports person (a tennis player, gymnast, runner, etc.) who drops his racket, falls off the parallel bars, or trips during the last 10 yards. Discuss what the player might do, think, and say. Have students write a poem using these circumstances.

10. Read the book *The King Who Rained*, then discuss figures of speech. Brainstorm figures of speech such as, I've got a frog in my throat, I'm a little hoarse (horse), I'm playing bridge, etc. Have students write and illustrate their own books and then read them to younger children.

CHARACTERISTICS OF AN INSTRUCTIONAL DAY

In the upper grades, school is usually departmentalized according to subject matter areas and students are often grouped by ability. Consequently, rather than spending all day with one teacher and a heterogeneous group of students, upper grade students see several different teachers each day and are often homogeneously grouped with other students of similar ability. All this is further complicated by the fact that in many school districts there is no formal reading instruction in the upper grades except for those students who are reading well below grade level. Each content-area teacher provides instruction in the attitude, process, and content goals.

The unique characteristics of the upper grades greatly influences the reading instruction provided there. Because reading instruction is confined to content area textbooks, it is not unusual for both students and teachers to begin ignoring reading. However, if students are to move through the application stage of developmental reading growth and go on to the power stage, teachers must consciously integrate into their content instruction appropriate attitude and process goals.

SUMMARY

Upper grade reading instruction is often dramatically different from instruction at earlier levels. Not only are students in a new building, where they move from teacher to teacher rather than stay with one teacher all day, they often do not have a subject designated as "reading." Instead, upper grade content-area teachers integrate reading instruction into the teaching of their content specialty, a technique referred to as content-area reading. The focus, therefore, is on content goals, particularly as they relate to subjects being taught in the middle or junior high school. However, process goals continue to be emphasized, especially critical reading and study strategies, and attitude goals also receive emphasis. Since a typical instructional day in the upper grades is divided into separate periods for separate subjects, the hardest thing about teaching reading at this level is integrating reading instruction with content in ways that help students develop wholistic understandings about reading.

SUGGESTED ADDITIONAL READING

ARMBRUSTER, B., ANDERSON, T., ARMSTRONG, J., WISE, M., JANISEH, C., & MEYER, L. (1991). Reading and questioning in content area lessons. *Journal of Reading Behavior, 23*(1), 35–59.

BARROW, L. H., KRISTO, J. V., & ANDREW, B. (1984). Building bridges between science and reading. *Reading Teacher, 38*(2), 188–192.

BERGQUIST, L. (1984). Rapid silent reading: Techniques for improving rate in intermediate grades. *Reading Teacher, 38*(1), 50–53.

CARR, E., DEWITZ, P., & PATBERG, J. (1989). Using cloze for inference training with expository text. *Reading Teacher, 42*(6), 380–385.

CONLEY, M. (1992). *Content reading instruction.* New York: McGraw-Hill.

CUNNINGHAM, P., & CUNNINGHAM, J. (1987). Content area reading-writing lessons. *Reading Teacher, 40,* 506–513.

DEGLER, L. S. (1978). Using the newspaper to develop reading comprehension skills. *Journal of Reading, 21*(4), 339–342.

DWYER, E. J. (1982). Guided reading in poetry: Combining aesthetic appreciation and development of essential skills. *Reading Psychology, 3*(3), 261–270.

FLOOD, J. (1986). The text, the student and the teacher: Learning from exposition in middle schools. *Reading Teacher, 39,* 784–791.

FREEMAN, R. H. (1983). Poetry writing in the upper elementary grades. *Reading Teacher, 37*(3), 238–242.

GREENE, B. (1992). Teaching test-wiseness: Can test scores of special populations be improved? *Reading Psychology, 13*(1), 99–104.

HELMSTETLER, A. (1987). Year-long motivation in the 8th grade "reluctant" class. *Journal of Reading, 31,* 244–247.

HOLBROOK, H. T. (1985). The quality of textbooks. *Reading Teacher, 38*(7), 680–683.

LANGE, J. T. (1983). Using S2RAT to improve reading skills in the content areas. *Reading Teacher, 36*(4), 402–404.

MCWHIRTER, A. (1990). Whole language in the middle school. *Reading Teacher, 43*(3), 562–565.

SMITH, L. B. (1982). Sixth graders write about reading literature. *Language Arts, 59*(4), 357–363.

STAHL, S., & KAPINUS, B. (1991). Possible sentences: Predicting word meaning to teach content area vocabulary. *Reading Teacher, 45*(1), 36–43.

STOTT, J. C. (1982). A structuralist approach to teaching novels in the elementary grades. *Reading Teacher, 36*(2), 136–143.

SULLIVAN, J. (1986). The Global Method: Language experience in the content areas. *Reading Teacher, 39,* 664–669.

THOMPSON, L.,& FRAGER, A. (1984). Teaching critical thinking: Guidelines for teacher-designed content area lessons. *Journal of Reading, 28,* 122–127.

WIDMANN, V. F. (1978). Developing oral reading ability in teenagers through the presentation of children's stories. *Journal of Reading, 21*(4), 329–334.

WOOD, K. D., & MATEJA, J. A. (1983). Adapting secondary level strategies for use in elementary classrooms. *Reading Teacher, 36*(6), 492–496.

THE RESEARCH BASE

ANDERSON, T. H., & ARMBRUSTER, B. B. (1982). Reader and text-studying strategies. In W. Otto & S. White (Eds.), *Reading expository material.* New York: Academic Press.

ANDERSON, T. H., & ARMBRUSTER, B. B. (1984). Study skills. In P. D. Pearson (Ed), *Handbook of reading research.* New York: Longman.

ARMBRUSTER, B., ANDERSON, T., & MEYER, J. (1991). Improving content area reading using instructional graphics. *Reading Research Quarterly, 26*(4), 393–416.

BROWN, A. L., CAMPIONE, J. C., & DAY, J. C. (1981). Learning to learn: On training students to learn from text. *Educational Researcher, 10*(2), 14–21.

GAYLOR, B., & SAMUELS, S. J.   (1983). Children's use of text structure in the recall of expository material. *American Educational Research Journal, 20*(4), 517–528.

KONOPAK, B., MARTIN S., & MARTIN, M.   (1990). Using a writing strategy to enhance sixth-grade students' comprehension of content material. *Journal of Reading Behavior, 22*(1), 19–37.

SIMONSEN, S., & SINGER, H.   (1992). Improving reading instruction in the content areas. In J. Samuels & A. Farstrup (Eds.) *What research has to say about reading instruction.* 2nd ed. (pp. 200–219). Newark, DE: International Reading Association.

ACTIVITIES FOR REFLECTING, OBSERVING, AND TEACHING

Reflecting on Teaching Grades Five Through Eight

PURPOSE: A major factor in your success as a literacy instructor lies with your ability to embed the teaching of skills and strategies in genuinely important activity. The unit on resolving conflicts provided as a sample in this chapter is an example of such activity. You will need to create similar units for your own teaching. This activity is designed to give you experience in doing so.

DIRECTIONS: Using both the sample unit provided in this chapter and the suggestions provided in Chapter 14, create a unit which will involve fifth through eighth graders in authentic literate activity in pursuit of a genuine goal. Include specific content, attitude, and process objectives, and a day-to-day schedule of activity.

Watching Others Teach Reading in the Upper Grades

PURPOSE: Watching other teachers gives you ideas about how you want to do things yourself (and, sometimes, about how you do *not* want to do things). This activity is designed to help you set up an observation of a teacher of grade five, six, seven, or eight with the intent that you will extend your experience with teaching and, in the process, know how to be a better teacher yourself.

DIRECTIONS: Arrange to observe a fifth, sixth, seventh, or eighth grade teacher. In schools where instruction is departmentalized, it is usually best to watch the teacher teach the same class for several consecutive days. During these observations, note specifically the following:

- the instructional emphasis (relative to Table 19.1)

- the literate environment

- the instructional approach used, particularly as it relates to developing attitudes

- what strategies are taught and how they are taught (look particularly for comprehension strategies such as using word choice and detecting propaganda and study strategies such as efficient study, locational strategies, and organizational strategies.

- what content is taught and how it is developed

- whether activity is organized into units and, if so, the nature and characteristics of the unit

Trying It Yourself

PURPOSE: You will get better and better at teaching the more you teach. This activity is designed to help you capitalize on opportunities to expand your teaching experience.

DIRECTIONS: When observing in an upper grade classroom, look for opportunities to assist the teacher, relieve the teacher, or take over the class for the teacher. On those occasions when you can teach, use the suggestions in this chapter to guide your decisions about what to do and how to do it.

Part 5

Continued Professional Growth

One of the distinguishing characteristics of professionals is that they continue to learn and to grow. The chapter in Part 5 provides suggestions for how you can continue to learn and grow as a teacher, thereby assuring your status as a professional. When you finish this chapter, you should have an understanding of what it takes to maintain a sense of professionalism and vitality while working in the reality of classrooms.

20 Continued Professional Growth

GETTING READY

As lifelong learners, professional teachers make a conscious effort to remain professionally fresh and vibrant. Learning how to continue your professional growth throughout your career is an important part of being a teacher. This chapter describes why continued professional growth is important and makes suggestions about how to ensure that your teaching remains fresh and vital throughout your career.

FOCUS QUESTIONS

- What happens when teachers do not make conscious efforts to continue their professional growth?

- How can you assess your professional growth?

- What are some professional activities that ensure your continued professional growth?

- What personal things can you do to maintain your freshness and vibrancy as a teacher?

- What are the rewards of continuing your professional growth?

This book began by pointing out two truths about reading instruction in today's schools: First, some teachers are more effective than others, and, second, many teachers teach more like technicians than professionals. Consequently, this book has emphasized what makes teachers effective and how they can become professional decision makers who maintain cognitive control of their instruction rather than technicians who merely follow the directions in a teachers' guide.

However, no single book, course, or degree program can do all that is needed in this regard. Rather, professional decision making in teaching requires a lifetime commitment to new learning and a career-long effort to grow as a teacher. In short, when you receive your initial certification to teach, you have not finished your preparation—you have just begun it. The following sections describe some of the ways to continue your professional growth throughout your career.

ASSESSMENT PLAN

Continued professional growth depends upon how well you assess your capabilities so you can use your strengths and overcome your weaknesses. While preparing for a teaching position, you need to ask yourself: "What are my strengths and weaknesses? What needs to be worked on now? What needs to be worked on later?" This self-assessment can be structured around the following four areas: students and their needs; the reading curriculum; the role of the teacher; and the classroom environment.

Students and Their Needs This category involves assessing what you know about reading growth and your ability to apply this knowledge to students' reading needs. Do you feel knowledgeable about reading stages, instructional reading levels, the influence of verbal aptitude on reading growth, student interests, etc.? Can you effectively use these concepts in classroom teaching? Organize these into two lists, one labeled Strengths and one labeled Needs.

Reading Curriculum This category involves assessing what you know about and what you can do to improve the typical reading curriculum. Are you knowledgeable about the three instructional goals of reading? Do you have objectives and activities for each instructional goal? Are you familiar with the strengths and weaknesses of basal reading materials? Do you understand state assessment tests and standardized tests and their role in the reading curriculum? Can you effectively use these in your instruction? Add these items to your list of strengths and needs.

Role of the Teacher This category involves assessing your knowledge of the teacher's role and your ability to perform it. Can you assess students in terms of the three curricular goals? Can you provide instruction for the three goals? Can you find, develop, and organize materials for instruction? Which of the above can you do effectively? What are you concerned about? Add these to your list of strengths and needs.

Classroom Environment Finally, assess your ability to create a literate classroom environment. Do you know what constitutes a literate environment? Can you create one? Do you know how to account for and create good social-

Teachers must be able to assess their knowledge of their role and their ability to perform it.

emotional, physical, and intellectual environments? Add these to your list of strengths and needs. Figure 20.1 is a check list you can use to assess yourself.

PROFESSIONAL DEVELOPMENT PLAN

Once your self-assessment is completed, use the data to create a professional development plan. Your plan for continued professional growth can be divided into two areas. Begin by setting goals for yourself. How can you improve your classroom work based on your assessment of yourself? Your planning should include both long- and short-term goals, since both are crucial to lifelong professional growth. Successful completion of short-term goals provides incentive and rewards for continuing the effort, and successful completion of long-term goals provides a pattern of thinking and action that supports lifelong professional growth.

You set goals as you search for ways to improve. In fact, the heart of professional growth is the ongoing search for improvement. The best teachers are the ones whose motivation to excel has them constantly looking for ways to improve. In short, they are always experimenting with better ways to do things.

FIGURE 20.1   Teacher Self-Assessment

	Strength	Need
A. Student variables		
1. Do I have knowledge of		
a. Reading stages		
b. Instructional reading levels		
c. Independent reading levels		
d. Influences on verbal learning and atitudes		
e. Student interest		
B. Curriculum variables		
1. Do I have knowledge of		
a. Instructional goals		
b. Objectives and activities for goals		
c. Strengths and weaknesses of basals		
d. State assessment tests		
e. Standardized tests		
2. Can I use		
a. Reading stages		
b. Instructional reading levels		
c. Independent reading levels		
d. Influences on verbal learning and attitudes		
e. Student interests		
C. Teacher variables		
1. Do I have knowledge of		
a. Student assessment		
b. Student instruction		
c. Environment conducive to learning		
d. Developing and organizing materials		
2. Can I use		
a. Student assessment data		
b. Instructional strategies		
c. Classroom environments conducive to learning		
d. Developed and organized materials		
D. Classroom environment		
1. Do I have knowledge of variables		
a. A literate environment		
b. Social-emotional environment		
c. Physical environment		
d. Intellectual environment		
2. Can I use		
a. Literate environment		
b. Social-emotional environment		
c. Physical environment		
d. Intellectual environment		

RESOURCES FOR IMPROVEMENT

The teaching profession offers both formal and informal resources for improvement and updating.

Formal Resources

The primary resources in this category include professional organizations, professional journals, and graduate work in universities. Professional organizations tend to divide into ones with an interest in particular kinds of problems (for example, reading problems or early childhood problems) and those with an interest in particular curricular areas (social studies, language, mathematics, etc.). All these organizations have annual conferences where teachers gather to exchange ideas and to hear speakers present information on the most recent innovations in the field. These conferences are often highly exciting, intense, and satisfying experiences where teachers obtain many ideas and return to the classroom stimulated and renewed. A list of organizations that have a particular interest in the teaching of reading are included in Figure 20.2.

Second, teachers can get new ideas and innovations from various professional journals, of which many are associated with professional organizations such as those noted in Figure 20.2, but others are published independently. In either case, these journals contain teaching and curriculum ideas that have been submitted from all over the country and, sometimes, from all over the world. By subscribing to one or more of them, you are assured of intellectual stimulation and continued growth as a teacher. Figure 20.3 contains a list of journals of particular assistance to teachers interested in improving reading and writing instruction.

FIGURE 20.2   Professional Organizations

Association for Supervision and Curriculum Development
125 N. West St.
Alexandria, VA 22314–2798

International Reading Association
800 Berksdale Road
PO Box 8139
Newark, NJ 19711

State affiliates of International Reading Association

National Council of Teachers of English
1111 Kenyon Road
Urbana, IL 61801

State affiliates of National Council of Teachers of English

FIGURE 20.3   Professional Journals

Elementary School Journal
University of Chicago Press
PO Box 37005
Chicago, IL 60637

Instruction
PO Box 6099
Duluth, MN 55806-9799

Journal of Reading
IRA 800 Berksdale Road
PO Box 8139
Newark, NJ 19711

Learning Magazine
530 University Avenue
Palo Alto, CA 94301

Reading Psychology
1010 Vermont Avenue, NW Suite 612
Washington, DC 20005

Reading Teacher
IRA
800 Berksdale Road
PO Box 8139
Newark, NJ 19711

School Library Journal
PR Bowher Co.
PO Box 67
Whitinsville, MA 01588

Finally, many colleges and universities offer programs of graduate study for teachers. These institutions offer a wide range of courses and workshops relating recent trends and findings to the problems of teaching. Participation in such graduate education is an effective way of pursuing both short-term and long-term goals. It not only broadens your perspective on your classroom work, but serves as the basis for salary increases in many states.

Informal Resources

Helpful ideas can come from a variety of informal sources: students, colleagues, your school district, and your own travel. The most accessible and possibly the most overlooked resource is your students themselves. By listening to students and questioning them about their interests and concerns, you can get many useful ideas for modifying your instruction and for incorporating student interests into your materials and activities.

A second informal resource is other teachers. Teaching is an isolated profession in which you spend most of your professional time with children, and very little with professional colleagues. Yet, interaction with colleagues such is one of the most helpful ways to maintain professional growth. One way to ensure interaction is to have a "buddy system" in which you team with another teacher from your own school or from another school in the area. You can periodically exchange ideas, materials, and innovations that have worked. This plan can also include exchanging visits to one another's classrooms. Adapting good ideas of other teachers is encouraged in teaching. If somebody else has a good idea, borrow it and see if you can make it fit your own situation; if you have a good idea, encourage your colleagues to use it with their classes. This kind of exchange promotes the growth essential for teaching.

School districts also provide informal sources for professional growth. Most school districts, for instance, provide resource centers where the most recent ideas about instructional improvements are cataloged and displayed so that teachers can use them. Many districts have "professional days" in which teachers can take time off for professional growth. A visit to another teacher's classroom is an excellent way to spend this time because it gives you another perspective on your own work. Finally, school districts offer various in-service programs. Whether attendance is voluntary or mandatory, these programs are an excellent way to develop yourself professionally. Also, many of these in-service programs are backed up by a formal, district-wide staff-development program where participation can earn you salary increases or other incentives. All such district-level activities are excellent sources of ideas and innovations.

Finally, your own travel can be a resource for growth. For instance, you could plan your travel around a professional theme, such as traveling in foreign countries to visit and compare school systems or traveling through our country with the goal of collecting local folklore for use in your classes. In short, there are many formal and informal resources available to teachers who want to grow and get better at their profession.

MONITORING AND EVALUATING PROGRESS

In addition to taking advantage of available resources for professional growth, you need to monitor and evaluate your progress toward the goals you have set as part of your professional plan. At designated points, you should sit down and examine the data you have collected regarding how well or how poorly you are achieving your goals. Data gathering and evaluation need not be formal. However, it does need to be regular and honest.

Increasing Your Impact on Students

There are many ways to collect data about your impact on students. One way is to keep careful records of your students' progress toward the goals you have set and to evaluate yourself in terms of how well your students achieve these goals. For instance, if you want students to develop certain concepts about reading, you must keep records of their progress and review these periodically. Likewise, if you want students to develop certain attitudes or to become more aware of how reading works, you must keep track of this. If you want students to become better writers, you must keep samples of their writing throughout the year and periodically review their progress. By setting goals and then reviewing the data regarding how well your students are achieving these goals, you will find yourself modifying your teaching in order to meet these goals. Such change is evidence of professional vitality and growth.

In addition to keeping track of student progress on academic work, you should also keep track of their awareness of lesson content. It is a good practice to periodically interview students after lessons, asking them what they think you

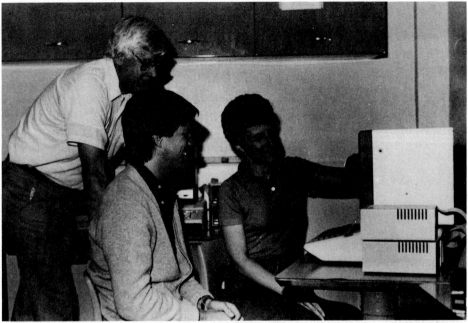

School district in-service programs help keep teachers current.

were teaching, why you were teaching it, and how to do it. If several students give responses which indicate misconceptions about the lesson, you should re-evaluate your teaching and make changes that will improve your students' awareness of what is going on during instruction.

Reflective Journals

A second way to keep track of your professional growth is to keep a reflective journal. Either daily or several times a week, write your thoughts about your progress. Note what is going well and what is not going so well. Include your ideas, thoughts, and feelings and periodically evaluate your journal and yourself. Ask yourself if you are progressing the way you want to or if there is a problem that needs to be resolved. If possible, share this information with another professional and have that person help you evaluate it. Decide with that person whether to continue as you have been or to make changes.

Self-Monitoring

A third way to monitor and evaluate your professional growth is to tape record (or videotape) your own instruction. It is very difficult to be aware of what you are doing while engaged in the act of teaching. However, you can be much more objective and perceptive when you listen to yourself or watch yourself.

It is particularly helpful if you look for only one thing at a time. For instance, listen to the tape once to determine how many times you were distracted from the main focus of the lesson; listen another time to determine whether each student was given an equal opportunity to respond, listen another time to see how explicit you were in showing students how to do the task, and so on. Each time you will note things to improve your teaching. Once you are aware of these shortcomings, you can take steps to improve them. If you are not aware, however, you can never improve. Again, sharing and discussing the results of these analyses with a colleague is better than solitary evaluation.

IMPORTANCE OF PERSONAL GROWTH

Teachers should be well-balanced people. They must not only be competent professionals, but also be interesting persons. This means that professional development is not enough—it must be accompanied by personal development.

Because teaching is such a demanding task, it can become all-absorbing. You can become so devoted to helping students achieve and grow that all of your time is allocated to professional tasks. In short, you can become a highly professional drudge.

Having a variety of personal interests helps balance the demands of classroom teaching.

This must be avoided. Teaching is person-to-person interaction and, in the final analysis, your impact on students will depend both on your professional competencies and on how interesting you are as a person. Your students' desire to interact with you will depend on how they see you as a person. Attention and respect is not awarded to drudges, it is given to teachers who are alive and vital in their private lives as well as their professional lives.

To achieve vitality as a person, you have to cultivate interests beyond the classroom. You have to know what is going on in the world around you, and you should become involved in community, state, and national affairs. This does not necessarily mean that you must be a political activist, merely that you should take an active interest in contemporary affairs. You do this by reading more than just professional journals.

Your personal development means developing your own interests and aptitudes. Because teaching is stressful and absorbing work, it is particularly important that you have a rich family and social life and that you have hobbies and activities that absorb your energies and attention once school is done. In short, you should be a multidimensional person who has a variety of interests—someone who paints, or gardens, or flies airplanes, or refinishes furniture, or runs marathons, or explores caves. These other interests will help balance the professional devotion required to be a classroom teacher.

FACING THE REALITIES

All the previously mentioned plans for continuing your professional growth are helpful. However, one major problem remains. It involves the realities of classroom life, which often force otherwise dedicated teachers to become technicians who follow prescriptions rather than professionals who exercise professional control.

It is alarming that so many teachers act like technicians. At a time when the teaching of reading must be thoughtful, we find too many teachers who are mechanical, routinized, and procedural. The result is students who respond to reading in mechanical ways, who see reading as tasks to be completed rather than genuine communication, and who rarely choose to read once school is over.

It is not accurate to say that such technical teachers are simply unwilling to put forth the necessary effort. Most teachers try hard and want to do well by their students. However, the complexities of the job simply overwhelm many teachers. There just seems to be too much to attend to and not enough help, too many demands and not enough time, too many pressures and not enough reward, and too many students who have difficulty learning and not enough techniques that work. Eventually, some teachers stop trying to be innovative and fall back on prescriptions of others, which they can follow in routinized ways.

The typical scenario proceeds something like this. A new teacher accepts a position in a school district that uses a mandated basal text program and expects high achievement on the state assessment test. The principal frequently visits the new teacher's classroom to ensure that the basal is being followed and the students are being prepared for the test. Following the lead of the veteran teachers in the building, the new teacher uses the basal text prescriptions and prepares students for the test. Instruction lacks interest or relevancy, students get bored, the success rate is low, and students become unmotivated. Soon the teacher becomes discouraged and casts about for "the answer." The school district and the state either encourage the use of another prescription or closer adherence to the one already in use. The teacher follows these directions but the results are the same. Yet another prescription is suggested; the teacher tries to implement it but has little success. The teacher's frustration and boredom continue, and eventually all signs of freshness, innovation, and vibrancy disappear. The teacher either gives in to mindless technical behavior, or gives up the profession entirely.

This is a dim picture. Does it have to be this way? We think not. The source of technical behavior in teachers is rooted in the reality of the workplace, but there are ways to deal with these realities and to fight off the pressures to become a technician. Three suggestions follow.

Be Realistic Classroom teaching in our society *is* difficult. The pressures are great and the rewards in terms of money and prestige are small. Teachers are expected to be public servants who can work miracles with large numbers of students with a minimum of resources. They must have the strength to maintain cognitive control over their own teaching while fighting off the pressures for conformity and regimentation that come from school and society. They are expected to resolve inherently unresolvable problems while working in isolation from their colleagues.

The task is difficult, and you must be realistic. You need to understand that students will not always respond with enthusiasm, that not all students make dramatic progress, that there is a bureaucracy in teaching, and that classroom teachers often seem powerless. You must also understand that there are no panaceas in teaching. There will never be one right way to teach reading to all students; we will always be seeking better ways. The nature of teaching is to constantly strive to improve.

Accept Dilemmas You must also learn that teaching is full of dilemmas. You must understand that survival in the classroom demands keeping students busy, but that this is not necessarily teaching. You must understand that your task is to demonstrate how to cognitively process language, even though no one knows for sure how this cognition occurs for different people. You must think in terms of "real world" applications of reading, even though the school district, the state, and our society seem to place more value on test scores that measure the performance of isolated skills. And you must stress cognition, strategic awareness, and mental processing when the instructional materials you are required to use often stress memory, rote, and accuracy.

Maintain a Vision Finally, you should have a vision that transcends the constraints of the workplace. Reading is more than skills and more than a subject;

you must see it as part of a language communication system. You must view the goals of reading not only as getting the message, but also as positive responses and accurate concepts of what reading is. Teaching is a person-to-person interaction that no script or machine or prescription will ever replace. It will be helpful to keep the following in mind:

1. The rewards of teaching lie in presiding over nondramatic growth, which you witness daily in various kinds of students.

2. No outside authority governs what happens when you close your classroom door and begin teaching.

3. No day will be like any other.

4. No matter how long you teach, there will always be new challenges.

5. The cliché "the youth of America is in the hands of its teachers" is not a cliché at all, but the truth.

To summarize, you must love and value teaching but not romanticize it. It is a demanding and difficult task, and progress results more from diligent planning, the reflective application of pedagogical knowledge, and tenacity in making and sticking with decisions than from flashy demonstrations, intuitive interactions, or dramatic confrontations. It can demand all your time and effort and produce few tangible results. When these realities are consciously acknowledged and dealt with, teachers can fight off burnout and the temptation to be technicians. To know what the realities are is to arm against them. If your expectations are realistic and you are prepared to deal with them, you cannot be surprised.

SUMMARY

Effective teaching is associated with vital teachers who make their own decisions and, in so doing, maintain control of their instruction. Teachers who do not make conscious efforts to remain vital by continuing their professional growth become professionally stale. Consequently, the best teachers continually search for better ways to do things, develop realistic ways to assess their own work, and develop programs of professional development for themselves. In addition, the most effective teachers make conscious efforts to be well-rounded, interesting human beings since personal development often carries over into professional work. And, finally, effective teachers are realistic about the demands of teaching. When you make the effort to continue your professional growth while also being realistic, teaching can offer you a fulfilling professional life.

SUGGESTED ADDITIONAL READING

BAILEY, M. H., & GUERRA, C. L. (1984). Inservice education in reading: Three points of view. *Reading Teacher, 38*(2), 174–176.

BEAN, R. M., & EICHELBERGER, R. T. (1985). Changing the role of reading specialists: From pull-out to in-class programs. *Reading Teacher 38*(7), 648–653.

CALDERHEAD, J. (1989). Reflective teaching and teacher education. *Teacher and Teacher Education*, *5*(1), 43–52.

CASSIDY, J. (1977). Reporting pupil progress in reading—parents vs. teachers. *Reading Teacher*, *31*(3), 294–296.

COCHRAN-SMITH, M., & LYTLE, S. (1990). Research on teaching and teacher research: The issues that divide. *Educational Researcher*, *19*(2), 2–11.

CUBAN, L. (1990). Reforming again, again and again. *Educational Researcher*, *19*(1), 3–13.

CUNNINGHAM, P. M. (1977). Match informal evaluation to your teaching practices. *Reading Teacher*, *31*(1), 51–56.

DREHER, M. J., & SINGER, H. (1985). Parent's attitudes toward reports of standardized reading test results. *Reading Teacher*, *38*(7), 624–632.

FLODEN, R., & KLINZING, H. (1990). What can research on teacher thinking contribute to teacher preparation? A second opinion. *Educational Researcher*, *19*(4), 15–20.

LAMPERT, M., & CLARK, C. (1990). Expert knowledge and expert thinking in teaching: A response to Floden and Klinzing. *Educational Researcher*, *19*(4), 21–24.

LAPP, D., FLOOD, J., & GLECKMAN, G. (1982). Classroom practices can make use of what researcher learn. *Reading Teacher*, *35*(5), 578–585.

LEINHARDT, G. (1990). Capturing craft knowledge in teaching. *Educational Researcher*, *19*(2), 18–25.

MCGAGHIE, W. (1991). Professional competence evaluation. *Educational Researcher*, *20*(1), 3–9.

RICHARDSON, V. (1990). Significant and worthwhile change in teaching practice. *Educational Researcher*, *19*(7), 10–18.

SMITH, M. (1991). Put to the test: The effect of external testing in teachers. *Educational Researcher*, *20*(5), 8–11.

VUKELICH, C. (1984). Parents' role in the reading process: A review of practical suggestions and ways to communicate with parents. *Reading Teacher*, *37*(6), 472–477.

THE RESEARCH BASE

BARNES, H., PUTNAM, J., & WANOUS, D. (1979). Learning from research adaptation. *Adapting educational research: Staff development approaches*. Normal, OK: University of Oklahoma Teacher Corps Research Adaptation Cluster.

BYRNE, B. (1991). Burnout: Investigating the impact of background variables for elementary, intermediate, secondary and university educators. *Teaching and Teacher Education*, *7*(2), 197–209.

CALDERHEAD, J. (1991). Images of teaching: Student teachers' early conceptions of classroom practice. *Teaching and Teacher Education*, *7*(1), 1–8.

DUFFY, G. & ROEHLER, L. (1986). Constraints on teacher change. *Journal of Teacher Education*, *37*(1), 55–59.

DUFFY, G., ROEHLER, L., & PUTNAM, J. (1987). Putting the teacher in control: Instructional decision making and basal textbooks. *Elementary School Journal*, *87*(3), 357-366.

MALIK, J., MUELLER, R., & MEINKE, D. (1991). The effects of teaching experience and grade level taught on teacher stress: A Lisrel analysis. *Teaching and Teacher Education*, *7*(1), 57–62.

OLSON, M., & OSBORNE, J. (1991). Learning to teach: The first year. *Teaching and Teacher Education, 7*(4), 331–344.

ROEHLER, L. (1983). Moving toward integration through inservice. In B. Busching & J. Schwartz (Eds.), *Integrating the language arts in the elementary school.* Urbana, IL: National Council of Teachers of English.

ROEHLER, L., WESSELMAN, R., & PUTNAM, J. (1984). *Training teachers for instructional change in reading: A descriptive study* (Research Series No. 143). East Lansing: Michigan State University, Institute for Research on Teaching.

SCHWAAB, J. (1969). The practical: A language for curriculum. *School Review, 79*, 1–23.

WEINSTEIN, C. (1990). Prospective elementary teachers' beliefs about teaching: Implications for teacher education. *Teaching and Teacher Education, 6*(3), 279–290.

ACTIVITIES FOR REFLECTING, OBSERVING, AND TEACHING

Reflecting on Your Professional Growth

PURPOSE: There are no observing or teaching activities associated with this chapter because it is difficult for one to observe some else's professional growth or to practice professional growth yourself. However, you can reflect on how you will continue your professional growth and set up a plan for ensuring that you do continue to grow. This activity is designed to help you do so.

DIRECTIONS: The basic premise of this chapter is that the realities of teaching often overwhelm teachers, causing them to abandon thoughtful teaching in favor of technical teaching. The focus of continued professional growth is to perpetuate the vitality and vigor of thoughtful teaching, and to fight off the temptation to be a technician who merely follows the directions of one or another teacher's manual.

The concept of "teacher as researcher" is one way to ensure that you continue to be a thoughtful and vital teacher. It means that teachers continue to learn by studying their own work. They read professional literature and attend formal and informal professional gatherings, use ideas garnered from those sources to form hypotheses about how to improve their teaching, and set up little "mini-studies" in their classrooms in which they try to systematically study their own work by collecting data about their effectiveness and then use the results of their data collection to make decisions about how to modify their instructional practices and, thereby, continue to learn and grow.

You can begin the process of "teacher as researcher" now by anticipating a way in which you might study your own practice when you have a classroom of your own. For instance, you can read professional journals such as those suggested in this chapter, looking for ideas you could try in your classroom. Using those ideas as a stimulus, you can begin planning how you might study your own work by doing the following:

1. Describe the idea as it was presented in a professional journal or in a formal or informal professional encounter.

2. State your hypothesis—your hunch of what will be improved by incorporating this idea into your teaching repertoire. Usually, you will be looking for improved literacy performance from your students, but you need to specify what exactly they will be better at if you implement this idea.

3. Describe how you will implement the idea. What will you do in your classroom?

4. What data will you collect? That is, how will you document what you did? How will you document whether your students were any better off because you did what you did?

5. How will you analyze the data? What will the data need to look like in order for you to decide that your hypothesis was correct?

6. What do you anticipate the significance will be for your work as a teacher? How do you think you will grow professionally as a result of this study? What might you change in your teaching of literacy?

Glossary

Note: Italicized words in definitions denote other entry words in the glossary.

Ability group   Teacher-assigned instructional group in which all student members have about the same reading level; used primarily for developing *content and process goals*; contrasted with collaborative groups.

Academic task   The work students engage in.

Accountability   Holding teachers and students responsible for student achievement; frequently associated with assessment testing mandated by state law.

Activate background knowledge   Accessing prior knowledge about *topic*, author's *purpose*, and text structure for the purpose of making initial predictions about what will happen; *initiating strategy*.

Activity flow   Maintaining a smooth, uninterrupted flow of classroom activities as a way of keeping students on task.

Affix   A prefix, suffix, or inflectional ending added to root word; used in *structural analysis for decoding*.

Allocated time   Designated amount of time assigned to academic content; the time when reading is normally taught, for instance.

Application   Ability to *transfer* what has been learned from the classroom to the real world; using reading strategies for reading *recreational or functional text*.

Application stage   *Stage of developing reading growth* typically associated with grades 5 through 8; curricular emphasis is on *content*, such as social studies or science; contrasted with *emergent literacy, initial mastery, expanded fundamentals, and power stages*.

Assessment   Collection of data to be used in making decision; crucial to instruction, especially *direct instruction*, because good decisions cannot be made about instructional objectives until student performance is assessed; may involve *formal or informal tests*.

Attitude   Concepts and feelings one possesses about a particular activity or idea; in this book, the concepts and feelings students possess about reading and writing.

Attitude goals   One of the three major curricular goals in reading; consist of developing a positive response to reading and an accurate *concept* of what reading is; viewed as the foundation of an effective instructional program because little can be learned unless students have accurate concepts and positive feelings about reading.

Auditory discrimination   Ability to distinguish one sound from another; in reading, for example, the ability to distinguish the sound of the letter *d* from the sound of the letter *b*; contrasted with *visual discrimination*.

Authentic Assessment   Collections of data that reflect the actual learning of students that are relevant to their lives, their families, and their community lives.

Author's chair   A technique in which a student writer is interviewed by student peers about something he or she has written.

Author's purpose   Author's reason for composing *text*; readers analyze author's purpose to aid in understanding text meaning; contrasted with *topic* and *text* structure.

Basal reading textbook   The reading textbook used in most U.S. classrooms; each text program consists of a students' edition of stories written to match the average ability level of the grade at which it is to be used, a teachers' edition containing instructional suggestion, and a variety of supplementary materials.

Basal text approach   Organizing reading instruction around the stories and books in a basal text series; students read each story in each *basal* reading *textbook* and complete associated workbook and text materials under the supervision of their teacher; contrasted with *language experience* and *literature-based reading approaches*.

Book part strategy   *Locational study strategy* used to find information in books; includes table of contents, index, glossary, etc.; contrasted with *library, reference source*, and *graphics strategies*.

Buffer   Person recruited by a teacher to assist with routine classroom tasks; can be an adult, an older student, or a student in the class.

Cognition   Act of knowing; associated with the *mental processing* readers do to make sense out of *text*.

Collaborative group/sharing   Teacher-assigned or self-started temporary grouping structure used primarily for developing *attitude goals*; students with varying abilities work together to solve a problem or to complete a project; important aspect of the *social-emotional environment;* contrasted with *ability groups.*

Combined approach   Organizing reading instruction by combining a variety of approaches; occurs both directly (with *basal text activities*) and less directly (with *language experience and literature-based reading activities*); teachers use each approach to develop specific reading goals.

Comprehension   Process of making sense of an author's or speaker's message; reconstructing an author's message for *recreational or functional* purposes.

Comprehension strategy   Used by readers to determine text meaning; includes *initiating, during-reading, and post-reading strategies;* all are *metacognitive.*

Concept   Understanding students have of a particular phenomenon; the sum of one's *direct* and *vicarious experiences* with that phenomenon; organized into a network of related understandings (the *schema/schemata* for the phenomenon).

Concept book   Children's book written to help preschool and primary grade students develop a particular idea; examples: a book on colors or a book on clouds.

Connected text   Printed matter that represents a complete message being communicated within a meaningful environment.

Connotative language   Using words that trigger emotional responses; example: "arrogant" has a negative connotation, but "confident" has a positive connotation.

Constraint   Limits on a teacher's freedom to perform various tasks of teaching; example: society has certain expectations that teachers must take into consideration when making instructional decision.

Content   Message conveyed by a *text* or speech.

Content area reading   Textbook reading done in various content areas such as science, social studies, etc.

Content goals   One of the three major curricular goals in reading; consist of guiding students to an understanding of the messages conveyed by particular *functional or recreational texts.*

Context   *Semantic* elements of *text* or speech that immediately precede or follow a sentence or word and can be analyzed to predict meaning.

Context clue   Clue embedded in *text* that helps readers decode unknown words; contrasted with *structural analysis and phonics.*

Contract   Written agreement between a teacher and a student stating what a student will be accountable for on a particular project.

Controlled text   Text created by teachers for purposes of providing students practice with a particular skill or strategy; contrasted with *natural text.*

Cooperative group   See *collaborative group.*

Critical question   Question that requires students to make a judgment about the meaning an author is conveying in *text;* requires readers to go beyond reconstructing the author's message to make a value judgment about the message; contrasted with *inferential* and *literal questions.*

Critical reading   Making a judgment about the meaning an author is conveying in *text;* requires readers to go beyond reconstructing the author's message to make a value judgment about the message; usually associated with *post-reading strategies;* emphasized in upper grades.

Curriculum   That which is to be taught and how it is organized for instruction; in reading, it includes experiences with being literate and *attitude, process,* and *content subgoals.*

Decode   To figure out what an unknown word is; to use *context clues, structural analysis,* or *phonics* or a combination of these to identify an unknown word.

Denotative language   Using neutral terms that tend to be objective in nature; example: Referring to a person as "slim" rather than "skinny."

Developmental progression   The steady, progressive pattern that most students follow in learning to read; the instruction provided in a particular grade is part of a development progression; the different points along this line of development are called *stages of development reading growth.*

Direct experience   An experience one actually has; contrasted with a second-hand, or *vicarious,* experience; example: seeing the Empire State Building.

Direct instruction   Developing curricular goals by overtly interacting with students; often characterized by teacher direction or teacher explanation; used primarily for *process* and *content goals;* contrasted with *indirect instruction.*

Direct teacher mediation   Teachers' attempts to guide students' understanding; usually through instructional dialogue; contrasted with *indirect instruction.*

Directed listening activity (DLA)   A technique for structuring listening activities to ensure that students understand the content; includes introduction, purpose setting, listening, discussion, and closure.

Directed reading lesson (DRL)   Structuring reading activities to ensure that students understand the content; includes introduction (*topic*, words, *purpose*), reading, and discussion (clarifying, summarizing, extending understanding).

Directed reading-thinking activity (DRTA)   Structuring reading activities; similar to the *Directed reading lesson*, except that students are involved in making predictions about the purposes for reading.

Drafting stage   Stage of the writing in which the writer composes a first draft of the message.

Drill-and-practice model   Technique for teaching *routine skills* through *direct instruction;* emphasis is on repetition and memory; format includes introducing, *modeling, practice*, and *application*.

During-reading strategy   *Metacognitive strategy* readers use while reading text to monitor their understanding and to repair any blockages to meaning; contrasted with *initiating, post-reading*, and *study strategies*.

Editing stage   Stage of the writing process in which writers revise drafts of the message for purposes of clarity and precision of meaning; contrasted with *planning* and *drafting stages*.

Editing table   A technique in which students (or teachers) assist student authors as they revise their drafts.

Emergent literacy stage   *Stage of developmental reading growth* typically associated with preschool and kindergarten; curricular emphasis is on building positive responses to reading and accurate concepts of what reading is; contrasted with *initial mastery, expanded fundamentals, application* and *power stages*.

Evaluating strategy   *Post-reading strategy* used to make judgments about the text's message; example: discriminating fantasy and reality; see *critical reading*.

Expanded fundamentals stage   Stage of *developmental reading growth* typically associated with grades 3 and 4; curricular emphasis is on learning and applying the fundamental skills of reading, particularly comprehension; contrasted with *emergent literacy, initial mastery, application*, and *power stages*.

Expectation   Tendency of humans to do what is expected of them; example: children from homes where reading and learning are valued tend to have positive expectations about learning to read.

Explanation   Process of providing students with information and assistance needed to construct a *schema* about a particular phenomenon; associated with *direct instruction;* uses explicit statements, *modeling*, and *guided practice*.

Expository text   *Text* written primarily to inform; contrasted with *narrative text*.

Expressive language mode   The language modes of speaking and writing, both of which are used to express meaning; contrasted with *receptive language mode*.

Fix-it strategy   *During-reading strategy* used to repair a meaning blockage; contrasted with *fluency* and *monitoring*.

Fluency   Relative smoothness of constructing meaning from *text;* fluent reading reflects the reader's clear understanding of the vocabulary used, the *topic*, the author's *purpose*, and the *text structure* and is evidenced by correct intonation and an absence of interruptions.

Formal test   *Assessment* device published by testing companies and used by teachers in accordance with specified procedures; contrasted with *informal test*.

Frustration reading level   Traditionally, reading materials too difficult for a particular student to read; student fails to recognize at least 95 percent of the words instantly or fails to answer 75 percent of the questions posed about the content of the text; contrasted with *instructional* and *independent reading levels*.

Functional text   Created to inform; examples: textbooks, encyclopedias, and catalogues; see *expository text;* contrasted with *recreational text*.

Function word   In the English language a word that signals a *syntactic* meaning as opposed to a *semantic* meaning; example: prepositions are function words because they signal the beginning of a prepositional phrase rather than provide a lexical meaning.

Graphic strategies   *Locational study strategies* used to find information in graphics such as maps, tables, charts, and graphs; contrasted with *book part, library*, and *reference source strategies*.

Guided practice   Attempting to move students gradually to a point where they can use strategies independently.

How-to-change pattern   Routine teachers establish regarding what students are to do when changing from one activity to another.

How-to-start pattern   Routine teachers establish regarding what students are to do when starting new activities.

How-to-stop patterns   Routine teachers establish regarding what students are to do when they finish their work.

Independent activity/practice Activities students do by themselves while the teacher is teaching other students in a reading group; often referred to as *seatwork*.

Independent reading level Traditionally, reading materials comfortable for a particular student to read; student recognizes at least 99 percent of the words instantly and answers 90 percent of the questions posed about the content of the *text*; contrasted with *frustration* and *instructional reading levels*.

Indirect instruction Developing curricular goals by providing a *literate environment* designed to help students "discover" certain things; characterized by an absence of direct guidance by the teacher; used primarily for *attitude goals*; contrasted with *direct instruction*.

Individualized reading Synonym for *personalized reading* and *literature-based reading*.

Inference/Inferential Process of constructing the meaning an author implies but does not state explicitly; requires readers to make predictions using a combination of *prior knowledge* and text-based clues.

Inferential question Question that requires students to make an inference; students must determine the meaning an author implies but does not state explicitly; contrasted with *critical* and *literal questions*.

Informal test *Assessment* device that depends heavily on teacher judgment; these are often teacher-made tests; contrasted with *formal tests*.

Initial mastery stage *Stage of developmental reading growth* typically associated with grades 1 and 2; curricular emphasis is on learning and applying the fundamental skills of reading, particularly word *recognition*; contrasted with *emergent literacy, expanded fundamentals, application,* and *power stages*.

Initiating strategy Metacognitive strategy readers use as they begin to read a text; involves making initial predictions about a *topic*, author's *purpose*, and *text structure*; contrasted with *during-reading, post-reading,* and *study strategies*.

Instruction Intentional use of academic work, *presentations*, and interactive dialogue to provide information students need to build *schemata* regarding desired curricular goals; contrasted with *learning and teaching*.

Instructional reading level Traditionally, reading materials that a student can read with teacher assistance; student recognizes 95 to 99 percent of the words instantly and answers 75 to 99 percent of the questions posed about the content of the *text*; contrasted with *frustration* and *instructional reading levels*.

Integration Forming into a whole all four language modes in the classroom; listening, speaking, reading, and writing are interrelated; an important characteristic of the *literate environment*.

Intellectual environment. Part of the classroom *literate environment*; characterized by expectations that language will be used meaningfully and by challenges to get involved with meaningful language communication; integrated with *physical* and social-emotional environments.

Interaction pattern Routine teachers establish regarding conversation and other socialization in the classroom.

Internal motivator Motivator teachers can use to stimulate particularly good responses from students; examples: giving students choices, opportunities to act like adults, and opportunities to alter or create language.

Invented spelling Unorthodox spelling of words that young children invent during *preliterate stages*.

Language arts Curriculum subject that integrates listening, speaking, reading, and writing.

Language convention Procedure of dealing with language that has been agreed on in the interest of expediting communication; example: left-to-right progress across a line of print; *routine skill*; contrasted with *linguistic unit*.

Language experience approach (LEA) Organizing reading instruction around materials written by students; students engage in experiences, talk about the experiences, write about the experiences, and then read what they have written; contrasted with *basal text* and *literature-based approaches*.

Library strategy Locational study strategy used to find information in the library; includes looking at the card catalog and knowing the Dewey Decimal system; contrasted with *book part, reference source,* and *graphics strategies*.

Linguistic unit Units of printed symbols associated with written language; examples: letters, words; *routine skill*; contrasted with *language conventions*.

Literacy Proactive, enthusiastic use of language and higher-order thinking in the service of controlling and enriching one's destiny.

Literacy cycle A teacher-developed structure for organizing reading and writing opportunities in the classroom.

Literal question   Question that requires students to answer in terms of what is written on the printed page; contrasted with *critical* and *inferential questions.*

Literate environment   Classroom environment permeated with examples of literacy and language in action; various kinds of student communications, both oral and written, are encouraged; *integration* of the four *language modes* is emphasized in classroom activities; includes the *physical, intellectual,* and *social-emotional environments;* contrasted with *direct teacher mediation.*

Literature-based reading   Organizing instruction around literature books, usually selected individually by student from school or room library; see also *personalized reading* and *individualized reading.*

Locational strategy   *Study strategy* used to locate information; examples: *book part, library* and *graphic strategies;* contrasted with *rate, remember, organizing* and *study habit strategies.*

Long-term memory   Information accessible to recall for long periods of time after experiences; contrasted with *short-term memory.*

Look-back   Used during reading; a *fix-it strategy;* when a problem is encountered in reading *text,* readers look back in the text for *semantic and syntactic cues.*

Mainstreaming   Placing students with special learning problems (and who would normally be taught by special education teachers) in regular elementary classrooms.

Mediation   Thinking about something and, in the process, constructing and altered meaning; see *direct teacher mediation.*

Mental modeling   Teachers explain their own thinking process identified in a *task analysis* by showing students how they themselves use it.

Mental processing   Reasoning done to construct meaning from text; associated with *metacognitive strategies.*

Metacognition   Conscious awareness of how thinking is done; in this book, conscious awareness of the reasoning involved in making sense out of written text.

Metacognitive control   Being consciously aware of how reasoning is done so that it can be monitored and controlled; see also *self-regulation.*

Metacognitive strategy   Strategy students use in a conscious way to meet *process goals;* awareness of what to do and how to do it; includes *initiating, during-reading, post-reading,* and *study strategies.*

Model   Showing students how to do a task with the expectation that they will then emulate the model; in reading, modeling often involves teachers talking about how they think through a task, since much of reading is *cognitive.*

Modified directed reading lesson (MDRL)   Structuring a reading lesson so that skills and strategies are taught before reading the story in which they will be applied; format includes an introduction of the story, instruction of the skill or strategy, purpose setting for both story content and skill or strategy application, reading, discussion of the story and the skill or strategy application, and closure.

Monitoring   *During-reading strategy;* process of keeping track of one's own meaning getting while reading; includes monitoring for unknown words, unrecognized words, author's meaning, and beyond author's meaning; contrasted with *fluency and fix-it strategies.*

Motivation   Condition affecting student perseverance; affected primarily by the degree to which students value the activity being pursued and by the amount of success experienced while pursuing it.

Narrative text   *Text* written primarily to entertain, contrasted with *expository text.*

Natural text   *Text* that has not been altered from the form in which the author(s) publish it; contrasted with *controlled text.*

Nook-and-cranny time   Short periods of time during the school day when no academic tasks are being pursued; useful for additional reading instruction.

On-your-own strategy   Strategy readers use to relate questions about content to answers in the *text;* readers rely on their background knowledge; contrasted with *right-there* and *think-and-search strategies;* see QARs.

Oral round-robin reading   Traditional technique for listening to students read orally—each student reads aloud in turn while the teacher listens.

Organizing strategy   Includes *study and post-reading strategies.*

Personalized reading approach   Organizing instruction around materials students select from the school or room library; students select a book of their choice, read at their own pace, and receive individual help from teachers in conferences; see also *literature-based reading* and *individualized reading.*

Phonics/Phonic analysis   Proces of using letters and letter sounds to sound out and *decode* an unknown word; contrasted with *context clues* and *structural analysis*.

Phonogram   Common phonic spelling patter; examples: *at* in *cat*, *bat*, and *sat* and *et* in *bet*, *met*, and *set*.

Physical environment   Part of the classroom *literate environment*; characterized by physical evidences of literacy and by physically attractive areas that encourage students to engage in meaningful reading; integrated with *intellectual* and *social-emotional environments*.

Planning stage   Stage of the writing process in which writers gather and organize information in preparation for composing; contrasted with *drafting* and *editing stages*.

Portfolios   Systematic collections of student growth in reading, writing, speaking, and listening as they are used across curriculum content.

Post-reading strategy   *Metacognitive strategies* readers use after reading a selection; involves reflecting about a selection's content for purposes of reorganizing and evaluating what was read.

Power stage   *Stage of developmental reading growth* typically associated with grades 9 through 12; curricular emphasis is on the highly technical aspect of reading and studying; contrasted with *emergent literacy, initial mastery, expanded fundamentals*, and *application stages*.

Practice   Repetition and drill of an act to make it habitual.

Preliterate writing   Doodling preschoolers and kindergartners do to "write" stories before they learn how printed language works.

Preprimer   First book in the *basal text approach*; consists of pictures and a limited number of words and short sentences.

Presentation   Part of the lesson in which teachers present information to students; usually includes lesson introduction, *modeling*, and *demonstrations*.

Primer   Book after the *preprimer* in the *basal text approach*; an easy reading book.

Print awareness   Awareness of what printed symbols are and how they work; first stage in *word recognition*; associated with *language conventions* and *linguistic units*.

Prior knowledge   Background experience (*direct* and *vicarious*) accessible for use in making sense out of text.

Procedural pattern   Predetermined organizational procedures that become classroom routines.

Process   Means by which students attain a goal; in this book, the means by which students comprehend *text*.

Process goals   One of the three major curricular goals in reading; consists of understanding how the reading system works and how to apply strategies when reading.

Purpose   In this textbook, why students read a particular text; the particular information being sought from a printed text reflects the purpose; see also *author's purpose*.

Question-answer relationship (QAR)   Technique for comprehending *functional text* in which students analyze the relationship between what the question asks for and what the text offers; includes *right there, think-and-search*, and *on-your-own strategies*.

Rate strategy   Study strategy in which students decide the most efficient rate of reading for the situation; examples include *scanning, skimming*, and careful pacing; contrasted with *locational, remembering, organizing*, and *study-habit strategies*.

Readiness   A term formerly used to designate the *emergent literacy* stage of developmental reading growth; see *emergent literacy* stage.

Reading program   Organizing structure used to teach reading; most teachers use either the *basal text approach*, the *language experience approach*, the *literature-based approach*, or a *combined approach*.

Receptive language mode   The language modes of listening and reading, both of which are used to receive meaning; contrasted with *expressive language modes*.

Recreational text   *Text* created to entertain or enrich; examples: stories, poems, and plays; see also *narrative text*, contrasted with *functional text*.

Reference source strategies   *Locational study strategy* used to find information in reference sources; includes dictionaries, encyclopedias, atlases, etc.; contrasted with *book part, library*, and *graphics strategies*.

Remembering   Recalling at a later time information comprehended in reading or listening situations.

Remembering strategy   *Study strategy* in which students consciously attempt to retain information; includes SQ3R, summarizing, and stating main ideas; contrasted with *locational, rate, organizing*, and *study habit strategies*.

Repeated reading   Technique for developing fluency; students are directed to read a passage over and over again until they can read it smoothly.

Restructuring   Combining prior knowledge with new knowledge; the result is usually a somewhat different meaning from what the author or speaker intended, or a "restructured understanding."

Right-there strategy   *Strategy* readers use to relate questions about *content* to answers in the text; readers examine what is right there on the page for clues to disrupted meaning; contrasted with *think-and-search* and *on-your-own strategies;* see also QAR.

Routine skill   Procedure readers can employ from memory without conscious awareness of what they are doing; a *process goal;* includes *language conventions* and *linguistic units.*

Safety valve   Learning center or activity available to students, not changed daily; need not be associated with academic work in the classrooms; tends to be viewed by students as fun; examples: vocabulary games, board games, journal writing, and recreational reading.

Scanning   Very fast rate of reading; used as a *study strategy* to quickly locate information about a phenomenon; based on direct and vicarious experiences; see also concept.

Schema, pl. schemata   Mental structure of one's concepts about a phenomenon; based on *direct* and *vicarious experiences;* see also *concept.*

Scope-and-sequence chart   Chart published by basal-text companies that visually displays all the skills and strategies taught throughout students' K-8 reading programs.

Seatwork   Work teachers give students when they are not working under the teacher's direct supervision.

Self-concept   Image that people hold of themselves, developed from perceptions of what they and other people think of them.

Self-efficacy   The I-can-do attitude affecting student feelings of empowerment.

Self-fulfilling prophecy   Phenomenon of human behavior characterizing the tendency of humans to fulfill the expectations they set for themselves.

Self-regulation   Imposing personal control over comprehension of text; see also *metacognitive control.*

Semantic   Meaning associated with words in cluster of words.

Semantic Map   *Organizing study strategy;* requires grouping *concepts* and labeling the grouped concepts.

Short-term memory   Information accessible to recall for only short periods of time after experiences; contrasted with *long-term memory.*

Sight word   Word readers recognize instantly when encountered in *text;* a routine skill.

Skimming   Moving eyes rapidly over text; used as a *rate study strategy* to search likely sections of text for key words that signal the desired information; contrasted with *scanning* and careful pacing.

Social-emotional environment   Part of the classroom literate environment; characterized by warmth, acceptance, and agreed-on procedures for the interchange of ideas; factors include social interactions and *collaborative sharing;* interchanged with *physical* and *intellectual environments.*

SQ3R   *Remembering study strategy;* SQ3R stands for survey, question, read, recite, and review.

Stages of developmental reading growth   Different points along the line of *developmental reading;* includes *emergent literacy, initial mastery, expanded fundamentals, application,* and *power stages.*

Standardized tests   Developed by testing companies; field-tested on large samples of students; used to measure ability; norms are established and used to compare students' performance with students in other places.

Story structure   Elements that organize a story; usually include setting, character(s), problem, story events, and resolution of the problem: see also story structure.

Story map   Analysis of a story according to its structure; usually based on elements such as setting, character(s), problem, story events, and resolution of the problem; see also story structure.

Strategic   Flexible, adaptable, and conscious use of knowledge about reading and how it works.

Strategic behavior   Actions and thoughts in which students use strategies.

Structural analysis   Using prefixes, suffixes, inflectional endings, and root words to identify words and decode their meanings; contrasted with *context clues* and *phonics.*

Structured overviews   Technique for graphically displaying key words associated with a topic and how they are related; used primarily with *functional text;* contrasted with *QARs* and *study guides.*

Student engagement   Getting students to focus attention on the academic task and to keep on that task.

Study habit   *Study strategies* that aid in organizing time and promote efficient study; examples: prioritizing study assignments, allocating time, following directions, and test taking; contrasted with *locational, rate, remembering,* and *organizing strategies.*

Study strategy *Metacognitive strategies* expert readers use to efficiently gather and use information from a variety of text sources in response to the demands of study; includes *locational, rate, remember, organizing,* and *study habit strategies.*

Survey, question, read, recite, and review (SQ3R) Five-step process used in teaching *content goals;* designed to help readers recall information.

Syntactic Meaning associated with the grammatical structure of a language; includes word order, function words, and so on.

Task analysis Process in which teachers decide what steps are involved in performing a particular task.

Teacher-pupil planning Process by which teachers and students, through discussion, decide what will be studied and how it will be studied.

Teaching All the tasks associated with being a classroom teacher; does not necessarily refer to developing intended curricular goals; contrasted with *learning and instruction.*

Text Sum of the message being read or spoken; authors compose text to communicate messages or ideas; the meaning is the author's; the text carries the meaning, but readers must reconstruct the author's meaning from the cues embedded in the text.

Text structure Way a written text is organized; example: newspaper articles have a structure different from epic poems, plays, and so on; readers use *prior knowledge* about text structure to aid in constructing meaning from text; contrasted with *topic* and *purpose.*

Think and search strategy Strategy readers use to relate questions about *content* to answers in the *text;* readers examine and think about information implied by the author as a means of repairing disrupted meaning; contrasted with *right-there* and *on-your-own strategies;* see also *QAR.*

Topic What a written selection is about; readers use *prior knowledge* about topic to aid in constructing meaning from *text.*

Transfer Ability to use in one situation what was learned in another situation; in reading, the goal is that strategies learned in school will be used in reading done outside school; see also *application.*

Typographic cues Punctuation (such as question marks and exclamation points) and other devices (such as underlining and italics) help readers determine an author's meaning.

Uninterrupted sustained silent reading (USSR) Activity during which all students and the teacher read books of their choice; often called sustained silent reading or DEAR (drop everything and read).

Unit Unified learning experience that may encompass several days or weeks; develops a variety of related objectives; include several lessons; characterized by a logical progression of activities moving toward predetermined goals; often offers opportunities for integration of language; is situated in authentic activity.

Verbal learning Aptitude for learning language; characterized by the ability to understand and respond to language instruction; influenced by background experience, culture, and language.

Vicarious experience Not a *direct experience;* example: seeing the Empire State Building is a real experience, but seeing a picture of the Empire State Building is a vicarious experience.

Visual discrimination Ability to distinguish one visual form from another; in reading, for example, the ability to distinguish the printed form of *d* from the printed form of *b;* contrasted with *auditory discrimination.*

Vocabulary Knowing the meaning of words; contrasted with *word recognition.*

Vocabulary strategy Used to figure out the meaning of unknown words.

Voice A condition in which an individual's unique perceptions and perspectives are available for others to hear.

Whole language A philosophy of literacy that emphasizes an integrated conception of language and in which instructional activities focus on meaningful uses of language in pursuing genuine literacy events.

Word analysis/attack Category of *fix-it strategies* that focus on what to do when a word is not recognizable at sight; also called *decoding;* three major methods of word attack are *context clues, structural analysis,* and *phonics.*

Word caller Students who accurately pronounce words encountered in text but do not know what the words and the text mean.

Word recognition Recognizing the printed form of a word; successfully pronouncing a word.

Word recognition strategy Used to identify unknown printed words.

Index by Author

Index by Subject